HORN, SAHEL AND RIFT

STIG JARLE HANSEN

Horn, Sahel and Rift

Fault-lines of the African Jihad

HURST & COMPANY, LONDON

First published in the United Kingdom in 2019 by
C. Hurst & Co. (Publishers) Ltd.,
41 Great Russell Street, London, WC1B 3PL

Printed in India

Distributed in the United States, Canada and Latin America by Oxford University Press, 198 Madison Avenue, New York, NY 10016, United States of America.

A Cataloguing-in-Publication data record for this book is available from the British Library.

ISBN: 9781849044141

www.hurstpublishers.com

CONTENTS

PREFACE

This book originated in an interest in African jihadist organisations. It is the product of a dramatic intellectual journey: friends have been tortured and killed, both by the organisations described here and by their enemies. The book is an attempt to ground a comparative analysis in detailed local studies. It is my belief that in order to discover general trends, one needs to study the particular in depth. The book also strives to give voice to individuals not often heard in the literature, thereby illustrating for example that rural violence targeting farmers may be more important for the dynamics within jihadist organisations than grand terrorist attacks on international targets and global ideologies.

Along the way, many colleagues, friends and fellow researchers have contributed to my work. In Harvard, Christopher Anzalone, whose office was located just metres away from me, has, through our frequent conversations, stimulated and enriched my reflections on the subject. His unique archive of jihadist videos has proved very helpful for the book. Aisha Ahmad, at the University of Toronto, commented on my ideas and helped secure the grant that made possible the field studies on which this book draws. Yahiya Ibrahim at the University of Florida has been exceptionally helpful, as has Yahya Hagi Ibrahim of Benadir University in Mogadishu. Ilmari Käihkö, Linnea Gelot and Stian Lid have all contributed to my conceptualisation of the subject. I am also very grateful to Mohamed Husein Gaas, Jacob Zenn, Ballama Mustafa and Adam Sandor for their invaluable comments on various chapters. Presentations at Harvard and the University of Florida, presided over by Stephen Walt and Terje Østebø, have all contributed to my thinking. Tor A. Benjaminsen and Gry Synnevåg shared their local networks and knowledge with me.

The book benefited immensely from a number of my students, especially Clifford Collins Omondi for his rich knowledge of Majengo, Nairobi, and Brenda Jimris (who won a prize for the best thesis at the Norwegian University of Life Sciences during the period in which I wrote this book) for her knowledge of Kenya and the Swahili coast. Umar Abdi Mouhamed, Adam Egal and Asha Adam shared their understanding of Somalia, and El Hadj Djitteye guided me through the politics of northern Mali. Adolphe Bazengezi watched over my steps in Congo. Isma'il Alfa Abdulrahim did the same in Nigeria. Ida Bary gave invaluable help, translating Arabic texts and enhancing my knowledge of East and North Africa and the Middle East.

The patience of my publisher, Michael Dwyer, has been amazing. Lastly, but perhaps most importantly, thanks to my wife and family who have been persistently patient with me. Two children were born during my work on this book, yet my wife found the strength to allow me to finish it.

Professor Stig Jarle Hansen
Maiduguri, Borno State, Nigeria
October 2018

ABBREVIATIONS

ADC	Democratic Alliance for Change
ADF	Allied Democratic Forces
ADFL	Alliance of Democratic Forces for the Liberation of Congo-Zaire
AFISMA	International Support Mission in Mali
AI	al-Islax
AIAI	al-Ittihad al-Islamiya
AMISOM	African Union Mission in Somalia
AMYC	Ansar Muslim Youth Centre
ANC	African National Congress
AQAP	al-Qaeda in the Arabian Peninsula
AQEA	al-Qaeda East Africa
AQIM	al-Qaeda in the Islamic Maghreb
ARS	Alliance for the Re-liberation of Somalia
ATNMC	Alliance Touareg du Nord-Mali pour le Changement
ATT	Amadou Toumani Touré
AU	African Union
CATIA	Groupe Autodéfense Touareg Imghad et Alliés
CCM	Chama Cha Mapinduzi
CJTF	Civilian Joint Task Force
CMA	Coordination des mouvements de l'Azawad
CUF	Civic United Front

CVF	Countering Violent Extremism
DDRRR UN	Disarmament, Demobilisation, Repatriation, Resettlement and Reintegration Programme (UN)
DSR	Defenders of Sanaag Resources
ECOWAS	Economic Community of West African States
EIJ	Eritrean Islamic Jihad
ELF	Eritrean Liberation Front
FAC	Forces Armées Congolaises
FIS	Front Islamique du Salut
GIA	Armed Islamic Group
GSPC	Salafist Group for Preaching and Combat
HCUA	High Council for the Unity of Azawad
IARA	Islamic African Relief Agency
IIRO	International Islamic Relief Organisation
IPK	Islamic Party of Kenya
IRO	Islamic Relief Organisation
IS	Islamic State
ISGS	Islamic State in the Greater Sahara
ISI	Islamic State of Iraq
ISIL	Islamic State of Iraq and the Levant
ISIS	Islamic State of Iraq and Syria
ISRA	Islamic Relief Agency
ISS	Islamic State in Somalia
ISWA	Islamic State in West Africa
JMNTF	Joint Multi-National Task Force
JTF	Joint Task Force
JTJ	Jama'at al-Tawhid wal-Jihad
LIFG	Libyan Islamic Fighting Group
MAA	Arab Movement of Azawad
MDC	Operational Coordination Mechanism
MINURSO	United Nations Mission for the Referendum in Western Sahara
MINUSMA	United Nations Multidimensional Integrated Stabilisation Mission in Mali
MLF	Macina Liberation Front
MNA	National Movement of Azawad
MNLA	Movement for the National Liberation of Azawad

MOJWA	Movement for Oneness and Jihad in West Africa
MONUSCO	United Nations Organisation Stabilisation Mission in the Democratic Republic of the Congo
MPA	Popular Movement of Azawad
MRC	Mombasa Republican Council
MSA	Azawad Salvation Movement
MUJAO	Movement for Unity and Jihad in West Africa
MYC	Muslim Youth Centre
NALU	National Army for the Liberation of Uganda
NIF	National Islamic Front
PAIC	Popular Arab and Islamic Council
PMPF	Puntland Maritime Police Force
SSDF	Somali Salvation Democratic Front
UAMSHO	Association for Islamic Mobilisation and Propagation
UMFF	Ugandan Muslim Freedom Fighters
UMSC	Ugandan Muslim Supreme Council
UNDP	United Nations Development Programme
US	United States
UVIKITA	Tanzanian Muslim Youth Union

INTRODUCTION

Over the last sixteen or so years, the world has witnessed a surge of violent jihadist organisations in Africa. New bodies like Ansar Dine, Harakat al-Shabaab, Boko Haram, al-Mourabitoun and al-Hijra emerged or else older groups consolidated themselves, the Salafist Group for Preaching and Combat (GSPC) for instance becoming al-Qaeda in the Islamic Maghreb, in the process being reinvigorated. All of these organisations have shown a surprising degree of resilience and, despite the enormous resources and efforts that have been channelled into defeating them, they are still present in some form, surviving government offensives, arrests and even assassinations of top leaders, and notwithstanding their ideological differences.

Their resilience has surprised many observers. When I travelled across Somalia after 2013, I was astonished to hear the many commentators who claimed that Shabaab was disappearing; they were believed to have been defeated in the field, incapable of holding larger cities in the face of the African Union's forces. In Nigeria, I heard similar stories, this time how territorial losses would lead to Boko Haram's demise, how the new 7th Division (established in 2013) and, later, the Chadians and a newly elected northern president would bring about an end to the conflict. Yet the organisation survived one crisis in 2009, it survived another in 2013, and will probably survive its fragmentation today. The same pattern was repeated during my stay in Mali, where people talked about the final victory that was still to come. In all, it was a case of, as the Somalis say, '*Hadal haan ma buuxsho*', words do not fill a vessel. The comments I heard in these countries made me wonder whether there was something the world failed to understand when it came to these organisations, something about the mechanisms of resilience in the jihadi movements which enable them to survive defeats and transform themselves. This book is about these transformations, and it outlines their mechanisms of survival, which may have a bearing outside Africa as well. Several of the organisations analysed here pioneered a modus operandi that was followed later by the more famous al-Qaeda in the Arabian Peninsula and by the Islamic State. African jihadist organisations took and held large swathes of territory some years prior to the expansion of the Islamic State. The Harakat al-Shabaab, for example, was in control of large areas as early as 2009, and attracted a substantial number of foreign fighters as early as 2008, while Boko Haram expanded its territories in 2012 and then again in 2014.[1] Yet the lessons from the African examples have often been neglected.

When the jihadist organisations established permanent territorial control in their various areas, they became different from the kind of small clandestine group that executed the 9/11 attacks in 2001. Territoriality challenges our understanding of how jihadist organisations function, what kind of activities they can carry out, what kind of instruments of cohesion they can use. However, over the last five years or so, a new transformation has been taking place among the African organisations, after they began to lose territorial control. This was often seen as the first step on the path to final defeat.[2] Nevertheless, Boko Haram, the Shabaab and Ansar Dine, although they lost control over territory, were not conquered but were instead transformed. This transformation involved a reversion to the 'old ways', the ways in which they had operated before they gained territorial control. They changed their structure, and proved quite successful in absorbing the body blows aimed at them. This book will study how these changes happened, and how the organisations managed to survive.

Not all jihadist organisations gain territorial control: in some cases the state they face is too strong. Indeed, in Africa state capacities vary, and this book examines how movements in some of the stronger states, such as Tanzania and Kenya, acquire a different form of organisational dynamics from those based in places like Somalia and the periphery of Mali. Last but not least, some of the jihadist organisations have been employed by the local state, and have actually enjoyed a good relationship with state leaders and institutions during periods of their history.

The book is also a comparative study of jihadist organisations in Africa. It sets out to offer an analysis of all the major violent African jihadist groups, comparing them in respect of the way their organisational dynamics have varied over time, and how they have been influenced by their context, such as the weak presence of their enemies, the existence of stronger states, or attempts to employ them as agents of state politics. In this sense the book is based on a dynamic rather than a static comparative framework: it explores variations over time in the different organisations rather than searching for a static, timeless 'essence' that can be used to classify an organisation within a larger model. The general comparative framework used is the variety of territorial presences that the different organisations experience, as chapter 2 explains.

The book also provides a general reference work for interested individuals. Finally, it presents the disagreements among analysts about the historical trajectories of the various organisations.[3]

Global versus Local

The history of the diffusion of militant jihadist organisations goes far back in time. Indeed, the word 'jihadism' was introduced into the English language in connection with the Sokoto Caliphate established in West Africa by Usman dan Fodio (1754–1817) and the threat of 'Mahdist jihadism' in the nineteenth century.[4] The 1980–5 Maitatsine uprisings by Islamist militants in northern Nigeria, and warfare engaged in by al-Ittihad al-Islamiya in Somalia in the early and mid-1990s, are also important in the history of violent jihadists, the latter even involving present-day Shabaab leaders.[5]

Yet these historical regional legacies do not tell the whole story of the organisations studied here. Outside forces and impulses combined with local ones to form the violent sub-Saharan jihadist networks. The Soviet intervention in Afghanistan from 1978 to 1989, for example, is of great significance. An early cadre of future leaders of radical, militant, often Wahhabi-inspired organisations participated in the mujahideen resistance to the Soviet army, such as Mokhtar Belmokhtar of al-Qaeda in the Islamic Maghreb (AQIM), the late Ibrahim Haji Mehad 'Afghani' of the Harakat al-Shabaab in Somalia, and also, so it is claimed, Jamil Mukulu of the Allied Democratic Forces (ADF) in Uganda. Although Mukulu probably did not take part in the war, all three men used their alleged or actual participation in Afghanistan as a 'badge of honour', something with which to attract followers, indicative of an attraction to and identification with al-Qaeda, its activities and its ideology.[6]

Al-Qaeda itself entered Africa in 1991 when Osama bin Laden established himself in Khartoum, Sudan. The early activities of al-Qaeda, in planning terror, supporting local insurgency movements and searching for funds, all set a pattern and precedent for the future. Their allies had large problems to do with unity and fragmentation. Al-Qaeda itself had problems in dealing with local realities and with tribal and clan politics. It had to adjust accordingly, as it had done in Afghanistan and Pakistan before, though local and regional interests often interfered with or were at cross purposes with al-Qaeda's global ideology, and vice versa. After Osama bin Laden was evicted from Sudan in 1996, direct support for local allies dwindled. In the wake of 9/11, there was a large expansion of al-Qaeda's local affiliates and other militant Sunni groups. This expansion was ideological, tactical and geographical: new tactics came to the fore, new organisations emerged, and there was greater interest in al-Qaeda's worldviews. As regards al-Qaeda-related or -inspired organisations, the first ten years after 9/11 saw the rise of al-Shabaab, Boko Haram, al-Hijra and the Movement for Oneness and Jihad in West Africa (MOJWA), as well as more independent groups like Ansar Dine. These years also saw what Valentina Soria calls the 'Africanisation' of AQIM, when it moved its focus southwards.[7] AQIM established itself in the border areas between Niger, Mauritania, Mali and Chad, and staged attacks on Algeria's southern neighbours. Today, traces of these organisations survive in Somalia, Kenya, Djibouti, Ethiopia, Tanzania, Uganda, the Democratic Republic of Congo, Burundi, Rwanda, Cameroon, Nigeria, Mauritania, Senegal, Sudan, Ghana, Sierra Leone, Niger and Mali. The most important groups spread out in what Ali Mazrui called the crescent of Islam in Africa: West Africa, North Africa, and East Africa or the Horn.[8] Not only did new organisations emerge, but old organisations turned more violent, and some moved south. And these second-generation jihadist groups came to control territories and prove themselves more efficient than their ideologically confused and fragmented predecessors, such as al-Ittihad al-Islamiya (AIAI) in Somalia and Eritrean Islamic Jihad (EIJ) in Eritrea.

Al-Qaeda's military techniques and tactics penetrated Africa as well. By 2006 Somalia saw its first suicide attack, and by 2011 so did Nigeria.[9] By 2006, the technique of improvised explosive devices had been taught to Somali jihadists by Afghanistan veterans, and it reached Nigeria in 2011.[10] The attack on a United Nations house in Abuja, Nigeria, in 2011, another in Aménas, Algeria, in January 2013, and the Westgate shopping mall attack in Nairobi, Kenya, in September 2013 gained much attention and demonstrated the significance of the surge in African jihadism to the rest of the world. In these attacks, non-Africans became involved both as victims and as hostages, thereby gaining attention from the global media. Sadly, the waves of Boko Haram attacks in northern Nigeria caused a greater number of deaths, but were fairly neglected internationally, at least until the organisation kidnapped two hundred schoolgirls in 2014.

As we have noted, these early developments in Africa divided analysts and commentators into two camps. On one side were the alarmists, who suggested that a new and close network of al-Qaeda was developing, thus fulfilling the old stereotype of the dedicated and fanatical militant Islamist. The instrumentalists or cultural determinists, on the other hand, originally saw the various African affiliates and Islamist organisations as isolated and mainly present for instrumental reasons, and unable to gain a foothold because of the cultural and ethnical realities of Africa. According to this approach, the new Islamist groups used the 'brand name' of al-Qaeda to gain foreign support, fulfilling the old stereotype of the African militant rent-seeker as basically avaricious and without ideology.[11] Over time, the two oversimplified views mutated into a more nuanced approach stressing the importance of local dynamics, including clan and tribal dynamics, and another stressing the importance of global connections and global diffusion. This cleavage is the source of most of the intense debates among analysts and scholars focusing today on African jihadist organisations, most intensely perhaps in the case of Boko Haram. Often area studies analysts will be situated in the 'local' camp, while terror analysts will be situated in the 'global' camp: the latter often more popular with the international press due to their simpler, more dramatic, and all-encompassing message.

This book, however, refuses to accept such a dichotomy.[12] As will be shown in later chapters, emphasis on the global or the local will vary according to what needs to be explained and even according to specific phases in the history of a jihadist organisation. In many ways, the local is most important. The reasons why the rank and file join a jihadist organisation holding territories, such as Boko Haram, Ansar Dine and the Shabaab, are not dominated by global visions: recruits are often influenced by clan/tribal issues, the need for security and economic rationales. The targets of these organisations also suggest that more local interests predominate. None of the organisations studied here have attacked targets outside Africa, and encouragement from al-Qaeda and the Islamic State has not changed their targeting policies. In large part they have had to navigate their way in a complex local political landscape, dominated by local conflicts and local interests, and they have put their local interests before any global agenda.

To see the organisations studied here as obedient members following the orders of global movements is misplaced. Yet, global networks and ideas have influenced the diffusion of strategies, especially when individuals have travelled between organisations inside and outside Africa. At times global ideas influenced the motivation for joining the organisation in question, especially in the early stage of its history, as well as in later stages (as with the Shabaab). There are cases where allied jihadist organisations supported each other directly with material aid, though primary evidence gathered so far indicates that these instances have been limited; nonetheless they were sometimes important. Sometimes there have been exchanges of people and ideas. At other times, and perhaps more frequently, the organisations studied here have participated in spreading global ideas online and in neighbouring countries. This means that African jihadist organisations have acquired global agency, albeit limited. Shabaab (see chapter 9) has produced videos attempting to persuade sympathisers in the West to attack

Western targets, and has also attracted Western foreign fighters. Boko Haram participated in propaganda videos attempting to sway al-Qaeda affiliates (like Shabaab) away from that organisation and into alliances with the Islamic State (see chapter 6). Some of the wider trans-border mechanisms have little to do with the specific ideology of al-Qaeda or the Islamic State, but draw upon the increasing importance of religion in conflicts in Africa. The real or perceived ability to provide justice has secured local support, partly because religious actors at times have been seen as more efficient in this respect because of the tenets of their faith, partly because some of these organisations actually do provide law and order in more efficient ways than their rivals. For example, both Jama'at Nusrat ul-Islam wal-Muslimin' (see chapter 4) and Shabaab (see chapter 9) have provided order in their home areas, often more efficiently than the Malian and Somali state; while Boko Haram (see chapter 6), although this is often forgotten, used 'anti-corruption' rhetoric and religion as a solution to corruption in its early propaganda.

Keeping a keen eye on the local dynamics, while at the same time not neglecting global dynamics and actors, enables us to discover surprising facts, for example how local dynamics in Sudan dominated al-Qaeda during its Sudan years (chapter 3). That al-Qaeda became part of a non-state governance network used by the Sudanese government to strike at its enemies, and to fund its activities, shows how one of the supposedly more global actors was captured by the local context. Indeed, the dynamics of the global actors also seem more complex than many acknowledge. Al-Qaeda, for instance, changed from a more centralised organisation prior to 2011, to a looser network of affiliates. Its new leader, Ayman al-Zawahiri, became more of a figurehead, a spiritual guide, rather than a general in direct command. The central leadership began to show more respect for local variations and opinions, and its power to instruct and command affiliated groups seemed to decline.[13] Perhaps this can be seen in Zawahiri's inability to mend fences between leaders within al-Qaeda in the Islamic Maghreb, as well as within the Shabaab, and in the problems he faced in dealing with the Islamic State of Iraq and Syria (ISIS).[14] At the same time, we have also seen the rise of the Islamic State, which, like many of the African organisations before it, chose to aim for the control and conquest of large territories, in the process gaining prestige in the violent Sunni jihadist community and attracting foreign fighters, including some from Africa. As a result, a new ideological beacon emerged for many African groups, rivalling al-Qaeda. Islamic State attempted to influence Shabaab, Boko Haram and al-Mourabitoun, but in the end this only had limited effects. Both the Islamic State and al-Qaeda have been used as tools in local power struggles, though the latter in particular has also tried to rein in what it saw as the 'unreligious' behaviour of its local allies, such as attacks against civilian Muslims.

Definitions

Terrorism as a concept is here defined in terms of action, following the works of Boaz Ganor.[15] Terrorism is a strategy – one among many – adopted in order to achieve victory in a political struggle. The use of Ganor as a point of departure allows us to acknowledge that insurgency organisations can include terror as part of their repertoire of activities, and that it is incorrect to use the term 'terrorist organisation'. The organisations studied here employ terrorism as a strategy, in combination with others, in a repertoire that includes guerrilla warfare, conventional warfare, and strategies to win hearts and minds.

Indeed, if terrorism is defined as a strategy by a non-state actor that targets the civilian population or civilian infrastructure outside a war zone, many organisations have employed it. For example, the African National Congress (ANC) of South Africa applied the strategy in order to fight for the redress of quite legitimate grievances, in its case ethnic domination by a white minority government. This illustrates an important point: radical organisations can be driven by quite legitimate reasons. Yet this does not mean that terror is acceptable. At the same time, it is important to understand the strengths and weaknesses of organisations employing terror. We need as well, in the context of the international law of war and peace, to distinguish between *jus ad bellum* and *jus in bello*, the legality of war and the legality of actions within a war, for an organisation can have some legitimate aims but at the same time commit atrocities.

This book studies violent jihadist organisations in Africa. Jihadism is a contested concept. The term is taken from Arabic, where its meaning also tends to be ambiguous. Jihadism can mean, among other things, an inner struggle for purification, as well as religiously obligatory campaigns of conquest directed against non-Muslims.[16] This book looks at violent jihadism, thus excluding peaceful moral campaigns to 'cleanse' individuals at a personal level or campaigns to change society peacefully. Violent jihadist organisations are willing to use violence, and justify that violence by pointing to Islam and the need to defend its tenets. An organisation will be defined here as an organised body of people with a particular purpose, but it is important to note that the exact boundaries of organisations are often hard to determine.[17] In some cases, this is intentional, as many of the groups in question need to operate clandestinely.

This book will explore the various African jihadist organisations on the basis of field studies, and offer a detailed description of each. It will do this in order to highlight local features as presented in area studies. In addition, it will examine similarities between the cases, recognising that such patterns are best identified if the depth of the individual cases is taken into account. In this way it attempts to combine an area studies approach with a more standard international relations approach that seeks to discover wider patterns.

Territoriality and Transformation

Many excellent books and articles have been produced on various jihadist organisations in Africa, though more comparative studies are generally lacking.[18] There are some exceptions. Gregory Pirio's book *The African Jihad* (2007) focuses mainly on East Africa (indeed it is subtitled '*Bin Laden's quest for the Horn of Africa*'), especially Somalia, and thus neglects other countries.[19] Hussein Solomon's *Terrorism and Counter-terrorism* (2015) focuses on Mali, Somalia and Nigeria. While it is excellent in introducing tribal/clan dynamics, it fails to examine Shabaab offshoots in Kenya and Tanzania, and the focus on local dynamics fails to explain the increase in violent jihadist organisations after 9/11. The global patterns in the rhetoric of these organisations are also neglected,[20] as are foreign fighters and ties to other jihadist groups. African jihadists are thus seen as isolated, not subject to influence from abroad, despite the diffusion of techniques, propaganda narratives and, in some cases, people from outside a state's borders, even from outside the continent. This tendency can also be observed in other works that emphasise local dynamics but fail to consider global currents: these often appear in academic journals with a regional focus.[21] As mentioned earlier, this book will recognise local dimensions, which are essential for an understanding of the dynamics of the organisations. At the same time, the book also acknowledges that global currents influence African jihadists, as we have seen with the role played in Africa by foreign ideologies and conflicts, such as the war in Afghanistan.

Violent jihadism in Africa has been analysed as part of the debate about the supposed weakness or absence of the state in Africa. The so-called ungoverned spaces hypothesis is central to these discussions. This suggests that violent jihadism will emerge where there is a lack of authorities and institutions to stop it.[22] The hypothesis has been criticised on several grounds. One is that 'ungoverned' spaces are seldom ungoverned, as tribal institutions, religious institutions and, at times, aid organisations often provide a semblance of governance.[23] The approach has also been criticised for minimising the role of state policies in facilitating the growth of jihadist organisations, at times through local agents of the state.[24] Some also maintain that jihadist organisations have had problems surviving in tribalised conflicts with various other armed factions in conflict zones that were supposedly ungoverned.[25] The hypothesis also tends to create the misconception that religious militancy is not present in states with relatively stronger institutions, something proven wrong by Hijra's activities in Kenya and Tanzania. These states may also exhibit some traits that can be taken advantage of by violent groups, such as corruption. Corruption can work to the benefit of militant Sunni jihadist organisations; it can enable banned organisations to survive. For example, the infamous 'White Widow' of Shabaab, Samantha Lewthwaite, quite possibly bribed her way out of the hands of the Kenyan police.[26] Corruption may also shield clandestine networks, which can be relatively hidden from the public, though this would not apply to large bases used for training jihadists. At no stage in Africa has there been an organisation mainly operating inside a functioning state that has attracted foreign fighters in large numbers. Indeed, large bases will turn out to be visible to foreign powers, which can put pressure on local states to close them down.[27]

The ungoverned spaces hypothesis, as well as the criticism aimed at it, does contain some truth, though both are, as will be shown in this book, inaccurate. The devil is in the detail. The regions of Africa involved in civil war usually have institutions that lack the powers of a functioning state, and may be less able to prevent a well-organised violent jihadist group from expanding. Shabaab, ADF, Jama'at Nusrat ul-Islam wal-Muslimin', AQIM and Ansar Dine all grew in areas without strong state penetration. However, some of them, such as ADF, started out in different settings where they faced stronger states. This book also studies organisations, like al-Hijra and Boko Haram in its early phase, that existed and survived in areas where the state had a presence. In the case of Boko Haram, the organisation was initially accepted by the state; the same goes for al-Qaeda in the Sudan, where it was actually supported by the state. Clearly, the presence of a state does not exclude the existence of a violent jihadist organisation. However, state penetration may influence the structure of the entity in question.

The book also shows that the areas in which Shabaab, ADF, AQIM, Ansar and MUJAO grew had government structures in place, and for this reason it is wrong to talk about 'ungoverned spaces'. Moreover, Shabaab, ADF and AQIM faced states that intervened from outside the organisation's territory, as well as these states' local agents. Nevertheless, local arms of government were often simply too weak to prevent the jihadists from growing. As I will show, in some instances traditional governing structures supported these organisations, seeing them as providing better services, for example law and order or security, than the central government.[28] Often local structures had little interest in reacting against these organisations, even when they had clear al-Qaeda connections. International politics and the pressure of foreign powers trying to prevent al-Qaeda's expansion were simply experienced as too weak at the local level, and other interests and concerns seemed more pressing for local elites.

This book will argue that a better approach would be to talk of weakness of governance rather than using the contested concept of 'ungoverned spaces', and to recognise that weakness of governance is also a matter of degree. The concept of ungovernability is fruitful in this regard. 'Ungovernability' can be broken up into four variables: (1) the level of state penetration of society; (2) the extent to which the state has a monopoly on the use of force; (3) the extent to which the state controls it borders; and (4) whether the state is subject to external intervention by other states.[29] This analysis does not take into account the possibility of non-state actors involved in governance or informal networks of governance. One example in this regard is the presence of what William Reno calls shadow states that run through society – parallel non-state structures of revenue generation, governance and extraction, often transcending borders.[30] There are also often non-state structures, such as tribes or clans, that are involved in governance, though these structures tend to be weaker than is common for a state. The important point here is that state penetration will influence the way a violent jihadist group is organised. It will not necessarily prevent such a group from appearing. Nevertheless, an efficient monopoly of violence on the part of a hostile state will make it advantageous for the jihadist group to develop a clandestine type of organisation different from a more openly operating armed faction.

The likelihood of rebellious activity will be determined by the advantages as well as the costs of rebellion. In some weak states, with weak institutions and informal governance networks, it will be easier for jihadists to conquer and hold territories.[31] Geography can also play a role. In some areas the nature of the landscape can make it difficult for a government to exercise control, such as in the Sahara, and a government can yield territorial control because of the need to save costs and resources, when the regime does not see it as necessary for its survival to patrol and surveil these areas. Such areas, left more or less to themselves, become a refuge in which violent jihadists can operate openly.

A common approach to African conflicts has been centred on the notion of opportunism, on the gains of instigating rebellious action or of joining a rebel movement. Many African conflicts have been analysed by using the now well-known concept of 'greed' developed by Anke Hoeffler and Paul Collier, according to which armed conflicts are said to occur because entrepreneurs who stand to earn from the hostilities have a vested interest in generating and maintaining violent conflict.[32]

This view was subsequently moderated and turned into an approach that studies opportunity costs. One way of looking at the causes of African insurgencies is to consider the ease with which wars can be started – for example, due to the terrain that can protect potential insurgents, the weakness of the army and police force opposing them, or the lack of an alternative income if one went to war. Against this can be set the potential gains made by joining or instigating a rebellion.[33] For the individual joining a rebellion, income can be generated and protection can be gained. Gains could involve access to natural resources or the spoils of taxation, or access to state bureaucracy and the ability to use this to reward followers. In these ways, militant action becomes the consequence of a cost-benefit analysis, weighing up the gains and costs of organising a militant movement, against those of remaining peaceful.

Such an approach has been rightfully criticised in the African context.[34] However, as an analytic approach, it allows us to consider economic advantages and financial gains as motives for jihadists.[35] In the study of radical al-Qaeda-aligned organisations, income generation very often seems to be a form of acquiring assets for terrorist or insurgency efforts. It is often a strategy to achieve a political target, rather than a strategy to gain wealth. As Andrew Lebovich has pointed out, it is possible to be both a criminal and a jihadist simultaneously. This is perhaps best illustrated by Somalia's Timojele 'Rambo', who was both a kidnapper and a Shabaab commander.[36] However, such combinations become less likely if the income opportunities presented by membership of an organisation are smaller, and the sacrifices are higher.

In general, with some notable exceptions, income, or the lack of it, is seen as unimportant for recruitment to violent jihadist organisations.[37] Krueger and Maleckova, for example, in a much-quoted study investigating Hamas and Hezbollah, concluded that there were no connections between poverty and membership of these organisations.[38] Yet there is clearly some ground for suggesting that poverty and terror are connected on a more macro level. Research indicates that states with a low GNP per capita experience more terrorism, and that rich terrorists can act 'on behalf of the poor', as Brynjar Lia and Katja Skjølberg argue, but this has mainly to do with elites that act out of solidarity with their brethren, not the poor themselves.[39] What has been neglected is the existence for example of categories of fairly poor Shabaab and ADF fighters, and the 'rent-a-hand-grenade' type of attacks all too common in Mogadishu, where Shabaab simply pays poor youths to throw grenades.[40] Several violent jihadist organisations maintain a permanent administration and exercise a more stable form of territorial control. These organisations can provide income opportunities, for instance in non-combatant positions in the administration, or the more common position of a fighter – work that can be relatively stable when the organisation in question controls territory over a period of time.

The logical conclusion from this discussion is that we can develop at least two different scenarios based on the extent of government penetration. At one end of the spectrum, where a hostile state exercises control through solid penetration of a territory, clandestine anti-government organisations can exist, though they cannot operate large-scale training facilities, since the government would react and stop them. At the other end of the spectrum is a jihadi organisation controlling territories, exploiting natural resources and exacting taxes on a large scale, and creating training facilities, courts and a bureaucracy. As Luis de la Calle and Ignacio Sánchez-Cuenca show, armed groups who hold territory have means and advantages at their disposal that are denied to groups without territory.[41] The latter have often tended to draw most attention in Africa, yet the former also exist.

These two opposing positions are not the only forms of territorial presence. The violent jihadist organisation could also be accepted, even endorsed, supported and used by a state structure, as the status of al-Qaeda in Sudan in 1991–6 or Boko Haram in Nigeria pre-2009 shows. However, a violent jihadist group may also exist as a semi-territorial organisation, facing the superior forces of a state that does not attempt to secure the countryside but ties up its army in garrisons and larger cities, thereby allowing the organisation to control the countryside in between military campaigns. In some of these scenarios where the state is strong and the population partly hostile, terror may be the main option for an organisation rather than other militant strategies such as taking over territory or ambushing the forces of the state. As in the case of al-Qaeda in the Sudan and even Boko Haram, the relationship with the state may in some phases be fairly peaceful, even to the extent of the state delegating governance tasks to the jihadists. In such a situation, far from being one of hostility, the relationship between state and organisation becomes one of cooperation. Thus, in some of these scenarios it becomes misleading to see the jihadists as insurgents only: they might choose to employ terrorism in areas with little or no armed conflict, or they might actually be tools of the state. A new typology is needed to understand how these dynamics vary.

This book develops a typology based upon varieties of territorial presence, introducing the concepts in the next chapter. It then proceeds to analyse al-Qaeda in its Sudan years in chapter 3. Chapter 4 introduces the various forces that in the end formed Jama'at Nusrat ul-Islam wal-Muslimin'; while chapter 5 introduces the Islamic State in the Greater Sahara. In chapter 6, Boko Haram is examined, while chapter 7 analyses the Allied Democratic Forces in Congo/Uganda. The book then proceeds to explore al-Hijra and al-Muhajiroun networks in chapter 8. Chapter 9 looks at the Harakat al-Shabaab, while chapter 10 considers the Islamic State in Somalia.

2

DEVELOPING A TYPOLOGY OF TERRITORIAL PRESENCE

Why have there been so many predictions of the downfall of African jihadists when most of the organisations explored in this book remain in existence after more than a decade? In fact, as this book shows, African jihadist organisations do not disappear on the whole. The question may actually deliver important answers about the surprising resilience of these organisations, including their ability to absorb military defeats and transform themselves, abandoning one form of territorial presence for another. The transformation in question involves changes in the organisation's 'toolbox', the techniques it uses to recruit, to create cohesion, and to control the local population. Simply put, these organisational features will depend on the kind of territorial presence a group adopts – whether as groups that exist as illegal clandestine networks, such as Hijra, and those that have some kind of territorial control, as the Allied Democratic Forces (ADF) once had in Congo.

Understanding that the type of teritorial presence not only varies between jihadi organisations but also varies over a single organisation's history will enable analysts to avoid treating the various movements as static, as having an unchangeable form, an organisational 'essense' when most of them have actually gone through immense changes. Indeed, any analysis of African jihadists has to take into account that the organisations in question change over time. Harakat al-Shabaab, for instance, is in many ways a different type of organisation today from when it controlled large territories. Boko Haram also changed from being a clandestine network to an organisation controlling territory but lost this control again. These changes are important; they can tell us something about the future trajectory of jihadi groups that suffer defeat, and the new organisational dynamics that can emerge after such defeats when territorial control is lost. They can also tell us about the mechanisms for survival available to organisations after their defeat at the hands of police forces, military forces or local militias.

This book presents four ideal types of territorial presence for the organisations studied here, depending on the kind of hostile force each faces. Does it face a hostile state with relatively efficient state structures? Does it face a relatively friendly state? Does it face meaningful opposition? Or does it simply face superior enemy forces that win open battles during short campaigns but lack a more permanent presence afterwards?

The Clandestine Network

The clandestine network depicts the type of violent jihadi organisation active in countries with relatively well-functioning state structures, such as Europe, the United States and China. This type of territorial presence is exemplified by organisations like the Red Army Faction and the Weathermen, though it also describes al-Qaeda's pre-9/11 presence in the West.[1] But the clandestine network is also to be found in Africa, even though the African state is often referred to as 'weak', perhaps because academics often tend to focus on the various samples of 'weak' states.[2] Yet they are many countries in Africa with relatively strong state structures that penetrate society to a large degree, such as Eritrea, Tanzania and Ethiopia. In some African countries the state is hierarchical and all-encompassing. In Ethiopia, for instance, the Amharic expression '*Ye Mengist*' comes to mind, illustrating the unity that exists here between the ruler, the state and the party,[3] although there are large changes taking place in this country at the time of writing. Other states have less solid governance structures, but still maintain relatively standard functions, including a considerable law-enforcement capacity. A relatively functioning state with a capable police and security force can maintain and enforce a certain monopoly of violence against militant organisations within it. This situation has consequences for jihadists, which are important to explore, as the case of al-Hijra/al-Muhajiroun illustrates (see chapter 8). Large-scale training bases are hard to build up in countries where there is a relatively stable hostile state. In such a situation, the groups have to organise in a way that avoids drawing attention from the state. In the post-9/11 world, moreover, financial transactions as well as communication channels are much more closely monitored, and this also limits the size of the income transfers possible for the jihadists.[4]

As later chapters illustrate, those African countries that have stronger state structures, such as Ethiopia and Tanzania, have been relatively successful in curtailing and prosecuting jihadists. They still face societal dynamics that encourage the creation of new groups, and they still have clandestine jihadist networks in their territories. Yet one cannot speak of a jihadist 'insurgency' in their territories. Here the jihadists consist of small clandestine networks rather than guerrilla groups, which seldom engage in open battle with military forces but choose instead to use terror. These terror attacks often take the form of 'waves': attacks are launched, the police prosecute members of the networks behind them, and the networks are broken up; subsequently, in some cases, a new network will launch fresh attacks. In the case of Ethiopia and the Shabaab, few such attacks have occurred, and the response of Ethiopian security services has been swift and efficient. In the case of Tanzania, domestic clandestine jihadist networks have launched a greater number of attacks, but these have also been curtailed and contained by the state. The Kenyan government has been less effective, but it has been able to contain several of the domestic networks. At the time of writing large-scale attacks in the centre of Kenya, prominent a few years ago, have ended, and attacks in the border areas near Somalia have also declined.

In the clandestine network scenario, an active state seeks to destroy or root out the violent jihadist organisation within its territory. The state effectively promotes strategies to limit the group's income, to break it up and arrest its members. Organisations that want to survive in such a hostile environment have to maintain secrecy and adopt a clandestine structure. Steps have to be taken to avoid the arrest of even one member for this could lead to the destruction of the group itself, as the organisational chain of command is commonly used to identify members. Consequently, violent jihadist groups often take the form of small secretive cells, in which members are organised to survive in a repressive environment.[5] The mode of operation is not dissimilar to that of resistance groups in Europe during the Second World War, and it is a notable feature of the jihadist networks operating in Kenya and Tanzania. To hide the identities of members and to conceal their strategic goals becomes essential for survival.

Such an organisation will have several traits that will influence its repertoire of activities and internal dynamics. Firstly, it is actually advantageous if the various leaders have limited contact with and knowledge about one another. This will keep sub-groups separate and make the organisation less vulnerable. When a small sub-unit is dismantled by the security apparatus or police, other parts of the organisation may survive.[6] As a result, organisational hierarchies and mechanisms of command cannot be open or known, or else the whole organisation will be vulnerable.[7] In this situation, organisational bureaucracy is of less value as a means to create cohesion.

Personal conflicts within the group, sometimes over lovers, sometimes over money, can have deadly results and lead to the demise of the entire group. The organisational hierarchy (if it exists at all) is often too weak to rein in such conflicts. Organisational sanctions are of limited value because they may lead to defections, which can give the police important information. Inasmuch as the clandestine nature of the group makes the membership unclear even for the leadership, this can lead to fragmentation and ideological confusion. The apparatus of organisational indoctrination lacks the means to maintain ideological homogeneity, which can be further eroded when contacts between the various cells are limited or broken. The existence of opinion formers within cells may become more important than remote ideological leaders, particularly in setting the ideological agenda, as we shall see in later chapters. At times this might lead to tolerance within cells for ideological differences: Islamic State and al-Qaeda followers may, for example, exist in the same networks. In other situations, however, the existence of ideological differences can create clashes between members.

In this kind of organisation, small-group cohesion is often strong and fosters group loyalty and identity. However, a small and closely knit group structure can also lead to what Cronin calls the generation gap, where group members fail to transfer their knowledge to the next generation of potential activists.[8] The organisational hierarchy has few means of systematically training new recruits or recent arrivals. In addition, the lack of bureaucracy means that systematic weapons training and other learning exercises are harder to implement. Training could well be feeble, consisting of the kind of backyard training in Pakistan that Petter Nesser describes in his analysis of the Operation Crevice group arrested in the UK in 2004, or small-scale, ad hoc attempts to rent or use buildings suitable for clandestine training.[9] As Nesser describes it, there seems to have been pressure on network-based organisations to obtain practice and training on the battlefields of jihad, perhaps as a consequence of the constraints put on training in territories controlled by a hostile and relatively efficient state.[10]

The second characteristic feature of clandestine networks is that the risks of joining are high, as potential members can easily be arrested by the police and lose everything. One has to search actively for the group in order to be able to join it, for the group has to maintain secrecy in order to survive. Recruits also face the threat of prosecution by the state. Accordingly, the effort needed to join an organisation is great: it takes real dedication to become a member. Yet it is hard for a terror organisation to be careful and discriminating when it comes to the quality of recruitment if it lacks regular bases or a stable population pool, although the latter disadvantage can be negated by the internet.[11]

It is important to note that most of the literature on disengaging people from extremism focuses on this type of violent jihadist organisation, facing hostile institutions in the form of the government, especially police officers engaged in crime prevention and civilian NGOs involved in disengagement.[12] Europe and the West take centre stage in theories of de-radicalisation, and it is thus not strange that these theories conform to the scenario closest to the situation in the West. However, as will be shown later, not all violent jihadist organisations are clandestine networks, and so disengagement and CVE (Countering Violent Extremism) programmes need to be adjusted to the organisational mode of the group in question.

The third characteristic of this ideal type is that small cell-based structures have difficulty generating an income, as they are under constant watch by the police and are vulnerable to police action.[13] After 9/11, new financial control mechanisms were created by authorities in the West, leading to reduced opportunities to transfer money.[14] Crime, including forms of protection rackets, may be employed to finance the organisation, but this strategy may cause the group to be exposed, especially if large sums are involved. Financial control and surveillance limit income generation, including fundraising activities among sympathisers and even covert support from foreign states. Large-scale 'taxing' of locals will also be hard to achieve.

In this kind of scenario it would be easier for members of these groups to defect, as defectors can get protection from police forces. Even corrupt police forces will have to act, as the defectors would be hard to hide, and continued operations by the group might hurt both the prestige of the country's leaders and its relationship with states hostile to the violent jihadist group. A reluctance to act would lead to pressures from the international community. Corruption may give opportunities to the jihadist networks, as in the case of several African states, yet international pressure and the need for control by the local elite will limit any excesses committed by jihadist groups. Corruption may therefore provide a means for building up cells and escaping arrest, but not for building up militias or establishing larger training facilities.

Lastly, the advantage of a clandestine group operating in a fairly well-functioning society is that it can be active close to attractive targets, like tourist destinations, foreign business companies or large international organisations. Terrorism then becomes a more functional strategy, because the targets are closer geographically.

In many ways, all these features give rise to a situation where there are relatively dedicated recruits, who have smaller sources of financing than the other types presented later. The group also has fewer bureaucratic tools with which to construct their ideology, enhance their training and maintain unity. As a result, fragmentation and ideological confusion become more likely. Law enforcement is perhaps the most important weapon in countering such an organisation, but there is also a role for CVE programmes conducted by municipalities and NGOs.

The clandestine network has been the most commonly studied form of jihadist organisation in academic work, although this has changed somewhat due to the rise of the Islamic State.[15] The operations of these small groups do not constitute an insurgency or a war but bear greater resemblance to what West Germany faced during the Red Army terror campaigns of the 1970s.

The Accepted Presence: Jihadists as a Governance Tool

As Caitriona Dowd and Clionadh Raleigh have correctly suggested, states can be directly involved in promoting violent jihadist groups.[16] This support can be clandestine, but a state can also openly host a jihadist organisation in its own territory, and even manipulate it for its own purposes. Such an organisation might be tolerated, encouraged, and even used for governance purposes by a state. In the case of Boko Haram, it should not be forgotten that the organisation existed openly for more than five years. Moreover, several sources claim that it, or its members, were used for governance purposes by the local Borno government.[17] This is not a new phenomenon: religious extremist groupings in Pakistan were tolerated and even encouraged in the late 1970s, 1980s, 1990s and even the early 2000s.[18] As the next chapter shows, al-Qaeda in Sudan was accepted by the Bashir government from 1991 to 1996, and its members were even used as instructors for insurgent movements supported by the Sudanese.[19] If one regards the Taliban as the sovereign government of Afghanistan between 1996 and 2001, the relationship between Afghanistan and al-Qaeda can be seen as of a similar nature.[20]

In this sense, the 'ungoverned spaces' theory is wrong: a jihadist organisation can be supported by a government in the government's own territory. In Africa, as in the Middle East, there has been a tradition for such groups to be used as agents for the government, as a form of rule by non-state proxies, to save money, maximise income or avoid responsibility for actions. Alex de Waal, commenting upon East African politics, says that 'political life can be described as an auction of loyalties in which provincial elites seek to extract from one or other metropolitan centre the best price for their allegiance'.[21] A sub-group can be used as a tool by a state centre, and receive benefits in return. In some cases, this kind of configuration can be part of a governance strategy to delegate violence to sub-groups in society.[22] Indeed, according to Metz, this has perhaps been one of the most common strategies of state structures in the past.[23] Local factions are seen as tools by local and central authorities, and their independence and their potential or occasional disloyalty may be tolerated.[24] They can easily become part of governance structures and networks outside the state and employed as such by a ruling elite to gain control or extract income. As will be shown later, it was profits and income that motivated state support for al-Qaeda in Sudan.

A violent jihadist group can be allowed to have permanent organisational facilities, bases and even training camps by a relatively well-functioning government. In this case, the organisation will be separate from the hosting state, and not necessarily share the latter's ideology. Al-Qaeda, for example, held a different outlook on foreign policy from both Sudan and the Taliban. Each of them formed a separate entity with a distinguishable ideology, while interacting with the wider society and at the same time isolating themselves from it (see the next chapter).[25]

Importantly, the type of organisation we are discussing here is surrounded by an efficient state apparatus and will, to a certain extent, be limited by that state. If it oversteps the limits defined by the state, there will be consequences. The state might punish excesses or misdemeanours. It will have to approve and tolerate training camps. It will want to approve income-generating mechanisms in general. The state may also attempt to take financial advantage of the organisation, trying to obtain a share of the jihadists' income. If the organisation grows too powerful, there may be sanctions as well. The state may fear a rival. It will want to feel that it maintains sovereignty while hosting the organisation in question. Often the relationship, as with al-Qaeda in Sudan, ends on a sour note. If the organisation becomes a liability for the state, or even if it becomes less useful, the relationship might be brought to an end.

An accepted organisation does not need to be clandestine; it can have both a strong hierarchy and a strong bureaucracy, ensuring training capacity, capacity to handle small-group problems, and control over information reaching the members. It can also earn money, as far as this is allowed by the host state; it can conduct military training, when allowed; and it can recruit new members fairly openly. Information that reaches members can also be controlled by the organisation, and indoctrination can take place relatively freely.

As long as it has a friendly relationship with the host country, ordinary CVE or disengagement programmes are ineffective, and the accepted organisation can even prosecute such efforts by going to court or by forms of harassment. Such a group can maintain a hierarchy and can discipline members and address organisational crises and conflicts. It can engage in large-scale training, as long as it does not frighten the host state. The same goes for income-gathering efforts. The constraints within which the organisation operates may create tensions with the host state, and lead to a collapse or transformation into another form of territorial presence. The problem of an accepted organisation that is seen as troublesome by the international community can also be addressed through pressure against the host state, as happened in Sudan in 1996.

Once again, this scenario does not amount to war or insurgency. The jihadists may participate in wars outside the core areas of the state, but the relationship between the state and the jihadists can be positively friendly. At times, the state may be able to get away with such a relationship if the organisation is of a relatively limited size or because of ignorance and lack of knowledge on the part of the international community. Alternatively, the state might be willing to face demotion to the status of an international pariah.

A Semi-territorial Presence

A semi-territorial presence in many ways reminds one of the traditional insurgency scenario, where, after supposedly large-scale victories over a jihadist organisations, what the president of the South West state of Somalia, Sharif Hassan Sheikh Aden, called 'fly-over territory' is more or less left to the jihadists. Rural security is neglected; territories far from the larger cities, where terror attacks tend to create global headlines, are left alone; and government and international forces entrench themselves in large camps and provide little protection for villagers.[26] Yet it is these very villagers who provide one of the most important sources of income needed to sustain the jihadists of sub-Saharan Africa.

In an interview held in 2016, former US ambassador to Nigeria John Campbell commented on the territorial holdings of Boko Haram. He warned that the question whether Boko Haram still held territory in northern Nigeria was an open one because of the ways in which it could be interpreted.[27] He focused on how the Nigerian military and its allies had dislodged Boko Haram, but also stressed that 'when soldiers leave, the terrorists later return'. In this way Campbell perfectly described the notion of semi-territoriality: in essence, how territory can be controlled and harnessed by a violent organisation despite the presence of a superior hostile army in striking distance. Another good description was given by one of Somalia's senior clan elders interviewed by the writer in 2016: 'These are remote areas and nobody is patrolling them, so they [the Islamic State] come and go as they please. The government only goes after them when their whereabouts become public, and the criminals use their slogans of "we took over certain areas".'[28]

In many cases the enemy of a violent jihadist organisation lacks the resources or the will to patrol or fully secure their areas of operation, although they have the manpower to overwhelm the jihadists in any direct confrontation. The causes of this situation can be many. To fully secure an area, they have to spend resources on police and security; at the same time they have to protect the locals where they live. Thus semi-territoriality can be the result of a strategy of cost avoidance. If it is a peripheral area, an alternative is to retreat from it, to use the funds thus saved for other purposes. This is sometimes combined with attempts to use local non-state networks to wield forms of control, though analysis in later chapters will show that this is often inadequate to stop a violent jihadist organisation.[29] In addition, as Herbst notes, some geographical features simply make control harder to exert, such as in the Sahara.[30] However, semi-territoriality can also be an outcome of military tactics, the attempt to save manpower and negative media attention – not too different from the American strategies in Iraq under General George Casey. The US general stressed the need to reduce US vulnerability and visibility, thus limiting patrols, and to provide security locally.[31] The emphasis was on 'force protection via mounted patrols; deployment in large, fortified bases; and operations in large formations without sustained informal contact with the population'.[32] What the United States was in practice doing was abandoning local control to the insurgents in the periods between mounted patrols.

Some organisations will be able to extract resources, because they are present in borderlands that neighbouring states have a hard time controlling, as parts of al-Qaeda in the Islamic Maghreb (AQIM) have done in the Western Sahara, or the Allied Democratic Forces (ADF) on the Ugandan–Congolese borders. Resources become available when the organisations temporarily dominate local villages or are geographically situated in areas critical for trans-border trade. Formal state control in the periphery may also be weak. In such a situation insurgents simply move from an area cleared by the odd hostile campaign by superior enemy forces, to other safer areas where the enemy's presence is weak. This leads to a deterioration of the security situation elsewhere: such a balloon-squeezing phenomenon prevents security from improving overall.[33] To paraphrase a famous Stephen King short story, the problem is 'Sometimes they come back'. After the odd offensive that 'squeezes the balloon', it simply reverts to its old form.[34]

This situation has several consequences. Firstly, potential local supporters of the enemies of a violent jihadist organisation can easily be punished. Al-Qaeda in Iraq, for example, killed members of the Albu Nimer, the Albu Mahal and the Fahad groups in Iraq, and ended their resistance prior to 2007, partly because the United States seemed uninterested in ensuring security in their tribal areas.[35] This kind of response will have the potential to remove local support for forces trying to fight the group in question. To resist simply becomes too risky when no protection is forthcoming from the more powerful enemies of the jihadist group.

Secondly, the violent organisation becomes a part of day-to-day life, something local people have to live with. By intermarrying with the jihadists, for instance, you can make your existence safer.[36] By joining the jihadists, you might ensure that you and your family receive protection.[37] You can make your existence safer by obeying their orders, or by paying protection money.[38] In the words of an *amenokal* (leader) of the Tuareg in Mali, who wished to be anonymous:

'Sometimes people don't have choice when the Islamists occupy this area, they join to save their lives.'[39]

In this situation, a police force controlled by a state cannot be established because it is simply too insecure.[40] As Alice Hill says, 'once violence reaches certain levels they [the local police] either support the insurgents, or they disappear or they are killed. This is notable in rural areas where police are rarely present.'[41] What often happens instead is that police engage in counterinsurgency missions, focusing more on combat and less on actual policing. In this scenario, as a local you cannot expect justice save perhaps from the violent jihadist groups or from other non-state actors. At the same time, the jihadist group also becomes a point of contact when you want justice. Moreover, the religious image of the organisation might encourage the perception of them as justice providers, and indeed sometimes they are better providers of order than the state. David Kilcullen observed a similar situation in Afghanistan where the Taliban provided a semblance of order. In Africa Jama'at Nusrat ul-Islam wal-Muslimin' and Shabaab have both provided order and forms of justice in areas they control, or where they have a semi-territorial presence, in the form of mobile Sharia courts or Sharia courts in adjacent territories.[42] As a businessman in Mali said: 'Islamists provide the best environment for business because they secure their areas and do not live on the backs of people. They do not charge taxes and do not request contributions from people.'[43] Significantly, as Kilcullen shows, this creates local sympathy and support for the group. What is more, you don't need to implement 'fair' justice to create this effect, but just be able to inject a sense of predictability and order, a sense of safety in chaotic day-to-day life. There is much variation in justice provision among the organisations studied in this book: Boko Haram has shown little interest in providing Sharia, instead focusing on extraction, while Nusrat ul-Islam and Shabaab showed rather more. Semi-territoriality illustrates how these jihadist organisations do not need full control of a territory to implement rudimentary forms of governance, contrary to the conclusions of many scholars analysing rebel governance.[44]

Semi-territoriality also opens up the possibilities for recruitment. In his brilliant essay 'The ontology of political violence', Stathis Kalyvas higlights the way local actors and factions use a wider war to gain allies in their own local conflicts. In Somalia clan groupings have attempted to hijack Shabaab, while in Mali lineage conflicts among the Tuareg have influenced the inner dynamics of the Ansar Dine. Semi-territoriality makes possible this type of attempt to manipulate jihadist organisations.[45] At times the jihadist organisations will attempt to infiltrate powerful local actors as well, such as clans and tribes, and manipulate them in turn.

Thirdly, semi-territoriality also increases income-generating options. Where violent jihadist groups have a semi-territorial presence, the income from taxation or protection money is likely to increase, as locals and even businessmen operating in these areas need to pay to conduct any form of business, including transit through the area.[46] A semi-territorial presence also makes possible the rudimentary control of exports and imports to and from an area as long as the government is absent, thus enabling direct involvement in illegal trade, for example of diamonds, ivory or drugs. The jihadi group may end its illegal activities during government offensives, only to resume them once government forces have withdrawn. Another option is to move activities during enemy offensives to more secure areas.

Illicit trade – in humans, cigarettes, cocaine and hashish – can provide significant income for members of a jihadist group. For example, Mokhtar Belmokhtar, leader of al-Mourabitoun and former leader in al-Qaeda in the Islamic Maghreb, became famous as 'Mr Marlborough' for smuggling cigarettes.[47] In some areas, such 'business ventures' can be fairly profitable. AQIM, according to Levy and Thornberry, earned an estimated $70 million from hostage-taking in the Maghreb from 2005 to 2011, using the Sahara desert to hide their victims.[48] Harakat al-Shabaab earned, according to the United Nations Arms Monitoring Group for Somalia and Eritrea, over $25 million from the charcoal industry in southern Somalia alone, often from checkpoint fees taxing goods in transport.[49] Many of these checkpoints are not permanent, and disappear during the odd government or African Union campaign, only to return afterwards.[50]

These forms of income generation – checkpoints for taxing trade, taxes from businesses that want to travel through your territory, and taxes imposed on small villages – are probably the most important source of revenue for African jihadists. Admittedly, clandestine networks are able to do much of the same, but they cannot tax as efficiently, as the security forces of a functioning state are able to disrupt illicit trade on an almost daily basis.

Fourthly, semi-territoriality provides a stronger role for the command hierarchy of the jihadist group in disciplining their ranks. It becomes simply harder to flee, and one's safety can only be ensured if one escapes to larger enemy army bases or away from the area in question. The fact that local villages are dominated by the jihadists also enables them to employ reprisals against the families of potential defectors without the interference of a functioning police.

With a semi-territorial presence, the organisational toolbox of the jihadist group enlarges to include economic redistribution, a stronger command hierarchy, and increased opportunities for punishing defectors. It does not need to remain clandestine, as it does not face law enforcement within its territory from outsiders. On the modern battlefield it does need to maintain forms of clandestine activity because of drones and surveillance, but not in the same way as a cell-based structure within a state that controls a monopoly of violence.

Semi-territoriality is in many ways key to the many transformations that African jihadists have gone through, and explains why frequent predictions of their demise have proved untrue. Although it is increasingly used for all forms of jihadism, this is the scenario where the term 'jihadist insurgency' really becomes useful, as the scenario resembles the situational dynamics described in many of the academic works on counterinsurgency and insurgency, which are often not relevant for the clandestine network and accepted network scenarios.

The last scenario in our discussion, that of territorial control, concerns a situation where jihadists have stable control of an area over some time, and where they have often started to build up public and more permanent governance institutions,[51] more reminiscent of a state formation process than what is commonly perceived as guerrilla warfare.

Territorial Control

The Islamic State and its expansion took the world by storm in 2014–15, though what the Islamic State did – building institutions in its quest to control territory – was actually nothing new. Organisations like the Taliban, al-Qaeda in the Arabian Peninsula (AQAP) (at least in 2010–11) and the Somali Shabaab had previously controlled large territories at times, and attempted to build up institutions to govern them. Yet with the rise of the Islamic State many started to realise that a violent jihadist organisation could build up something resembling a state structure and have a more permanent presence in a region.[52] The word 'state' is misleading, as the Islamic State's expressed end goal is a global caliphate, for violent jihadism transcends states, although some writers like Brynjar Lia have defined these entities as 'jihadi proto-states'. The long-term goal of most of the Islamic State, mirroring the claims of many other jihadist organisations, is not to be a state in the ordinary sense of the world – they disdain conventional borders – but rather a resurrection of a wider Islamic '*ummah*' (community) as a political entity. Indeed, the Islamic State's announcement of its caliphate was literally called 'Breaking/shattering the borders'. While not all jihadists aim at statehood, those that do will attain it not because of any inherent capacity to govern, but rather because of friends in the international system. Jihadists lack such friends at present, and they will probably not achieve statehood despite having the institutions.[53]

The jihadists who wield territorial control face a situation drastically different from small cell-based, more traditional terrorist organisations, such as Shabaab in Kenya or indeed al-Qaeda in Europe. Some analysts, like Berger, maintain that this is the future of al-Qaeda, that al-Qaeda's affiliates are increasingly controlling more territory, turning them into statelets.[54] The fact remains that windows of opportunity need to be present for such expansion to occur. Extensive territorial control has occurred three times in Africa – in Mali, Nigeria and Somalia – and has been created by the possibilities of civil war, save in Nigeria where the territorial control was short-lived. In the case of the Sahel, the state often lacks the capacity or ability to fully secure the wasteland territories, opening them up for organisations like AQIM. In stronger states, like Kenya or Tanzania, jihadists are doomed to remain smaller, hidden networks for the near future, unless there is a meltdown of the state.

It should be remembered that several Islamist groups, even al-Qaeda affiliates, hold or have held territories. These groups have been exposed to needs and possibilities very different from those of small clandestine organisations in the West, as well as in China and Japan, that use terror to win attention in order to further their goals. The benefits of leading a jihadi organisation that can hold territory, in places like Pakistan and Yemen, and also in Mali and Somalia, are clear. Firstly, as Robert W. McColl argues in his classic article on insurgent bases, territorial control provides a relatively safe haven for leaders, and a safe base that can be used for further development of the movement, including organisational development.[55] Training facilities can be established, indoctrination facilities set up, and a school curriculum both at primary and secondary level developed to indoctrinate the youth. Like-minded ideological recruits, including those from abroad, have a more identifiable territory to which they can travel, and more stable bases in which they can be trained. This may create a wider problem, when returning foreign fighters cause trouble, or even initiate extremist groups in their own countries, as happened in the Horn of Africa.[56]

Secondly, territorial control is prestigious. It provides proof of the jihadist organisation's success on the battlefield, proof of their ability to stand up to their enemies. It offers a clear alternative to other entities that claim to govern the areas that have been conquered by the jihadists.[57] Thirdly, as McColl suggests, it also gives advantages when harnessing resources, making possible the establishment of stable income-generating businesses.[58] If one has more permanent territorial control, extraction can take place in the open, with little need for secrecy or protection against government offensives. It gives an organisation the opportunity to act as a stable income-provider in the territory it controls, as well as offering incentives for long-term planning and 'good governance', and limiting outright predatory behaviour that can ruin future income possibilities.

Much of the literature on African conflicts is focused on opportunity costs, especially in the work of Collier and Hoeffler, where conflicts are depicted as an activity driven by income-seeking rather than grievance or ideology.[59] Besides becoming one of the more stable income-providers on the block, a violent jihadist organisation that holds permanent control of a territory has other incentives to offer. In such a situation, it does not require only frontline fighters, but also administrative functionaries, religious judges, tax collectors and policemen. You do not need to be part of the front line in order to work for the organisation: this makes it more tempting to join out of opportunism. For the jihadists, growth becomes easy, but at the same time it is harder to prevent opportunists from entering the organisation. There is a possibility of infiltration by other social groups, such as tribal groups, clans or criminal networks trying to control part of the organisation. This may also happen in a semi-territorial phase, but the likelihood increases when there are relatively permanent and stable bases and institutions, which make it easier for outsiders to reach, contact and even infiltrate these hierarchies, knowing as they do where to go.

Fourthly, the scenario potentially gives organisational control of recruits and members.[60] Increased control, and the lack of contestation by other armed factions, hinder desertion, for example, although McLauchlin believes that the nature of the terrain can negate this advantage.[61] Indeed, the tendencies to foster cohesion increase with territorial control to include a stronger command hierarchy and increased opportunities for punishing defectors. As Kalyvas suggests, as territories become uncontested, one is more able to punish defectors.[62] At the same time, the quality of the command hierarchy grows in importance as it is able to play a larger role. The organisation no longer needs to maintain a clandestine existence, but can use its resources and facilities to attempt to develop networks and relations outside the areas that it controls.

Fifthly, the governance aspect of the organisation may become more important than in the other scenarios. In his discussion of stationary versus roving bands, Mancur Olson stresses that a more permanent type of territorial control provides an incentive to avoid predatory practices and to plan for long-term forms of taxation and extraction, since one needs to ensure that locals will provide income in the future as well. Investments to increase income might become advantageous.[63] It is also important to note that locals might become more cooperative as the jihadists' control endures, as commonly happens with other actors in armed conflicts.[64]

Full territorial control (rather than semi-territorial control) can of course have other effects as well. During my stay in Gaza in 2013, I was reminded of this by a former cabinet minister in Hamas's Gaza administration, who claimed that it was impossible to be a hard-core ideologist when having to interact with neighbours, 'amongst others having to depend on Israeli hospitals for types of treatment'.

It is important to note that territorial control is not only advantageous, but can be disadvantageous as well. To establish permanent institutions in the open, to wield an army instead of a guerrilla force, indeed to hold territory at all, makes a group more vulnerable. If larger and superior forces intervene, loss of prestige is inevitable; it is then hard to hold on to what you have gained. The organisation in question will face the possibility of loss of income (through taxing) and loss of status and may have to transform back into a clandestine organisation again. Furthermore, developing a state structure is not cheap: funds that could be used by the military may need to be diverted to creating a territorial administration.

What Does This Mean?

What this discussion means is that the organisational behaviour of jihadist groups is partly dependent on the type of territorial presence they hold. There is no 'one size fits all' approach. Organisations with territorial and semi-territorial control have more flexibility and more organisational tools available to them. Many of their recruits are present for reasons other than global ideological goals. Both a semi-territorial presence and full territorial control can counter government attempts to disrupt income-gathering and indoctrination or educational activities. On the other hand, clandestine networks and organisations with an accepted presence are more easily constrained by the state. The former have to survive in a hostile environment, while the latter can easily be a victim of policies of the state that supports it, and its excesses might easily be punished.

An organisation will often change territorial presence. Boko Haram started out as an accepted organisation, turned into a clandestine network, and then took semi-peripheral control. Shabaab started out as a clandestine network, acted as an accepted organisation during the time of the Sharia Courts movement, then turned into a clandestine network once again. Subsequently, it became semi-territorial, and then took territorial control. Now it is reverting to semi-territoriality. An organisation can have clandestine networks as offshoots, despite having territorial control. In fact, its bases may serve other clandestine networks for training purposes or safety, in the way that Shabaab has served Hijra and Boko Haram. We must remember that it is not inevitable that an organisation will transform from a clandestine network (or from having an accepted presence) into semi-territoriality or territoriality. Yet, if such a transformation takes place, the organisational characteristics will change. In the Rift, the Horn and the Sahel, such change has been mistaken for defeat, yet it was rather a matter of transformation. At the same time, transformation, especially away from semi-territoriality and territoriality, makes organisations vulnerable in their transitional phase, and they may face heavy losses. However, when the transition ends, a new period of stability may ensue.

We now have a model based on several common assumptions, with which we can attempt to categorise the organisations in the Horn, the Rift and Sahel.

Territoriality: Status of African Jihadist Organisations Today

Organisation name	Jama'at Nusrat ul-Islam wal-Muslimin'	The Islamic State in the Greater Sahara	Allied Democratic Forces (ADF)	Shabaab	Al-Hijra/al-Mujahiroun	Islamic State in Somalia	Boko Haram, both factions
Type of Control	ST	ST	ST	T/ST	C	ST	ST

ST = semi-territorial, T = territorial, C = cell-based

There are several warnings that should accompany this model. The first is that it becomes important not to mistake transformation from one form of presence to another as defeat. To lose all larger cities, as Boko Haram and Shabaab have done over the past years, does not mean being conquered, as you can operate freely in a periphery where your enemies are hardly present. To be vanquished as an accepted organisation does not mean the end if you have a periphery to flee to, nor does the dismembering of a cell structure signals its demise. Military victories in open battle mean nothing if the countryside is not secured for the locals.

The model also contains precautions for the 'ungoverned spaces' theory. While ungoverned spaces might be governed by tribal or clan groupings, or local patrimonial agents of foreign governments, these may easily become too weak to stop a violent jihadist organisation and, moreover, may lack loyalty to the organisation's global enemies, thus causing them to refrain from combating the jihadists. Secondly, a violent jihadist organisation may exist both in a setting with a fairly well-functioning state (of which, contrary to the stereotypes, there are many in Africa) and in a setting without or with few state institutions, in 'ungoverned space'. Depending on which setting it finds itself in, the configuration of the organisation will vary.

How does Transformation Occur and What does It Say about the Future?

Transformations give us a good tool for understanding the dynamics that may influence these organisations in the future. What this comparative study suggests is that so far many groups have moved from an accepted presence into a clandestine network, then further into a semi-territorial presence. Many of the organisations studied here have at times functioned as a tool for states or, in the case of Shabaab, an organisation (the Sharia Courts movement) in control of territories. As will be shown later, al-Shabaab, al-Qaeda, ADF, Ansar Dine and, to a certain extent, Boko Haram all served such a purpose at various stages of their history. For most of these organisations, this phase seemingly often manifested itself in the 1990s and early 2000s, when several other jihadist groups were ignored and allowed freedom of operation in their initial phases (e.g. Hijra). Increased attention given to jihadism by international actors has probably limited such opportunities for now, but one can speculate that increased international focus on power politics and great power rivalry may at some stage in the future open up such possibilities again. After changes of power in the countries that hosted them, or as a result of international pressure, these groups were forced to transform, as the state intensified its attempts to curtail them, and they mostly, but not always, transformed into clandestine networks.

The clandestine network phase is the great filter of jihadist organisations. Some do not make it beyond this stage, some are defeated or seriously curtailed, and they cease at that point. To enter the stage of territoriality or semi-territoriality there need to be weakened opponents in some form. Shabaab took advantage of rural anarchy and the minor presence of the Somali government and Ethiopian forces to establish itself in the Somali countryside. Boko Haram and ADF took advantage of the weak presence of state forces in the Borno countryside and the Rwenzori hills respectively. Ansar Dine took advantage of a military coup in Mali, and the fighting between the Movement for the National Liberation of Azawad (MNLA) and the state. In this sense, an absence of efficient state structures, and very often (though not always) a preceding civil war, provided the conditions under which transformation into semi-territoriality could take place. In some cases, where organisations like Boko Haram, Ansar Dine and Shabaab managed to defeat their enemies, they achieved territorial control. However, in Africa, territorial control by a jihadist organisation has always resulted in foreign intervention, as regional powers and in some cases international actors simply do not tolerate territorial control by jihadists. There are good reasons for the lack of tolerance: as shown by the various Malian jihadists and also by the Shabaab, attacks by organisations that exercise territorial control can lead to the establishment of new groups or the reinvigoration of old ones outside the area of control.

What happens when the jihadists lose territorial control? A military campaign can oust a jihadist organisation from control of an area, as happened in the cases of Shabaab, Boko Haram, Ansar Dine and the ADF. Yet these military victories have so far not amounted to total defeats, as success in large campaigns simply does not fully bring an end to African jihadist organisations, although it forces the jihadists into a costly transformation. The key to understanding this failure is the transformation from territorial to semi-territorial control in the African countryside. Events in the countryside of Africa seldom gain international attention. Villagers' lives are in this sense cheap, often neglected or at best regarded as of low priority by the urban political elite, and attacks do not gain much coverage in the international media. Yet, as will be shown in the various case studies in this book, the income-generating possibilities in rural Africa are large. An organisation can keep itself alive for decades by preying on locals in the rural areas.

The semi-territorial presence is perhaps the most durable of all the scenarios in this book. Such a presence ensures that the groups can take advantage of the most important income source for African jihadists: not financial support from remote organisations like the Islamic State or the central al-Qaeda, but the taxation of rural farmers and businessmen operating in the areas where the jihadists are active. The cattle thefts carried out by the Islamic State of Sahara, the '*koormeer*' of the Shabaab, the villagers pillaged by Boko Haram, all create the income needed for the organisations, as the locals are not protected. The jihadists even gain followers because of locals' need to integrate with the organisations for security reasons. And the jihadists become durable: they are there for the long run, able to go on the offensive when regional intervention ends, or when some sort of conflict erupts between their enemies. However, without such occasions, there will be no territorial control, just a bloody stalemate, in which the rural population suffers and the jihadists sponsor terror in the wider region.

There are variations in territorial presence beyond those described above. An interesting fact concerns the newcomers, the African affiliates of the Islamic State, both the Islamic State in Sahara and the Islamic State in Somalia. When facing a strong al-Qaeda affiliate, the Islamic State groups tend to end up on the peripheries of the al-Qaeda organisation's area of semi-territoriality or territoriality. They are not able to survive in the core areas of the al-Qaeda affiliates, save in some areas, as small clandestine networks. In the case of Boko Haram, this did not happen, as Boko Haram never was an al-Qaeda affiliate. Boko Haram remains, even after its split, the Islamic State's strongest affiliate in sub-Saharan Africa. However, in cases where jihadists only have a clandestine network presence, the exact boundaries between Islamic State and al-Qaeda sympathisers become much less clear, as shown by the Tanzanian groups, many of which never took sides.

While the weakness of state institutions in peripheries is important in explaining semi-territoriality and territoriality, these peripheries do have governance structures, and hence they are not ungoverned. The cases in this book show the importance of 'traditional' structures of governance, popularly known as 'tribe' or 'clan', in an understanding of jihadist organisations. At the outset we can define the tribe or clan, loosely following Olivier Roy, as a segmentary solidarity group based on a real or perceived lineage, with an internal system of regulation, cultural traits and forms of local notables.[65] As Mohamed Husein Gaas remarks, the study of such structures has been confused: there is a pre-colonial tendency to see them as carved in stone, as primordial and given; subsequently a modernist approach dismissed these notions altogether; while an instrumentalist approach sees them as entities used by elites to further their interests.[66] Gaas correctly points out the errors of such views, and instead sees tribal identity as fluid, but with a more slowly changing core identity that often enables tribal agency.[67] People can hold several, overlapping identities, giving rise to different loyalties. Jihadists might have a tribal membership, despite joining the jihad as individuals. There might be an equally strong tribal and jihadi identity among recruits to a jihadist group, and tribal or clan structures might interact with other hierarchies in society to establish hybrid forms. Gaas points to the example of Somalia's warlords in the 1990s, whose identity drew on clan, though few of them were clan leaders, and to the selection of members for the most recent Somali parliament, which drew on clan structures, but was also influenced by patrimony, religious affiliations and personal relationships.[68]

Admittedly, there are several studies, for example Gabriel Koehler-Derrick's account of al-Qaeda in the Arabian Peninsula (AQAP), that dismiss tribalism as important for jihadists.[69] Yet his study was limited to two provinces only, and to an organisation, AQAP, that then lacked territorial control in tribal areas, although it gained this later. AQAP attempted to woo Yemeni tribes, but recruitment was not systematic in clan or tribal areas, as it was for example in Somalia, and the Yemeni branch of al-Qaeda did not have semi-territorial or territorial control at the time. Analysts also assumed that a stable alliance between the two, where the tribe in question permanently and collectively sheltered al-Qaeda, was the ultimate confirmation of tribal importance.

Gaas's work introduces much-needed nuance to our understanding of the tribe/clan, while Virginie Collombier and Olivier Roy's edited volume suggests a complex pattern of interaction between tribes and jihadists. Tribes/clans can have agency, in the sense of trying to co-opt jihadist networks, to rival them, to ally with them. Tribes/clans have been defeated by jihadists, but also have beaten them. Jihadism has been used as a tool against oppressive tribal structures by tribes/clans (or members thereof) viewed as inferior by others.[70] The clan/tribal leadership may not have any influence on the tribal/clan traditions that jihadists take advantage of, and it could be tribal/clan-based business networks or tribal/clan solidarity that allows a Kanuri jihadist from Borno to escape into Kanuri villages in Cameroon and receive support, despite these villages being far from jihadist in their inclinations.[71] As Hosham Dawod suggests, tribes may vary in importance, as national leaders choose to empower them, or as they become more important as providers of security.[72] In addition, tribal identity will overlap with other identities, such as national identity and even a global jihadist identity. Tribes are seldom the only source of identification, and they may have unclear boundaries. As an illustration of the flexibility of and the differences between the various tribal systems, one should recall that Ansar Dine did not recruit only from specific sub-tribes of the Tuareg in Mali, but also from caste groups as well.[73]

In this book, several consequences and benefits of clan and tribal networks are identified. They can provide shelter to individual jihadis fleeing an enemy. Tribes/clans can also offer an advantage when a jihadist organisation moves into new areas, for jihadists with a local clan/tribal background can be sent first into the new territories, as happened both in Somalia and in Mali. This feature is essential in explaining developments in these two areas. Tribes/clans can attempt to manipulate the jihadists, and also use them to settle tribal/clan scores. As Gaas argues, one has to be cautious about the idea of primordialism: the loyal, eternal jihadist clan does not exist, loyalties come and go, alliances shift, and individual clan/tribe members act differently. Yet clan/tribal networks can be drawn upon, even beyond traditional clan/tribal leaders, and alliances between tribes and jihadist organisations may in fact be forged.

Where tribal/clan structures exist, the jihadists have to interact with them in the semi-territorial as well as territorial phases. The tribes need to be governed, they need to be taxed, and tribal conflicts that disrupt jihadist operations need to be settled: thus we see jihadists mediating in tribal conflicts. At the same time, tribes and clans need to hedge themselves against attacks from the jihadists, which they do by marrying some of their women to jihadists, or providing recruits, and in some cases even attempting to capture whole organisations. As a result, organisations that come from outside will develop roots in new areas, as AQIM did in Mali, though it should be remembered that such roots are often the result of forms of occupation.

In areas with stronger state structures, the state has often curtailed tribal power, or entrenched it within the state structure through forms of hybrid arrangements, such as tribal voting in Kenya. In consequence, the tribal/clan networks become less important in an accepted presence or clandestine network scenario. Clan/tribe networks may facilitate contacts, but the traditional structures of tribal governance do not really matter. Yet, in the cases of semi-territoriality and territoriality, tribalism is an underestimated ideological current in most of the jihadist organisations discussed in this book. It influences the jihadists' policies, for they need to play the tribal game in order to survive, and they often need to interact with those tribal institutions and leaders that are important in their surroundings.

Some of this holds true for other collective beliefs within jihadist organisations as well. Ideology tends to be more fluid than is often assumed. Ideology can, for example, be used by 'non-believing' impostors in order to gather support, or by unbelieving individuals as an instrument to gain legitimacy. However, even those who want to manipulate ideology for their own gains have to act according to some of its tenets if they want to be regarded as a follower of that ideology. This means that in such situations ideology can still have an impact on action. Moreover, the instrumental use of religion actually underlines the potential importance of ideology: it means that ideological assumptions do attract followers, for otherwise it would be impossible to gain recruits by pretending to adhere to specific ideological tenets. If ideology matters for followers, it also can influence their behaviour at a micro level.

Ideological assumptions may of course also have a direct influence on leadership and on the organisation as a whole.[74] Ideology enables individuals who believe in it to identify an in-group of whom they are a 'part', such as a class, *ummah* (community), race or nation. It can also influence strategies, which may be defined by the ideology itself.

If the leadership of an organisation believes in a specific ideology, this ideology may define how the group identifies itself and which allies it seeks to establish connections with. Such beliefs may also define what type of aims the organisation has, some of the rationale of individuals who want to join the group, the strategies that are prominent for them, and the strategies that are unacceptable: in all these ways they act as a frame of reference.[75]

However, there are pitfalls in understanding ideology. It is possible to homogenise ideology too much, especially when studying Islamist organisations. Such groupings often claim that their policies are directly based on the Quran and the Hadith, yet they often vary from group to group. As Scott Appleby argues, to use religion for the purposes of violence is often to suppress one aspect of it and highlight another.[76] Any jihadist position is a reconstruction, a reinvention of aspects of the Islamic religion. One interpretation, containing several specific assumptions, could be preferred over others, but this interpretation, and its assumptions, are far from the only ones. Sub-religious categories like Wahhabism, neo-Wahhabism, Salafism and neo-Salafism are often employed when studying many of the movements explored in this book. Although related to the behaviour of the groups in question, the definition of these groups varies, as does their propensity to use military power. Ultimately, there are too many internal variations to employ these categories meaningfully.[77]

What is important is that the assumptions behind the ideological positions adopted by jihadist organisations need to be studied in more detail, thereby breaking down the ideology into more fine-tuned and precise elements, which can be shared at times by individuals outside a particular ideological strand, such as Wahhabism or Salafism.[78] Such an approach will also enable us to explore ideological reconstructions, the elements of grander Islamist ideologies that have changed and been adapted to local circumstances. This will allow us to recognise that ideologies overlap, as do ideological tenets. Indeed, it is one of the findings of this book that none of the organisations studied here are dominated by a single type of Islamic ideology. Organisations are rather arenas where different elements of ideologies meet, including non-Islamic ones such as clannism, nationalism and tribalism. As will be shown later, these latter elements can form part of the ideology espoused by a violent jihadist organisation, where they are dressed up in a jihadist language.

A focus on wider ideological systems can lead a researcher to ignore the fact that one person might actually believe several different ideological rationales. It is possible, for example, to merge conventional views from Marxism, liberalism and nationalism with forms of Islamism, as in the work of the revolutionary socialist Ali Shariati in pre-revolution Iraq, in this way gaining a wider audience.[79] It is possible for jihadists to take advantage of ideological openings created by merging popular elements from seemingly different ideological positions. For example, Islamists in Ansar Dine exploited the animosity of Tuareg clans and castes against the central leadership in Mali in 2013, in the process merging clannism and Islamism as well as class issues.[80] By doing so, the organisations in question present themselves as an answer to specific grievances that plague the clan groups from which they recruit members. Indeed, I will argue that such ideological openings, events or tendencies, which allow radical Islamist organisations to gain legitimacy through sympathy for parts of their ideological programme shared by other parties in a conflict, are vital in explaining the territorial conquests of Islamists in the Horn, the Rift and the Sahel. Overlaps in common assumptions help radical Islamists to impose other, more alien assumptions on societies, because they are seen as allies of nationalists or ethnic groups or mere champions of justice. Some parts of their ideological repertoire may be able to attract followers to a larger degree than others, because they resonate with local opinion or the local situation.

While one needs to see ideology, and indeed the assumptions of religion, as intrinsically fluid and liable to change, this does not mean that they are unimportant.[81] Ideological preferences change over time, but such processes of change can take a long time, and thus create some stability in the meantime. As Sanín and Woods remark, there has been a tendency in the literature to abandon the focus on overarching ideological typologies and move towards ideological elements that characterise specific patterns of actions or institutions. This book will follow that tendency.[82] We examine here specific elements that prescribe action or loyalty towards one or other reference group. Such ideological assumptions can be found in speeches and direct interviews with organisational leaders. As leaders may be detached from regular members, who might hold different assumptions, it is important to triangulate the opinions and actions of the former with those of the latter.

As will be shown later in this book, an examination of ideology that goes beyond a study of Wahhabism, neo-Wahhabism, Salafism and neo-Salafism may produce some surprising results. Wahhabism is, for example, supposed to be universal, transcending ethnic, tribal or clan borders, yet nationalism or ethnicism can be a surprisingly potent mobilising factor even for an Islamist group claiming to be universalist. Although somewhat contradictorily, nationalism and a more global idea of a unified *ummah* can be combined, as the Shabaab leader Ahmed Godane did when appealing for support against Ethiopian forces in the African Union contingent in Somalia in February 2014, by focusing on Somalia's special position in the *ummah* and on Islam as part of Somali identity.[83] Ethnicity, tribe and clan may also infuse an organisation, partly for operational reasons. As mentioned earlier, territorial control over an area inhabited by a particular clan or tribe may influence recruitment and membership of a group. Tribal conflicts can also manifest themselves within an organisation; indeed, tribalism and ethnicity are often alive and well within Islamism.[84]

Even jihadists can have goals that resonate with grievances in a larger population, especially if there is no alternative organisation that effectively promotes similar goals. At times, the fact that militants have a religious image, in a corrupt society where trust is rare and where dedicated religious individuals are regarded as more trustworthy, can be a valuable asset. Religiosity can be seen as projecting trust, as well as law and order, especially in an early phase when the exact nature of the militant agenda is not well known. This happened in Somalia during the Sharia Courts movement, in Pakistan during the Taliban offensive in the Swat valley, and in Afghanistan during the Taliban's expansion in 1996–2001. The fact that other solutions, more secular movements, have tried, and failed, to uphold law and order gives legitimacy to the alternative. There is thus a trajectory which promotes militant Islamism as a solution, but this trajectory can be disturbed when alternatives exist, or when a state (or local factions that are strong enough) actually exists to uphold a minimum of law and order and curtail jihadist efforts. Specific rationales of jihadist groups may be influenced by conceptions of justice grounded in religious perceptions, by local conditions, or by expectations directed towards religion in poorer and corrupt countries, where religion inspires trust and may induce hopes of the provision of justice and redistribution as well as just governance.

Writers like Shaukat Ali and Dr Mohammad al-Burray have shown the immense number of written Islamic texts that draw a link between Islam and good governance.[85] These links can involve a set of assumptions in which radicals truly believe and for which local populations and citizens yearn, perhaps because of existing corrupt or limited governance. Such assumptions can create an ideological opening, enabling the insertion of other ideological assumptions that are more alien to locals. Indeed, justice as a concept plays a crucial role in the thoughts of some strategic thinkers of militant Sunni Islamism. One example is Abu Bakr al-Naji and his focus on managing 'savagery' by 'establishing Sharia justice among the people who live in the regions of savagery'.[86] Abu Ubayd al-Qurashi was concerned with how zones of territorial control could become enclaves for social and economic justice and thereby showcase the achievements of militant Islamist organisations to a wider population.[87] Providing Islamic governance to a local people can be a highly popular ideological assumption among potential recruits, especially if alternative governance institutions are abusive or corrupt. It is in many ways a 'heart and minds' strategy to win local support, yet it is also part of the new Islamic society envisaged as an end result. Governance has featured in the propaganda or actions of al-Qaeda affiliates and allies in places as far apart as Yemen, Afghanistan, Pakistan, Somalia and Mali.[88]

Governance is hard to exercise without territorial or semi-territorial control, but it can still figure in propaganda and thus be important for recruitment Indeed, references to governance have emerged in the propaganda of all of the organisations studied in this book.[89] Even if it is used instrumentally, as a mere tool to attract followers, it nevertheless is important to them and thus for the organisation in question. Governance can be implemented rigorously, or it can be mere rhetoric, yet even in the latter case it can influence the motivation of recruits, and the way the organisation attempts to be perceived and thus its actions.

There are other ideological assumptions that are more commonly cited by researchers. One of these concerns both reference group and motivation, more specifically the existence of a form of pan-Islamic motivation. This can be seen in speeches focusing on the resurrection of the caliphate, or an even wider obligation, as for example in Abdullah Azzam's classic book *Join the Caravan*, to fight for the protection of 'Muslim lands' under attack from non-Muslim enemies, in this way launching a pan-national identity. For Azzam, ethnicity, tribalism and nationalism do not hold the same importance as solidarity based on religion. Azzam quotes the medieval Sunni theologian Ibn Taymiyyah: 'When the enemy has entered an Islamic land, there is no doubt that it is obligatory on those closest to the land to defend it, and then on those around them, ...for the entire Islamic land is like a single country. Also, [it is compulsory] to go forth to meet the enemy without permission from parents or people to whom one is in debt. The texts of [Imam] Ahmad are quite explicit regarding this.'[90]

Although people like Azzam fought for the abolition of secular borders and the establishment of a state based on the Muslim *ummah*, an *ummah*-based identity can coexist with a local identity, and both together might spur conflict. Azzam himself saw the resurrection of a Muslim political entity as a long-term goal, and pragmatically accepted the existence of other political entities, as well as the establishment of local Islamist entities, allowing some space for local interests.[91] For those acting on *ummah*-based solidarity, this means that there is no need for the political unity of the *ummah*. What is required is just solidarity. It is not necessary to turn the *ummah* into a state but rather the aim is to create a religious community inspiring loyalty.[92] Others focus on the resurrection of a political entity consisting of Muslims; while yet others focus on an expansion of this territory into non-Muslim lands. The aim can thus be a global Islamic state, the political union of existing Islamic states, or simply the protection of existing Muslim states, but for all of these versions the enemy becomes global as well as local forces attacking an imagined pan-Islamic entity.[93] All three versions are found in African jihadist organisations, or at least in their rhetoric. Such wider identities can of course coexist with ethnic identities, just as European Union identities can coexist with local ones. It is important to note that such coexistence does not mean that a conflict is 'local'. A local identity does not necessarily prevent global action; and solidarity with a perceived global *ummah* under attack may coexist with a more local clan solidarity.

This book shows that other global currents, such as Takfirism, are important. This term is used here to describe the desire by some Muslims to condemn other Muslims for their beliefs.[94] An element of Takfirism can be traced back to Saudi Arabia and Abd al-Wahhab, the main founder of what outsiders term Wahhabism. Wahhab was a crucial actor in the establishment of Saudi Arabia, bestowing legitimacy on Saud ibn Abd al-Aziz, the founder of the current Saudi monarchy. The latter launched several attacks on the Ottoman state, a supposedly Muslim state, claiming that the Sunni Muslim Ottomans were disbelievers and polytheists. Abd al-Wahhab enabled the Saudi dynasty to send a harsh message to the Ottomans accusing them of being un-Islamic, thus starting a tradition, within what was named Wahhabism, of condemning other Muslim strains, such as Sufism and Shiism, for not being Islamic.[95] Later Saudi scholars like Abd al-Aziz ibn Baz continued this tradition by expressing condemnation of 'deviant Muslims' such as Sufis – charismatic Sunni Muslims – and Shias, in brochures and booklets distributed free in Africa, and sponsored by the Saudi Arabian ministry of information.[96] Such views also often draw upon specific, and contested, interpretations of the works of the Egyptian Islamic writer Said Qtub.[97] A Takfir assumption is potentially problematic for an Islamist organisation, for a staunch critique of the rest of Islam will alienate potential allies. It is in itself a potential driver of conflict. In the Sahel, the Rift and the Horn, this can be seen in the attacks by the Shabaab on Sufis in Somalia.[98]

Yet another ideological assumption is anti-modernism. Here Islamism becomes the protector of traditions in a moving and changing world in which knowledge is increasingly based on the values of the European Enlightenment and supplied by outsiders, often Westerners or East Asians. The object of the attack here is social change and the onslaught of foreign habits, including those that may be sinful. The wish is to return to the pure habits of the past. It should be noticed that many of the previously discussed assumptions are based on a reinterpretation of the past, on the claim to go back to the roots of things. The same is true for ideological assumptions which have the aim of protecting old values. In this sense, an anti-modernist assumption will have similarities with an *ummah*-based assumption: Islam is seen as under attack, but in a cultural rather than a military way. What is seen as Western knowledge, even simple assumptions such as that the earth orbits round the sun, can be criticised, as Ibn Baz did, or when the Boko Haram leader Shekau objected to Western knowledge and Western-style schools in Nigeria.[99] In this way Islam becomes more than a reference group, but an *ummah* conceived of as a political entity under attack, and the war to defend it becomes something that is fought in the mind as well. There is thus a virtual *ummah*, and its ideas, as much as its borders, need defence.

There may be other rationales of jihadist organisations as well, though what we have described so far will provide useful tools in understanding the movements studied in this book. There are, for instance, also opportunists, individuals who attempt to use the banner of religion to gain power for their own sake, or individuals who join Wahhabist-inspired jihadist organisations because they need financial support from them. This opportunism does not mean that these assumptions fail to influence the individuals: even opportunists sometimes have to pretend to adhere to the 'belief set' if they want to use it for mobilisation. The assumptions thus influence the types of action taken and the rhetoric employed.

One important question here is the role of transfer channels – above all, the international media – for ideological elements. The media contribute to the existence of grievances on behalf of an 'imagined community', an ideological or religious macro-group such as the global Muslim *ummah*. The media also transfer brands and trademarks, such as al-Qaeda, which acquire the signification of success. One way of exploring the growth of radical Islam is to see al-Qaeda as a brand name, which, given the focus on the original organisation, helped direct considerable attention to local organisations, indeed local youths, after 9/11.[100] Another approach is to see both doctrines and tactics as transferred through international networks, by recruits who, after fighting in Afghanistan and Iraq, returned to their home countries: this applies to the Shabaab and AQIM, and perhaps also (though this is contested) to Boko Haram.[101] As we shall see, among the organisations studied in this book both of these channels have been in operation.

It is important to stress again the limitations of a clandestine network in attempting to homogenise beliefs in an organisation and to discipline members into following orders despite their divergent beliefs. On the other hand, jihadists in a semi-territorial or territorial mode may believe in many things, but there are disciplinary mechanisms to keep them in line. The introduction of ideological deviances in the Sahel, the Rift and the Horn, as the Islamic State came to the fore on the world stage, led to the fragmentation of semi-territorial organisations loyal to al-Qaeda only at the periphery, not at their centre.

Setting the Stage for the Case Studies

This book takes a comparative historical approach to the wave of violent jihadist organisations that spread over sub-Saharan Africa during the last twenty-five years. Such an approach makes it possible to trace the intellectual and historical roots of al-Qaeda, both as a structured organisation (where there are clear organisational links) and as a looser movement of ideas (where there are ideological overlaps). The book first explores al-Qaeda's historical roots in the region, starting with its years in Sudan and its transition from an organisation that largely performed a military advisory role in the region, to an organisation that staged terror attacks on Western targets. It also explores the history of the major militant Sunni Islamist movements in the Horn, the Rift and Sahel, starting with AQIM and its move to the south, and the case of Jama'at Nusrat ul-Islam wal-Muslimin'. It then moves on to explore the Islamic State offshoot in the Sahel, the Islamic State in Greater Sahara. The book continues by analysing the Boko Haram and all its factions (within one chapter because of the claims of both fractions to be the 'real' Boko Haram), as well as the Allied Democratic Forces. It then proceeds to the Horn and the Rift, studying the networks of the Swahili coast, and Shebaab and the Islamic State in Somalia. In the conclusion, it draws comparative lessons from Africa which could have a wider validity. The study also provides an opportunity to observe militant Sunni Islamist organisation in a tribal/clan setting. It deals with actors that are unfamiliar to many Western readers, but important in the settings facing al-Qaeda in Iraq, Yemen and the tribal areas of Pakistan.

The book is based on field research in Nigeria, Somalia, Mali, Congo, Uganda, Egypt, Sudan, Kenya and Tanzania, and on secondary sources relating to other countries. I also had the pleasure of drawing upon regional partners conducting qualitative interviews for me in Mali, Somalia, Kenya and Nigeria. Secondary sources include media reports, United Nations reports, works of analysts and other researchers, as well as the publications of the jihadi organisations themselves, often available online or through jihadist forums. The book will analyse the growth of each organisation, exploring the reasons for growth, at the level of individual members, of the entrepreneurs who created and developed the organisations, and of the society that surrounds them. It will then proceed to compare the various groups.

The book is based on several methodological principles. It assesses the credibility of sources, emphasising the closeness of sources to the events the book analyses, and the direction of their potential bias. Bias does not necessarily make a historical source worthless; it can actually strengthen its historical value if the source contradicts its expected bias. It nevertheless becomes important to gain information about the source itself, so as to understand its role and bias. The propaganda arms of Ansar Dine, Boko Haram and other organisations have several audiences to which they may want to tailor their messages. These organisations speak to a global audience as well as a local one, to followers and potential followers as well as enemies. Their messages might vary according to which audience they target, and so the messages need to be examined and compared. Rhetoric has to be compared with action as well, and thus locals who are outsiders need to be interviewed. Triangulating sources becomes important, and it is a principle that will be followed in this book.

3

PROLOGUE: AL-QAEDA IN SUDAN

Perhaps the most overlooked jihadist organisation that led its operations from the Sahel, the Rift and the Horn areas is al-Qaeda. Al-Qaeda was commonly viewed as an 'outsider' in Africa, but this is not true for a period during the 1990s. Admittedly, it had its origins outside Africa, and in many ways was a global organisation when it moved to Africa in 1991. But after 1991, its top leaders were Africa-based, and the Khartoum years were in many ways formative in respect of its ideology. In addition, the organisation created networks that were to prove lasting.[1]

The study of al-Qaeda in these years is not without its problems. The primary sources for the Sudanese years of al-Qaeda are limited, and many of the available accounts actually draw on the same sources, especially the testimonies of the defector Jamal al-Fadl.[2] Some accounts put forward interesting narratives but fail to refer to reliable primary sources, leaving many of their claims in doubt.[3] The presence of al-Qaeda in Africa has also been politicised. Several Sudanese leaders have, for example, attempted to promote an image of Osama bin Laden, for years after he left the country, as pacific and isolated in order to appease Western critics, thus also hampering access to primary sources, while hostile neighbours had an interest in stressing al-Qaeda's presence. Documentation found in Afghanistan and Pakistan has removed some of the problems, and it seems certain that al-Qaeda was active both politically and militarily in Sudan and had connections with several movements in neighbouring countries.[4] However, what has been overlooked is its real embeddedness in Sudanese politics, and the parallels between al-Qaeda's role in Sudan and its influence on other non-state actors in African politics.

As this chapter will show, al-Qaeda was more than just an organisation based in Sudan. It was in fact frequently employed by Sudanese leaders for foreign and domestic policy purposes. In this sense, it was a part of a governance strategy not so different from that of other countries of sub-Saharan Africa. Governance functions (including security) have in many African countries been delegated by the state to other actors. In this regard, armed groups and non-state networks built around specific leaders play a significant role, at times even equalling formal state institutions in importance. Indeed, over the last twenty years, this type of outsourcing has been characteristic of the Sudanese war effort, including that in areas like Darfur.[5]

This is not to say that al-Qaeda was a 'puppet' of the Sudanese government. Al-Qaeda also acted independently, it had an agenda and an ideology that differed even from the Turabists in the Sudanese government, and it supported organisations that were only of peripheral interest to Sudan's regime. Al-Qaeda's stay in Sudan helped it to connect to several regional groups; some of which continue to supply present-day jihadist organisations with recruits. Al-Qaeda also facilitated the development of networks that would be useful for future jihadist organisations, including four studied here: ADF, al-Shabaab, al-Muhajiroun and AQIM. However, when al-Qaeda fell out with the Sudanese authorities, it experienced the drawbacks that come with being an accepted organisation existing within a state, and the Sudanese authorities forced it to flee in 1996. Al-Qaeda thus serves as an excellent example of the advantages of the status of an accepted organisation, as well as all the disadvantages.

Al-Qaeda's move to Sudan

Al-Qaeda's origins were mainly among Arab fighters who travelled to Afghanistan to resist the Soviet invasion from 1979 to 1989. A charismatic Palestinian, Abdullah Azzam, had acted as a mentor for the younger, wealthier Osama bin Laden, who raised funds in Saudi Arabia for volunteers to fight the Soviet Union in Afghanistan. Bin Laden rented a house in Peshawar and set up an organisation in about 1984 called the Service Bureau, which at the start acted as a publishing house for Azzam's publications and a hostel for jihadists.[6] After a while, the Service Bureau also engaged in 'matchmaking' for newly arrived Arabs in Peshawar, tying them up with organisations inside Afghanistan.[7]

The Service Bureau developed in a context where Pakistan, Saudi Arabia and the United States had all been actively searching for proxies inside Afghanistan to further the resistance against the Soviet invasion. Through his old family network, Bin Laden enjoyed access to the Saudi Arabian top leadership.[8] There were disagreements over the focus of the Service Bureau, as Bin Laden wanted to concentrate on the Arab foreign fighters in order to avoid their being influenced by the factionalism among the Afghan resistance organisations, but also because 'they had stronger battlefield morals'.[9] On 18 August 1988, al-Qaeda al-Askariya was founded in Peshawar, with only sixty fighters, according to Abu Rida al-Suri.[10] The original intention was to create a base for jihadist activities, outside Afghanistan and Pakistan as well, and initially there were overlaps with other organisations, in that al-Qaeda trained members of other groups, for example.[11] The foundation of al-Qaeda itself signalled an important change, to a focus on establishing separate Arab units, involving a move away from embedding foreign fighters in local units in Afghanistan and Pakistan.

The formal creation of al-Qaeda took place late in the Soviet–Afghan war, close to its end. American support for Afghani resistance organisations began to dwindle as the Soviet Union prepared for its withdrawal. At the same time, the Islamist-inspired Zia-ul-Haq was on the verge of losing power to the more secular Benazir Bhutto in Pakistan, the main base for the early al-Qaeda. When Bin Laden sided with the military in its rivalry with Bhutto, the government exerted pressure on the military and Saudi Arabia to get him to return to that country. In November 1989, Osama bin Laden left for Saudi Arabia, taking with him several hundred recruits of Saudi origin, and hosting several non-Saudis in his house in Jeddah.[12] It seems that some training facilities remained open in Peshawar. Bin Laden then returned to Pakistan in late 1991 and stayed there until early 1992. With his base in Pakistan, he engaged in peace-making between warring Afghan factions, and at the same time al-Qaeda organised its first international terror attack, against the Afghan king in exile, using a Portuguese convert.[13] However, inside Pakistan, still the main base for al-Qaeda's operations, the environment facing the organisation became more and more hostile.[14] In 1992 Bin Laden and a considerable number of his supporters again moved, this time to Sudan.[15]

According to the al-Qaeda member Jamal al-Fadl, contact with Sudan was first established when Bin Laden sent envoys to that country as early as 1989 after hearing about the Sudanese revolution.[16] It should be remembered that al-Qaeda was 'young' when it moved to Sudan, and its ideology was not clearly or fully formed. Admittedly, it was based around a loose network that was much older. However, as the al-Qaeda ideologist Abu Musab al-Suri argues, the Sudan years may have been formative when it came to ideology.[17]

Sudan was in many ways a good match for the early al-Qaeda. On 30 June 1989, Colonel Omar al-Bashir led a bloodless military coup against the democratically elected government of Sadiq al-Siddiq. Although he was imprisoned just after the coup and then released, Hassan Turabi was one of the ideological 'movers' in the new regime.[18] Turabi was a leading ideologist of Islamism in the late twentieth century, and had already made a mark on wider Islamist discussions.[19] He actively tried to unify different Islamist organisations, including Shia ones, as well as support the wider jihad in the world, even before the 1989 coup. One element in this plan was the Popular Arab and Islamic Council (PAIC), founded by Turabi himself. The PAIC was far more eclectic in its membership than al-Qaeda would ever be, containing representatives from secular rebel factions such as the Palestine Liberation Organisation, Hamas, Ayman al-Zwahiri's Jama'ah al-Islamiyah (the Islamic Jihad in Egypt) and the Philippine group Abu Sayyaf.[20] East African jihadist organisations joined as well, together with Osama bin Laden's network. Some of the East African member organisations would later be trained by al-Qaeda and supported by Sudanese intelligence. Turabi maintained that PAIC would have positive effects for Sudan: participants could ensure the survival of the Islamic Republic of Sudan, and the network could provide assets for Sudanese development and for Sudanese foreign policies. Yet one should not make the mistake of equating the Turabists with the Sudanese state, as they each had separate agendas, and the PAIC, for example, was Turabi's organisation rather than Bashir's.

At about the same time the Sudanese regime had to face a troublesome civil war in the south of the country, and sought to quell a vibrant insurgency with limited economic means. It also had to face regional rivals, some provoked by Turabi and Sudan's support for local Islamist organisations. The new regime chose to employ small non-state groups to fight its wars inside and outside Sudan and to provide intelligence, probably as a cheap alternative to doing so itself, though in this it also followed Sudanese traditions.[21] The distressed economy was also an issue, prompting an interest in securing foreign investors and capability in building up infrastructure. Given the wealth amassed by Osama bin Laden, the nascent al-Qaeda network could actually serve all three purposes, and it did. Firstly, Bin Laden acted as a lender to the Sudanese government, funding wheat purchases and providing money for government purchases of oil. He acted, through his company Al-Hijrah Construction and Development Ltd, as a road constructor, and, according to himself, he also invested in agricultural projects in the al-Jazirah state in Sudan.[22] Another company, the Wadi al-Aqiq, handled trade while Al-Themar worked in agriculture with four thousand employees. Taba Investments was a trading company; the Blessed Fruits Company grew fruit and vegetables; Al-Qudurat dealt with transport. Bin Laden invested in the Al-Shamal Islamic Bank in Khartoum and he even owned his own sweets factory, the Al-Ikhlas.[23] Veterans from Afghanistan were employed in his businesses, but most of his employees probably knew little about his militant activities.[24]

Secondly, Bin Laden could aid Sudan's foreign policy by staging clandestine operations. The al-Qaeda network for example smuggled weapons to Yemen, to aid Turabi's allies, under the oversight of the Sudanese intelligence.[25] Some of the accounts of such activities require more in-depth analysis, as these allies were to become important for al-Qaeda at a later stage. One of the organisations supported (at times) by Turabi and Sudan was the Eritrean Islamic Jihad (EIJ) movement, whose members were employed as storm troopers by the Sudanese state, as well as being trained by al-Qaeda. This was a somewhat fragmented group from the start, organised around Islamist remains of the old Eritrean Liberation Front (ELF). Several of the future leaders (for example, Ismael Addow and Hamid Turki) had been imprisoned in 1978, and severely tortured because of their Islamist leanings.[26] When these members were released, they founded the Islamic Vanguard, which joined with another organisation, the National Islamic Front for the Liberation of Eritrea, in a partnership from 1982 onwards.[27] Several smaller groups, including the Popular Committee for the Defence of the Oppressed Eritreans and the Committee for Islamic Harmony, joined with the two larger organisations and created the Eritrean Islamic Jihad in November 1988.[28] This body also drew upon the grievances of the Beni Amer ethnic group in the Gash Barka border areas of Eritrea–Sudan, which had been exposed to ELF forced recruitment for years.[29] The result was an odd organisation with ideological tensions – combining as it did elements of Wahhabism, Ikwhan (an Arabian religious and military brotherhood) philosophy and nationalism, all existing in parallel – and there were great operational tensions to boot.

The EIJ probably included individuals with connections to the al-Qaeda network from a very early stage. Notes written to Eritrean Islamists have been discovered in both Bosnian and Afghan sites that are associated with al-Qaeda, and they were also mentioned in other al-Qaeda documents.[30] Moreover, the Eritrean government claimed to have captured Afghanistan veterans and foreign fighters among raid parties that crossed the border into Eritrea prior to 9/11, when such claims were far less likely to attract Western financial support, and thus Eritrea had fewer incentives to falsify the information.[31]

EIJ early on crystallised into two groups, a military wing around the former Afghanistan veteran Mohammed Ahmed Saleh (Abu Suhail) and a civilian wing, often named the Arafa faction, after Sheikh Ahmed Mohamed Arafa, who at the time was in prison but acted as a symbolic leader for the group. The disagreement between the two groups concerned political strategies. In 1993, after a congress boycotted by the Abu Suhail group, the Eritrean Islamic Jihad formally splintered into two.[32] Confusingly, both groups still used the same name for some years.[33]

The EIJ had been one of Turabi's regional allies, although the relationship between Sudan and the Eritrean Islamic Jihad varied over time. The EIJ was one of the negative factors in the relationship between the relatively new Eritrean state and Sudan, having received Sudanese support from 1989.[34] The support could have been directed against the regime in Addis Ababa, the so-called Derg, which ruled Ethiopia from 1974 to 1987, and which sponsored the anti-Sudanese movement for years. However, support continued after the change of power in Ethiopia and Eritrea's de facto independence in 1991. During an Eritrean–Sudanese honeymoon in 1992–3, the Sudanese regime attempted to curtail the movement, but by the end of 1993 the EIJ was attacking Eritrea again, and receiving Sudanese support, even to the extent of having Sudanese forces fighting alongside them. After the collapse of the organisation, it was the Abu Suhail group that became the most active, under the mantle of the old name, Eritrean Islamic Jihad.[35] Sudan's relationship with both Eritrea and Ethiopia grew more and more hostile because of its sponsorship of Ethiopian and Eritrean Islamist organisations.

Some of the support for the EIJ seems to have been channelled through al-Qaeda. Defectors alleged that Bin Laden's network operated a base in Hamesh Koreb along the Eritrean border, before it was overrun in 1997, and that EIJ representatives sat on an advisory committee for al-Qaeda created by Bin Laden.[36] According to the testimony of Tariq al-Fadel, al-Qaeda transferred at least $100,000 to the EIJ, although it is unclear if this was the pre-1993 organisation or the Arafa group that later split off from it.[37] Sudan's ally was in this case al-Qaeda's ally: al-Qaeda was acting as an agent for Sudan, although it had an independent agenda.[38] The EIJ had the same relationship with the Sudanese state: it could be launched against Sudan's enemies, but it also created hostilities with neighbours in periods of détente. In this sense, both al-Qaeda and the EIJ shaped Sudanese foreign policy, though it was also formed by Sudan and its elites. In the end, the EIJ (or at least all of its successor groups after its split) became, ironically, an ally in the United States war against terror launched against Eritrea when Eritrea supported the Harakat al-Shabaab in Somalia.

The al-Ittihad al-Islamiyah in Somalia was actually very similar to the EIJ: like the latter, it helped shape Sudanese foreign politics, had strong tendencies towards fragmentation, and was supported by al-Qaeda. Ittihad had its deeper roots in the religious awakening in Somalia in the

57

late 1960s and early 1970s, when, first, scholarships from Sudan and Saudi Arabia and, then, the secular family laws of Siad Barre spurred the formation of several Islamist organisations. Al-Ittihad al-Islamiya was formally established in 1983 in Hargeisa in Somalia/Somaliland.[39]

Ittihad has tended to be misunderstood, at times being seen as closer to al-Qaeda than it really was, and is often said to be the progenitor of today's Harakat al-Shabaab. While there were important individuals who went from Ittihad to Shabaab, and elements of Ittihad clearly had al-Qaeda contacts, the organisation was perhaps even more fragmented than the EIJ. Not unlike the latter, it was formed by the union of two different sub-organisations, Jamaaca Islaamiyah, a more radical Salafist breakaway group of Ahl al-Islam (originally a Sufi-inspired Islamist group), and Waxdah, a more eclectic body, mainly founded as an umbrella for Islamist resistance against cultural impulses and influence from the West.[40] Initially at least, Ittihad was an umbrella body, containing Sufi-, Wahhabi-, Brotherhood- and individually inspired Islamists. It was ideologically divided, and the fusion between the two constituent bodies was far from complete, so that a distinct northern and southern organisational identity remained.[41] It did, however, have one common denominator in the sense that it looked towards Turabi (not to the Sudanese state at the time) for support.[42] In fact, Turabi and his National Islamic Front (NIF), just after his parting of the ways with the Egyptian Brotherhood, set up a separate office in Mogadishu in 1982, attempting to create connections with Somali Islamist organisations. Al-Ittihad al-Islamiya officials were later to frequent the office there.[43]

When the Somali Islamists began to realise that the Barre regime was nearing its end, Islax (the Somali Muslim brotherhood) and Ittihad stepped up their rivalry, struggling to control the elites – the students – in the universities. Paradoxically, the two organisations also attempted to move closer together. When it was clear that the Barre regime was at its end, Islax also reached out to engineer a wider coalition, attempting to bring Ittihad and others into a grand Islamist organisation. The Islamists saw the potential end of the regime as the opportunity for a form of Islamist revolution, totally underestimating the consequences of civil war. The Ittihad that faced the internal upheavals was a confused body. As Somali society descended into civil war, the organisation became vulnerable to fragmenting clan forces.

Parts of Ittihad in the south participated in the organisation's first conflict in that region, the battle for the Arrale Bridge.[44] In April 1991, members of Ittihad's militias from the Darod clan were convinced by other factions from the same clan to fight against the advancing forces of General Mohamed Farah Aideed, all recruited from the Hawiye clan.[45] Aideed sent a former colonel from his clan, Hassan Dahir Aweys, to negotiate with the Ittihad militias, but Aweys defected to them after the negotiations had failed.[46] The battle ended in a rout, and al-Qaeda and the northern branch of Ittihad were highly critical of the way the Islamists had been manoeuvred into participating in clan warfare.[47] All the same, Aweys was to become a future leader of Ittihad and, later, somewhat hesitantly joined Harakat al-Shabaab.[48]

Most of the remainder of the organisation fled to the north-east of Somalia, where another part of the organisation had convened under the protection of a regional insurgent group, the Somali Salvation Democratic Front (SSDF), which saw them as potential allies against the Aideed faction in the south.[49] In June 1991, a large meeting was held where Ali Warsame became leader and Hassan Dahir Aweys his deputy.[50] The organisation gained finance from control of the port of Bosaso, and also from Saudi charities such as the International Islamic Relief Organisation (IIRO) (a part of the Muslim World League).[51] From letters from Afghanistan, we know that al-Qaeda was in contact with the group even at this stage.[52]

By mid-1992 the relationship with the SSDF and local clans became extremely strained, and in June 1992 Ittihad attacked the SSDF and captured several of their leaders, after the SSDF had threatened to cut off Ittihad's income from the port. The SSDF and local clans retaliated and Ittihad was chased away to neighbouring Las Khorey in the Sanaag province.[53] Here, local clans once again forced Ittihad activists out, and installed a replacement for Hassan Dahir Aweys in the leadership of the organisation.[54] The withdrawal from Las Khorey led to fragmentation. Ali Warsame was replaced as chairman by Sheikh Mohamud 'Isse', a southerner, and many members returned to their home areas. One sizeable contingent went to the Ogadeen region, and another went to south Somalia in August 1992. The latter group was under the leadership of Hassan Turki, later a (not very willing) Shabaab member. A sub-group was set up in Luuq, where it established territorial control, building up institutions and exercising governance, in a period in Somalia when few other factions bothered to do so.[55] In Ogadeen, Ittihad established other bases, in one instance – in Quray Shighut – assisted by al-Qaeda, who were joined by the veteran al-Qaeda commander Saif al-Islam in 1993 after coming directly from Afghanistan.[56] The result was the Khalid ibn al-Walid training camp.

However, the expansion of Ittihad's sphere of interest (or, rather, that of the Turki sub-group) and the activities of the sub-group that fled into Ethiopia began to draw attention from, among others, the Somali National Front, the most powerful local rebel movement. Ittihad's Ethiopian sub-group also launched a campaign of terror against the Ethiopian government, including an assassination attempt on the Ethiopian minister of transport and a bomb attack on the popular Blue Tops restaurant in Addis Ababa.[57] This drew hostile feelings towards the movement from the Ethiopians. Additionally, parts of Ittihad had always stressed non-violence, and when the top leadership attempted to sway the organisation away from violence, the Ogadeni sub-group declared its independence, as did Hassan Turki with his group in the Ras Kamboni area.[58] In 1993, according to notes from his meeting with al-Qaeda officials, Hassan Dahir Aweys also expressed scepticism about armed struggle.[59]

Despite this confusion, al-Qaeda engaged in the training and support of Ittihad forces in this period. The training scheme in Luuq was rather large. Documents from Afghanistan name five trainers active as part of the al-Qaeda mission, training perhaps as many as 140 men.[60] The same documents also describe interaction with the Sudanese intelligence services, and reveal that Saif al-Islam was active with the Ogadeni branch.[61] The documents show too that Hassan Dahir Aweys went to Khartoum for coordination meetings.[62] Al-Qaeda's Saif al-Adl visited the group active in Ras Kamboni, and was impressed.[63]

In 1996, Ethiopia intensified its warfare against the various sub-groups of Ittihad, and ended the Islamic rule in Luuq, as well as severely damaging the independent Ittihad group in the Ogadeen. Twelve al-Qaeda fighters were killed in the intervention: this signalled the decline of al-Qaeda's role in Somalia, as well as of Ittihad's activities. The attack was not only the beginning of the end of the organisation, but also a battle in which several of al-Shabaab's future leaders participated. In 1996, sub-groups of the organisation changed their name to Jama'at al-I'tisaam bil-Kitaab wa Sunna, excluding the former Ethiopian components.[64] In 1998, some elements of Ittihad sued for peace with Ethiopia, but other elements, including the future Shabaab commander Mukhtar Robow, continued to voice their opposition to such a decision. However, the organisation was by now too fragmented to present itself as a viable ally for Sudan or al-Qaeda.

Ittihad had served as a training ground for the future leaders of al-Shabaab. Yet it is misleading to say it was the predecessor of al-Shabaab: it contained so many ideological trends, was plagued by clannism, and had a continuous history of fragmentation from 1993 until its end. In many ways it was very similar to Somalia's other factions in the 1990s.[65]

While Ittihad's history is relatively familiar, the history of al-Qaeda and Sudan's partner in Uganda is less clear. According to Human Rights Watch, the Bin Laden network operated a base close to Uganda's borders.[66] The Islamic forces of Sheikh Abdullah in Uganda were also included in Bin Laden's advisory committee.[67] Abdullah was later to become part of the Uganda Muslim Freedom Fighters, which in turn became part of the Allied Democratic Forces (ADF) in Uganda, as described in a later chapter. Indeed, Sudan had been involved in the formation of the nucleus of this organisation through its funding of the efforts of the Tabliqi, a Sunni missionary movement, to take control of the Islamic Council of Uganda. Sudanese pragmatism showed itself in supporting as well Christian-based rebel movements in Uganda. However, during the founding of the PAIC, only religious activists from Uganda were invited.[68]

In Algeria, Sudan supported the Front Islamique du Salut (FIS).[69] After the FIS was removed from power in the military coup of 1992, Osama bin Laden sent Qatri el-Said to meet with refugees, and channelled $40,000 to aid their struggle. The more radical offshoot of the FIS, the Armed Islamic Group (GIA), included Afghanistan veterans, some of whom had friends in Bin Laden's network.[70] Later, they attempted to get support from Bin Laden, then in Khartoum. Nevertheless, Bin Laden refused them because of what he saw as their excessive use of violence.[71] GIA continued, nevertheless, to maintain offices in Sudan and retain Turabi's support.[72] In this way Algeria illustrates how Sudan and al-Qaeda were on a collision course in

61

this period. The other organisation that was a source of tension was the Egyptian Islamic Jihad, which was in many ways very close to al-Qaeda after Ayman al-Zawahiri, Abbud al-Zumar and Sayyed Imam al-Sharif fled to Afghanistan from Egypt in 1986. The Egyptian Islamic Jihad moved to Sudan in the years when Bin Laden operated from that country, but tensions arose when the Egyptians became unruly. They were targeted by both Ethiopia and Egypt, as well as the United States, for the failed attempt to assassinate Egyptian President Hosni Mubarak in Addis Ababa in 1995. Another incident that fuelled tension was the execution of two boys who had been spying for Egypt, against the wishes of the Sudanese government.[73]

The dynamics in Sudan were multi-layered, consisting of several sub-groups with varying interests within the state, which also established or attempted to influence militant groups outside the state to achieve their goals, and at the same time pursued their own interests. Al-Qaeda was one of these: a group that defectors claimed was used for training and courier purposes. It also participated in the economic sphere, which was increasingly dominated by actors in the new regime who sought to enrich themselves. If one believes the information in Fayizah Sa'd's interview with Bin Laden in 1996, these spheres also overlapped. Bin Laden used his construction firms to build training bases for militants. Similar information came in the testimony of Jamal al-Fadl, on day six of the *United States* vs *Osama bin Laden* court case, who pointed to the twofold use of the Damazin farms in Sudan for military training and for business.[74] The training was also meant for militias used in the Sudanese civil war. Bin Laden actually saw the Sudanese wars as part of a global clash of civilisations: 'Muslims are always reproached when they defend themselves. For the past few decades, plots have been hatched to partition Sudan from there. These plots are hatched in Nairobi. As is widely known, the US Embassy in Nairobi is the agency that is doing this. The greatest CIA center in eastern Africa is located at this embassy.'

It is not Always Easy to have an Accepted Presence

Al-Qaeda was not a puppet of the Sudanese state, nor was the Sudanese state unitary, for there were considerable differences in interests, for example, between Bashir and Turabi. Al-Qaeda's role in Sudan is perhaps best viewed as yet another non-state actor empowered by an elite. It was a non-state organisation that was allowed to build bases in Sudan to provide training for militias. It also provided infrastructure and, in the case of Somalia, field operatives attached to allies of Turabi or Sudan.

While it successfully promoted its own global agenda, and managed to stay active in Afghanistan and Somalia, al-Qaeda was at the same time vulnerable. Firstly, given the fragmented nature of power, the Sudanese government was not able to fully guarantee the security of the group. Bin Laden was, according to his own account, exposed to two assassination attempts, one at the al-Thawrah mosque in Omdurman in 1993/4, and another targeting his house in 1993.[75] The attackers were from the Takfir wal-Hijra.

Secondly, the Sudanese government and al-Qaeda differed over which groups to support and which not. L'Houssaine Kherchtou, later a defector from al-Qaeda, explained:

> There was a pressure from the Libyan government on the Sudanese government that all the Libyans must leave the country, and they informed Usama bin Laden that if you have some Libyans you have to let them get out from the country. And Usama bin Laden informed these guys and he told them that you have to leave, because if you don't leave, you will be responsible for yourselves, and if somebody caught you, I am not responsible. What I can do for you is I can give you twenty-four hundred bucks, plus a ticket with you and your wife if you want to live somewhere, but the Libyans, most of them, they refused the offer of Usama bin Laden. They were very upset and angry because they couldn't.[76]

Al-Qaeda in the end chose to sacrifice its allies in the Libyan Islamic Fighting Group (LIFG), at considerable cost in the form of hostility between Libyan jihadists and al-Qaeda after 1995. The decision was not popular within the organisation. Despite securing some advantages, such as exemption from tax, al-Qaeda also had to pay heed to the Sudanese. Indeed, the Sudanese could evict al-Qaeda if it was in their interests, and this is what they did in the end. The majority of the pressure probably came from Saudi Arabia, as well as Egypt and the United States, which increasingly started to view Bin Laden as a threat. Bin Laden's publications criticising the famous Saudi scholar Ibn Baz's endorsement of the Oslo treaty plan enraged the Saudis, while his closeness to the Egyptian Islamic Jihad, which was behind the 1996 attack against Hosni Mubarak, angered both Ethiopia and Egypt.[77] Osama bin Laden quickly began to prove a liability for Turabi and Bashir, and as his funds dwindled, he had less to offer for his stay. Turabi attempted to pressure al-Qaeda and Bin Laden to leave, and in 1996 he did so. Al-Qaeda then resettled in Afghanistan, under the sponsorship of the Taliban. Yet several of al-Qaeda's networks were left behind, and in 1998 it managed to stage a successful attack against the US embassies in Nairobi and Dar es Salaam, using remnants of its East African structure that operated from Sudan.

By moving to Afghanistan, al-Qaeda had liberated itself from one set of chains, the chains of Turabi and Sudan. Its remaining members in East Africa thereafter operated as clandestine networks, rather than as an accepted organisation. Overall, al-Qaeda had a lasting effect on the jihadi movement in sub-Saharan Africa, and many of the networks that it had established, often with Sudanese aid, continued after Bin Laden departed.

4

JAMA'AT NUSRAT UL-ISLAM WAL-MUSLIMIN'
GREY BORDERS IN THE DESERT

The Nusrat ul-Islam was founded as late as March 2017. Four older organisations, the Ansar Dine, the southern branch of al-Qaeda in the Islamic Maghreb (AQIM), the larger part of al-Mourabitoun (the part of the organisation that refrained from declaring loyalty to the Islamic State), and the Macina Liberation Front joined forces to create the new body. While these organisations had their separate histories, they also had many common traits, and shared a connected history. All of these groups originated either in AQIM or in the circles around Ansar Dine's leader Iyad Ag Ghali, and had been products of splits or re-establishments in new geographical areas by members of these bodies. The organisations in questions have had a history of extensive cooperation in the past, before the current union, and increasingly since then.[1]

Yet they are also different. Ansar Dine and its offshoot, the Macina Liberation Front, were more firmly entrenched in a Malian context than AQIM and its offshoot, al-Mourabitoun. Indeed, AQIM has its origins mainly in the Salafist Group for Preaching and Combat (GSPC), rooted in Algeria. GSPC itself was an offshoot of the Armed Islamic Group (GIA), which rose and fell in Algeria in the 1990s. The GIA was in turn a product of the Group for Defence against the Illicit, formed in 1979 around a former veteran of the Algerian civil war, Mustafa Bouyali, to pressure the Algerian government to take religion more seriously.[2] In 1981, the Algerian government accused the group of launching violent attacks.[3] Boyali fled from the police, and violence escalated.[4] Subsequently, another more violent organisation, the Algerian Islamic Armed Movement, was started.[5] After counter-measures by the Algerian state, this organisation was largely defeated, and Boyali died. However, most of the leaders were released after an amnesty in 1991. Mansour Meliani, leading a breakaway faction, established the Armed Islamic Group (GIA, from the French name Groupe Islamique Armé), particularly because of disagreements with the main leadership in the Islamic Armed Movement over how to handle the overwhelming success of the more peaceful Islamist party, Front Islamique du Salut (FIS), in working through democratic channels.[6] The nascent GIA leaders wanted to continue to use violent means.[7] In the heated atmosphere after the 1991 elections, in which FIS actually won the democratic elections but was denied power by the military, more moderate Islamists also joined the GIA. GIA's use of violence was seen by many activists as the only way forward after FIS's participation in democratic processes had failed.

GIA enjoyed some support from al-Qaeda during its early years.[8] Yet the relationship soon turned sour, for reasons that mirrored some of al-Qaeda's later criticisms of Shabaab (and, indeed, local Islamic State affiliates' criticisms of parts of Boko Haram and Shabaab). Al-Qaeda grew at odds with the GIA, because of the latter's targeting of civilian Muslims. The whole situation ended with a humiliating defeat for Osama bin Laden when one of his envoys, later an important al-Qaeda ideologist, Jamal Ibrahim Ishtaywi al-Misrati, was kidnapped and held for one week by GIA.[9]

Inside Algeria, the GIA started to expand the scope of its attacks. As early as 1996, GIA declared war on the remnants of FIS, just as the Algerian government had done. GIA also turned on its own members, launching attacks on the so-called Jazarists and Afghanistan veterans.[10] In 1997 the organisation also declared that all Algerians who did not support it deserved death.[11] A veritable fight to the death between the GIA and other Islamists began brewing. External jihadist organisations, including al-Qaeda, were angered by the way GIA targeted Muslim civilians and other Islamists.[12] Simultaneously, a sub-group of GIA leaders, including Hassan Hattab, Shaykh Abou al-Baraa and Amari Saïfi 'El-Para', grew increasingly estranged from the rest of the GIA leadership, and Hattab broke with the group as early as 1996.[13] A new group, the Salafist Group for Preaching and Combat (GSPC), was created in 1998.

The Algerian government became increasingly successful in offering amnesty to Islamists, but it failed to attract enough GSPC members to be able to dismantle the organisation. By 2002, the government renewed its campaign against the group, but without success. A new generation of leaders started to emerge, including Nabil Sahraoui, Abdelmalek Droukdel (aka Abu Musab Abdelwadoud) and Amari Saïfi 'El-Para'. Several of these leaders moved against Hattab, who left the organisation, according to his own account, because of disagreements over al-Qaeda's role, as well as the increased focus southwards.[14] Nabil gained control of the organisation, but this was quite short-lived, as he was killed in a gun battle with Algerian forces, and Droukdel took over.[15] Indeed, Algerian counter-terrorist efforts seemed quite successful in stopping the GSPC: it declared an amnesty in 2005, and at the same time forced the movement into the eastern Algerian mountains. However, the GSPC also increasingly turned its eyes southwards to the Sahel, an area with a weak Algerian state presence, porous borders and fewer threats to the GSPC.

GSPC Goes South

Southern Algeria and its Saharan region became an important source of revenue for the GSPC when it started to conduct kidnappings there in 2003, establishing a pattern that exists till today. The leader behind the kidnappings, a former Algerian paratrooper turned GIA turned GSPC, Amari Saïfi (Abou Haidara, alias 'Abderrezak El-Para'), fled into Niger, Mali and Chad. He married into both the Tuareg and Becharabe tribes, establishing two other patterns for the future: of AQIM leaders marrying into local groups, and of using the porous borders to escape from enemies, since government forces in general were reluctant to cross these borders. His demise also set another precedent: he was captured by a Chadian group and in the end handed over to Algeria.

Just as Mali would do later, Algeria chose to draw upon non-state actors to implement its policies in the Sahel.[16]

Another GSPC leader, Mokhtar Belmokhtar, a northern Algerian (from Ghardaïa), entered the Sahel, after developing extensive contacts in the region.[17] Belmokhtar was born in northern Algeria in 1972. He was also a veteran of the post-1991 Afghanistan civil war. He later joined the GIA, after forming his first militia in Algeria, the Martyrs' Brigade. Like many other GIA members, he left the organisation in anger, to join the GSPC. As early as 2003 he was active in the south, slowly establishing his networks there.[18] In 2006 he managed to gather enough militiamen to lead a relatively fierce attack on Lemgheity, an isolated Mauritanian border post between Mali, Mauritania and Algeria.[19] Belmokhtar operated with considerable autonomy from GSPC's leadership, because of the disruption of communication lines by the Algerian government, but also because of the distances. Additionally, Belmokhtar had a separate history with the central al-Qaeda leadership, a factor that contributed to his estrangement from GSPC's central leadership already from an early stage.[20] Later, his ability to tap into smuggling networks meant that he would generate more income for the organisation and also gain financial independence for himself.[21] At this stage AQIM, which became the new name of GSPC, chose Abdelhamid (Hamidu) Abu Zeid as commander of a region east of Belmokhtar's core areas.[22] The two commanders were formally placed under the control of Yahya Djouadi, who was based in north Algeria.[23]

AQIM's southern operations steadily grew in importance.[24] Operations in the south also proved easier to conduct. According to a Mali military commander quoted by Peter Pham, Belmokhtar enjoyed freedom of operation from the Malian forces at the start, allowing him carte blanche as long as he refrained from attacking Malian targets.[25] Indeed, there are statements from Malian officials that can be interpreted as giving support to the GSPC.[26] The early relationship between the GSPC and the Malian state was perhaps best expressed by the Malian president, Amadou Toumani Touré, to the US Embassy on 10 November 2006. The president stressed that GSPC had not yet attacked any Malian installations, and thus Mali would not risk any retaliation by launching campaigns against it. Touré also noted that the Malian military had attempted an action against the GSPC in 2003, but had sustained serious casualties in the process.[27] There was thus no real fighting engagement with AQIM from the Malian side between 2003 and 2009. In fact, in the interview Touré even warned the Americans of the danger of provoking the GSPC. Perhaps this attitude was rewarded by AQIM, which, in this period, actually intensified its targeting of neighbouring Mauritania, while Abu Zeid staged kidnappings in Niger.[28]

Mali functioned as a kind of safe haven for AQIM members operating in the country. GSPC was accepted by the Malian state, and so had a more or less stable presence there. Although AQIM was probably not directly supported by the state, there was a fluidity in relations between the two in the north. Militiamen and former rebels were also mayors, members of the security services, military officials and local notables, and some of them might also have had connections with AQIM.

The Malian state lacked the financial means to build up a credible army or an ability to develop its outreach in the north. It was also constrained by the 2006 Algiers accords that limited its military presence in the region. Mali chose rather to use agents in the north – militias – which in turn had their own interests and at times acted against the central Malian authorities.[29] Mali was not a perfect safe haven for the jihadists. Algeria attempted to attack the GSPC and supported Tuareg militias hostile to AQIM, encouraging them to attack the latter.[30] AQIM also faced local rivals: the Democratic Alliance for Change (ADC), ironically led by the future Nusrat leader Iyad Ag Ghali, fought a minor battle against them on 23 October 2006, when an ADC patrol got too near AQIM forces. Moreover, AQIM had to interact with other groups. At times, this was mutually beneficial. Tuareg tribal leaders, including Iyad Ag Ghali for example, earned money from AQIM's kidnappings by acting as negotiators and middlemen, for a percentage of the profit. AQIM also used human smuggling and drug smuggling networks for arms transport and actively stationed members in key points along these routes, in order to tax the smugglers.[31] The arms markets of Mali allowed easy access to arms for the GSPC.[32] Because of the freedom Belmokhtar enjoyed, he was increasingly integrated into the Saharan smuggling networks. It seems that GSPC attracted mercenaries to its cause because of the lucrative business, including kidnappings, that it handled.[33]

AQIM's activities in Mali increased. In 2009 a hostage was killed and the relationship between AQIM and the Malian state worsened, as Mali retaliated and Abu Zeid responded in turn.[34] Simultaneously, Algerian patience with Mali began to run out and newspapers loyal to the regime in Algeria launched a large-scale media attack on the country's handling of AQIM.[35] In 2010 a joint Malian and Mauritanian army offensive against AQIM was launched, but the campaign was restricted in time and could not secure the countryside. AQIM was left free to come back when the army units returned to their barracks.[36]

AQIM's internal unity was also under pressure. Firstly, a new breakaway group active in the Sahara was formed. In October 2011 the new group kidnapped three European aid workers from a refugee camp in southern Algeria.[37] The group made its first jihadi video in December 2011. Their leader, the Mauritanian Arab Hamada Ould Mohamed Kheirou, declared war upon France and said that its aim was to impose Sharia on West Africa. It claimed to be carrying on the legacy of Usman Dan Fodio, Cheikou Amadou and Umar Tall.[38] It also said that it consisted of defectors from AQIM. The group called itself the Movement for Oneness and Jihad in West Africa, mostly known by the initials of its French name, Mouvement pour l'Unicité et le Jihad en Afrique de l'Ouest (MUJAO), and recruited many jihadists from among Mauritanian and Malian Arabs.[39] Its initial targets were mostly Algerian, but some had connections with Western Sahara.[40] Many of the leaders that were to emerge in the organisation, including Ould Kheirou, the famous Islamist smuggler Sultan Ould Badi, and Ahmed Ould Amer (Ahmed al-Tilemsi), were close to Belmokhtar, and had worked for him before. It is far from certain that they distanced themselves from him, at a time when he was himself drifting away from AQIM.[41] Over the months the organisation recruited among Songhai villages that had previously been inspired by Salafist visions of Islam, and among the Fulani, and these groups grew in numbers.

Within AQIM, Zeid and Belmokhtar remained rivals though the central leadership of AQIM favoured Zeid. Belmokhtar tried actively to refer matters, when he felt he was being treated badly by AQIM, to al-Qaeda's central leadership. Several letters from this correspondence were found in Timbuktu after the French intervention, and they allow us to glimpse how Belmokhtar drifted away from AQIM, while remaining loyal to al-Qaeda. Issues like Belmokhtar's lack of respect towards couriers and his lack of transparency over money seem to resurface in the correspondence. Belmokhtar in the end asked for a separation in a letter to both al-Qaeda central and AQIM, suggesting the creation of a new organisation, al-Qaeda in the Islamic Sahel – this after outflanking his mother organisation by moving forces into Libya without permission. Droukdel answered by focusing on an argument drawn from Sharia. Despite these internal conflicts, AQIM's emir of the Sahara, Djamel Okacha 'Abu Yahya al-Hammam', attempted to work for a greater union of all Islamist groups, in an Islamic State of Azawad under the Islamist Tuareg leader Iyad Ag Ghali, a person with unique contacts on most sides of the Malian conflict.[42]

Enter Iyad Ag Ghali and Ansar Dine

AQIM's activities in northern Mali drew upon the peripheral status of the territory and the fact that even though the organisation had de facto enemies (notably, Algeria and allied militia groups), it nevertheless did not have rivals who could secure the rural areas. AQIM had achieved a kind of semi-territoriality. Withdrawing in the face of rare Algerian offensives (often just across the border), and of the extremely rare and weak Malian offensives, it became an organisation that could easily return to its former bases after its enemies had ended their campaigns. Local allies of its enemies, including Tuareg militias allied with Algeria, were too weak or too uninterested in the conflict to change this picture.

In part, the state of semi-territoriality was aided by the lack of Algerian–Malian cooperation, and also by the local context. Northern Mali had been a periphery, even during the colonial era, with many, though not all, Tuareg tribes resisting occupation by France and actually wielding de facto control for long periods over the countryside.[43] Tuareg rebellions were frequent. Seen in this way, the build-up in the early 1990s of a renewed Tuareg rebellion, known as the al-Jebha, was only one of many waves breaking on the shore of the Malian state, the first having taken place on the eve of independence in 1962.[44] A part of this longstanding ritual involved negotiation. In January 1991 the parties signed a ceasefire agreement, agreeing to give northern Mali an ill-defined 'special status' that was practically equivalent to autonomy for the Tuareg. In this way, a considerable amount of Malian control was forfeited.

In this situation, the Tuareg movements fragmented beyond recognition, often following tribal lines. Other people, like the Songhai, mobilised militarily as well. The north became a hotbed of non-state armed groups. A locally initiated peace process, the Bourem Pact, was established by tribal chiefs in 1996, and was to last for a decade. Yet the peace was far from perfect: violence was common and the area was drawn into a global economy of trading in hashish, cocaine, weapons, humans, oil and other merchandise, which businessmen transported across the Sahara. A notable name in these power struggles was Iyad Ag Ghali, who was regarded as a nationalist leader of the Tuareg, if not the major leader of the rebellion in the 1990s.[45] Ghali, the son of a nomadic stock farmer who had died in the 1963–4 Tuareg rebellion, hailed from the sub-lineage Kel Ireyakkan (also called Kel Ouzeyen) of the Ifoghas tribe and the Kidal region in Mali.[46] He had been for some time a refugee in Algeria, and was involved in the early al-Jebha li Takhrîr ash-Shimâl al-Mali, a Libyan-sponsored Tuareg-based rebel organisation, which in the 1980s was used by Libya in the conflicts in Chad.[47] Ghali was, in the early 1990s, initially seen as a moderate, a leader who rejected the Tuareg desire for independence.[48] Before the Malian government rewarded him with a diplomatic position in Saudi Arabia in 2007, he was regarded as a key figure in negotiating hostage releases with the GSPC, in which process he gained contacts with this organisation and at the same time expressed hostility to it in public.[49] At this time, Ghali had a relationship with the Tabliqi sect and, according to his own account, made increasing contacts with religious activists.[50]

Internal Tuareg conflicts led to the founding of the Democratic Alliance for Change (ADC) in 2006, one of the major leaders being Iyad Ag Ghali. The ADC directed its anger against what it perceived as the state's failure to distribute resources from the Malian centre to the periphery. Many saw the ADC as an Algerian tool to attack the GSPC, and there were several clashes between the two at the time, although occasionally the ADC also paid taxes to the GSPC when moving through their territories.[51] However, in hindsight, Ghali's antipathy towards the GSPC may have been less pronounced than many believed at the time, for fellow ADC leaders complained that he had directed sub-tribe members away from the current fights with GSPC, which led to internal conflict in ADC.[52]

Another peace settlement was made in 2007. Ghali, having expressed that he was tired of northern Malian intrigues, was appointed to a diplomatic position in Saudi Arabia. Yet, several Tuareg leaders were dissatisfied with the settlement and in September 2007 founded Alliance Touareg du Nord-Mali pour le Changement (ATNMC), led by Ibrahim Ag Bahanga, an ex-ADC leader, largely based around the Ifergoumessen sub-tribe of the Ifoghas Tuareg.[53] Mali was this time able to recruit former Tuareg guerrillas into special forces units that destroyed the ATNMC in 2010.

However, trouble was still brewing, and the conflict was renewed again with the founding in October 2010 of a new northern organisation dominated by Tuaregs, the National Movement of Azawad (MNA). By 2011, the MNA and the Tuareg Movement of Northern Mali (NMA) had created the National Movement for the Liberation of Azawad (MNLA), once more promoting autonomy for the north.[54] Many returning fighters from Libya joined the new organisation (although their number is hard to estimate).[55]

Iyad Ag Ghali's role in all of this was barely noticed internationally (although the locals were aware of him). He was seen as a broker even when he was in Saudi Arabia, but in 2010 he was declared persona non grata by the Saudi Arabians, who seemed to dislike his connections with the Tabliqi. Upon his return to Mali, he was initially not so prominent, and he failed to be elected *amenokal* (tribal leader) of his Kel Ifoghas lineage.[56] Subsequently he also failed to become a leader of the new MNLA in 2011, some sources claiming that this was because he wanted the organisation to implement Sharia.[57] Ghali drifted away, but was still initially seen as part of the MNLA, although he established his own organisation, the Ansar Dine (Defenders of the Faith), calling for an Islamic republic and the application of Sharia in northern Mali. This was first reported in the media on 15 December 2011.[58] Amid tensions provoked by the Malian president's 'security and development' programme, Ansar Dine's new leader, Iyad Ag Ghali, started his insurgency as early as December 2011.

Allies with Territoriality

On 17 January 2012 the MNLA attacked Malian forces in northern Mali. The Malian response was feeble, and the army was weakened even more by a successful coup against President Amadou Toumani Touré on 21 March. Ansar Dine was accepted as an ally by the MNLA from the start of the latter's military offensive. In one sense, this was unsurprising, as links between Ansar Dine and the MNLA had been close from the start. Some Ansar Dine commanders had recently been part of the MNLA, and there were attempts to merge the two organisations. However, Ansar Dine's relationship with AQIM and MUJAO strained the relationship with the MNLA. Ansar Dine took a relatively anti-nationalist stand, explicitly saying that they were not fighting for independence for northern Mali, but rather for Sharia.[59]

Ansar Dine was not bothered by the tensions. In fact, MUJAO and AQIM were crucial for Ansar Dine's battlefield operations.[60] Following a common pattern in northern Mali, Ansar Dine delegated tasks to and drew upon the resources of AQIM. Iyad Ag Ghali had established considerable family links with the latter, most importantly perhaps through AQIM commander Hamada Ag Hama, Ghali's cousin. Several AQIM leaders fought alongside Ansar Dine, while others, like two long-time AQIM members from northern Mali, Sanda Ould Bouamama and Omar Ould Hamaha, presented themselves as Ansar Dine officials.[61] Very often, tribal lines explained which AQIM leaders took up arms for Ansar Dine, and AQIM commanders with tribal brethren in Ansar Dine joined the fight first.[62]

Ansar Dine's relationship with MUJAO and AQIM was highly unpopular with the MNLA. Yet organisational overlaps, and perhaps the fact that Ag Ghali was a veteran among Tuareg rebels, prompted MNLA to negotiate with Ansar Dine for a merger. At the start, it did so from a position of strength. The MNLA, for example, played a major role in the battle of Aguelhok from 18 to 25 January. Indeed, the MNLA was highly successful on the battlefield from February–March onwards. However, the International Crisis Group saw the battle for Amachach–Tessalit, in February–March 2012, as a turning point.[63] The Amachach base was besieged and a negotiated withdrawal of Malian forces took place on 10 March. Ansar Dine played a crucial role in all this. After the fall of the city of Gao, Kidal and Timbuktu fell too.

The role of the Ansar Dine and AQIM as well as MUJAO under these circumstances was remarkable, and different in kind from that of the more anarchic MNLA. Ansar Dine established a form of governance in the area, taking on the task of maintaining public order. It created a 'hotline' to contact its members, and set up Sharia courts as well as sponsoring charities.[64] AQIM even managed to organise such essential services for locals as health, food, water, electricity and gas, and at the same time avoided provoking the MNLA.[65] Ansar Dine indicated that it had attempted to set up neighbourhood committees already in April and early May, and was working to curtail crime against the local population, while MUJAO claimed that it set up Sharia courts in Gao in April.[66] However, at this early stage it seems that each city administration was established separately, with little contact between the cities.[67] Sometimes AQIM's and Ansar Dine's governance attempts were fused where the borders between membership of the two organisations overlapped. The new Islamist chief of police in Gao in 2012, for example, claimed membership of MUJAO, Ansar Dine, Boko Haram and al-Qaeda.[68]

Ansar Dine and its allies began slowly to overtake the MNLA. The financial strength of Ansar Dine made inroads. It attracted members of MNLA, and started to sway the tribal hierarchy, as for example Alghabass Ag Intallah, the favourite in the race to become the future *amenokal* of the Ifoghas.[69] Indeed, Ansar Dine drew a large proportion of its fighters from the Ifoghas. The MNLA was, for its part, reluctant to fight Ansar Dine. A last round of negotiations between MNLA and Ansar Dine in May 2012 led to a draft agreement in which Ansar Dine recognised independence for Azawad, while MNLA accepted that legislation should draw upon the Quran and the Sunna, although there may have been factions in the MNLA hostile to this.[70] MNLA also attempted to push Ansar Dine to distance itself from AQIM and MUJAO, but failed.[71] Ansar Dine claimed that it was not a part of al-Qaeda, and did not accept their methods, which, it said, were the outcome of foreign (Western) influence. It claimed that many Muslims were pressured to accept al-Qaeda's methods because of foreign interference. Moreover, Ansar Dine stated that it welcomed foreign mujahideen.[72] Although a formal merger between Ansar Dine and MNLN was declared on 26 May 2012, it came to nothing. MNLA accused Ansar Dine of having changed its views (to saying that Sharia – rather than the Quran and the Sunna – was the basis of law).[73] On 4 June 2012 the general secretariat of the MNLA announced unilaterally that it would participate in an interim council to run the country's affairs, thereby angering Ansar Dine.

The tense situation seems to have led to clashes after demonstrations targeting Ansar Dine erupted in Kidal. Ansar Dine attributed these demonstrations to the MNLA.[74] Following the death of a municipal councillor in Gao, a significant portion of the population blamed the crime on the MNLA. MUJAO used the situation to drive the MNLA out of the city on 27 June 2012.[75] On 29 June, Ansar Dine took control over Timbuktu. By and large the MNLA had been defeated by Ansar Dine and its allies before the end of the summer. MUJOA ended up having a strong presence in Gao, while Ansar Dine dominated Timbuktu and Kidal. As the three groups expanded their territorial holdings, the Malian government's old technique of setting armed militias against their enemies backfired when fighters from the ethnically Songhai group Ganda Koy ended up as allies with Ansar Dine.[76] MUJAO also captured Ménaka, close to the Niger border, on 20 November, with AQIM forces fighting alongside them.[77]

Ansar Dine and MUJAO were now in de facto control of the land. Like Shabaab, they started systematically to expand their governance functions. In the words of one of the Tuareg *amenokals*: 'AQIM recruited police, created police, made police commissioners, financed Quran schools, they could even build you a well or a mosque. They would pay the imam of the mosque, they could pay teachers, even pay double to be popular.'[78] In Kidal, Ansar Dine complained about the state of the hospital and tried to stop it being plundered:

> We went to the hospital to inspect the hospital and help the wounded. When we entered the operations room, I really was shocked, it was a mouldy room, the operations room was mouldy, you can say it was more a dustbin than a hospital. As for the medicine there was a store or two stores for the medicine, and we Alhamdulillah managed to secure them from the sabotage that happened here, and you know that we came here late, and found the city partly destroyed, but the thing that we found from

facilities we managed to secure, like the water and electricity companies, and also the hospital, also the remainder of communication equipment.[79]

There were small signs of an increased level in implementation of Sharia. Human Rights Watch, for example, reported the case of the stoning of a young unmarried couple by MUJAO and Ansar Dine in Aguelhok on 29 July 2012.[80] AQIM claimed to have successfully banned handguns in Kidal, and curtailed freelance militias.[81] Yet they also asserted that the population was not yet ready for *Hudud* punishment (under Sharia law), and that it would take time before this could be carried out. In an interview an Ansar Dine leader expressed the belief that Sharia could be implemented over time, and that a mix 'between the implementation of Sharia and educating the people about the reality of Islam' was the optimal short-term step.[82]

Abu Omar al-Taarki was put in charge of Timbuktu city (this later changed), and Islamic police stations were set up. Ansar Dine seems to have been quite proud of this, and published detailed accounts of some of the court cases through Sahara Media, as well as a jihadi video which shows members patrolling the market who caught a car thief.[83] Yet Ansar Dine officials also admitted that they had problems with the implementation of justice, just as the Shabaab had in Somalia; they lacked experienced *qadis* (judges) for their court, and had difficulty managing land conflicts. Lack of resources and differences in customs between tribes were also seen as challenges.[84] An Islamic emirate of Azawad was declared, with Iyad Ag Ghali at the head, and a special council was put in charge of each state, the administrative divisions being kept the same as those of the Malian government because of 'locals habits'. Sheikh Abu al-Fadl became responsible for the affairs of the Kidal state, while Sheikh Abdul Hamid Abu Zayd was appointed governor of Timbuktu state. It also seemed as if there were some attempts to draw traditional leaders, including the *amenokals*, towards the groups. In the words of a local observer: 'During the 2012 crisis, politico-military armed groups reduced their criticism of traditional leaders for the sake of inclusion. Their other objective was to mobilise as many communities as possible to join their project.'[85]

AQIM also stressed its alliance with Ansar Dine and MUJAO, claiming 'a convergence of goals and objectives [between it and Ansar Dine] and even in the means, since everyone seeks to implement the Sharia of Allah', while still maintaining that they were separate organisations. In practice, northern Mali was divided between Ansar Dine and MUJAO: the Timbuktu region and north-east were controlled by the former, and Gao by the latter, and AQIM was largely embedded within Ansar Dine. MUJAO expressed pride in cooperating with AQIM units.[86] Ansar Dine and MUJAO were also able to tax the locals.[87]

According to Bill Roggio, the new situation attracted foreign fighters from Togo, Benin, Niger, Nigeria, Guinea, Senegal and the Ivory Coast, as well as Egyptians, Algerians and Pakistanis. At least two training camps were established in Gao, the largest city in northern Mali.[88] The groups also attracted many fighters from the central regions of Mali, often from the Fulani ethnic group. This period was to some extent presented as a golden age by Ansar Dine, and the reduction in criminal violence that was achieved was later used as an argument in Ansar Dine's propaganda. Indeed, interviews conducted by the International Crisis Group seem to indicate that MUJAO's ability to prevent crime actually impressed locals in Gao.[89] As MUJAO and Ansar Dine advanced into central Mali, local ethnic groups would join, such as the Ntéréré from Macina and nomadic Fulani from the Douentza, sometimes seeking protection from other armed groups.[90] Among the Fulani joining MUJAO was Amadou Koufa, a Fulani preacher previously active in Macina, and known in the early 2000s for the popularity of his taped religious sermons.[91] Indeed, the territorial phase was to attract followers from other parts of Mali and from beyond, individuals who in some cases were to return home and create new groups in their home areas. However, the situation of permanent territorial control was not to last, nor was the process of institution-building.

Intervention and Transformation

Besides facing strong criticism from MUJAO, neighbouring countries were worried by the fact that all three organisations attracted foreign fighters from the region, as well as by their ties to al-Qaeda. Foreign intervention thus became more and more likely. France initially committed 2,000 troops to fight in northern Mali as part of a cooperative military intervention organised by the Economic

Community of West African States (ECOWAS). The United Nations Security Council approved a regional intervention force, the International Support Mission in Mali (AFISMA), in December 2012. A UN Security Council resolution, no. 2085, was also issued, asking the parties in the conflict to abstain from contact with AQIM, and mentioning that the United Nations had listed MUJAO as a terror organisation.[92] Yet, it was France that first acted, responding officially to a request from the Malian interim president, Dioncounda Traoré.[93] The French forces were soon joined by a Chadian contingent and in January also by contingents from Nigeria, Togo and Benin.[94]

On 11 January fast mechanised columns of the French army, ideal for defeating Ansar Dine and its allies in open combat, struck and advanced quickly. With 4,500 well-trained troops, France conducted a blitzkrieg in northern Mali, which was well suited to getting MUJAO, Ansar Dine and AQIM to flee.[95] First, French Special Forces destroyed a column of Ansar Dine moving south.[96] On 18 January, Malian forces with French supervisors moved on Konna. Then from 21 January to 1 February 2013 France moved on the Niger bend, launching forays towards Gao and Timbuktu.[97] In general, Ansar Dine avoided conflict and withdrew in front of the French forces. MUJAO faced a French air assault on Gao, resisted and lost.[98] As early as 28 January, Chadian and Nigerian forces moved towards the eastern Malian towns of Ménaka, Ansongo and Gao.[99] On 29 January, Timbuktu Airport was cleared. While the rapid advances were impressive, only French air units actually inflicted losses on Ansar Dine, and the jihadists on the whole withdrew in a relatively orderly fashion.[100]

The French campaign continued north, again conducting an air assault on Kidal on 30 January, with Chadian forces moving on the ground against the city.[101] Another air assault took place on 8 February, when French Special Forces attacked the Tessalit airfield.[102] As a portent of things to come, MUJAO fighters attacked the French with suicide vests and small arms in Gao on the same day, with some of the attackers withdrawing into the mountainous Adrar des Ifoghas.[103] Here, Ansar Dine still held some artillery pieces and BM-21 Katyushas (rocket launchers), but these were destroyed in costly Chadian and French offensives in February, leading to the apparent loss of 140 jihadists.[104]

By the end of February, the French and their allies were the masters of open combat in the north. Neither Ansar Dine nor MUJAO nor AQIM elements could in reality hope to defeat larger French or Chadian units here. Yet, despite the media attention in the West and the conventional success of the French, the Chadians and their allies, the outcomes were in many ways similar to the story told in this book about Boko Haram, Shabaab and the ADF.[105] The Ansar Dine and its allies were not defeated; they had merely transformed. The claim made in September 2013 by President Hollande of France of victory in the struggle against the terrorists seems hollow today, and indicated a lack of understanding of the dynamics of this transformation.[106] The jihadists could still operate in the vast distances of the Malian Sahara and beyond. The French (now reduced to 2,000 men) and their allies simply did not possess the manpower to secure the countryside. Moreover, in central Mali the Malian army failed to bring peace and security and instead was allegedly involved in several local massacres.[107] What the war did do was to disrupt AQIM's taxing of the drug trade.[108] Estimates, although unconfirmed, gave the number of members of MUJAO, AQIM and Ansar Dine killed as 2,000, with 430 taken prisoner.[109]

On 25 April 2013, the United Nations Security Council passed Resolution 2100, creating the United Nations Multidimensional Integrated Stabilisation Mission in Mali (MINUSMA), which would involve up to 12,600 soldiers and police.[110] A reduced French contingent was to remain in the country as a rapid deployment force for MINUSMA, and the West African forces were rehatted for the mission.

The transformation away from territoriality, brought about by Operation Serval, led to several losses for Ansar Dine. Parts of Ansar Dine defected, and some factions sought appeasement with the international forces and the Malian government. In May 2013 the Intallah Ag Attaher, the *amenokal* of the Kel Adagh Tuareg, and two of his sons formed the High Council for the Unity of Azawad (HCUA), an Ifoghas-dominated organisation that successfully attracted disillusioned Ansar Dine members.[111] Other militias, like the Arab Movement of Azawad (MAA), also had similar success. However, a hard core of Ansar Dine and members of AQIM and MUJAO stayed loyal to their leaders in opposition to the intervening forces, the Mali government and the Tuareg organisations seeking peace.

Semi-territoriality and Unifications

These three groups also 'reshuffled' their cards between them. A part of this apparently even took place before 2011 when Belmokhtar increasingly became estranged from AQIM. During the territorial phase in northern Mali, this rupture was formalised when AQIM announced that Belmokhtar had been 'suspended' from command of the group, owing to his supposed deviations from the group's aims.[112] In December 2012, Belmokhtar appeared on video for the first time to broadcast his creation of a new group, al-Mouwakoune Bi-Dima ('Those Who Sign with Blood'), a reference to the name of the GIA detachment responsible for the 1994 hijacking of an Air France flight.[113] But what Belmokhtar did *not* do – a fact that several commentators got wrong – was to publicly state that he had left AQIM.[114] Belmokhtar also remained in close contact with MUJAO and Ansar Dine.[115] The three organisations continued to overlap in membership. Sultan Ould Badi, for example, went over to Ansar Dine.[116] Some members, such as Omar Ould Hamaha, seemingly switched between the organisations on a relatively frequent basis.[117]

Belmokhtar's and MUJAO's old hostility to the central AQIM leadership may have influenced the alliance between the two, as did past ties and friendships. That common interests existed between Belmokhtar and MUJAO was confirmed by a merger between Belmokhtar's faction and MUJAO in August 2013, with the creation of al-Mourabitoun.[118] The merger was also a confirmation of realities on the ground where the two factions had cooperated closely for quite a while. The two organisations staged an attack on a uranium mine in May 2013 in Arlit in neighbouring Niger, as well as a parallel attack against a military base in nearby Agadez. There were also rumours of the existence of a common *Shura* (council) in January 2013.[119] In a sense, the new unit was left in command of the jihadist field when the French killed Belmokhtar's old rival, Abu Zeid, on 25 February 2013; he was replaced by the Algerian Djamel Okacha.[120] Yet there were still signs of sympathy between Belmokhtar and AQIM, and there were never any direct statements from Belmokhtar confirming that he had left AQIM.[121] Correspondence between the two continued, despite a negative tone in many of the letters, and despite Belmokhtar's attempt to establish direct lines of communication with al-Qaeda.[122] Ansar Dine managed to keep contact with all factions, and AQIM published videos involving Iyad Ag Ghali.[123]

By late 2013, these loose allies had undergone a transformation, at some cost, including the death of Abu Zeid and others. Al-Mourabitoun lost one of its founders when Ahmed Ould Amer 'Ahmed al-Tilemsi', who was also one of the founders of MUJAO, was killed in a French Special Forces raid in December 2014.[124] However, by late 2013 the organisations were able to threaten locals and exact taxes, as long as their enemies were absent, and could conduct forms of governance such as peace negotiations between Tuareg tribes. A very similar transformation happened to the Shabaab in Somalia after 2012 and to Boko Haram in Nigeria after 2015.

The pattern of attacks by the allied jihadists in late 2013 demonstrated their military potency. Assaults were launched on a military camp in Timbuktu on 28 September. MUJAO shelled military installations in Gao on 7 October, and the airport in the same city on 30 October. They also attacked Chadian peacekeepers at Tessalit on 23 October, and a suicide attack was staged against Ménaka barracks on 30 November. A terror attack was launched on a bank in Kidal on 14 December, while the shelling continued in Gao.[125]

The jihadist allies also managed to involve themselves in both governance and taxation. Ansar Dine staged a large meeting in Boughaessa with the local population, and even established Sharia police services in Beyra in February 2014.[126] MUJAO forces managed to set up interim roadblocks at Djebock, near Gao, vanishing after a while, much like Shabaab in Somalia. AQIM held popular meetings in villages and even made videos of the events.[127]

The organisations operated in a setting in which shifting patterns of population influx and departure spurred conflicts, including at a local level, which were often not managed or understood by the international intervening forces. In the words of the mayor of Timbuktu:

> Since 2012, there has been an exodus among the population. Some have moved towards the capital and the south of the country while others left for the neighbouring countries and settled in the refugee camps in Niger, in Mauritania, Burkina Faso and Algeria. This has significantly affected the

demographics of the city. But with the liberation of the areas occupied by the jihadists, there was a massive return of population despite the presence of some in the refugee camps. The reasons for these displacements are many: the arrival of occupants whose rule cannot be tolerated by the residents, especially with the abuse suffered by the population. The new situation created a tension between certain ethnic groups; some preferred to abandon the city.[128]

Many saw the ethnic composition of the Islamist groups as leading to an Arab domination of several cities, especially as local people fled. Locals also complained of a change of values, as the Islamists had tried to break with the past. Traditional leaders, and religious leaders from before 2012, were seen – by some of the leaders themselves – as having being weakened, for example in Timbuktu.[129] The changes upset many, while lack of security and the general corruption of the factions created a feeling of insecurity.

> Before the crisis, there were the political actors, administrative actors and civil society; but the political actors were the most influential because in democracy the primacy goes to the politicians. During the occupation, there were the armed groups like the MNLA and the MAA, an Arab movement, along with the Islamists who appeared under the name of Ansar Dine relying on the High Islamic Council to bring the people to pledge allegiance to them. Their purpose was to create the Islamic Republic of Azawad. The actors have changed in theory, not in reality, but fear and threats have brought anarchy. The liberation and the peace agreements were an opportunity to put back in place the administration and regular politics; however, there has been a real setback due to corruption. So, in conclusion, there has been no positive change.[130]

Anarchy and insecurity were the reality for many. However, some benefited from the international intervention: entrepreneurs were granted contracts with the international forces from 2014 onwards, and when humanitarian NGOs returned to the north, business improved. In fact, several entrepreneurs in Kidal saw these as boom times:

> The construction market is very dynamic. Fifty per cent of their products come from Algeria and the rest from Mali. It is a booming activity whose volume has even tripled. This is due to the expressed need and the markets offered by the UN mission in Kidal, which is spending a lot of money

in the construction and rehabilitation of public infrastructure destroyed during the conflict or else vandalised. Humanitarian organisations and even the state are taking to spending a lot in this activity.[131]

Yet, many businessmen and women expressed respect for the order provided by the jihadists, even the businessman just quoted: the jihadists remained more trusted in the area of justice provision, and were seen as less corrupt.[132] A point made by several interviewees in Kidal was that, although many of them benefited directly from the international intervention through building and construction projects, the jihadists had usually refrained from collecting taxes. 'All the [secular] actors mentioned are involved in the conflict and all are worth less than the jihadist groups. Because they do not charge and they ensure the safety of areas under their control. And they know how to serve justice when people complain to them.'[133]

The state of semi-territoriality assumed by the Islamist groups was not only present in northern Mali, but in parts of southern Algeria and western Niger as well, and was growing in central Mali. Ansar Dine led the organisations on the ground, being the largest jihadist body in northern Mali. Yet, there were geographical differences, with al-Mourabitoun being strongest in MUJAO's old area in Gao, and AQIM being strongest in Timbuktu, Taoudenni and Kidal, although local Tuareg leaders dominated the last-mentioned city.[134] The limited size of the international and Malian forces contributed to this development, as did the tension between the Malian army and the MNLA, the latter repelling the former from Kidal in May 2014. As a result the Malian army confined itself to barracks or in the Niger River area south of it.[135] The withdrawal of the Malian forces, and the lack of protection offered to civilians, even led to the emergence of new, often ethnically or tribally based armed self-help groups, and tribal rivalry and conflicts became frequent. However, the presence of the Sahara enabled the Ansar Dine to raid villages where its enemies had little presence, and begin taxing again, as well as pressuring locals into supporting the group, not only in Mali, but even in Algeria and Niger. While it was the resurgence in attacks against the international forces that the international press most often wrote about, the incidents where the jihadists punished locals resisting them were perhaps more significant.[136]

Moreover, recruits who had been attracted to MUJAO and Ansar Dine returned to central Mali. In January 2015, a new organisation, led by a former Ansar Dine member, Amadou Koufa, was created, the Macina Liberation Front (MLF).[137] Memories of ancient Fulani grandeur influenced the organisation, which took its name from a nineteenth-century Fulani state.[138] There remains a lot of confusion about this group. Leaflets distributed in mosques in central Mali were, for example, most commonly signed by Ansar Dine, or used the name of Dina, a Fulani theocracy of the nineteenth century. A video posted on the internet by a group active in central Mali, distributed on 18 May 2016, claimed to be that of Ansar Dine's 'Katibat Macina'.[139] Tactical overlaps between the two organisations were common.[140]

The International Crisis Group suggests that three groups were active. One consisted of Fulani and Tamasheq combatants with roots in Ansar Dine and leaders close to Iyad Ag Ghali. A second group, active in the Ténenkou and Youwarou regions, was mainly recruited locally but included veterans from MUJAO and Ansar Dine. A third, more trans-border group consisted of nomadic Fulani, namely the sub-groups Seedoobe (from Mali), the Djelgobe (from Burkina Faso) and especially the Toleebe (from Niger), most of them being MUJAO veterans.[141] In the south, Souleymane Keita, a southerner who commanded the Khalid ibn al-Walid combat unit, nominally under AQIM, also cooperated with the MLF.[142] Further away, Ansaroul Islam, led by the radical Burkinabe preacher Dicko (more commonly known as Malam Ibrahim Dicko), started a relatively weak insurgency in Burkina Faso's northern provinces of Soum and Oudalan. Dicko was later to gravitate towards supporting the Islamic state.

The tension in central Mali also has to be seen in the light of local conflicts. Some of these involved conflict between animistic groups within the Fulani and the more settled Dogon and the generally Muslim Fulanis, who usually won, since they were better equipped. In a sense this was a symptom of the long tension between nomads and settled groups, which created an environment in which the MLF could thrive. In addition, many Fulanis saw the national security forces as biased and supporting the Dogons in this conflict, creating animosity towards the state and support for the jihadist groups. Yet the Fulanis also had their own internal conflicts, for example between the Soosoobé and

Salsalbé, sub-groups which had been at conflict on several occasions since 1936. In November 2016, jihadists sent an unsigned letter in Arabic to the two communities, giving the Soosoobé grazing claims priority, perhaps because of the Salsalbés' stronger connection with the traditional nobility of the Fulani. In the end the support of the jihadists tilted the balance of power in favour of Soosoobé away from the old Fulani elite. The conflict dwindled away and the jihadist intervention was adhered to by both parties. Benjaminsen and Ba claim that both Salsalbé and Soosoobé individuals joined the jihadists, partly to prepare for future conflicts between the two groups, in a move, as often happened in Somalia, that had little to do with global or even Malian jihadist revolutions.

The exact boundary between jihadists, bandits and self-help groups at times became blurred.[143] However, there was an element of resistance by Fulani herdsmen against national security forces as well. Amadou Koufa has highlighted the current struggle as a continuation of the anti-colonial struggle against European invaders, but also against a corrupt and unfair state, resembling the propaganda of the early Boko Haram, and emphasising the struggle as one against infidels as well.[144] Ibrahim Dicko later attempted to rival Koufa as 'the Fulani leader' in his speeches.

Perhaps the main conclusion of this discussion is that, as in Kenya, the boundaries between the various jihadist organisations were blurred in the south. Perhaps the best example was the 20 November 2015 attack on the Radisson Blue hotel in Bamako, where three groups took responsibility for the attack, of which two, AQIM and al-Mourabitoun, admitted that they cooperated, while the Macina Liberation Front also claimed responsibility.[145] The most likely explanation is that the event signalled closer cooperation between AQIM and al-Mourabitoun, drawing upon their networks in the south, including members of the Macina Liberation Front, which in itself was a loose configuration. The propaganda of Ansar Dine about attacks 'south of the river' became more and more frequent, and Ansar Dine and al-Mourabitoun increasingly shared propaganda statements in the north.[146]

While the reach of the jihadists spread and different factions of AQIM merged, there were also signs of problems within the new organisations. The unification that led to al-Mourabitoun had left out some MUJAO leaders, such as Adnan Abu Walid al-Sahrawi, who had refused initially to acknowledge the group's new leadership.

Unity is in a way a strange word. Many of the southern activists were involved in clandestine networks. While the northern leaders in general had a background in either AQIM or Ansar Dine, the geography hampered command lines, as did the authoritarian personalities and the various ethnic backgrounds of the groups. Yet there were clear signals of an increased willingness to cooperate between the groups, which led eventually to the founding of the Jama'at Nusrat ul-Islam wal-Muslimin' on 3 March 2017. In the video announcing the formation, AQIM's Sahara region, represented by its leader Djamel Okacha and Abu Abd al-Rahman al-Sanhaji; al-Mourabitoun, represented by its second-in-command, Mohamed Ould Nouini (al-Hassan al-Ansari); Ansar Dine, represented by Iyad Ag Ghali; and the Macina Liberation Front, represented by Koufa, all declared their unity. They swore allegiance to the emir of al-Qaeda, Ayman al-Zawahiri, and to the 'emir of the Islamic Emirate' in Afghanistan, Haibatullah Akhundzada, to which the central al-Qaeda also swore allegiance. The new group was to be led by Iyad Ag Ghali, though it also swore an oath to AQIM's leader, Abdelmalek Droukdel.

Geography and different organisational traditions may possibly limit cohesion and coordination within the group, but the tendency towards some limited centralisation was there before the declaration.

On the ground the groups were still seen as different by local actors, from whom they raised money. The groups seemingly did not participate in the trade routes that went through northern Mali but rather taxed them. Yet, the exact amount of money that the groups received from the trade is hard to estimate, as the local business community is reluctant to speak about it. In the words of a businessman from Timbuktu involved in the transport sector: 'We cannot evaluate the informal taxes we pay to armed groups and even Islamists. Because they are confidential taxes, which secure all our business and even our own security.'[147]

The business sectors in the north had turned as a result of the civil war towards the basic goods trade. Plunder and taxation conducted by the armed groups, as well as by forces allied with the government, were the order of the day.[148] According to local businessmen, the jihadists maintained a presence in the larger cities in the north, 'being everywhere, but invisible', and collected taxes from traders passing through territory outside the cities.[149] Yet many, especially in Kidal and Gao, saw such taxes as being fairer than those imposed by other groups. Indeed, the organisations that were supposed to be hostile towards Nusrat ul-Islam, including government officials, seem to have been integrated into the illicit economy, and interviewees in the region frequently mentioned informal taxation exacted by a variety of secular militias. There were rumours of collaboration between groups, in the form of the Coordination des mouvements de l'Azawad (CMA), but Nusrat ul-Islam targeted CMA leaders at a local level. In many instances the rumours could have originated in the fact that some jihadist commanders had previously left and joined the CMA.

The new group, Nusrat ul-Islam, faced challenges in the form of Algiers accords between the Malian government, the MNLA and several other armed groups in the north. Indeed, some observers have wondered if the peace agreements were one of the causes of the union among the jihadists.[150] Yet at the same time, Nusrat ul-Islam enjoyed many advantages. While the various groups within the union were expelled from the larger cities, they were allowed to operate relatively freely in the countryside. Rida Lyammouri, for example, tells the story of how AQIM openly visited the village of Boudjbeha in November 2015, speaking publicly to the crowd and warning them against collaborating with outside forces.[151] In one sense this scene could have come from Somalia, where AQIM was able to warn and scare locals in supposedly 'liberated zones'.

The vast distances of the Sahara, and the limited capacity of the Malian state as well as the foreign intervention forces, will enable the new body to remain semi-territorial quite easily, and for some years to come, while it also develops more network-based organisational modes in central Mali. The assassination on 9 September 2018 of a commander of the MOC, a body set up by the Algiers agreement to create joint security efforts, also showed an ability on the part of the organisation to take steps to enhance local security, as previous attacks on MOC units had indicated, and serves as a warning to locals not to cooperate with such efforts. Rural security remains troubled. The reported death of Amadou Koufa in November 2018, was a blow to JNIM in central Mali, but the local grievances remain and can be taken advantage of by new leaders. The size of the Sahara will ensure that Nusrat ul-Islam can pull back in the face of enemy offensives, and return to tax and recruit locals as soon as these offensives dwindle, while at the same time it sponsors terror attacks in southern Mali. The transformation from territoriality had its price, but that price has now largely been paid.

5

THE ISLAMIC STATE IN THE GREATER SAHARA
ON THE PERIPHERY OF THE PERIPHERY

The Islamic State in the Greater Sahara is also a relatively new organisation, born out of a leadership struggle within al-Mourabitoun, one of many similar struggles that have plagued the Saharan groups in the past. At the time when it emerged, however, there was a new global organisation that could provide one of the factions with legitimacy, and could influence its ideology from outside: the Islamic State then establishing itself in the Levant.

The most important leader in the formation of the Islamic State in the Greater Sahara was, and is, Adnan Abu Walid al-Sahrawi, whose real name, some say, is Lehbib Ould Ali Ould Saïd Ould Joumani.[1] According to *La Tribune du Sahara*, Walid al-Sahrawi was born in El Aaiún to a prominent Western Saharan family of the Reguibat–Lebouiha tribal confederacy, which was later to supply the Movement for Jihad in West Africa (MUJAO) with many members. He fled to Algeria in 1990.[2] At some point, he joined Ejercito de Liberación Popular Saharaui (ELPS, or Sahrawi People's Liberation Army), the military wing of the Polisario Front, which fought for the independence of Western Sahara, and was trained in the Shahid el-Ouali camp in Muqataa just before the first ceasefire, probably in 1991–2.[3] Perhaps disillusioned with the lack of progress of ELPS, Walid al-Sahrawi drifted towards jihadism, and into the Salafist Group for Preaching and Combat (GSPC), where he befriended Hamada Ould Mohamed Kheirou (Abu Qum Qum), a Mauritanian firebrand sheikh, who allegedly left for Iraq in 2003.[4] Together with the half-Tuareg, half-Arab Malian Sultan Ould Badi and a Lamhar Arab from Gao, Ahmed Ould Amer (Ahmed al-Tilemsi), they belonged to a heterogeneous group of non-Arabs within units of the very independent al-Qaeda in the Maghreb (AQIM). This group became important for the foundation of MUJAO in late 2011.

There is much speculation about the founding of MUJAO.[5] One factor may have been the reluctance of AQIM's leadership to allow Sultan Ould Badi and Hamada Ould Mohamed Kheirou to create a separate unit recruiting from Sahelian Arabs and the Lamhar tribe. Although primary sources are scarce, this story seems plausible, especially in the context of Mokhtar Belmokhtar's increased independence from AQIM's central leadership, and his close bonds with the future leaders of MUJAO.[6] Moreover, it explains the initial Saharan profile of MUJAO, before it expanded its recruitment in Mali. Interestingly, the pattern was to be repeated in the future Islamic State in the Greater Sahara. It was initially dominated by Mauritanians and Sahrawites, as well as Saharan Arabs, and was later joined by other southern ethnic groups, while the Algerian leaders so common in AQIM were absent. Algerians who wanted to join the Islamic State belonged to other organisations, primarily Jund al-Khilafah, and also the al-Ansar brigade in central Algeria, the Protectors of the Salafist Call (Humat al-Da'wa al-Salafiya) based in west Algeria, the al-Ghurabae brigade and the Ansar al-Khilafa brigade, all groups from AQIM that defected to the Islamic State.

After its creation, MUJAO cooperated with many other jihadist organisations such as Belmokhtar's group and Ansar Dine during the period of jihadist territoriality in Mali described in the last chapter and during its transformation into semi-territoriality.[7] Given this pattern of extensive and eclectic cooperation, it was not strange when in 2013 MUJAO chose to join Belmokhtar's faction and create al-Mourabitoun.[8] On the ground, the situation was confused, with many keeping the name MUJAO and having limited interaction with the leadership. The unification created conflict as it left out some MUJAO leaders, like Walid al-Sahrawi, who initially refused to acknowledge the organisation's new leadership.[9] There are few primary sources on the event but, according to Rida Lyammouri, MUJAO's first leader,

Abu Bakr al-Masri, was an external, compromise candidate chosen to bring the two factions together.[10] Even though a compromise was reached, several MUJAO leaders were sceptical about the union. The veteran Ould Mohamed Kheirou refused to join and Sahrawi remained uncertain before he finally joined.

The initial problems might have been overcome if al-Masri had the chance to consolidate his leadership position. However, in April 2014 French forces killed him. A new leader, the MUJAO veteran Ahmed al-Tilemsi, was selected by the organisation's *Shura* (council) to become the new emir after Belmokhtar allegedly refused the position because of an agreement with Walid al-Sahrawi that he would not take up leadership of the organisation.[11] Tilemsi was killed by the French in December 2014. A leadership struggle now flared up, and it seems that Sahrawi called a *Shura* and was elected as the new leader. The composition of the *Shura* was controversial, and Belmokhtar, who was not in Mali at the time, contested the whole process. When he refused to pledge allegiance to Sahrawi, tensions rose. At the same time, Belmokhtar began talks with AQIM about reintegration. MUJAO distanced itself strongly from AQIM, while Belmokhtar had always declared his loyalty towards the central al-Qaeda leadership, and had an ambiguous relationship with AQIM, for example publishing videos that paid homage to AQIM's dead leaders and celebrated them as martyrs.

In this way, the conflict contained many of the characteristics common to the fragmentary processes among jihadists in the Sahara: struggles over leadership, and problems in controlling organisational structures, which were exacerbated by the vast distances and by the possibility of rebellious units moving away to avoid sanctions from the mother organisation. Yet something new was added to the mix. Whereas in the past al-Qaeda had been the only global organisation in the militant jihadist camp, this had now changed. The Islamic State had emerged on the scene. This organisation had its origins in Abu Musab al-Zarqawi and his Jama'at al-Tawhid wal-Jihad (JTJ), founded in 1999, which joined the al-Qaeda network in 2004, changing its name several times until it started to call itself the Islamic State of Iraq (ISI) in 2006. There were many problems between the Islamic State of Iraq and the central al-Qaeda, and the relationship declined rapidly from April

2013. The Islamic State expanded from Iraq into Syria, challenging another al-Qaeda affiliate operating there, the Jabhat al-Nusrah, which the Islamic State actually declared it had absorbed.[12] Fighting between Jabhat al-Nusrah and the Islamic State over the next year made the conflict more severe, and in February 2014 al-Qaeda disowned the Islamic State.[13] The forceful reply from the Islamic State was to declare a resurrected caliphate a few months later. A caliph is seen as a supreme leader of Muslims and, in theory, all Muslims are required to obey him. What this declaration did was to question al-Qaeda's leading role, and insist that all jihadists should be loyal to the Islamic State. This declaration might have had limited effect if it was not for the Islamic State's astonishing battlefield victories in the years from 2012 to 2014, giving it an aura of invincibility, which helped attract followers. The use of extreme violence also put the Islamic State on the map.

For Sahrawi and other former MUJAO leaders, the Islamic State offered an alternative to standing alone or allying with the hated AQIM. MUJAO's tradition of being hostile towards AQIM, and leadership rivalries between Sahrawi and Belmokhtar, may have set the stage for what was to happen. In May 2015 Sahrawi declared al-Mourabitoun's loyalty towards the then expanding Islamic State in the Levant.[14] Sahrawi claimed that the declaration was made because of ideological reasons. However, the leadership struggle with Belmokhtar must also have influenced the process, as well as the old animosities with AQIM's leadership.[15]

Struggling on the Periphery of the Jihadists

The declaration of loyalty to the Islamic State had limited success. Belmokhtar dismissed the move and announced that al-Mourabitoun was following him, not Sahrawi.[16] Matters would get worse. In August, Belmokhtar convened his own alternative *Shura* for al-Mourabitoun, which elected him as leader.[17] Local newspapers reported that Belmokhtar attacked Sahrawi's militia near Gao and the clashes allegedly left several of Sahrawi's men dead and Sahrawi himself possibly injured, although this is hard to verify.[18] The activities of the Sahrawi group were limited over the next year, indicating that the new organisation was weak and no recognition was forthcoming from the

Islamic State. There may have been contacts between Sahrawi's Greater Sahara outfit and AQIM in order to create some form of peace, but this came to nothing.[19] It seems as if the new organisation, called the Islamic State in the Greater Sahara (ISGS), settled down in the border area between Niger and Mali around Bouratam, and members married into the local Fulani tribe.[20]

In 2016, however, the organisation was revitalised. On 4 May 2016, Sahrawi made his first public appearance for over half a year, giving a speech in which he threatened to attack posts of the United Nations Mission for the Referendum in Western Sahara (MINURSO) in the area as well as Moroccan forces, tourist groups and Western organisations.[21] Interestingly, the threat was not circulated by the main media outlets of the Islamic State, indicating a possible lack of contact between the two.[22] However, by the autumn of 2016 ISGS stepped up its direct attacks, not against groups loyal to al-Qaeda but against government and civilian targets in the border area between Burkina Faso, Niger and Mali. In September 2016, the ISGS attacked a Burkinabe military outpost near the border with Mali. A second operation occurred near the site of the first and left three Burkinabe soldiers dead. In October 2016, they attempted a prison break at Koutoukalé prison, in Niger, near the capital of Niamey.[23]

Perhaps it was because of the increased activities of the organisation that the central Islamic State became more forthcoming. On 30 October 2016, the Islamic-affiliated Amaq News Agency announced the formal acceptance of ISGS's allegiance by Abu Bakr al-Baghdadi, ISIL's leader, but the ISGS was not acknowledged as a *wilayat*, a formal region, perhaps indicating some distrust on the part of the central Islamic State leadership. This recognition was also again followed by a period of relative silence. Despite the Islamic State in the Greater Sahara having an able Fulani leader in the person of Nampala Ilassou Djibo, it remained relatively quiet. It exerted influence in the Oudalan province, as well as in the Liptako-Gourma region in Burkina Faso. In addition, it was active in the wider Ménaka region of Mali, but here it seems to have attracted counter-measures from the local militias and from Moussa Ag Acharatoumane, a leader of the Dawshahak (Daoussak) Tuareg, of the Azawad Salvation Movement (MSA), established in September 2016. It also clashed with General Ag Gamou, the leader

95

of the Tuareg self-defence group loyal to the government, Groupe Autodéfense Touareg Imghad et Alliés (GATIA). In both cases, the Islamic State was initially on the losing side.[24] There were also rumours about some leaders being supposedly loyal to al-Qaeda, including Boureïma Dicko (Malam Ibrahim Dicko) and Amadou Koufa.[25] Koufa was accused of negotiating with Nampala Ilassou Djibo for a possible merger with the Islamic State.[26]

Yet, slowly but steadily the Islamic State carved out a niche for itself. Part of that niche was around Ménaka, where the organisation engaged in cattle rustling and providing cattle 'protection' for the locals. It also became involved in local conflicts. There are communitarian tensions between the Dawshahak and the Toleebe sub-group of the Fulani of Ménaka–Tillabéry, many of the latter having been formerly active in central Mali. In this context, the Islamic State in the Greater Sahara presented itself as the defender of the Fulani against Moussa Ag Acharatoumane and the MSA. As a result several chieftains like Dondou Cheffou (aka Khalid al-Fulani) and Ilassou Djibo (aka Petit Chaffori) sided with Sahrawi to defend the interests of the Toleebe Fulani. These Toleebe groups straddled the border with Niger, and thus gave Sahrawi a welcome foothold in that country, a situation not dissimilar to the spread of Boko Haram into Cameroon.

Although some observers believed the Islamic State took the side of the Fulani against the Dawshahak, the latter were split, as many chieftains and elders resented the pre-eminence of Moussa Ag Acharatoumane, who relied on the international forces of the French Barkhane and MINUSMA (the United Nations Stabilization Mission in Mali) to solidify his hold. Some Dawshahak leaders feared that this could put them at risk when the Barkhane force exited. In fact the Islamic State managed to secure the support of some Dawshahak leaders who had local popularity, and who had challenged the leadership of Moussa Ag Acharatoumane (previously known as al-Mahmoud Ag Baye, also as Ikaray), Mohamed Ag Almouner (also known as Tinka) and Almahmoud Ag Akawkaw (also known as Royal). Moussa was also opposed by several ethnic sub-groups, among them the Ansongo and the Iguodiritane. Tinka and Ikaray are members of the Iguodiritane, whose traditional leader was provoked by the conflicts to seek allies outside, both in the Islamic State and the MSA.

During 2018, fighting between the Islamic State and its enemies flared up, involving the killing of Dawshahak tribesmen. The Islamic State also staged assassinations. The most infamous attack occurred when four American Special Forces soldiers and five soldiers from the Niger were killed during an ambush by the Islamic State in Tongo Tongo, a few kilometres from the Malian border, on 4 October 2017. Yet this action may have damaged the Islamic State, as Moussa Ag Acharatoumane and Tinka Ag Almouner are said to have died during the ambush, thereby weakening the fragile foothold of the Islamic State among the Dawshahak, though this was denied by local sources. The episode demonstrates the fragile nature of the Islamic State, and could explain its attempts to cooperate with al-Qaeda affiliates again in 2017.

In many ways, the Islamic State in Greater Sahara seems to have carved out a niche for itself on the periphery of the periphery, where it has been opposed by both Islamists and more secular hostile movements, as well as government forces. Yet it has been able to implement a form of contested semi-territoriality, where it has had to face local militias and has been defeated by them in several battles.

6

BOKO HARAM/THE ISLAMIC STATE IN WEST AFRICA
FROM TERRITORIALITY TO FRAGMENTATION?

Jama'atu Ahlis Sunna Lidda'Awati wal-Jihad ('People Committed to the Prophet's Teachings for Propagation and Jihad') has long been better known by the name Boko Haram (loosely speaking, 'Western education is sin'), given to it by outsiders. It was among the four most active organisations carrying out terrorist attacks in 2014.[1] It also exemplifies many of the changes experienced by Sunni-inspired African militants. The organisation developed from a small accepted group into a clandestine network, then into an organisation with semi-territorial control, then into one that controls territory, before most of these territories were lost again.

As such, Boko Haram provides a test case of variation in organisational dynamics as a group expands and contracts, and it is one of the few groups in this book which at some stages were legal in their home country. Ideologically, it also presents an interesting case study. Boko Haram's connections to Shabaab are today well proven, as are its interactions with al-Qaeda in the Islamic Maghreb (although the scope of this interaction is hard to assess), yet it is not an ideological copycat.[2] Boko Haram exists inside an evolving discourse in which local redefinition of foreign ideological impulses creates a complex ideological platform, which has varied over time.[3] The present leader of one of its factions, Abubakar Shekau, appeared until 2015 in many videos focusing on his persona, a quite different presentation from, for example, Shabaab's media clips of its leaders that contain ample references to global issues and quotes from the Quran and the Hadith.[4]

There are great methodological problems in studying the organisation. Its centre of gravity has always been the Borno province in Nigeria, where few researchers have done thorough fieldwork. This may be the reason for the historiographical controversies around the organisation. The first concerns the origins of Boko Haram itself. Most analysts trace the formation of the group back to the initiative of Sheikh Mohammed Yusuf in the early 2000s, though some go even further back, to the late 1990s.[5] The exact structure of the organisation is also unclear. Some analysts maintain that there is a tendency to inflate attacks supposedly conducted by Boko Haram but in reality committed by local strongmen and conflict entrepreneurs, often a common tool employed in Nigerian politics; consequently, this creates confused statistics and leads to an overestimation of the size of the organisation.[6] Blurred lines between this group and others make it hard to assess both its ideology and international connections, though this situation is mirrored in the case of other organisations in the Rift, the Horn and the Sahel. Fortunately, ideas manifest themselves in action and speeches, and even when they are presented to achieve instrumental purposes they have to resonate either with a foreign audience which can provide support and means, or with the local population. By using these sources, combined with press reports and local interviews, one can map the trajectory of the organisation.

Origins: A Relatively Accepted Status

How did Boko Haram originate? The northern regions of Nigeria where the organisation has recruited members is poorer than the rest of the country.[7] Researchers and commentators also point to the problem of the Almajiri system of education in the country, in which young boys attend traditional religious schools, usually begging to survive while students, and often ending up as unemployed afterwards, as their religious training is ill-suited to modern Nigeria. The system is seen as creating a pool of potential recruits for Boko Haram, although some researchers, like Hannah Hoechner, contest this.[8] Indeed,

Hoechner makes the point that the Almajiri system is simply too large to explain the phenomenon of Boko Haram, and that most Almajiri students become peaceful members of Nigerian society.

Corruption and nepotism are also said to have alienated the local population from the Nigerian state, and northern grievances – such as a relatively high poverty rate in the north-east, and an increase in poverty locally after the oil boom of the 1970s – are often claimed to have created animosities against the central government.[9] Additionally, local political elites have not scrupled to create, arm, employ and tolerate private armed gangs, seeing them as useful political storm troopers. In this way they created an environment in which it was easier for Boko Haram to grow.[10] There is no doubt that all these factors are important, yet they lack explanatory power. Many large variables such as poverty, alienation and migrant status are often identified in order to explain recruitment to radical groups, yet these variables influence large segments of a population who never become founders or members of radical organisations.[11]

The missing link in the early stages of the organisation could be, as Gilles Kepel, Olivier Roy and Quintan Wiktorowicz suggested in respect of other militant Sunni fundamentalist groups, some kind of personal or social ties between members that facilitate mobilisation.[12] Yet its origins are controversial. According to Freedom Onuoha, citing information from Nigerian security sources, a small group emerged in 1995: the Ahlulsunna wal'jama'ah hijra (Muslim Youth Organisation).[13] This was started by Abubakar Lawan, and was on the whole peaceful: its message was that Sunnis had to find their path back to the ways of original Islam.[14] It was said to have been begun at the University of Maiduguri in the capital of Borno state, later one of the strongholds of Boko Haram. In 2002, there was a change in leadership when Lawan left for Saudi Arabia, and Mohammed Yusuf was appointed leader of the group.[15] This is not the only version of the founding story. Kyari Mohammed describes, on the basis of government sources, how the small organisation that was to become Boko Haram withdrew from the city of Maiduguri to the Kanamma area of Yobe state in north-eastern Nigeria, and counts 2002 as the founding year of the organisation, although others contest this.[16] Human Rights Watch reckons the founding took place in 2003, when members went into the countryside to create a parallel society.[17] The various names used for the organisation, both Boko Haram and what was to become its own name, Jama'atu Ahlis Sunna Lidda'Awati wal-Jihad, appeared later, the latter after 2009.[18]

The story emerging from the writer's own field research to a certain extent corroborates parts of the stories given above, though this mainly has to do with overlaps of networks rather than the founding of the group itself. The nucleus of the early Boko Haram seems to have been a youth rebellion of young scholars against the older leadership of a mosque, Maiduguri's Indimi mosque, led locally by Sheikh Abakar Adan, and from afar by the popular Sheikh Ja'afar Mahmud Adam, who was based in Borno. The early history of what was to become Boko Haram was actually very similar to the founding of Hijra and, indeed, of one of the important groups within the ADF: it was about conflict in a local mosque between youths and the central mosque leadership, although in this case there were also conflicts between different youth groups.

The future leader of Boko Haram, Mohammed Yusuf, was at the time a protegé of the famous Ja'afar Mahmud Adam in 2000–1. He was seen as very talented and given the position of leader of the mosque's youth group, and was chosen by Ja'afar to do charity work, such as giving away fatherless brides on their wedding day. In the words of someone who frequented the mosque:

> The first time I heard about Mohammed Yusuf it was early 2000. He was with Sheikh Ja'afar and was a very captivating person. He was just learning the Islamic teachings in the Indimi mosque. He used to argue with his teacher. He was Ja'afar's favourite, he was the most favourite of all Ja'afar's students. He did not have followers at the time, but he had a few friends, mostly students. They often abandoned school.[19]

At this stage the future leader of Boko Haram interacted with some of the leading local politicians who frequented the mosque, as well as with the network that Ja'afar may have secured. Ja'afar's sermons were fairly popular, but many observed an increasing tendency on Yusuf's part to challenge the elder sheikhs and, according to witnesses, his speeches contained some radical elements at that time: 'I heard about him in 2001–2. He said Western education is haram for females. I heard it in the loudspeakers from the mosque in our neighbourhood. I heard he lived with my grandmother here in Sabon Numba. He did not come often, but he came maybe monthly. He was preaching against my participating in school. I did not like it.'[20]

Yusuf was apparently was allowed to stand in for Sheikh Ja'afar when the latter was absent, and he also travelled to smaller mosques to give sermons. In this way he gained both fame and followers. The Indimi mosque's youth group, also known as al-Shabaab, had, according to members, been created in 1999, with Yusuf as its second leader. From 2001 onwards, several conflicts broke out in the group, and three groups formed, one around Bashir Mustafa, one around the leader of the Shabaab, Mohammed Yusuf, and an informal group around Ali Husseini and Abubakar Lawan. Some of the Shabaab members had belonged to the Ahlulsunna wal'jama'ah hijra (Muslim Youth Organisation), but there were members of this organisation scattered among all three groups. Bashir Mustafa and Mohammed Yusuf were rivals. Mustafa criticised Yusuf for his lack of understanding of the Quran, while the group of Ali Husseini, Mohammed Ali and Abubakar Lawan was more radical than both the other groups. It was to become known as the Kanamma group, also as the Taliban, and its leaders spoke often about global issues, such as travelling to foreign theatres for jihad, though eyewitnesses never heard any talk of al-Qaeda. As a leader, Yusuf was in the middle of the conflict, facing attacks from both Bashir Mustafa and the Husseini group, which at one stage actually tried to depose him.[21]

The discussions of the Kanamma group drew upon a religious resurgence partly created by the reinvigoration of the Salafist movement by young Salafist sheikhs returning from Saudi Arabia in the 1990s.[22] Most of these sheikhs never joined Boko Haram – including Yusuf's mentor Sheikh Ja'afar, who later was to attack Yusuf and his group in many speeches – but they contributed to a general mode in religious discussions that paved the way for the future Boko Haram by confronting older authorities and attacking Sufism.[23]

Boko Haram's early years were influenced by several other trends in Nigeria: the increasing number of self-help groups claiming to provide justice after the reintroduction of democracy in Nigeria in 1999, and the adoption of the Sharia penal code by the Governor of Zamfara state, Sani Yerima, in 1999, which helped set the stage. Boko

Haram was not the only one of its kind; several other sects existed, some offshoots of the Yusufia.[24] A number of these groups were part of an elaborate scheme of patronage by which activists and armed groups were incorporated into governance structures. Yusuf, for example, was appointed to the Sharia Implementation Council in 2001.[25] Clustered around Yusuf were several other leaders, including the future head of Boko Haram, Abubakar Shekau, and Mohammed Ali, who jihadist publications claimed was actually Boko Haram's first leader. The group around Ali Husseini and Mohammed Ali chose to establish a separate segregated colony outside the village of Kanamma, which flew Taliban flags; they later attacked a local police station.[26] However, this group should not be mistaken for Boko Haram. Nominally they remained part of the Shabaab, the mosque's youth group, and Mohammed Yusuf was in theory their leader, but in reality he had little influence, and in fact he criticised their move.[27] Indeed, Yusuf seems to have been in Saudi Arabia for three months in 2003–4.[28] The group was in the end defeated by the police and many died, including Ali Husseini. Some, however, would later enter what was to become known as Boko Haram. The demise of the Kanamma group at the hands of the police might also have pushed Yusuf in a more extreme direction.[29]

Boko Haram did draw upon former members of the Kanamma group, but most of the future leaders in Boko Haram had other origins. Membership of the Indimi mosque enabled Yusuf to deliver speeches around Maiduguri, and he attracted many in this way, including the future Boko Haram leader Abubakar Shekau.[30] In his speeches and sermons Yusuf drew upon the content of Saudi Arabian and Syrian books, circulated during the later 1990s and early 2000s: he cited the well-known Syrian Salafi quietist Nasir al-Din al-Albani (d. 1999) and the Jordanian Salafi jihadist Abu Musab al-Zarqawi in his speeches.[31] He engaged audiences outside Boko Haram, and in some of the question-and-answer sessions held by the organisation, though his views were often contested by the audience.[32] Moreover, Yusuf addressed in his speeches a wide spectrum of issues, including public morals, how to follow Sharia, the heliocentric view of the solar system (which he criticised) and other relatively narrow topics. Yet, perhaps the most important element was a critique of the rich and powerful, of the lack of justice, and corruption in the Nigerian system.

According to a document written by Yusuf, Nigeria was 'a failed state that cannot provide jobs and basic necessities of life to its citizens'. He said that Boko Haram 'aims to kill all government officials, including security operatives, to set up a system of government that ensures justice and equitable distribution of resources'.[33] Witnesses repeat this story: 'He targeted the mind of the masses, he set up the ruling class against the masses, whenever the masses heard about the rich they would go against them, that was his method, that they had been cheated. What he said was 95% true, the last 5% was his strange ideology.'[34] In addition to the vigorous strain of anti-corruption rhetoric in his propaganda, Yusuf also focused heavily on protests against being governed by a non-'Islamic' state.[35] In this way, the early Boko Haram sought to create an image of itself as an alternative to the corrupt practices of the Nigerian state, both at a regional and national level.

At the same time, Yufu's teachings were not welcomed in the Indimi mosque and the Shabaab. His relationship with other sheikhs, and in the end with Ja'afar, hardened as Yusuf challenged Ja'afar's authority openly, and gave interpretations of the Quran that were seen as erroneous by the Indimi leadership. These conflicts had been simmering since 2001, but they grew stronger and stronger. After a while, a pattern developed in which Ja'afar would demand public retractions from Yusuf, Yusuf would yield in closed meetings but he would never make his apologies openly.[36] In 2004, the final break came between the Indimi mosque and Yusuf and his followers, when Ja'afar distanced himself from Yusuf after returning from hajj and Yusuf was evicted from his position in the Shabaab.

After being evicted from Indimi, Yusuf, with the help of businessman and sponsor Baba Fu, who owned much of the area, established himself close to the railway station in an interim mosque, and later in a larger mosque, Ibn Taymiyyah Masjid. The latter's name indicated a belief in Takfirism, since Ibn Taymiyyah was an important symbol of radical Sunni Islamism.[37] A radical interpretation of Taymiyyah suited the group's orientation, as Taymiyyah, inspired by the Mongol invasions and the conversion of Mongol fighters to Islam, clearly had a strong reason to declare some Muslims non-Muslim, which is an important part of Takfirism. The mosque became known locally as the Markas mosque, and was built by voluntary workers, both from the group and among locals supporting the project.

The new group included many members from the Shabaab, but also gained followers in other circles, such as a group around Aminu Mohamed 'Billi Tashe'. 'Billi Tashe', who once had the reputation of a frequent party-goer and a drinker, had gathered a group of students around him, including the son of the owner of the land where the Indimi mosque was located. These students now joined Boko Haram.[38] Another early joiner was Mamman Nur, a young sheikh from the neighbourhood around the Indimi, though he was never a member of the Shabaab. Yet, of the new group, now known as the Yusufia, the most important members were individuals whom Mohammed Yusuf had won through his speeches. The group gained a lot of new followers. A loose *Shura* (council) structure was created. Many traders joined and were given positions, such as Mustapha Kawadima, a perfume trader with considerable money who contributed to the group and who was killed in the 2009 conflict with the government; Alhaji Bor, a businessman selling textiles, who was killed by the government in 2011; and a petty trader with a kiosk who used to give out free water close to the mosque, and who fled in 2009. In this way, the Yusufia could access finances for its operations.

Another important member who joined in this period was the future leader Abubakar Shekau. He was seen as an 'original' by many, a comic but alarming sight in Maiduguri as he drove around without a helmet on his motorbike, carrying his religious books, always ready to stop and utter angry comments when he saw something that he deemed unIslamic.[39] According to his neighbour:

> Shekau was born in Gaida, the village's name was actually Shekau. His parents sent him alone to Quranic school. His teacher was Mallam Taibu, he was sent to study Quran here, he got a diploma in Islamic studies at the Muhamad Gumi College of legal and Islamic studies. I saw him for the first time when he was playing football very often in the early 2000s. Seven years later, during 2007, I met him again, a tiny man riding his motorbike, he had a lot of books, he was sometimes reading his Quran while driving, very dangerous, and shouting, and not wearing a helmet. When he preached he had a very jumpy style of preaching and just shouted.[40]

Other Shura members were youngsters, who broke with their parents because of the demands of the increasingly cultish group. One was Baba Sainna, described by members of the group as 'a very gentle guy' and a very good reciter of the Quran, but he was disowned by his father when he joined the Yusufia. Disowning was indeed a very common result for Yusufia from well-to-do families, though at times it was the youths who disowned their parents. The new group wielded considerable influence and exerted social pressures, as one young woman experienced: 'I remember in 2005, their speeches, very often repetition. My neighbour came to us, with a speech from Shekau about girls participating in school. He wanted me to stop attending school. What could I do? I just laughed and said yes, yes yes, then I did whatever I wanted.'[41]

Although it was not without its troubles for the government, Boko Haram was on the whole legal and tolerated for at least six years. Some writers allege that it at times had close relationships with certain politicians such as Ali Modu Sheriff, whom it assisted in the 2003 election, although this has been challenged.[42] Others, finding little evidence for such connections, contest the view that the two were linked, yet it is a fact that Yusuf's associate Buji Foi, later to be killed by the Nigerian police, was appointed as a minister by Sheriff.[43] Local sources interviewed for this book say that Sheriff attempted to persuade the Boko Haram to become his allies in 2006–7.[44] Yet, Buji Foi was a local civil servant before the establishment of the Yusufia/Boko Haram and might have been a natural choice anyway, nor did he wield much power in his position. Some of Yusuf's sympathisers were also offered limited positions in the political administration, such as being in charge of selecting individuals allowed to go on pilgrimage.[45]

The group was open, it was easy to join, and it impressed many youths:

> We sat there with him [Yusuf] at a public gathering, he was so friendly, and he had a good method of teaching. His lectures were held in so many places, like Unguwar Doka. He talked about what was haram, people should be very wary about doing haram, they should be very wary about taking care of religion, they should be aware of the government, because it is so many bad things that government does. Shekau was speaking when Yusuf was unable to be present. He was not like Mohammed Yusuf. He

was aggressive in his approach, he also publicly condemned government action. If they don't do exactly the way he does, he would say this is not the way it was then [in the time of the Prophet]. If both Shekau and Yusuf was away, Mamman Nur would preach, he was also not very aggressive, but more than Yusuf, less than Shekau. The day you joined Yusufia, they call you to attend the preachers, they will then tell you to follow them in their prayers and other activities, they will say, 'Don't work for the government, anything who is haram, it is forbidden, stop doing it'.[46]

Yet, the organisation was also disciplined and well structured:

They were very organised, they were well disciplined, even when they prayed, they order themselves, they had high respect from the leaders, when he emerged from the house [Yusuf], they worshipped him, they were more disciplined than the army. They were people into commerce, people gathering information, people spreading the gospel, they had their own female group. Some joined together with their family.[47]

The organisation may have staged attacks against their opponents as early as 2005–6. Then in 2007, Yusuf's old patron, Sheikh Ja'afar, was killed. The killing may have been conducted by followers of Yusuf, although this is not entirely clear. Conflicts between the Yusufia and neighbours over mundane issues such as parking, and with the police over the refusal of many members to wear motorbike helmets, also created tension. Yet the group remained popular, and it did not need to exert pressure to gain either recruits or finances.

The relationship between local politicians and Boko Haram did, however, turn sour. In 2008, there was a serious incident when the organisation attacked a Maiduguri police station on 13 November, leading to the death of 17 Boko Haram members and to the arrest of Yusuf. In 2009 Boko Haram accused the police of killing one of their members. The rhetoric of the organisation grew more violent in the preaching of men like the future commander Mamman Nur, a non-Kanuri member from Maroua, the capital of Cameroon's far north region, and Abubakar Shekau.[48]

While Yusuf was released after the 2008 incident, his deputy was arrested twice in early 2009.[49] In 2009, the intensity of clashes with the state also increased, as a new joint police–army campaign in the region, Operation Flush, was set in motion.[50] A famous incident occurred on 11 June 2009 when the organisation staged a motorcycle procession for the funeral of one of their members who had died in a car accident on the Biu–Maiduguri road.[51] Several of the members did not wear motorbike helmets and the police decided to make arrests.[52] There are several alternative accounts of the incident, including that the police acted against Boko Haram because it had attempted to stockpile arms for a future offensive, or that it wanted to bury one of its victims in secret.[53] Tensions mounted when the police attempted to confiscate weapons, after an alleged Boko Haram bomb-maker, Hassan Sani Badami, was killed in an explosion in his house. What followed involved what many saw as the most intense fighting in Maiduguri so far.[54]

Boko Haram retaliated in a way that showed either that they were very well organised and prepared, or that they had many sympathisers outside the Maiduguri area. On the morning of 26 June, Boko Haram or its supporters attacked a police station in Bauchi, capital of the Bauchi state. On the 27th, attacks were also launched in Potiskum in Yobe state and in Wudil in Kano state, in addition to attacks in Maiduguri.[55] More attacks followed, affecting five northern states (Bauchi, Borno, Kano, Katsina and Yobe), and in the end forces from the army, parts of the 3rd Armoured Division, were deployed in Maiduguri. Nigerian newspapers celebrated the police and army counter-measures as a great success. Indeed, Yusuf was captured, and the organisation became leaderless. Boko Haram issued statements that were defensive, saying that they had acted in self-defence. According to Khalil Zarqawi, their alleged leader in Yobe: 'We are attacking police because they killed our brothers in Jos and Bauchi … There isn't good leadership in Nigeria. Muslims are being killed daily and the authorities are doing nothing about it. These are the reasons why we are retaliating against the police, because they are the ones who killed our brothers.'[56] However, there were also clear sectarian aspects to these events, and local newspapers reported on the killing of Christians and the torching of churches.[57]

The large-scale use of the army and police, as well as the widespread attacks against the government after the 11 June incident, demonstrated that Boko Haram had acquired a great potential for violence, and a large number of followers and sympathisers in the north. At the same time, the Nigerian police and security services resorted to practising the type of collective or random arrests, even possibly random killings, that are familiar from other settings, like Kenya, thereby serving to alienate a segment of the local population that was probably larger than the Boko Haram group itself. This practice was to continue for the next few years.

Nevertheless, it is important to avoid simplistic claims that the events of 26–30 July 2009 created the Boko Haram problem in Nigeria, as incidents in 2007 and 2008 had clearly indicated that the situation was getting out of hand. Indeed, many local sources claimed that the Nigerian authorities had acted too late and that the problems had been known long before the clashes occurred.[58]

Boko Haram had been allowed to develop a presence in Nigeria. It had played on concerns in the wider population, about corruption and lack of governance within northern Nigeria, while acquiring a Takfiri strain. Unlike other similar organisations, it had so far enjoyed a legal existence inside Nigeria. But this period was now over.

A Clandestine Network with Tendencies of Fragmentation (2009–13)

The clashes in June 2009 eventually led to Mohammed Yusuf's arrest. His death while in custody infuriated members of the sect even more, and set the stage for Boko Haram's phase of existence as a clandestine organisation. Although the Nigerian police and army reported that they had inflicted large casualties on Boko Haram, not all of the police targets were members of the organisation: there are many stories of the Nigerian police targeting ordinary civilians and then claiming they were Boko Haram activists.[59] The Nigerian security services managed to arrest the future leader, Abubakar Shekau, but he was released, whether because of corruption, mistaken identity or the influence of friends inside the Nigerian government.[60] Overall, however, Boko Haram's activities did dwindle quite drastically, perhaps because of its losses, but perhaps also because of the need for readjustment. Once again, what many saw as annihilation was in reality a transformation: Boko Haram was to survive.

The first year after the 2009 crackdown was a year of rebuilding. Boko Haram had to transform from a public into a clandestine organisation, with hidden command lines, hidden command structures and separate cells, in order for it to survive government surveillance and police actions against it. Many of its key members had fled Nigeria. Mamman Nur, one of the more prominent leaders, accused of masterminding the 2011 suicide attack against a UN headquarters in Abuja, fled from Nigeria for Somalia.[61] Jacob Zenn notes that Khalid Barnawi and Adam Kambar allegedly fled to Algeria, seeking shelter and training from al-Qaeda in the Islamic Maghreb (AQIM).[62] Others hid within Nigeria in order to avoid capture. In Borno state Boko Haram still had some popularity, and one eyewitness for example describes how the Boko Haram fighters were received in quite a friendly way in Bama in 2009.[63] Seemingly, the crackdown of 2009 had led to increased decentralisation, indeed to confusion, within the organisation.[64] The exact leadership structure at the time seems to have been unclear. Several sources point to Sanni Umaru as leader during a short interim period, although in practice, as with European resistance organisations during the Second World War, there may have been many people in charge.[65] Boko Haram's leadership was nevertheless in disarray, key members had left the country, and the organisation was under pressure from the Nigerian police and armed forces. For the first year after the 2009 battles, the Borno state was quiet. Superficially, it seemed that the Nigerian army and police had scored a notable victory.

All the same, Boko Haram held several advantages. Firstly, it may have enjoyed local support, although its extent is hard to establish, but expressions of support were made to international reporters in 2010, some of it because of government executions without trial of several alleged Boko Haram members. Locally, the Nigerian police could have been seen as welcome targets, being feared across Nigeria for their brutality and corruption. Such targeting may have contributed to Boko Haram's recruitment. Secondly, a leadership consisting mainly of ethnic Kanuris dominated the organisation, and it had a clear recruitment base among north-eastern Nigerian groups. Operating as it did against the central state, it could thus be perceived as aligned with resistance against the state (although Kanuri elites later became important in the fight against Boko Haram).[66] Popular support was probably enhanced by local ignorance of the many malign sides of Boko Haram's ideology. The organisation itself made relatively drastic pronouncements and stated, for example, 'In fact, we are spread across all the 36 states in Nigeria, and Boko Haram is just a version of al-Qaeda, which we align with and respect. We support Osama bin Laden, we shall carry out his command in Nigeria until the country is completely converted to Islam, which is according to the wish of Allah.'[67] This statement has to be seen in the light of Boko Haram's position two weeks after the crackdown in 2009. It represents a claim by a new leader in uncertain times, trying to impress both members and outsiders, and convince his own people that there was still hope for the Boko Haram cause.

After the initial confusion, Boko Haram rebounded, but they did so in a way that alienated many civilians:

> In 2010 the killings started, killing the traditional leaders, the lowest leaders in the traditional system, they saw them … they continued to kill targeted individuals, first the police, then expanding to other people who exposed them. They assassinated one outside our door. In 2010 they killed security operatives, tried to take their guns; there were no heavy attacks. They had to hide. Their popularity waned, the people instead supported them out of fear.[68]

By the summer of 2010, there were indications in Borno state that Boko Haram was on the rise again. In June and July, drive-by shootings of government officials, fired at by assassins sitting on the back of motorbikes, started to become frequent. Rumours surfaced of some members training in remote border areas adjacent to Chad and Niger.[69] More importantly, movies of the then allegedly dead Boko Haram commander Abubakar Shekau started to appear, in which he claimed he was now the leader of Boko Haram.[70] It was in 2010 that Harakat al-Shabaab and al-Qaeda in Iraq each produced a propaganda video in support of Boko Haram, focusing on the extra-judicial killings of Boko Haram members.[71] Boko Haram also received direct support from al-Qaeda in the Islamic Maghreb, including the transfer of €200,000 in July, the contact between the two being confirmed in original documents from AQIM.[72] Further overtures were made. Shekau wrote a letter to al-Qaeda's central organisation (later discovered in Osama bin Laden's Abbottabad mansion in Pakistan). But the central Al-Qaeda may have been reluctant to make any commitment, as Boko Haram lacked the Afghanistan veterans that Shabaab and AQIM included among their members.[73] Claims that Boko Haram was a member of al-Qaeda at the time are erroneous.

On 7 September 2010 Boko Haram hit back at the Nigerian state, showing that it was resurgent by attacking a prison in Bauchi in the north-east of Nigeria.[74] The attack itself was well planned, and started at 6.40 pm, shortly after the breaking of the Ramadan fast, thus ensuring that the prison was weakly manned and that police reinforcements would take time to appear on the scene. The attack was a success, in the end freeing 127 alleged Boko Haram members and more than 600 other prisoners. Boko Haram now undertook an assassination campaign targeting local religious leaders, political leaders and government officials.[75] More worrying perhaps was that Boko Haram also chose to attack police stations, first in Borno, and actually managed to launch several heavy insurgency-like assaults as early as 24–27 December 2010.[76] The Nigerian army stepped up its presence, while Boko Haram spread its posters abroad in Maiduguri.[77] Yet locals felt that the police and the army failed to look after them, and many members of the petty business class paid money to Boko Haram out of fear.

Around 2011 my neighbour received a letter, saying we need to have money to do the work of God, they got money. My younger brother was working in UBA Bank, he was building a new house, he went to the house, they called him, and demanded the 100,000 naira at that time, threatening to kill him, they tell him to deliver the money in Kumshe area, in the west end. He got the money. As he went there he saw a little boy, and asked him, What are you doing here? The little boy asked him, Are you X?, and he confirmed. The little boy says, Give me the money, and then he disappeared. The second time he was asked, he went to Kaduna. My other brother was also working in a bank, his wife worked in the ministry of finance, they shot my brother in six places, and killed his pregnant wife. They ask him, Are you a lawyer? He said no, we businessmen are only using courts. They said they made a mistake, and that he should give them money, 2 million naira, but now you should go to the hospital. He left the area and went to Abuja. The problem happened in poor people's area, even now Jare is separate from Wangi. In the rich parts, they did not know … many did not know what happened in their own city.[78]

It was in this context that local self-help groups developed. Some of them were organised along Kanuri tribal structures, in part influenced by Boko Haram's targeting of traditional tribal leaders, who were seen as government informers. Indeed, in 2009 many of them had been crucial informants for the Nigerian police.

In early 2011, the Joint Task Force (JTF), an ad hoc formation of military, police and security units, was set up, bringing in 3,600 men and some fresh resources. Small contingents from Chad and Niger joined a Joint Multi-National Task Force (JMNTF), but they were too small to have any real impact.[79] Attacks continued and shoot-outs occurred in Maiduguri.[80] By Christmas 2011, Boko Haram was also attacking sectarian targets once again, outside Borno as well, for example the bombing in Madalla, near Abuja, said to be in revenge for sectarian attacks against Muslims in Jos during Eid ul-Fitr. Indeed, it is notable that warnings against further prosecution, and presentation of the attacks as a consequence of past actions against Boko Haram members in particular and the wider Muslim community in general, were common in the narratives used to justify attacks in 2010–12.[81] Simultaneously, the attacks widened in scope, civilians were killed, and banks were targeted, both in Maiduguri and Bauchi. Maiduguri residents were full of stories of fear, which emboldened local resistance over time.

Civilian casualties created internal discord within Boko Haram.[82] A new organisation, called Ansaru, or Jama'atu Ansarul Muslimina fi Biladis Sudan in full ('Vanguards for the Protection of Muslims in Black Africa'), announced itself publicly on 1 January 2012, criticising Boko Haram for indiscriminate killings.[83] The veteran Boko Haram leaders Adam Kambar and Khalid Barnawi, who both claimed to have been trained by al-Qaeda in the Islamic Maghreb, were said to be leading the new organisation. As with Shabaab, it was the most pan-jihadist elements who concerned themselves with the ethical issues of killings. The new organisation based its economy on kidnappings, even before it declared its existence.[84] Ansaru used kidnapping on a larger scale than Boko Haram ever did. But the debate about Muslim casualties did not seem to influence Boko Haram, which continued to stage attacks resulting in mass killings.

Boko Haram did enjoy some popular support, the exact scale of which is hard to estimate.[85] Their voices often mirrored Boko Haram's propaganda, which played on injustices against the organisation and against the wider Muslim world.[86] Indeed, the local population in Borno feared the security services as well as Boko Haram. Police corruption aided Boko Haram, both at the level of propaganda and operationally, for the police allegedly leaked information and ignored the logistical needs of their rural forces. Nor did the police respond quickly to the pleas of locals. People became angry with the police for not protecting them and many stopped supplying information to them. Moreover, those individuals who provided information were not protected, their identities were leaked, and Boko Haram in many instances assassinated such informers.[87] What also contributed to an atmosphere of animosity towards the Nigerian state was the fact that a southerner, Goodluck Jonathan, won the presidential election in April 2011, in a process that many northerners saw as manipulated. Moreover, the Nigerian police forces in Borno often came from outside the province, thus lacking local tribal connections.[88] The official propaganda warfare, which often claimed to have killed top Boko Haram leaders, whom Boko Haram later paraded to prove they were still living, also contributed to creating popular distrust in the Nigerian government.

To remedy the injustices suffered by its members seems to have been a theme in the Boko Haram press statements that surfaced about negotiations between the government and Boko Haram in the period.[89] Over time, the government began to pay more attention to the option of negotiations. These negotiations revealed the problems associated with clandestine organisations, including the difficulty of determining who the members were. On occasion, the central Boko Haram claimed that the individuals supposedly negotiating for them were not actual members.[90] In other instances, 'negotiations' in reality took the form of some local officials paying 'protection money' to Boko Haram.

Slowly but steadily the organisation changed. Its outliers – those parts outside Borno and its surroundings (including neighbouring regions of Nigeria, Niger and Cameroon) – became less active compared to its core. Perhaps, as the alleged press spokesman Abu Qaqa suggested after he was captured, the discrimination shown by Kanuri leaders towards Boko Haram leaders of other backgrounds could explain this change. Command lines were also easier to maintain in the Borno region.

On 1 January 2012, President Goodluck Jonathan declared a state of emergency in 15 of the northern provinces, including Borno, Yobe and Plateau states.[91] The types of violent activity carried out by Boko Haram remained attacks on checkpoints, ambushes of patrols, and terror attacks on government or religious targets. In 2013, this seemed to change. At least 55 people were killed and 105 inmates freed in coordinated attacks on army barracks, a prison and police post in Bama town on 7 May 2013.[92] In April 2013, a veritable battle was fought over the city of Baga; at least 187 Nigerians were confirmed dead, in what reminded observers more of a regular infantry assault than a terror attack.[93] In the countryside of the north-east, Boko Haram was able to control several smaller towns during 2013, and to dominate even more, as Nigeria's army increasingly withdrew into the capital of Maiduguri. Incidents also occurred where corruption in the form of Nigerian officers selling arms and supplies to the black market, even to Boko Haram, hampered efforts to defeat the organisation.[94] Beyond Nigeria, there were also increasing signs of a Boko Haram presence in Niger, which was used by the organisation as a rear area for logistics, and attacks in the border areas of Cameroon. The wider world neglected these developments, being more focused on Boko Haram's terror attacks than on its tactical gains. The complexity of some of the battles of 2013 also indicated that, while being fragmented over the north of Nigeria, Boko Haram was actually more hierarchically ordered in its core areas in Borno and adjacent provinces. The Nigerian government clearly saw the seriousness of the situation, and declared a full state of emergency in the Borno, Adamawa and Yobe states.[95] They also put new forces into Borno, creating the 7th Division, consisting of forces from Nigeria's other divisions as well as veterans of Nigeria's mission in Mali.[96] The army thus became increasingly involved in the conflict in the north-east. In many ways, from 2013 onwards Boko Haram was fighting an insurgency.

In Maiduguri the picture was slightly different. Vigilante groups had gained ground and became more active. Some vigilantes used traditional magic to fight Boko Haram, instilling a sense of self-confidence in their struggle, while home-made pistols were also common.[97] Vigilantes describe a much better relationship with the army in 2013, and by the end of the year Boko Haram's attacks inside the city had dwindled and Maiduguri became safer, although not completely so. In the surrounding countryside, however, an insurgency was raging: Boko Haram had established semi-territoriality.

Waging Guerrilla Warfare: Semi-peripheral Control (2013–14)

Although the military presence in Borno and surrounding states was strengthened, this did not mean increased security for the locals. For one thing, the Nigerian army failed to target their counter-measures on Boko Haram members, arresting and killing civilians as well. In April 2013, following a Boko Haram attack on a military patrol, security forces for example rounded up hundreds of men and boys and detained them, treating them inhumanely and killing some of them.[98]

The declaration of an emergency on 14 May 2013 and the creation of the 7th Division as well as the transfer of fresh troops in August created some momentum. The Nigerian army launched many offensives: in May–August, the army was active, and in September 2013 it launched counter-offensives in the north-east, attempting to clear the Bama–Banki road and the Kayfa forest area. In October, military operations continued with government offensives against Ajigi, Kafa, Izza and Galangi and two alleged Boko Haram bases. However, by November, the momentum had disappeared from the Nigerian offensive, and Boko Haram simply withdrew in front of the Nigerian forces, mostly to the Sambisa forest and the mountains around Gwoza, and also, according to Virginia Comolli, into Niger.[99]

The situation that developed thereafter was similar to that in Somalia at the time of writing. Because of the government withdrawal, and government failure to provide smaller villages with protection, Boko Haram dominated them, not with a permanent presence, but as a result of successive raids that scared locals into submission. In the Benisheik attack in September 2013, between 80 and 120 men attacked the town, managed to harass its citizens, and then withdrew. This was typical of the larger attacks of Boko Haram at the time. Boko Haram raided two cities in September 2013 (and were defeated during the raid against one of them), eleven in October and nine in November. During most of these attacks, the villages in question had little or no support from government forces or the police. At times there were vigilante forces present, but these militias were poorly equipped, often not even having guns, and were poorly trained. They were targeted by Boko Haram for assassinations, to the extent that Abubakar Shekau promoted a video threatening them in 2014.[100]

These attacks failed to attract international attention, yet they were very important for the organisation. Boko Haram plundered the local villages for livestock and supplies, which became a valuable source of income for the low-cost insurgency group. Moreover, Boko Haram used its semi-territorial control to forcibly recruit girls for logistical positions and as wives of Boko Haram fighters.[101] The organisation started to dominate larger parts of the Borno countryside in the latter part of 2013, and was able to recruit members by force and to tax the locals. Forced conscription took place in exposed cities like Bama, as the International Crisis Group recorded as early as June 2013.[102] It also became active in cross-border smuggling operations, being able to exercise control over smuggling routes to Niger.[103] Boko Haram was now a semi-territorial organisation. On the whole it did not put up fights against the Nigerian army, and withdrew in the face of determined attacks by the 7th Division and other units, but continued to harass the countryside and controlled villages for days when larger army units were not present. By doing this, it could return to the villages when they were defenceless, and punish them if they did not contribute to Boko Haram's funds.[104] Boko Haram thrived in these circumstances and grew increasingly able to challenge Nigerian army units.

In December, all hell broke loose for the 7th Division when Boko Haram, demonstrating a relatively unified command structure and good coordination in battle, launched an attack against an airbase inside Maiduguri with between 200 and 500 men. Later the same month, it carried out a similar attack against the Mohammed Kur barracks of an armoured battalion in Bama. Although both ended in Boko Haram's withdrawal, the fact that it was able to launch heavy attacks against important military units showed a large degree of sophistication as well as centralisation of tactical command.

Although Boko Haram had, and still has, offshoots acting independently, by 2014 these had been seriously weakened, and some, like the Ansaru, were barely active. Other factions inside Boko Haram were struck down by the government (they were in parts of northern Nigeria where Boko Haram was still operating as a clandestine network and thus vulnerable to police crackdowns), or their leaders in some cases were even killed off by the central leadership of Boko Haram. As the Borno operations indicate, Boko Haram seems to have become more unified around its representatives in the Borno province, which was much more efficient than the Boko Haram cells outside the north-east.[105]

The terror attacks conducted by Boko Haram continued and increased despite their having gained extensive territorial control. These included, during 2014, a greater use of female suicide bombers. The terror attacks usually targeted lower- and middle-class individuals, as well as schools, and won Boko Haram few tactical advantages.[106] The Borno countryside continued to suffer. In February 2014, eight raids were staged, in addition to two raids in neighbouring Adamawa. In March, a heavy attack followed on Maiduguri's Giwa barracks, probably to free prisoners. Six towns were also raided in Borno, and one inside Cameroon. Seven were raided in April, as well as a larger military camp.

In Bardari on 4 June, Boko Haram fighters ordered the villagers to gather by the mosque. Many of the poor local farmers complied. Boko Haram then opened fire, killing at least 45 people, and afterwards torched the village and stole the livestock. Village raids in the neighbouring Adamawa state intensified, where vigilantes were less organised. Boko Haram actually encountered less resistance when attacking the north-eastern villages.

In August, the city of Madagali, in Adamawa state, was completely captured. Much of the heavy equipment used by Boko Haram had been seized from the Nigerian army, including armoured cars. It seems that Boko Haram intended to stay in Madagali, making no moves to pull out. In September, this was followed by the capture of Michika, also in Adamawa, as well as Bara and Banki. Moreover, Boko Haram announced its intention to hold the territories it had captured and declared an Islamic state in the regions it had occupied.[107] Indeed, as early as April, some witnesses reported statements about the existence of an Islamic 'Boko Haram' state: 'You are no longer in Nigeria. You are now in an Islamic kingdom. Here, women's rights are respected, not like in Nigeria where women are made to work, farm, fetch water and firewood, and where you have all types of discrimination. This is the reason why we are rescuing Christian women like you. In our Islamic kingdom, there will be no discrimination because everyone will be Muslims.'[108] From April 2014, there were indications that Boko Haram had started to hold territories on a more permanent basis. Yet there were few signs of governance, and small villages remained vulnerable and were taxed to the brink of survival.

> From the Boko Haram of the islands of Chad, the mother of one of the commanders was to come to Maiduguri. They passed the woman and the letter, until she reached Maiduguri. Boko Haram coordinated her passage through their own checkpoints. The locals were taxed, the poor, because the wealthy would flee. They will come at random, after a certain period of time, you have to sell your stock, you have to sell the cows, gather one million for one community, they will come by themselves, preach and collect money. There was no government there, so it was easy. However, they would not stay, because the government would come in force.[109]

Yet, not all villagers joined because of fear of Boko Haram: 'In 2013–14, they [Boko Haram] were successful, locals could join, youth started admiring them, especially in the villages. You would get one motorcycle and one AK-47. They will return to the villages, and say, come and join.'[110]

The Rise and Fall of 'Boko Haram Land'?

In October 2014, the successes of Boko Haram continued. It captured Abadam in Borno, although Nigerian forces recaptured the town shortly afterwards. In Adamawa, the city of Mubi fell, and this time the Nigerian army failed to act. By October, a territorial Boko Haram entity was in existence, and by December, Boko Haram managed to launch heavy attacks inside Cameroon. Some analysts saw the expansion as a strategy to isolate the capital of Borno, Maiduguri, from the rest of Nigeria.[111] While this is uncertain, it seems that the attack on Baga in early 2015 was well coordinated, routing two Nigerian battalions as well as international contingents.[112] The attack may indeed have been the largest tactical victory ever by a sub-Saharan jihadist organisation, and indicated a tactical ability to centralise planning.

What effect did the aspiration for a more permanent status have on Boko Haram? One noticeable consequence was the professionalisation and centralisation of the Boko Haram media effort, which saw the establishment of a new media entity, al-Urwah al-Wuthqa. However, the process was not without flaws: not all videos were distributed through this channel and some that were contained spelling mistakes in the Arabic, including the name al-Urwah al-Wuthqa itself.

Boko Haram's victories and its establishment of a territorial caliphate also created weaknesses for the organisation. Firstly, the transformation from a guerrilla band into one that attempted to stand its ground against conventional forces made Boko Haram vulnerable when facing the means available to modern armies, such as artillery, armour and aircraft. This was also demonstrated by the American–Northern Alliance attacks against Taliban in Afghanistan in 2001. Secondly, a hostile organisation that establishes full territorial control becomes more visible as a threat, not only in the country in which it is present, but also in the whole region. In Boko Haram's case, its transformation into a territorial organisation drew wide attention. Its worldwide notoriety was confirmed by Boko Haram's kidnapping of 278 girls on 14–15 April 2014 in Chibok. (Ironically, more females had probably been kidnapped previously during the various town raids of Boko Haram, but they did not draw the world's attention.)

Boko Haram is often seen as an organisation that failed to exercise governance in the same way as Ansar Dine and Harakat al-Shabaab during their territorial phases. However, in its territorial episode it did implement Sharia, as their videos revealed, with the whipping of alleged alcohol drinkers and the stoning of adulterers as well as the punishment of ordinary crimes.[113] Yet Boko Haram never produced anything like the crime and punishment videos of the Shabaab, nor the law and order rhetoric of the Ansar Dine. What Boko Haram did produce was a defence of slavery, a position unique in Africa.[114] It seems that major elements of Boko Haram also cared less for the hearts and minds of the local population. Public knowledge of the atrocities of Boko Haram became widespread, making it harder to maintain a rhetoric focused on 'hearts and minds'. Boko Haram also declared war on cities and towns, arguing that these had entered into conflict with it – not too dissimilar to Shabaab's declaration of war on clans. They were still able to recruit villagers by force.

> I was force-recruited by Boko Haram in 2015. Our community is a village, there was no road, so to the village they came on motorobike, they were four. I look well nourished, so they said that I was not one of the villagers, but the villagers testified that 'he came from the village'. I explained that I was a kind of stranger since I lived in the city. They then cut out the magical amulet from the arm, they took that off my body, they took me alone, they came back later to pick up my brothers, they said I was a unbeliever, because I worked as a private guard in the Niger delta, because I was paid by unbelievers. The brothers were taken because my parents were bringing them to the city. I was lucky. Before they came I was told, 'Whatever you are told to do you should do.' I said to them, 'I cannot handle a gun, but if it is business then I can.' I was then transported to Elagarne in Dambao, formerly a settlement for people, but they were forced to flee, so [Boko Haram] had taken over the village. There were 1,000 men in the village, and I was questioned, 'Do you want to become an unbeliever by working, why are you here, have you accepted that if you are with us, you will not run into the bush.' They interrogated me over and over again. I was chained for two weeks on my legs, I still have the scar.[115]

The increased media prominence of Boko Haram and the prospect of presidential elections in 2015 meant that the Nigerian leadership, especially President Goodluck Jonathan, came under pressure to do something about the organisation. In the end the Nigerians allowed larger forces from its neighbouring countries, Chad, Cameroon and Niger, to participate in an offensive against Boko Haram. As described earlier, Boko Haram had expanded into Cameroon, and used its networks in Niger for logistical purposes. While Boko Haram had been active in Chad from at least 2014, expansion into Cameroon brought it close to the capital of Chad, N'Djamena.[116] This in turn led to an increased willingness on the part of the Chadians to intervene both in Nigeria and in Cameroon. The will to intervene was probably strengthened by the victory of Boko Haram in Baga on the shores of Lake Chad on 3 January, a town that had been systematically isolated over time by the organisation.[117]

Nigeria, together with small components from other regional forces, was unable to hold the city.

On 29 January 2015, the African Union approved a multinational force to assist Nigeria in the fight against Boko Haram. This was rather a formal authorisation, for Cameroon, Chad and Niger, for offensives that had already started. In the end, 8,700 multinational troops were involved. Nigeria also deployed other forces besides the 7th Division. Yet the high point of 'Boko Haram Land' had not yet been reached. On 1 February 2015, while controlling an area roughly the size of Belgium, Boko Haram launched its second major assault upon the Borno capital of Maiduguri. The attack failed, and forces from Chad, Niger, Cameroon and Nigeria slowly went on the offensive. On 21 February Baga was retaken. Boko Haram's attempt to conduct offensives across Lake Chad, in Niger and Chad, was contained.

Interestingly, the Baga battles led to the release of an interview with the up-and-coming Boko Haram commander and son of Mohammed Yusuf, Abu Musab Habeeb bin Muhammad bin Yusuf al-Barnawi, in which he attempted to justify the Baga attacks and to deny the killing of civilians. He maintained that Boko Haram saved individuals who were 'innocent', giving examples of villages that were spared.[118] The developments also led to a regionalisation of the war, with the first major suicide attack in Chad's capital, N'Djamena, taking place in June 2015. This also led to a wider targeting of Cameroonian and Chadian officials in Boko Haram propaganda.[119] Yet, as mentioned earlier, it is important to stress that the regionalisation had been ongoing for years in Niger and Cameroon. Niger to a certain extent had functioned as a safe haven for Boko Haram, with networks in Diffa being established as early as 2005, while recruitment in Cameroon had been in existence from 2012. In both places, ethnic networks were essential for creating local contacts.[120]

The battle-hardened Chadian troops as well as the reinforced Nigerian forces made a difference, and slowly Boko Haram lost its grip on its territories. At the same time, the Nigerian presidential election installed a northerner, Muhammadu Buhari, as president, creating the possibility that more resources might be allocated to solving Nigeria's northern issues. Yet, in the summer of 2015, Boko Haram still controlled several villages.[121]

In many ways some of the events of the transitional phase mirrored events in Somalia, where the Shabaab, facing regional intervention, pledged support to an external global jihadist organisation. In the case of Boko Haram, it was not al-Qaeda. Instead, it issued a *bayt*, a declaration of allegiance to the Islamic State of Iraq and the Levant (ISIL), or simply Islamic State (IS).[122] The latter had caught the attention of the global audience after expanding its territorial holdings drastically in 2013–14. Despite al-Qaeda's hostility to the move, it had declared a worldwide caliphate.[123] Boko Haram's alignment was accepted by the Islamic State one week later.[124] The declaration had an influence on Boko Haram's propaganda effort, for the first videos of its execution of prisoners, a common theme in IS propaganda, started to appear.[125] Moreover, the videos were now issued under the name of Wilayat West Africa, from June 2015. Another advantage of the *bayt* was to prepare a common ideological ground so as to forge an alliance with the remains of the Ansaru.[126] Ironically, Boko Haram now became referred to as the Islamic State's West Africa Province (ISWAP), although it was already on the verge of losing its territories.

Back to Semi-territoriality and the Cost of Transition

The organisation's phase of territorial control was simply too short for it to take advantage of some of the benefits of such control, such as the systematic ability to recruit by providing stable incomes, and a more permanent tax basis. Yet Boko Haram faced some of the inevitable losses that accompany loss of territory, such as prestige and probably also a large number of fighters when they attempted to hold on to territory. In the case of Shabaab and MUJAO, the strains involved led to leadership rivalries. Such rivalries did indeed take place in Boko Haram as well, partly fuelled by the old cleavage between Ansaru and Shekau. This had arisen not only from Shekau's concerns with the losses of Muslims and his willingness to declare certain Muslims non-believers, but also from the Islamic State's attempt to pass over Shekau and declare Mohammed Yusuf's son al-Barnawi as the rightful leader of Boko Haram.[127] On 3 August 2016, the Islamic State reported in its newspaper *al-Naba* that Abu Musab al-Barnawi was the new leader of their West African branch, and he promised a stronger focus on preventing Muslim losses.[128] The edition prompted a response from Shekau, who still maintained allegiance towards the Islamic State but denied that Barnawi had become the governor.[129] The debate hardened in August 2016.[130] The split was felt locally, and a former fighter who joined the Barnawi faction claimed that this was the first time he heard about the Islamic State, as allegiance was publicly declared in a sermon in his camp, long after Boko Haram had originally declared its loyalty.[131]

The heavy multinational military presence made the semi-territorial phase of Boko Haram slightly different from that before. After some negotiations, the renamed Boko Haram developed into two different clusters, one around Shekau in the south-east of Borno, and one under Barnawi, including former Ansaru members in the north. Barnawi remained in contact with the Islamic State, and had access to their propaganda outlets; he also gained the support of Mamman Nur. Local sources suggested that over time a ceasefire developed between the two factions. However, there were some clashes. In December 2017 several small hamlets were allegedly lost to the Barnawi faction by the Shekau faction.[132] Al-Barnawi's fighters also took over Umdarari, Jubul, Shuwari, Fulatar and Shunkori. His group was relatively well organised and his camps had frequent indoctrination lessons.

> They would gather people for what they called a 'reminder' after every two, three days, from 30 minutes to one hour; they will also refer to the hadiths, bukhari. They would gather you in the mosque or where you were, they formed something like a cluster, each cluster had a leader, but mostly led by people higher up. The fighters found themselves so indoctrinated. Very often they would talk about sin and paradise, but not of international jihad.[133]

A former fighter described a camp under the Barnawi faction as well organised, with clear divisions of labour, such as mechanics, firewood gatherers, vulcanisers for tyres, and 'businessmen' who were supposed to trade and secure supplies for the Boko Haram units. The units themselves were organised from a *kayid* with 1,000 men or more, to a *manzil* consisting of 300 to 500 men, and a *naqib* of 150 to 250. The smallest units were led by an emir and could be between 6 and 100 men. Recruits had about two weeks of training and could actually choose if they would fight or carry out another role such as 'businessman'.

It seemed that Barnawi once again wanted to take on the main forces of the Nigerian army, for example by launching a raid against the Kanamma barracks in Yobe state in January 2018. He also faced, at the time of writing, the heaviest counter-offensives yet seen. For their part, Shekau's forces maintained semi-territorial control over the Sambisa forest and parts of the Mandara mountains on the border with Cameroon. Both factions still managed to 'tax' local villages.[134] It seems as if the Barnawi faction still manages to exact levies on cattle transported through their territories, but is more restrained in its attacks on locals, while the Shekau faction still engages in armed action.

The authorities made attempts to fortify some villages to create safe zones for locals, yet the locals continued to suffer, and they were not adequately protected, enabling both groups to tax them. This may be changing. This time round, semi-territoriality may be less profitable, as the large stream of refugees have deprived Borno of many of its rural inhabitants, and plundering and extracting protection money will become harder. As long as the Nigerian government remains unable to provide rural-centred security measures to protect the local population, Boko Haram is in a good position to expand again. Simultaneously, police corruption and lack of targeted arrests may assist Boko Haram's future efforts to wage guerrilla war in Borno.

Analytically, Boko Haram's history remains surprisingly familiar in an African context. It started out as rebellion at a mosque, continued as a group that was accepted by the state, was transformed into a clandestine network, and then into semi-territoriality, before it gained territorial control. After having enjoyed territorial control, it lost it and was transformed once again. As with the other groups analysed in this book, the transformation undergone by Boko Haram was often equated by observers with annihilation, yet in fact the organisation has survived.

7

THE ALLIED DEMOCRATIC FORCES
OPPORTUNISTS IN DISGUISE?

A study of the Allied Democratic Forces (ADF) is the study of an organisation operating on the periphery of two states, the Congo and Uganda, taking advantage of their lack of ability to successfully control and secure these areas over time. For large periods of its history, ADF could control territories on a semi-permanent basis, withdrawing when the Ugandan army, United Nations or Congolese forces launched offensives, but returning afterwards, to collect taxes and at times to forcibly recruit locals. It situated itself in the local economy, drawing upon the timber sector and the local agricultural economy, and redistributing income to the local elite, and at times also to ethnic networks. Some commentators have seen this as marking its difference from other Islamist-inspired organisations.[1] Such traits bear resemblance to AQIM, the Shabaab and Boko Haram in their semi-territorial phases. For this reason, ADF was not so different from other African jihadist bodies that have become part of a war-economy system when operating in a semi-territorial or territorial mode. The organisation had to interact with the wider population, sometimes using fear, sometimes patronage and ethnic linkages, and at other times manipulating ethnic differences. For ADF and other organisations in a similar situation, semi-territoriality offers opportunities when it comes to harnessing income from locals. As long as the extraction of natural resources does not require a more permanent infrastructure, revenue can be secured again when state forces have withdrawn from the area after their campaigns.

The ADF is perhaps the most ideologically complex organisation studied in this book, being a union of several distinct groups, some of which have weak jihadist credentials. ADF has at times included non-Muslim groups, and their videos are by far the least religiously inspired of the movements dealt with in this book. It is not strange that the organisation, like Boko Haram, has stimulated a debate about the importance of international linkages as against pragmatism. Some researchers like Andrew McGregor have highlighted the international connections, while others, such as Lindsay Scorgie-Porter, Kristof Titeca and Koen Vlassenroot, and Gérard Prunier, have downplayed them, the first three highlighting economic opportunism instead.[2] This chapter positions itself closer to this view for most of the period, but traces ADF's jihadist credentials further back in time, arguing that it was stronger for parts of the organisation in the past and that the Islamic element grew in importance from 2007 onwards, as older non-Muslim leaders left the group. ADF has in many ways more in common with what I refer to in chapter 2 as the first-generation modern jihadist organisations in Africa: it contains a mix of different ideological elements and was influenced by Sudan in its early Bashir–Turabi phase: by its geopolitical strategies, and by Hassan Turabi's quest to unify various Islamist organisations across Africa. The confusion partly stems from the fact that the organisation had two components, one of which – the National Army for the Liberation of Uganda (NALU) – lacked any trace of Islamist ideology, being rather an ethno-nationalist organisation fighting for greater power for the Bakonjo-Baamba people.

The National Army for the Liberation of Uganda (NALU)

To some extent, the new Ugandan state, created in 1962, was superimposed on older existing governance structures, including the better-known kingdom of Buganda, as well as the kingdoms of Bunyoro, Busoga and Toro. The Bakonjo-Baamba people of Rwenzori had been forced to incorporate themselves into the kingdom of Toro by the British colonial power in order to support the latter, a British ally. Separate Bakonjo–Baamba governance structures remained in existence. After protesting against the Toro domination of the kingdom, the Bakonjo–Baamba attempted to secede, but lacked the resources to stand up to the new Ugandan state. From this emerged an armed protest movement, the Rwenzururu movement.[3] A second opportunity to renew the rebellion came on the eve of the Amin regime (1971–9), when the Ugandan army collapsed in the face of Tanzanian offensives and abandoned many small arms that could be used by potential insurgents. A new insurgency spread. As with the later ADF, the insurgents drew advantages from both the physical location of the Rwenzori Mountains and the fact that the Bakonjo–Baamba existed on both sides of the border with Congo (Zaire), in an area that was peripheral to both states. This meant that the permanent presence of both Ugandan and Zairean forces was limited, and the rebels could operate relatively freely. The Rwenzururu movement was in many ways ethnically defined, and had nothing to do with jihadism as such; in fact, it mainly recruited from animists and Christians. However, partly by acknowledging their grievances, and partly through granting amnesties, the various Ugandan governments managed to fragment the resistance, the largest amnesty taking place in 1982, when most of the leaders of the Rwenzururu movement opted out.[4] Popular support also dwindled. However, remaining hardliners formed NALU in 1988, with the support of Mobutu in Zaire and Daniel arap Moi in Kenya, both regimes seeing this as a chance to undermine a rival regime in Uganda.[5]

NALU only split from the Rwenzururu movement in 1991.[6] It did not perform well on the battlefield, losing several engagements, and its leader, Amon Bazira, was killed, probably by Ugandan intelligence, in Nairobi, Kenya, in 1982. It did, however, gain the attention of Omar al-Bashir in Sudan, who saw it as an ally in Sudan's struggle for regional hegemony, and a weapon to be used against Museveni's Uganda.[7] Bashir's and Hassan Turabi's strategies for Africa, which involved wooing African jihadist organisations, made it natural for them to search for allies for NALU from the Islamists of Uganda. At the same time, realpolitik imperatives were also important for Sudan: it sought to find the means to destabilise Uganda, which was then backed by the United States, and which supported the insurgency movements inside Sudan.[8]

The Second Component: The Islamic Salafi Foundation

During the regime of Idi Amin, the Ugandan state employed Islam as a kind of political tool, and played actively on the Israeli–Palestine conflict. Islam also functioned as an identity marker for Amin's own ethnic group and for his Nubian allies. The fall of Amin in 1979 led to the persecution of Muslims, especially in the south-west of the country, forcing them to organise themselves.[9] The Tabliqi movement became a vehicle for such efforts. This movement, which originated in modern-day Pakistan in the 1920s, practised forms of social segregation, with a focus on Islamic purity. Although initially apolitical, it has been used for political purposes, for example in Pakistan. In Uganda, it appeared just after the fall of the Amin regime.[10] It became activated as a political force through struggles with the Museveni regime over control of the Muslim faith and of mosques in Uganda. Following the example of many other East African countries, the government attempted to control its Muslim communities through the Ugandan Muslim Supreme Council (UMSC). At the time Idi Amin's regime, with its use of Islam to create legitimacy, was still fresh in people's memory, and such strategies were still seen as a threat by the Museveni government. This was how the Ugandan state came to be at odds with the Tabliqi. In 1989 a pro-government leader had been elected to the UMSC, leading to protests from Tabliqi leaders, including Sheikh Mohammed Kamoga, who was one of the coordinators of the resistance against government control. Many Tabliqi sheikhs attacked the government in their sermons.[11] In 1991 the conflict escalated when the Tabliqi and UMSC came to blows. Sheikh Kamoga had launched a verbal attack on the UMSC from the Nakasero mosque in the centre of Kampala, accusing it of abusing power and not sticking to previous agreements. The Tabliqis physically attacked the UMSC on several occasions.[12] In March the vice-leader of the Tabliqi youth at Nakasero mosque, Jamil Mukulu, a former Christian priest who had converted, and who had been trained in Arabic in Saudi Arabia, launched a strong and violent assault on the UMSC's headquarters. This time Tabliqi activists – not only from Kampala – came out in force, some sources say 400 strong, wielding clubs.[13] The Ugandan police had surveilled the Tabliqi for a time and responded with force, aided by the military police. Sheikh Kamoga allegedly attempted to stop the attack, but the UMSC compound fell to Mukulu for several hours, and four police officers died in the course of the conflict.

In a way reminiscent of the events that led to the ban on Boko Haram in 2009, the government reacted heavily, imprisoning many of the Tabliqi leaders, and taking decisive action against the Tabliqi youth and the Nakasero mosque leadership.[14] Mukulu and many others were imprisoned in the Luzira prison, where he met several future radicals, including Joseph Lusse and Tumushabe 'Benz', who later became a defector often featured in the Ugandan press. After Mukulu's release, there was a clear break with other Tabliqi organisations, and a separate organisation, the Salafi Foundation of Uganda, was established over time. Some defectors also claimed that a secret militant organisation, the Uganda Muslim Freedom Fighters (UMFF), was formed within the prison.[15] In this phase, while still legal, a clandestine organisation was set up to secure funds, and the Malkaz mosque in Katwe, a Kampala suburb, became the centre of its activities.[16] Increasingly, a military apparatus was also established, with a training ground in Buseruka in Hoima district at Kayera Gorge.[17] These developments were not acceptable to the Ugandan state, which launched a military offensive against the organisation on 25 February 1995, while simultaneously the police made arrests of suspected sympathisers. The remains of the UMFF had to withdraw. Mukulu and forty of his fighters escaped into Bunia, in present-day Congo, where Sudanese intelligence had established a presence. Sudan refitted the organisation, seeing it as an ally against Museveni's Uganda, and also transported members into Sudan, where they received training from Osama bin Laden and his al-Qaeda.[18]

Yet the pragmatism of Sudanese foreign policy was to show itself in the efforts Sudan made to fuse the UMFF with NALU, a non-Muslim organisation. The Sudanese also attempted to amalgamate these two with other smaller groups. While the attempt was successful, the NALU component dominated at the start, as they knew the area in which the new organisation was to operate, though over time the UMFF component would come to dominate.

The Henchmen of Mobutu: The Accepted Presence of Allied Democratic Forces

Bunia became the first base of the new organisation, followed by a second camp at Buhira. According to a defector, the new organisation elected Abdallah Yusuf Kabanda as a leader. His deputies were Jamil Mukulu and Hosea, a Mukonjo.[19]

At the start, the ADF led a perfectly open existence, as an accepted organisation supported with arms and supplies by the supposedly sovereign government of Zaire. It also received support from Sudan. The regime of Mobutu Sese Seko actively employed the young organisation for security purposes and it was allowed to sit on local security committees and recruit openly. According to an eyewitness at the time:

> When the ADF came in 1995, they were recruiting people in my village, they took my young brother. He was in fifth [grade], we did not go to study that day. I was coming from the field with my bicycle. I was told that my young brother was recruited by NALU. I stopped them, they listened in that period. One commander spoke Swahili. I told them he was under-age, he needed to study, they did accept. But my young brother did not want to quit. We saw them like special forces commandos, our soldiers used to call them 'uncle'. They were partners. They used to tell us, 'Our mission is to free Uganda, once we freed them you are going to get cars, benefits.' The youths took it as an opportunity. Once you were soldiers you were like kings. They were also recruiting Muslims, and integrated into local commerce.[20]

The commander, Abdallah Yusuf Kabanda, was highly visible at a local level, and the group was admired by many: 'They were not giving speeches, but they were to open a recruitment office in Beni at the time. They used money, 100 to 200 dollars, to attract fighters. They were just partners for the government, we did not care about them, they were a part of the government, the *garde civile*.'[21]

ADF was able to launch raids against Ugandan border posts and even conduct terror attacks inside Uganda. Several of these were quite successful.[22] Its Islamist credentials may have contributed to the support it received, according to the International Criminal Court, from the United Arab Emirates and Iran, the latter through local

Islamic charities. This in turn prompted Ugandan counter-moves, both against the ADF and against its sponsors. Uganda supported Laurent Kabila's forces against the Mobutu regime.

Into the Borderlands: A Semi-territorial Presence

Slowly but steadily the Mobutu regime eroded, and was eventually replaced by the new Kabila government. Ugandan forces also intervened in Zaire, causing the ADF to abandon its bases there.[23] But this did not lead to the ADF's destruction. Instead, it changed into a semi-territorial organisation operating close to the Rwenzori borderlands, withdrawing from its bases when a superior army faced it, and returning when these campaigns ebbed. The Rwenzori Mountains were ideal for such operations, as Lindsay Scorgie-Porter remarks: 'The nature of the Rwenzori space was a fundamentally transnational one, with the bulk of economic activity oriented outward and across the border, as opposed to inward toward the capital(s). The result of these dynamics was that the ADF was presented with a relatively welcoming and accessible atmosphere for pursuing various income-generating endeavours.'[24]

The borderlands, consisting of rugged terrain, were on the peripheries of the neighbouring countries and were weakly controlled. Although peripheral, several trade routes passed through them and could be taxed as long as the forces of the various governments, or later the United Nations forces, were absent, which was quite often. Moreover, the lack of a permanent presence by these forces meant that pressure and blackmail could be applied to local traders, who would be targeted as soon as the United Nations, the Ugandans or Congolese withdrew. The central bases of the ADF had to be evacuated during the campaigns of these forces, but could be re-established as soon as they ended. Moreover, the ADF could establish clandestine networks in adjacent areas as well, for they were often weakly controlled and served by corrupt police, and illegal border trade networks extended into them.[25] Various alliances within Congo also drove a number of Congolese groups, even the odd Hutu soldier who had fled from Rwanda, into the organisation.[26] Given the chaos in Congo, the Congolese army was not able to launch effective operations against the ADF. This enabled the ADF to force children and others into their ranks with relative ease, often by directly targeting schools and educational institutions.[27]

The influence of the ADF varied according to when campaigns were launched against it and which army it faced. At first, in the dying years of the Mobutu regime, it was highly active, using the border areas as staging posts for attacks into Uganda. The Ugandan authorities attempted to work actively against those supporting the ADF, including the Mobutu regime.

Museveni specifically raised the matter of the fierce attack on Mpondwe in November 1996 in the Ugandan parliament, arguing for the creation of a buffer zone.[28] The motivation for such a *cordon sanitaire* was not only provided by the ADF's activities, but also by those of other Zairean-supported organisations, such as the Lord's Resistance Army and the West Nile Bank Front, which operated in the region. The Ugandans at this stage had allies among the Rwandan leaders, who also faced hostile organisations on the Congolese side of their border. Another ally, hostile to Mobutu, was the Alliance of Democratic Forces for the Liberation of Congo-Zaire (ADFL), which, with Rwandan and Ugandan support, took control over large areas. By 1997, the old Mobutu regime was history. Yet the battlefield victories of Uganda and its allies did not defeat the ADF. The latter went on the defensive but managed to operate skilfully from the more remote Rwenzori area. The irony of the Ugandan operation was that, like Kenya's Somali intervention, it failed to conquer, or even to control, the enemy against which it had started its war.

By 1997, Uganda had a new ally in Zaire (now Congo), Laurent Désiré Kabila, who had ousted Mobutu. However, Kabila's regime lacked any capacity to pacify the border zone. His new Congolese army was chaotic, lacking proper command structures and mobility, and having diverging loyalties to a variety of ethnic and political groups. The Forces Armées Congolaises (FAC) were a heterogeneous group of soldiers, including former Mobutu loyalists, Tutsis (Banyamulenge), so-called Kadogos recruited during the 1996–7 campaign, and the Katanga Gendarmes, originally loyal to Angola and with little loyalty towards Kabila.[29] The resulting confusion, combined perhaps with the economic prospects that a campaign offered to Ugandan officers, led to a second intervention by Uganda into Congo with a force of around 8,000 men. ADF was put under pressure but refrained from engaging in combat, using the local geography to hide its forces. It also relied on the tendency of all warring parties to concentrate their forces in garrisons when not campaigning, thus enabling the ADF to operate in the vacuum created by this strategy.

The ADF increasingly concentrated itself in the areas between the Rwenzori Mountains and the Rwenzori forest, a terrain highly suitable for guerrilla operations, with few roads, high mountains and dense forests. They attempted to persuade local ethnic groups, always on the periphery of the state, to support them, such as the Bakonjo people, by using a combination of terror and propaganda to sway the locals, who received little protection from the Congo government. The ADF suffered losses and defection, and when part of the organisation under Hosea was cut off, he had to be replaced as commander by Fenahasi Kisokeranio. There is no doubt that it was an organisation under strain in this period, but it also saw successes, for example the downing of a Ugandan plane in 1999. The ADF tended to operate in smaller groups under pressure, as when it again faced a systematic campaign by the Ugandan army under Brigadier James Kazini, which also included local vigilantes.[30] The ADF was still perfectly able to launch terror attacks inside Uganda, such as in Kabarole, Kasese, Bundibugyo and the capital city of Kampala, and it also destabilised several Ugandan districts.[31] These operations included the infamous 1998 attack on Kichwamba Technical College, where students were burned alive. In this period the Islamic profile of the ADF was weak. It was often seen as consisting of 'rebels without a cause', and Islamic rhetoric was scarce in its publications.

By 1999, Uganda had intensified its efforts against the ADF and pushed them towards the north-east of the Congolese North Kivu province.[32] Operation Mountain Sweep was largely successful. The general secretary of the ADF, Ali Bwambale Mulima, was captured, and the movement was reduced to 200 or 300 men but it managed to survive in the Rwenzori Mountains.[33] The government also used a general amnesty to attract ADF fighters away from the organisation. However, Ugandan forces withdrew in 2003, and Congolese forces were not able to keep up the pressure.[34] In fact, the Congolese tended to garrison its forces in urban areas like Goma, Walikale, Butembo and Beni outside the 'campaign seasons', leaving ample space for the ADF to build up its forces and construct bases.[35]

A Local Anchorage

Outside support for ADF decreased, and over time the group became entrenched in Congo, where it recruited from Congolese ethnic groups, especially the Congolese Nande, who were ethnically close to the former NALU fighters. The 2005 Comprehensive Peace Agreement between Khartoum and the Sudanese People's Liberation Army ended Sudan's interest in playing geopolitical games in Congo, and Sudan's support for the ADF came to a halt in 2006.[36] The dwindling of external support led to a greater emphasis on local sources of income. Cross-border income-generating mechanisms remained important; moreover, illegal arms networks followed these channels, and enabled the ADF to obtain new arms.[37]

With its relatively stable local presence, the ADF became successful in recruiting locals for its army, who helped the ADF to become better acquainted with the terrain.[38] Such recruitment was enhanced by the old NALU's connections to the related Bakonjo people and by the intermarriage of ADF fighters with the local community. The ADF's stable presence also attracted recruits who were motivated to join for the pay. In addition, the ADF allegedly paid the tribal elites in the area they controlled. Some writers like Lindsay Scorgie-Porter see this as a form of social embeddedness, with the ADF becoming part of local society.[39] However, such a view underestimates the issues of semi-permanent territorial control. With its strong presence in the area, the ADF was, for the locals, still a force to be reckoned with. If one wanted to stay alive and prosper, one had to have a good relationship with them. The consequences could be severe if one did not adhere to the ADF's rules.[40] The combination of stable income possibilities, the threat of violence and the knowledge that the ADF usually returned after government campaigns ended must have been a powerful inducement for loyalty. It has to be said that the human rights record of the forces facing the ADF in the early 2000s was also abysmal: at best they left the local population to themselves, at worst they targeted the locals directly. It should also be noted that when there was a real chance that the ADF might lose semi-territorial control, as in 2005, it used harsh reprisals against civilians. The ADF also actively exploited its connections with local Muslims in the Eringeti–Beni axis in North Kivu, and was involved in the Eringeti mosque.[41]

Thanks to the failure of Ugandan and Congolese forces to provide adequate security in the countryside, the ADF could live off the land. It was able to tax locals on a semi-permanent basis, withdrawing in the face of enemy forces, but returning to harass local villagers when its enemies abandoned the villages to their own fate. The organisation was also able to take advantage of local timber, coffee and marijuana production, and taxed local businessmen who wanted protection in areas close to ADF guerrillas. These activities were so profitable that the ADF was able to tax Congolese officers who wanted to do business and at the same time pay off Congolese officials to look in another direction.[42] Lastly, but perhaps most importantly, the ADF managed to grow its own vegetables and add a substantial amount of self-grown food to its supplies.

Bringing Religion Back In?

Although it took large losses, its entrenchment in the Rwenzori Mountains enabled ADF to survive. It was able to take advantage of local resources, employ clandestine trade networks, and tax locals, and it seemed to have the potential to expand. Most observers estimated that its losses had weakened the organisation drastically, such that it entered into negotiations with the Ugandan government in 2001.[43] What commentators often failed to see was precisely the potential its semi-territorial status gave it, for it was for most of the time not militarily contested in its home area, save during intensive campaigns, which, when they ended, usually led to the withdrawal of its enemies from the local villages and trade routes that supplied it with income and recruits. This situation was to continue, although the organisation was to gain new enemies in the form of the United Nations Organisation Stabilisation Mission in the Democratic Republic of the Congo (MONUSCO) and the Congolese government forces, which for the first time were employed en masse against the ADF.

The NALU component of the ADF had slowly but steadily weakened.[44] NALU soldiers and officers often became sedentary and left the organisation. Some NALU soldiers tried to resettle in western Uganda, while a group led by Commander Kagwa split off and migrated to the Nyankunde, Tchomia and Marabo regions of Congo's Ituri province.[45] Seven top leaders of the old NALU surrendered to the UN Disarmament, Demobilization, Repatriation, Resettlement and Reintegration Program (DDRRR), leaving the NALU component in even greater disarray. Then in 2008 Uganda chose to acknowledge the kingdom of Rwenzururu, undermining the loyalty of NALU members even further.[46] The ADF's old Islamist component, admittedly with the addition of locals from Congo, became more dominant. Indeed, the increasing separation between NALU and ADF was seen by many as a cleavage between Muslims and non-Muslims. Islamist themes had always been present in Mukulu's speeches, who argued for attacks against Christians, but their importance now increased and Islamist rhetoric became amplified. This is shown by the letter the ADF produced to warn the UN and Congolese forces after their 2012 campaign:

> Earth solely belongs to Allahu Subhanau Waathala, not to MONUSCO or any other creature. Read the holy Quran, chapter 7, verse 128: said prophet Moses to the people. Pray from help from Allahu and wait in patience and constancy. For the word is Allah's to give heritage to such of his servants as he pleases. And the end is best for the righteous. So leave us alone in peace to worship our creator the true lord of the universe. If you persist then prepare for his anger wherever you be.[47]

The language here is different from that of all the other groups studied in this book, more defensive and with fewer sophisticated quotes from the Quran. It nevertheless says something about the image that the organisation wanted to project, as a group defending Muslim rights.

By 2001, the United States found evidence that ADF was using Islamist rhetoric in trying to obtain funds from the Middle East.[48] There was also other relatively clear evidence of contacts between the jihadist networks of the Swahili coast and ADF. Jamil Mukulu's son Hassan Mukulu was arrested in August 2011, but had his bail paid by members of the Muslim Youth Centre in Nairobi, which later became al-Hijra.[49] Furthermore, ADF was accused by Kenya of having Shabaab ties, and several of those behind the Shabaab attack in Kampala in 2010 were also alleged to be ADF members, although the court case is not finished at the time of writing. Beyond these allegations, and the clear evidence from the Hassan Mukulu case, the contacts do seem limited.

When a United Nations group of experts interviewed defectors, they found no traces of foreign links, but they did observe a tendency to focus on Muslims in the recruitment process, using relatives or Muslim sheikhs, although others were recruited through deception.[50] The inner circle of the ADF also used religion as an ideological glue, for example by praying together. ADF had notable religious leaders such as Seka Katende, the leader of the important Obedi mosque, located in what was then the ADF's main camp of Medina, and Sheikh Musa, who was in charge of Islamic education in the organisation.[51] It is significant that Shabaab and Hijra failed to mention Jamil Mukulu's arrest in 2014 when they sprang to the defence of other radical sheikhs in East Africa.

In the meantime, ADF faced the ebb and flow of enemy offensives. The 2005 Congolese–UN offensive ended the same way as previous Ugandan attempts had: ADF took heavy losses, but managed to retreat into the mountains, and the old jihadist Jamil Mukulu finally became the organisation's leader. ADF and the Congolese government initiated negotiations, but the Congolese government ended them, claiming that the ADF was only playing for time. These patterns were to repeat themselves when the Congo launched Operation Rwenzori in 2010. Although the Congolese army had help from Uganda, and was guilty of large-scale human rights abuses in the process (as was the ADF), the campaign was thwarted by an ADF that was more successful than ever in facing the army of a state. The ADF even went on the offensive. On 1 July 2011, ADF attacked Congolese forces at Chuchubo and Makembi and on 29 July at Bilimani. Although not all ADF attacks were successful, its opponents had clearly underestimated it. Another Congolese–UN operation, Rapid Strike, also failed to destroy the organisation, although the ADF was forced to change some of its base areas.

As a result, Medina camp, also known as the Madinat Tawheed Muwaheedina, had to be relocated. The name Medina was actually used for several bases, usually the one where Jamil Mukulu lived. Before 2010, this was the base at Chuchubo, but from 2011 until April 2014 it became the former Makayoba base (in the village of Nadui). In this area, ADF came close to wielding a form of territoriality. The base contained a hospital, numerous mosques, an orphanage and the Salaf Victory Primary School.[52] In addition to this, there were at least 70 'Bazana', or slaves, kept in the camp – individuals captured by the ADF on the periphery of the areas under their control. A two-level court system was established, with the lower court under the headship of Seka Baluku.[53] An elaborate network of posts was constructed to protect this version of the Medina base. All in all, the ADF was at the time estimated to consist of 400 to 800 men, a mix of Ugandans and Congolese, with Ugandans still dominating the top positions.

In 2014, another operation, this time without United Nations participation, Sukola I, was launched by the Congolese army. It was a little more successful than several of the previous ones, driving Jamil Mukulu into exile in Tanzania.[54] For a while the group fragmented, with 200 men leaving with Seka Baluku eastwards, and setting up a new base in the village of Kainama in early 2015. According to defectors, they received reinforcements from a defector from the Congolese forces who had established his own militia.[55] Other parts of the group fragmented, often following ethnic divisions, but over time drifted back towards Baluku, while yet others used local ethnic networks to find allies.[56] Baluku's rise to power may have created conflict between him and some of Mukulu's sons. Nevertheless, Mukulu was soon to become irrelevant. In March 2015, he was arrested in Tanzania and subsequently handed over to Uganda.[57] All these pressures effectively dismantled the organisational hierarchy. In 2016 other offensives – Operation Usalama I and Usalama II – were launched by the Congolese army and the United Nations forces, which compelled the ADF to vacate its new Medina base. Yet the Congolese and UN forces then withdrew, and the base was quickly reoccupied.[58] As offensives came and went, the survival of the ADF was assisted by the corruption of the Congolese armed forces, who at times sold arms to the ADF. The countryside meanwhile paid a heavy price through forced recruitment and kidnappings.[59]

The organisation still has the advantage of operating in the border areas, and it benefited from the failure of its opponents to carry out appropriate counterinsurgency strategies. Indeed, during 2017 the ADF launched many attacks, although a new offensive was mounted against them in early 2018. The ADF still managed to plunder villages and take advantage of the local population. 'They are investing in business still. They need the goods. They also collect from motorbike drivers. They come and steal from the farmers, and they will steal from the hospital in crisis. At times, they are killing and stealing from villagers. They don't communicate.'[60]

At the time of writing the ADF remains a slightly confusing organisation. There are also indications that the organisation, or at least local low-level sub-commanders, participate on different sides in the conflicts within local communities in the Congo. There are also rumours about tension between Muzamir Kasadha, ADF's deputy commander, and the leader, Seka Baluku, who remains close to Benjamin Kisokeranio, son of a former NALU leader, although the information has not been verified at the time of writing. However, the situation was indicative of a group that could find local allies and that was influenced by conflicts between other groups. During 2018, the Ugandan security services also accused the ADF of being behind the killing of sheikhs in Kampala, but they also stressed, perhaps paradoxically, that the ADF was only a minor threat to Ugandan national security.[61]

Although being the odd man out ideologically speaking in this book, the ADF's most prominent feature was that it started out with Takfirist ideas, though these ideas were diluted over time, to the point where Islam became important above all for self-identification and for justifying resistance, as Islam and ADF were deemed 'under attack' by outsiders. Today the organisation is taking small steps in the other direction, as jihadist rhetoric seems to be growing more and more important – at least it did so until 2017.

The ADF is an example of how a relatively large organisation can survive for years in the peripheral areas of a state, and how it can interact with the local environment, living off the land. In this sense, it serves as a reminder that transformation from territorial control does not necessarily lead to collapse, nor indeed to a complete loss of all aspects of territorialism, for taxation of locals might still be possible. This is a useful reminder, as several jihadist organisations, such as the Shabaab, Boko Haram and the Islamic State, may just face such a transformation in the near future. While some writers regard ADF's embeddedness as something unique to it, which separates it from other jihadist groups, it should also be viewed as the product of prolonged semi-territorial control. In other words, this embeddedness should be seen as the function of a monopoly of power, not a complete monopoly of power, but a monopoly that is restored when enemy offensives ebb. Consequently, locals are forced to integrate with the jihadists, marrying off their daughters and getting their sons to join, in order to appease the group and get them on side.

8

AL-HIJRA / AL-MUHAJIROUN, AND THEIR
UNCLEAR FRINGES

The jihadist networks along the Swahili coast (that is, the coast of Kenya and Tanzania, including the islands offshore), which also make inroads into the interior of these countries, are different from the groups operating in places like Somalia, Congo, Nigeria and Mali. Unlike Somalia, for example, Tanzania and Kenya have enforcement agencies able to suppress these networks, through both legal and extra-legal means. There have been many examples of successful investigations by police authorities in both countries, and jihadi cells have been closed down. The state institutions, including the army and the police, also have a solid presence in most areas of Kenya and Tanzania.[1]

In many ways, the situation in the two countries shares similarities with Western Europe, where law enforcement agencies follow up on investigations of jihadist networks, even though the same agencies have problems with corruption, human rights records and inefficiency. Yet both Kenya and Tanzania have seen increasing sectarian violence over the last ten years, the countries have produced their own jihadist videos, and have sent foreign fighters to Somalia. There is thus a jihadist presence. However, jihadists constitute clandestine and sometimes fragmented networks, structures that can more easily survive surveillance and counter-terrorism campaigns. To trace the activities of these networks is extremely hard, and the 'terrorist' designation has been used instrumentally by the two governments, whose ruling parties have adopted anti-terror rhetoric against many groups, including their political opponents.[2] Adding to the confusion created by such strategies is the fact that some oppositional organisations do have religious elements in their programmes, although they have limited ties to jihadi ideology. The Association for Islamic Mobilisation and Propagation – known as Jumiki or Uamsho (Awakening) in Swahili – in Tanzania and the Mombasa Republican Council (MRC) in Kenya were both accused of having jihadist agendas, yet it seems these bodies only have individual overlaps with jihadist organisations.[3]

The Kenyan and Tanzanian states, despite problems with their legal systems, have the capacity to suppress political and military opposition and to investigate jihadist cells. Any organisation that wants to operate in the two countries, with the exception of the north-eastern periphery of Kenya, has to be secretive and hide its command channels, in order to survive. This means that there are problems in identifying entities that are part of this network. Given the clandestine nature of the groups, it is personal connections, across borders and organisations, that tie jihadists together. At times the jihadists are found concentrated in sub-groups within an organisation, sometimes there are ideological overlaps where members of the same networks support both the Islamic State and al-Qaeda, and sometimes jihadists are accepted as members of organisations dominated by more moderate views. As this chapter will show, it is often hard to know where the exact borders of these networks lie, and not only within a single country, because the networks span national borders as well.

The jihadist networks of the Swahili coast often draw on historical grievances in their rhetoric. In 1698, Oman took control over Zanzibar, and Omani dynasties henceforth controlled the island, as well as parts of the coastline of both Kenya and Tanzania. Until 1856, the coast remained part of the Omani empire; after that, it became a tributary province, although later in name only. From 1884, the Omani dynasties of Zanzibar slowly but surely lost control over mainland Tanzania and Kenya. Germany first acquired possession of Tanganyika, but was succeeded by Britain after the end of the First World War. Britain also took de facto control over the Kenyan coast, while formally recognising Zanzibari sovereignty. The Omani dynasty in Zanzibar held power until a revolution in 1964 (the protectorate over the mainland had been ended in December 1963).[4] The revolution itself was later reinterpreted by radical Islamists as secularist in character, and a symbol of the oppression of Muslims; indeed, many fled the islands at the time.[5] This opened the way for a union with mainland Tanganyika in the new state of Tanzania. The more secular forces behind the coup in 1964 also drove the union itself. For this reason, Islam as a religion became a marker for resistance against the secular forces that had created the union with the mainland.

Yet this important cleavage in Tanzania has today a nationalistic strain to it – 'civilisational nationalism', as it has been called by Marie-Aude Fouéré, indicating a situation where Islam functions as a marker of national identity.[6] In this context, Uamsho has drawn attention to the links between violence, religion and politics in Zanzibar. The organisation was founded in 2001, advocating Zanzibari independence and a more radical version of Sharia.[7] It gained momentum when it became the only political organisation arguing for independence, especially after the other oppositional party in Zanzibar, the Civic United Front (CUF), decided to join the Tanzanian ruling party, the Chama Cha Mapinduzi (CCM), in a national unity government in October 2010. After the arrest of Uamsho's leader, Mussa Juma, serious demonstrations broke out, leading the Tanzanian state to ban the organisation.[8] There have been worrying signs about Uamsho. For one thing, pamphlets have been distributed in its name in Zanzibar, arguing for attacks against Christian targets.[9] The group was blamed by the government for a bomb attack in the Darjani district in Stone Town, Zanzibar, in June 2014, although it did not publicly claim responsibility. On 23 February 2014, the seafront Mercury Restaurant and Bar in Zanzibar, a popular tourist destination, was bombed, and once again the police pointed towards Uamsho. Yet the group did not claim responsibility this time either. There was also an acid attack against two British female tourists on the island, without any organisation claiming to be the author. These incidents, although serious, are small in number compared with those in mainland Tanzania, especially in the Arusha area.

Uamsho does not seem to have links with Shabaab at an organisational level.[10] Maybe one explanation is that Uamsho is to a certain extent the bearer of a Zanzibari nationalist ideology. Part of its supporters' rhetoric is admittedly aligned with a more radical form of Islam. Slogans presented in protests in Zanzibar can also call for radical versions of Hudud punishment.[11] Comments on international relations and events in the Middle East flourish, and are often anti-American in spirit. It is quite possible that the rhetoric on display at some of Uamsho's demonstrations may incite violence. However, allegations of connections with Shabaab have to be seen in the light of a 'Tanzanian tradition' where the Tanzanian government uses such allegations to discredit the opposition. What is significant is that a clear majority of jihadist-inspired attacks and videos in Tanzania have not been taking place in Zanzibar but on the mainland, and strong links with the Shabaab have never been proven.

The Mombasa Republican Council (MRC) is in many ways the Kenyan equivalent of Uamsho. It emerged in a situation where failed land reforms and political animosities created the foundation for an oppositional movement. As in Tanzania, the coastal elite had amassed power before the onslaught of European colonialism, centred upon Arab settlements that in some cases pre-dated Islam.[12] The coast resisted central control from the interior, partly basing their argument on the Omani and, later, the Zanzibari government, and developing the idea among Muslim coast-dwellers of a golden age when they were governed by Muslim rulers.[13] In Kenya's post-colonial setting, Christians from the interior in many ways outstripped members of the Muslim communities in the race for education and jobs. In the process the Muslim elites of the coast lost out to the Christian elites of the interior.[14] The struggle was influenced by conflict over the issue of decentralisation in Kenya, and how much power would be allocated to the coast. For a period, the drive towards centralisation was extremely strong, especially under the rule of Jomo Kenyatta, president from 1964 to 1978, and in the early part of Daniel arap Moi's presidency. This led to a sense of alienation among the coastal elites. The resulting animosities were over time fuelled by failed land reforms and government corruption.[15] The Kenyan authorities often succeeded in playing off different coastal sub-groups against each other. Indeed, at times, these groups fuelled such conflicts themselves.

In the 1990s, there was a move towards organising resistance, which began to flourish when the multi-party system in Kenya re-emerged after 1991. The MRC can be seen as part of this dynamic, as an organisation promoting autonomy for a region that to some extent had experienced a separate history from the rest of Kenya. The MRC itself was formed in 1999 to address perceived political and economic discrimination against the people of the coastal province. It also contested the treaties that had transferred control of the coast from Zanzibar to Britain.[16] The quest for independence began to gain ground in the organisation, which launched the slogan 'Pwani si Kenya' (in Swahili) or 'The Coast is not Kenya'.[17] However, it also attempted to address the grievances caused by land reform and marginalisation after Kenya was decolonised. From having been dormant for some time, the MRC was invigorated after the 2007 elections. Subsequently, it faced a legal battle with the Kenyan government, which attempted to ban it in 2010. This failed, and the move was, after a lengthy process in court, rejected in the Kenyan high court in 2016. But investigations and legal prosecutions of individuals within the MRC continued.[18]

MRC and Uamsho underline a more general point. The grievances of the coast, both in Kenya and Tanzania, were often geographically confined, their idea of a past 'golden age' was similarly restricted to a region, and ethnicity rather than religion played a significant role in marking identity. In fact, there were geographical and ethnic markers that in many ways contradicted jihadists' more global view of Muslims as a unified ummah. This had the disadvantage of making the recruitment of jihadists outside the coastal areas harder, by focusing on a conflict in which potential recruits had no part. Some jihadists attempted to resolve the problem by concentrating on coastal and Zanzibari grievances as those of 'Muslims' against foreign oppressors, though there were many difficulties with such an interpretation.[19] While some of the coastal grievances fuelled jihadism at a micro level, both Uamsho's and MRC's regional separatist agendas were vastly different from the unionist agendas of the jihadis, who claimed to be fighting for a larger ummah rather than a specific group or area. Although some of the grievances of the coastal areas enhanced recruitment for jihadist networks, the leaders of these networks did not come from either the MRC or Uamsho.

The Origins of the Kenyan Networks

In January 1992 the Islamic Party of Kenya (IPK) emerged just after political parties were again allowed in Kenya. A part of IPK's agenda focused on morality, with a concern to uphold morals among Muslims on the coast; a part was to alleviate the threat against Islam from the centre of Kenya and from a state elite dominated by Christians. A street preacher, Khalid Balala, soon gained influence in the party, taking power and leading it. Balala was to inspire several individuals who later became important for the jihadi networks of Kenya and Tanzania. One of these was Aboud Rogo Mohammed, an Islamic preacher of some fame, because of his resistance to the evictions of radical sheikhs from Tanzania in 1989. Rogo in the end even became a candidate for the IPK.[20] The IPK was banned by the Kenyan state, as the constitution excluded any party based on religion.[21] Although the ban led to severe protests, in which Rogo was active, the prohibition was carried out and the party broke up. We should note that fissures within the coastal Muslim population over issues such as race had inhibited the unity of IPK, and other oppositional movements, which at the start supported the IPK, had slowly backed out, so that when the party became illegal, it was already fragmented.[22] In the end, Balala was refused re-entry into Kenya after a stay in Europe.[23]

For his part, Rogo remained active, frequenting together with other IPK activists the Masjid Sakina, or Sakina mosque, in Mombasa. Rogo was, like several of the future radical leaders of the Kenyan jihadist networks, a Bajuni, an ethnic group with ties to Somalia. He hailed from the village of Siyu, where he later was allegedly introduced to al-Qaeda's Fazul Mohamed, who married a relation of Rogo's wife.[24] There were other connections between the al-Qaeda network and Rogo. Rogo probably received support from the East African branch of the Saudi Haramain charity, later closed down because of its use as a front for channelling money for al-Qaeda, and from a charity that had a connection with future Shabaab leaders.[25] While remaining active, Rogo and other IPK members found themselves the object of government harassment. By the mid-1990s, after the government put pressure on the Masjid Sakina in Mombasa, Rogo and other IPK members sought refuge in the more moderate Masjid Musa in the same town.[26] Masjid Musa was to become a hotbed of radical activity and a forum for radical speeches, though Rogo did not take outright control of the mosque. In fact, during an initial period there was a sympathetic relationship between him and the original mosque leadership, and only after Rogo's death in 2012 did the leadership committee lose out to Rogo's followers.[27]

This story illustrates several points about the radical takeover of mosques in Kenya. The radicals were initially not seen negatively by the wider community, and they coexisted over time, within the governing bodies of the mosques, with more moderate forces. For outsiders, the politics of these mosques were hard to grasp, and they were often viewed as unified in their views and either entirely radical or entirely innocent. The boundaries of the jihadi networks were, however, more blurred than many often believed them to be. All the same, members of the Masjid Musa and Masjid Sakina, the most important perhaps being the former Musa imam, Ramadhan Hamisi Kufungwa, were to join the Somali Shabaab, and give speeches promoting and defending violent global jihad.[28]

Rogo had various encounters with the Kenyan police during the early 2000s. He faced trial for the 2002 Paradise Hotel attack in Mombasa, but the court case collapsed.[29] It was also around 2002 that Rogo met another of Kenya's future radical preachers, Sheikh Abubakar Shariff 'Makaburi', who through his sermons was to influence a wider audience.[30] Rogo's prolonged court case and subsequent acquittal convinced many Muslims that he had been a victim of discrimination. Indeed, many innocent Muslims in Mombasa were targeted by the police, who had difficulty in identifying the jihadi promoters in the network. The situation probably contributed to Muslim radicalisation. Yet the problems can also be explained by the ineptness of the Kenyan police and prosecution at the time.[31]

Rogo successfully influenced several mosques and madrassas in Kenya, such as Sirajul Munir madrassa in Mtwapa and, as we have seen, Masjid Musa and Masjid Sakina in Mombasa, where a new generation of Islamist activists was educated. One of these activists was Ahmad Imam Ali, a student at Rogo's religious school in Mombasa, who later became a prominent Kenyan commander in the Shabaab. Imam Ali was also to become a frequent face on the videos of the Harakat al-

Shabaab.[32] Rogo often addressed Tanzanian students in his mosques, and gained the confidence of another important preacher, Samir Khan, although there was to be rivalry between them later. Both Rogo and Khan distributed firebrand distributed firebrand video talks on/via mobile phones; these reached many and gained popularity along the Swahili coast.

All these developments have to be seen in relation to events taking place in Somalia, where the rise of the Islamic Courts Union and its subsequent fall attracted some Kenyans. Kenyans from the radical networks started to travel to Somalia from 2006. Among them was Juma Ayub Otit Were 'Taxi Driver', from Majengo in Nairobi, an area with many coastal inhabitants, and bordering Eastleigh, Nairobi's most Somali-populated neighbourhood, which was readily influenced by events in Somalia.[33] It was in Majengo that the most tangible outcomes of the jihadist networks along the Swahili coast were to develop. The main mover was Imam Ali. He set about taking over the Pumwani Riyadha mosque in a slum area in Nairobi with many coastal emigrants. In the words of a sheikh in the mosque:

> They came with prayers like us, talked about religion. Ahmad Imam was sincere. Things went upside down. They became very active, they destroyed alcohol and other vices, we thought they are good. Many were Bajuni, many had parents from Majengo but had gone abroad to take education. They managed to get money to rebuild the mosque. They bought the place, building up the community, and won the election. They started to go to Somalia. He took people to Somalia.[34]

The followers of Imam Ali breathed fresh life into the Pumwani mosque, not only by injecting money but also by working against the sale of alcohol in Majengo, sometimes violently, and by constructing a new mosque. The older generation initially saw Imam Ali's followers in positive terms. However, the old, more moderate leadership was ousted in 2007 when Ali loyalists took control of the mosque's governing body. Imam Ali and his followers had thus gained a platform, and both Aboud Rogo and Samir Khan were allowed to use it to deliver radical speeches promoting jihad. The local community saw the development as a clash of generations, with the older sheikhs being driven out and forced to create a small rival mosque in Majengo.

The older generation also felt let down by the Kenyan authorities, which did not intervene on their behalf.[35] In 2008, drawing upon the Pumwani mosque, and the Pumwani Muslim Youth group, the radicals established the Muslim Youth Centre (MYC).[36] This was set up as a charity, to prevent crime and to protect the Muslim 'cause'.[37] Part of their activities involved disengagement work, attempting to draw youth away from crime, and it gained some popularity because of this.[38]

The MYC was to become a platform for jihadist propaganda and recruitment to Somalia. One of the platforms was the *Al-Misbah Magazine*, which was circulated in Kenya, containing reprints of the speeches of Anwar Awlaki of al-Qaeda in the Arab Peninsula, at the time one of the most important propagandists for al-Qaeda.[39] The focus of the magazine was international, as were many of the sermons hosted by MYC in the early days. These included the call to stop Muslim political participation in Kenya, as this was seen as a waste of time. In this way, MYC was very different from the IPK.[40] Over time, the Muslim Youth Centre developed a highly professional media centre, the Hijra. A network of business persons and other institutions also developed around the MYC, including sponsors and other mosques. At times these groups shared the MYC's ideology, at other times just parts of it. The network drew upon preachers from the whole of the Swahili coast, including Rogo's old connections. It seems that the network and the MYC were very good at providing Shabaab with recruits: even the MYC's leader, Ahmad Imam Ali, 'crossed over', in the term used by members of the MYC, to the Shabaab in 2009 and joined that group in Somalia.[41] Another key member was Sylvester Opiyo 'Mussa', who, unlike Ali, came from a poor background, was uneducated but charismatic; he was a Luo from a Christian family in the local Majengo area. Sylvester Opiyo looked after Rogo's logistics and escorted him around Nairobi when he visited.[42]

In this same period MYC organised jihad training sessions, and facilitated the travel of Kenyans who wanted to go to Somalia. Sylvester Opiyo himself 'crossed over' in late 2012. Rogo held large street prayer gatherings in Mombasa and Nairobi, the latter in the Majengo social hall where many of the initial debates between Imam Ali and the old Pumwani mosque leadership took place before they lost power to

Ali. The 'crossovers' in the Shabaab were also active and appeared in several Shabaab propaganda videos.[43]

During 2011 and 2012, several developments took place that led to a drastic increase in terror attacks. The most notable was the Kenyan intervention in Somalia which began on 16 October 2011, a decision taken by an inner circle of the government, possibly due to an escalation in hostage cases in the border areas. As a result, the Shabaab began to use its own forces in the very porous border areas between Kenya and Somalia, as well as striking directly at the heart of Kenya at times, as with the attack on the Westgate shopping mall in 2013. The Shabaab also increased its focus on recruiting Kenyan members and on producing videos with anti-Kenyan contents. Inside Kenya, several terrorist attacks were launched. Subsequently, the Kenyan mass arrests increased in scale, and several radical imams were targeted by assassinations. Samir Khan was assassinated in April 2012, and Aboud Rogo in August the same year.[44] Although there may have been other reasons for their killings, the previous use by the Kenyans of death squads in their anti-gang work makes it relatively likely that these assassinations were conducted by the police or rogue elements within the police.[45] The killings sparked animosity among Kenya's Muslims, many of whom saw them as an example of how the law in practice did not apply to Muslims, enabling executions without due process. Moreover, many Muslims were not aware of the radical agenda in their speeches, and saw Rogo and Khan rather as champions of justice.[46] Others were angered by the extra-judicial killings, and the issue was later even raised in the Kenyan parliament.[47] The distrust between the coastal population and the police reached new heights. Shabaab's propaganda units inevitably followed up on these narratives, using especially the killing of Rogo as an example of the lack of justice for most Muslims.[48]

The Kenyan police were frustrated with the slow-moving court system and problems with getting individuals sentenced in court, although they were empowered by a new law, the Prevention of Terrorism Act of 2012. Despite this, the situation in Mombasa turned explosive after Rogo's killing when large-scale riots broke out in August 2012. The pattern was repeated in October 2013, when Ibrahim Ismael, also known as Ibrahim Omar Rogo, was killed. The situation became tense. Sectarian violence increased when a church was fired at, killing at least six individuals in Likoni in March 2014. The old balance of power between radicals and more moderate elements in Masjid Sakina and Masjid Musa was destroyed. Supporters of Rogo took full control of the mosques in late 2013.[49] In both Masjid Musa and Masjid Sakina, hardliners gained the upper hand, and the Mombasa governor, Hassan Joho, was almost attacked by some of the radicals, despite being seen as a defender of Muslim rights by many.[50]

All this led to drastic measures from the Kenyan security services, who stormed the various mosques on several occasions, and made several arrests. In April 2014 Makaburi was killed, and later the same year the main radical mosques in Mombasa were closed by force, and the leadership changed. On two days in November alone (17 and 19) 360 people were arrested.[51] The heavy crackdowns forced some of the radicals to flee to Tanzania, and the Masjid Sakina and Masjid Musa were closed to the radicals. Kenyan investigation of the networks increased, including further inland, and targeted the MYC.

For outsiders, the politics of the Pumwani mosque were unclear and it was hard to assess where its ideological borders lay. The MYC was more than an organisation; it was a hub in a network. This network included other external individuals, board members of other mosques, and business companies who sponsored their activities. Among their supporters were those who saw the MYC as an alternative to criminal gangs, providing religion as an antidote to idleness. All the same, police arrests intensified.

It was in this context that MYC slowly distanced itself from the Pumwani mosque and by early 2012 it renamed itself Hijra. Increasingly, the network around the organisation and the organisation itself became more clandestine, according to the International Monitoring Group working in Somalia.[52] The increasing Kenyan crackdown was to put these networks under strain, and for their members secrecy became more than ever necessary.

New Names, Weakened Structures

The network behind the new name was not always very clear. Indeed, the Twitter account of the old Muslim Youth Centre did not change its name, and in fact its activities increased from January to September 2013, but the last press release was issued in September 2013.[53] Who operated the account was far from clear. The Twitter account itself claimed to operate out of Mombasa, Tanga, Korogwe and Majengo, with contacts among radicals along the Swahili coast and in Somalia.[54] The platform was also used to publish Ahmad Iman Ali's message on the 'Bayah of the Mujahideen' in March 2012, in which he swore allegiance to Shabaab's emir and to al-Qaeda. The platform, moreover, supported the leadership of the Shabaab in its struggle with the Shabaab opposition, and presented a blog from the so-called White Widow, Samantha Lewthwaite, the wife of one of the perpetrators of the 7/7 terror attack in London, who hid in Kenya and Tanzania.[55]

What the MYC network did not do was engage in large-scale, complex terrorist operations. The large-scale attacks on Kenyan soil, such as on the Westgate shopping mall in 2013, against Mpeketoni in 2014, and against Garissa University College in 2015, were the work of the Shabaab rather than its allied Kenyan and Tanzanian networks. Admittedly, these attacks at times took advantage of the presence of Kenyan and Tanzanian fighters, to the extent of organising a separate unit, Jaysh Ayman, that drew upon foreign fighters, but this was mainly operative in the border areas on the coast between Somalia and Kenya.[56] Indeed, for some of the members, the border between Kenya and Somalia was meaningless, as both Somalis and Bajunis had straddled the border for centuries and in many cases held dual citizenship. However, the attack teams were launched from Somalia, and had been trained by the Shabaab in Somalia. In Mpeketoni, locals were involved, but while the attacks in the Lamu region did take advantage of the grievances that had fuelled the coastal unrest, including land grabbing by the interior elite, the units carrying out the assaults were trained in Somalia, and were controlled by Somalia's Shabaab. The attacks by the networks inside Kenya were in general much simpler, involving hand grenades and simple bombs, with fewer casualties as a result, perhaps because of a lack of training among network members and an inability to organise larger attacks in view of the alertness of the Kenyan authorities. The largest of these attacks was probably that on the Gikomba market in September 2014. On the whole this episode was not noticed by the global press, probably because it targeted poor

Kenyans.[57] Even further on the fringes of the media's attention were sectarian attacks against churches inside Kenya. Shabaab did indeed criticise the Hijra network for lacking the capacity to launch larger-scale attacks. There was also some bickering between the two entities over command and control, Shabaab being less willing to yield control to Hijra.[58]

Although the networks continued to channel Kenyans into Somalia, it is wrong to see these channels as a definite organisation called Hijra, for, as Anneli Botha's research shows, recruitment often happened through friends.[59] Indeed, when the police crackdowns managed to remove the leadership of the two radical hubs, Pumwani mosque and the Masjid Musa, the replacements hubs were far from clear. Observers noted that informal youth gatherings and sports clubs began to acquire a similar function, while Islamic schools, now under close scrutiny, became less important.[60] The new networks were now more dispersed than ever before, and cells grew apart.[61] In this environment, the internet grew in importance: it was a way of communicating that did not require physical contact. A new set of internet-based Swahili-speaking publications, such as the *Gaidi Mtaani*, emerged from 2013. A jihadi magazine for women called *Al-Ghurabaa* was fully Swahili, not bilingual as was *Gaidi*, and, according to its front page, was produced in Dar es Salaam, indicating clear ties with Tanzania.[62] Indeed, the new group mentioned in this publication, the al-Mujahiroun, always signed off from a location inside Tanzania when issuing comments, and often seemed to comment upon Tanzanian-related issues inside the Shabaab.[63] The *Amka* magazine, issued only in 2015, was bilingual, English and Swahili, thus indicating a stronger focus on Kenyan audiences, yet it was also published by al-Mujahiroun. Hijra produced several publications, including the very short *Hijra Bulletin*, running through 2017. Although the organisations were active on the internet, they did not take responsibility for any terror attacks from 2016. There was talk, but nobody did the walk.

The crackdowns of the Kenyan police were successful in reducing the recruitment channels into Somalia and at times breaking the networks smuggling fighters and sometimes wives into Somalia. The Kenyans had to deal with other problems as well, as foreign fighters from Somalia started to return to Kenya from 2015 onwards, partly because of Shabaab's territorial losses, but also because of alleged racism within the Shabaab. The Kenyan government issued a general amnesty, which was somewhat confusedly implemented at a local level, leading to the arrest of several returnees seeking amnesty. Yet on the whole the Kenyan strategy in handling returning fighters was highly successful; for instance, the Supreme Council of Kenya Muslims' amnesty programme enlisted more than 700 returnees.[64] The programmes were mostly non-state-run.

All of these facts highlight a fragmented Kenyan jihadi scene. The clandestine networks in central Kenya were dispersed, and the command and control lines were in some cases difficult to define. At the same time, isolated groups became vulnerable to hijacking by other organisations: an Islamic State-friendly group was reported in Majengo, for example, but without any contacts with the Islamic State either in Somalia or in the Levant. Indeed, Kenyans left the country to join the Islamic State, while recruitment to Shabaab, though it declined, nevertheless continued.

Today, there are still jihadi networks inside Kenya, but with a weakened command structure and a weakened ability to conduct advanced attacks. The root causes are still there, and the networks can again be activated, but they have for now been curtailed by the state security forces.[65]

The Tanzanian Networks

The major incidents of jihadist-inspired violence and the first appearances of Tanzanian jihadi videos all emerged in mainland Tanzania, not in Zanzibar. The episodes when the police allegedly discovered Shabaab material, and when cells responsible for sectarian violence were captured, also took place on the mainland.[66] Significantly, in mainland Tanzania there were strong historical grievances. The Western colonial powers (Germany and Britain) were widely accused by Islamic activists of alienating Muslims through discriminatory policies in regulating access to education and job positions. Such accusations continued after independence, aided by the fact that the first president, Julius Nyerere, was Catholic. However, the phase of nation-building based on socialism led to a strong trend of secularisation, challenging both Islam and Christianity. The attempts of the government to control Islam in Tanzania, by establishing the government-controlled Baraza Kuu La Waislamu Tanzania (Bakwata) as an organisation for Tanzanian Muslims, was met with resistance from Muslim preachers. The controversial Sheikh Ponda Issa Ponda, who became a key figure in resistance against government control, was active in this struggle.[67] Ponda Issa Ponda has since the early 2000s appeared and reappeared in court cases, and he has been used as a symbol for Shabaab-affiliated groups such as the mysterious al-Muhajiroun.[68]

For a period, Islam and politics in Tanzania remained surprisingly detached from each other. However, this was to change. The development of new Islamist-inclined organisations in Tanzania was spurred by international developments. Firstly, scholarships were offered to Tanzanians by oil-rich Saudi Arabia from the 1970s onwards, some of which were tailored to students in religious studies.[69] These scholarship students were to be instrumental in the founding of the Ansar Muslim Youth Centre (AMYC). The returning students also spearheaded a form of youth rebellion against traditional Islamic institutions and practices, leading to heated debates over the exact timing of Ramadan, over government-controlled Muslim institutions such as Bakwata, over the practice of praying in mosques without shoes, and over traditional Sufism, partly spurred by Saudi influence.[70] The returnees were part of a larger trend of returning East African students, who often kept up their connections with one another across borders, and from this emerged trans-coastal Islamic networks from Mozambique through to Somalia. These developments should be seen as well in a wider political context, including the slow but steady weakening of the ideological assumptions of Tanzania's ruling party, until a multi-party system was declared in 1992, albeit dominated by the governing party, Chama Cha Mapinduzi. In a way, the developments created opportunities for revivalism, as old ideological assumptions were questioned, leaving openings for new ways of seeing the world.

The Saudi influence could also lead to quite different outcomes. Many returnees were not politically inclined and were isolationist, refraining from actively attempting to change Tanzania, save by sermons in the mosques. The Saudi form of Islam merged with other local revivalist traditions, which had a longer history in the area, to form what is known as the Ansar al-Sunna movement, a loose network of Islamic activists stressing the need for a return to the purity of Islam.[71] The movement itself was an ideological hybrid, its leaders for example quoting Muslim Brotherhood-related scholars like Yusuf Qaradawi. Nevertheless, it included an indirect emphasis on Takfirism in its condemnation of the practices of other Muslims, and its insistence that Muslims should follow the right path. In this critique lay a critique of the state itself and its public organisation for Muslims in Tanzania, the Bakwata. The Tanzanian state had traditionally been friendly towards Sufism, and Sufi leaders close to the regime could easily be seen as part of the corrupt culture of the regime itself. Inherent in the movement, therefore, was an anti-regime protest and an anti-corruption protest as well. The wider movement was a hybrid of local and global ideas, and contained a multitude of ideological elements.

However, not all of the elements of the wider Ansar al-Sunna movement maintained the same hybridity. The Ansar Muslim Youth Centre (AMYC) was based on the older Tanzanian Muslim Youth Union, which changed its name in 1988.[72] The AMYC provided a wide range of welfare services, with fifteen madrassas, two orphanages, more than ten nursery schools, four primary schools, a secondary school, a high school and a teachers' training college. It had branches in Bukoba, Mtwara, Arusha, Morogoro and Singida.[73] AMYC distributed newspapers as well. In 1990 the magazine *Al-Fikrul Islami* was launched, and *Al-Haq* followed in 1999.[74]

In 2012 the United Nations arms embargo commission pointed its finger at the AMYC and revealed its close connections to the East Africa office of the Saudi Haramain Foundation, which had been involved in the 1998 attacks on the US embassies in Dar es Salaam and Nairobi. The branch was later closed because of its al-Qaeda connections after the United States applied pressure.[75] After closure, several of the members of Haramain drifted towards the AMYC and its network.[76] One of these was Nur Abubakar Maulana, who was said to have travelled to Somalia from Tanzania; another was Laid Saidi (Sheikh Abu Huzhaifa), who was forcibly deported from Tanzania. According to the International Monitoring Group, Laid Saidi became close to the Masjid Shabaab in Dar es Salaam. The connections between Haramain and the AMYC illustrate the wide networks of the Sunni jihadists in

Tanzania, as parts of Haramain had links to the early Shabaab as well – in the person, for example, of Mohamed Kuno 'Gamadhere', later famous for his role in the Garissa attack in Kenya in 2015, an attack which also involved Tanzanian jihadists.[77] Haramain had also founded Masjid Mohamed in the town of Korogwe, led by Khamis Abubakar, a former sheikh in Tanga, who arranged competitions for youths to lure them into Somalia. The networks enabled a relatively large flow of potential jihadists from Tanzania to Somalia, possibly the second largest contingent of foreigners in the Shabaab.[78] Several of AMYC's financiers were involved in setting up a channel for Tanzanian foreign fighters travelling to Somalia.[79] AMYC itself exchanged students with radical Kenyan mosques like Masjid Musa and Masjid Sakina.[80] AMYC was also said to have been supported by the al-Muntada al-Islami Trust of Nairobi, an entity accused of being connected to terrorism by the International Monitoring Group.[81]

The picture of AMYC is not always clear and its ideological positions are not always consistent. For example, in 2013 Salim Abdulrahim Barahiyan, leader of AMYC, criticised another Ansar sheikh for arguing that agreements with non-Muslims were not to be respected.[82] The Facebook page of AMYC contains many postings about the need to curtail the anger of young frustrated Muslims, making them abstain from violence.[83] Yet sermons frequently criticised the nation-state and the state of the Muslim *ummah*. Barahiyan also accused Tanzania of being manipulated by the United States and of encouraging youths to enter non-Muslim schools, typical themes of Islamic sects.[84] That the AMYC had more than 75 different branches and that many mosques hosted sheikhs with AMYC affiliations ensured that various parts of the organisation could act on their own initiative. At the same time, it was also a structure that could aid radicals in hiding both their activities and their expressions of radical thought. Although the Tanzanian police put the AMYC under observation, the state seldom chose to prosecute leading members or financiers of the centre, save Juma Abdallah Kheri, who was arrested in 2013 for supporting jihadist networks in both Tanzania and Kenya.[85]

The outliers of the wider AMYC network are hard to map. The organisation itself is part of a wider network of ideas, contributing to a move to purify Islam in Tanzania. In general, there has been a drastic increase in religiously inspired violence in Tanzania, some of it launched by radicals who do not tolerate more moderate views within their own religion. One thinks here of the acid attack against Sheikh Mustapha Mohammed Kiago and Sheikh Said Juma Makamba of the Masjid Kwa Murombo, both incidents that took place in 2013 close to Arusha. Those involved included leaders of two mosques on the periphery of the Ansar network. One was Jafari Lema from Ngulelo, then in charge of Quba mosque (not the one in Zanzibar). Previously, the mosque had been a leader in ecumenical dialogue and its then head, Alhaj Ally Kisiwa, led Christians on tours in the mosque and even acted as a referee in a Christian football match. For these and other misdemeanours, he was dismissed in 2004, thereby opening up the position for Lema and his jihadist speeches.[86] Also involved in the acid attacks was Abdul-Azizi Mohamed, the leader of the larger Ijumaa mosque in Arusha.[87] The attacks were a part of a larger wave of assaults in Arusha, which also hit at Christian targets and tourist spots. By 2015, the Tanzanian police seem to have brought the activities in Arusha under control.

Several trends were rather notable after the collapse of the Arusha group. Firstly, a group referring to itself as al-Muhajiroun declared its existence. It published a magazine, *Al-Ghurabaa*, which was said to be produced in Dar es Salaam. The group also published biographies of martyrs that indicated clear activities within Tanzania, and it established support networks, as arrests in Kenya during 2015 attested.[88] In February 2015 the police clashed with a group of militants at Mikocheni Falls located at Amboni village in Tanga region and, in the face of much resistance, had to withdraw.[89] Initially, the police believed it was bandits that had challenged them. There were more worrying signs when a jihadi video was released in which a Tanzanian man with the nom de guerre of Abu Qays bin Abdullah appeared, taking responsibility for these and several other attacks. The video referred to Somalia, and contained declarations of admiration for Shabaab, but no direct reference to any organisation.[90] A second video called for Tanzanian recruits to join the Tanga group to fight for the Prophet.[91] The Tanzanian police also detected Shabaab-related materials in several confiscations they made.[92] A last worrying trend was the kidnapping of children, who were sent away to be taught Islam, allegedly by the Shabaab.[93]

The Arusha incidents illustrate the problems that Tanzania confronts with the jihadists. It faces networks that have channelled fighters to Shabaab, networks on the fringes that agitate for violence in Tanzania, networks that produce hate speech that could lead to violence. At the same time, the institutions that have radical sub-groups within them often have a more moderate majority, and they help orphans and the poor all over Tanzania. The jihadist networks in Tanzania are to a certain extent the product of Tanzania itself. They are shaped by the strength of the Tanzanian state, which does not allow jihadist organisations to exist on the periphery, as in Mali or Nigeria, but has the strength to prevent jihadists from assuming semi-territorial control and full territorial control.

However, in 2017–18 the killings started again. These could not be directly linked to jihadists and could have been the result of local conflicts at the village level between Christians and Muslims, and between the opposition and the government. Village elders were often targeted in this wave of attacks. Tanzania has had trouble in the past relating to resource distribution, which led to violence, and this could be an underlying factor in the recent attacks. No jihadist video appeared in the aftermath. There was greater clarity about another group of jihadists, formed in Cabo Delgado, Mozambique, and organised by a new movement known as al-Sunnah wal-Jama'ah, which in 2017 attacked a police station and barracks in the city of Mocimboa da Praia in northern Mozambique. Arrests indicated that there were members from Tanzania, Kenya and Somalia in the group.[94]

The connections between various groups and networks can be the result of individuals with double memberships, but also of common ideas. However, one does not need to share every idea in order to be a network member: there are varieties of views about world events and, indeed, about the concept of jihad within the known organisations described in this chapter. This enables the networks to tap into legitimate grievances against the state and the ruling party, criticising electoral manipulation, Tanzania's neo-colonial dependence, and the government's clumsy attempts to control the Muslim community in Tanzania, as well as expressing the alienation that some Muslim groups feel from the ruling party.

Developments in Tanzania have shown the importance of these networks. It was Somalia and the Shabaab that provided the major attraction to Tanzanians who chose to fight jihad abroad. The domestic jihadi videos in Tanzania were always linked to Somalia. Yet the local setting also created a fertile ground for recruitment. Nevertheless, the Tanzanian state was simply too strong for these networks to develop openly and take an active and above-ground role. The trajectory of the early Boko Haram was simply impossible in Tanzania. In Tanzania, the jihadist network had to remain just that; a network of relatively committed members. These networks can nevertheless be dangerous in the future, for a small, dedicated number of terrorists can cause a lot of damage. Political problems between the opposition and the government may also create opportunities for the networks to exploit.

The case of al-Mujahiroun and Hijra shows how clandestine networks may lead to organisational overlaps. It also illustrates how clandestine networks can be vulnerable to weaknesses in coordination and training. Yet it shows, too, how they can maintain themselves in situations where they are heavily prosecuted, and how they can draw on allies with a territorial and semi-territorial presence for training and propaganda purposes.

9

THE HARAKAT AL-SHABAAB
FROM TERRITORIALITY TO SEMI-TERRITORIALITY

The Harakat al-Shabaab in Somalia is a 'survivor'. It has survived several defeats: during the Ethiopian intervention against the Sharia Court movement of which it was a part, the Ethiopian withdrawal in 2009, and the Kenyan and Ethiopian (re-)intervention in 2011, as well as the re-establishment of a full (not transitional) federal government on 20 August 2012. Yet far from being defeated in these crises, Shabaab instead was transformed. This included returning to semi-territoriality in 2007, resuming territorial control in 2009, and then reverting in a slow, steady movement back to semi-territoriality from 2013 onwards. The transformations meant that Shabaab changed in all kinds of ways: the way it secured funds, the portfolio of its activities, and its very institutions. Indeed, the history of the Shabaab is the history of change and transformation, and also of successful adaptation.

The organisation started existence as a clandestine network. Several of Shabaab's members had a past history of involvement in al-Ittihad al-Islamiya (the links with al-Qaeda are analysed in chapter 3 of this book). Several of its future leaders had been fighters in Ittihad, while others of a younger generation had been pupils in Ittihad-affiliated schools. The hard core of the early Shabaab was a small group in Mogadishu that included many former Ittihad members. Yet it was different from Ittihad, with a high number of Afghanistan veterans.

The senior member of this original Shabaab group was Ibrahim Haji Jama Mead, also known as Ibrahim 'Afghani'. Afghani had even gone to the United States to study before travelling to Afghanistan in 1989. After his Afghanistan stay, he returned to Somalia together with other radicals, such as Mallim Kassim, Hassan 'Dheere' and Sheik Abdullahi Ahmed Sahal.[1] Yet, not everyone in the young group was an Afghanistan veteran, and not everyone had joined the Ittihad. Some members of the small group that was to become the Harakat al-Shabaab had actually left Ittithad, having seemingly retired. One of these was the current second-in-command of Shabaab, Abdirahman Mohamed Warsame Osman Diini 'Mahad Karate'. He was born in 1969 in Duusemareb in the Galguduud, Somalia, and hailed from the sub-clan Absiye, of the Ayr clan. He dropped out of secondary school, but did attend a karate club in Mogadishu, hence his nickname. Karate also attended a Quranic school, and joined al-Ittihad al-Islamiya, which, taking advantage of his past, presented him as a gym and karate instructor. Mahad was present at the battle of Arrare in 1991, the first major battle in Ittihad's history, but did not fight. He participated in Ittihad's conflicts in Bari, in Puntland State, and later went to the Luuq district. However, he then retired, left Ittihad, moved to Nairobi, and worked there as a businessman. Here the Kenyan authorities arrested him. He was sent to Ethiopia, possibly after a stay inside Somalia, and in the end he was again transferred, ending up in a Somaliland prison (Mandhera), from which he escaped, fleeing the region to Nairobi, and then to Mogadishu.[2] Karate's history is a good example of how Ittihad fragmented in the 1980s, with leaders and members leaving or defecting. Some of them would become the nucleus of the Shabaab. Shabaab itself was not to be as fragmented as the Ittihad.

The small group developing in Mogadishu had ties to al-Qaeda's East African cell, although the latter also kept its distance.[3] The group was under pressure, partly because of the Somalian civil war, in which different warlords fought among themselves, often with foreign powers on their side, and in the process attempted to tap into 'the war on terror' that had developed since 9/11 by designating their enemies as 'al-Qaeda'. The network's exact boundaries were unclear, at times on purpose in order to avoid members being caught. The network had to be secret, as individuals with al-Qaeda contacts were a commodity in Mogadishu at the time: warlords seeking favours and money in the West often tried to 'sell' such individuals to the West.[4]

There were parallel developments taking place that would empower the small network. The first trend was the decline of the 'warlord' system. From being dominant in the 1990s, the factions which the warlords controlled began to fragment beyond recognition, and became increasingly less able to tax, to provide protection to their allies, and less interested in providing security for their adherents. The territories controlled by the warlords dwindled, and the warlords' power waned.[5] In this situation, religious authorities grew in importance, functioning as sanctioning mechanisms for contracts because of the popular belief that they were just in view of their beliefs. Business companies also used religious titles like 'sheikh' to enhance their reputation for honesty, thereby improving their sales. Moreover, religious networks were used as vetting mechanisms for business partners; those that were devout were seen as more credible.[6] Religious leaders came to function as the providers of justice as well. In the early 1990s, so-called Sharia courts developed in Mogadishu. They were clan-based and, sometimes, as in the case of the northern Mogadishu Sharia court system, were sponsored by secular faction leaders. The courts were not necessarily extreme in their worldview and provided help for ordinary citizens in Mogadishu who had been targeted by criminals. What is more, the expansion of the Sharia court system was not linear: courts would attempt to come together in unions (usually following clan lines), and the unions would later dissolve again. Nor can it be said that the courts had a homogeneous theology; in fact, it seems that they were very heterogeneous until at least 2005. Some were led by Sufi sheikhs, some by Salafists, and others by sheikhs of more ordinary Shafia persuasions.[7]

The resurgence of religion in Somalia was in many ways not related to theological or ideological movements. Instead, it was related to the main tenets of Islam, of honesty and social justice (even though in some interpretations this might be harsh and barbaric). What Scott Thomas refers to as 'religious capital' – in this case, having trust in the reasonableness of transactions, and providing somebody to go to when you were in need of help – increased in importance in Somalia during the late 1990s and early 2000s.[8]

The small network that was to become the Shabaab was aided by the wider resurgence of religion. The network's members were seen as steadfast, just (in the sense of believing in Sharia), and able to transcend the limits of their clan. The reputation for justness may be hard to understand for someone outside a civil war context, given the atrocities that the Shabaab was later to conduct. However, the warlords and faction leaders in Somalia at the time cared little for the provision of any form of justice, and the extreme interpretations of Sharia held by several Shabaab members were relatively unknown to the wider local audience, who might also have regarded these views as far preferable to the anarchy of Mogadishu during the period 1993–2005.

The exact date of the founding of Shabaab as an organisation varies from source to source. The variance is perhaps due to the fact it was 'reborn' on several occasions. It was first formalised as an organisation in 2004–5, then restarted in September 2006 as a wider organisation inside the Sharia court system, and then reformed again after the fall of the Sharia courts.

The Shabaab itself developed from a network operating in an environment that was hostile, not because of the nation-state, but because of the warlords who held power in Mogadishu in the period 1991–2006. As with other network-based organisations, its borders were hard to define, and individuals continually left and re-entered it. Moreover, the network became embedded in the structures of several of the Sharia courts. Aden Hashi Ayro, one of the first publicly known Shabaab commanders, was, for example, allowed to join and, later, lead the militia of the Ifka Halane court.[9] It was this court, the Ifka Halane, that, in cooperation with others, drove a new process of unification among the Sharia courts. This process was supported, financially, militarily and vocally, by many members of the Somali business community, who saw unification of the courts as a possible source of protection for their businesses, which had been seriously hampered by taxes, tolls, theft, robbery and random violence.[10] The Somali business community was an important financial and military contributor to the new structures, and the courts at times aided them in their conflicts with the warlords. It was actually a businessman, Abokour Umar Adane who started the military expansion of the Sharia courts in late 2005. His quarrels with the warlord Bashir Raghe sparked the war that led to the rise to power of the Sharia court alliance.[11] Adane provided large sums of money to the courts, which thus became too important financially to be allowed to suffer defeat. The Sharia courts had to support him or else face a change in the balance of power in Mogadishu. Adane's opponent, Bashir Raghe, drew support from most of the warlords in Mogadishu. Early 2006 thus saw a face-off between the old warlords of the 1990s and the forces of the Sharia courts, which included both the Shabaab and a large number of forces provided by the businessmen of Mogadishu.

Adane's militias, together with the court militias, managed to secure control of the largest port of Mogadishu at the time and also Eisley airport. In this way, the courts controlled the most important sources of revenue in Mogadishu and won the upper hand in the fighting with the warlords.[12] By June 2006, the Sharia courts were in control. During these events, the Shabaab existed as a loose organisation within the Sharia courts. In the words of Omar Hamami: '[the leadership of the Shabaab] happened to be a bit of a coalition similar to the Courts, while simultaneously being inside the Courts'.[13] The Shabaab was to ride piggyback on the success of the courts, and would increase its powers drastically while being accepted as a legitimate organisation within the court system. They were to become trusted military and managerial leaders, at times handling the relatively large funds collected by the courts. Shabaab was thus ready for its first transformation, from a clandestine network into an accepted organisation that was able to act openly in the areas controlled by the Sharia courts.

An Accepted Presence, at Least Amongst the Sharia Courts

In September 2006, the formal foundational meeting for the new Shabaab organisation took place under the umbrella of the Sharia courts.[14] In southern Somalia, the Sharia court union now held large territories and attempted to develop governance structures. The Sharia courts were not a formal state, nor was it accepted as a state government by any foreign power. In a sense, it reminds one of the Taliban's status in Afghanistan in the period 1996–2001.

Yet, the Sharia court alliance of Mogadishu rode on a wave of popularity, which this writer witnessed when travelling in the city during the autumn of 2006. From June it had established peace and prosperity, as investment returned to the city. The Sharia court alliance also restored law and order to a city that had lacked this for years. The writer observed young women walking about without an escort at night, seemingly without any worries, in stark contrast to the atmosphere in 2005. The nascent Shabaab network drew heavily on this popularity: it was seen as a group of efficient fighters who had participated in bringing this development about. Its more extreme sides were relatively unknown, for it was very small, and just one of many within the Sharia court alliance.

The old Shabaab leaders became thoroughly integrated into the executive committee of the Sharia courts, their equivalent of a government. Fuad Qalaf Shongole led the department of education, while Ahmed Godane was secretary general.[15] Ironically, Mukhtar Robow, who later defected from Shabaab, was put in charge of looking after government defectors. Robow also rose to become the second-in-command of the armed forces of the Sharia courts. Ali Abu Otaiba gained the important position of unifying the courts. These promotions empowered the Shabaab, but also changed the balance of power, favouring some of the Shabaab leaders such as Ahmed Godane.[16]

The Shabaab was in part sceptical about the steps taken in relation to the wider Sharia court alliance. Some members, including the leader at the time, Abdullahi Sudi Arale, wanted to expand and create a broader Islamic salvation front, while others, like Godane, wanted a more ideologically focused organisation.[17] Yet the Shabaab remained unified in the face of external rivals, and was thus able to criticise the more opportunistic elements within the Sharia courts. At this time, the organisation was widened, and brought in new leaders. In its new form, it included present-day Western allies such as Ahmed 'Madobe', who had belonged to Hassan Turki's Harakat Ras Kamboni militias.

As part of the Sharia court alliance, the Shabaab was able to draw on funds and to build up training camps and active recruitment policies, targeting unemployed youths by promising them work. Its leaders could also, it seems, go behind the backs of the Sharia court leaders. Perhaps it was its ideological framework, its expanding training camp system, its multi-clan leadership and even its foreign fighters that contributed to the group's surprising unity. It managed to draw leaders from various clans, who systematically rebuffed attempts by clan elders to secure clan patronage.[18]

Shabaab seemed to take a much more aggressive stand than several leaders of the Sharia courts did. The balance of forces in this period was definitely against the courts, and such aggressive tactics are today hard to explain.[19] The aggression was to provide the spark that led to an Ethiopian offensive in December 2006, and thereby to the second important transformation in the history of the Shabaab, a turn to semi-territoriality and the re-establishment of the organisation. Instead of facing a friendly government, in the form of the Sharia courts, the Shabaab was now to face the superior forces of the Ethiopian army and the Western-backed Transitional Federal Government of Somalia. It was the military shock of December 2006 and January 2007 that prompted Shabaab's transformation, for it simply did not have the resources to withstand the advancing forces of its enemies, and of necessity had to transform. The professional Ethiopian forces were vastly superior to the Sharia court forces, including its Shabaab elements; they had good discipline, heavy artillery, air support and armour, and probably were numerically superior. Yet, despite the superiority of its enemy, the Shabaab, like Boko Haram in 2016, and MUJAO, AQIM and Ansar Dine in 2013, did not disappear.

Semi-territoriality in the Face of Superior Enemies

In 2007 many predicted that the Shabaab was history.[20] Indeed, the invading Ethiopian forces, perhaps as many as 20,000, had given both the Sharia courts and the Shabaab a big hiding. Many Sharia court leaders, including the later Somalian president, Sharif Sheikh Ahmed, fled to Kenya. Some Shabaab leaders remained undercover in Mogadishu, helped by the fact that Ethiopia and its Somali allies left parts of the city unoccupied until March 2007.[21] One man who slowly emerged as leader of Shabaab in Mogadishu was Mahad 'Karate', who built up an underground network. Many of the leaders, including Ahmed Godane, fled south into the forests of Ras Kamboni.[22] Former Shabaab leaders actually created two different camps in Ras Kamboni, one dominated by the more moderate Ras Kamboni militias.[23] The other was more ideologically extreme and was led by Ahmed Toosan; it was to become the nucleus of the reformed Shabaab.

In Mogadishu, Shabaab refrained from participating in the wider military campaigns against the government during the big battles of 2007. However, it became increasingly active in implementing terror attacks, suicide missions involving car bombs, and assassinations.[24] The Shabaab attempts were aided by the confused policies of the United Nations Development Programme (UNDP), Ethiopia, the United States and Norway, which attempted to build up the police forces and the army while neglecting the payment of wages. This led to the government forces pillaging and plundering in order to sustain themselves, or defecting, and in some cases being easily bribed.[25]

In this situation, Shabaab had several opportunities presented to them. Their enemy was a coalition of forces, some of which were not fully loyal to the anti-Shabaab agenda. In Bulo Marer the Shabaab bribed government forces, and stayed there by using the presence of government troops as a camouflage to build up a base that later was used by the organisation to expand in central Somalia. Shabaab also managed to manipulate the clan system by sending various of its leaders back to the home areas of their clans: local allies of Ethiopia were reluctant to arrest their fellow clansmen. Ethiopia did not have forces in these remote areas. Shabaab developed its own strategy, the so-called *koormeer*, whereby they attacked outlying Somali government positions and occupied villages with no permanent Ethiopian or government presence, holding them for a few days. During this time Shabaab would demonstrate to the locals that they had the power to punish supporters of the government, that they were to be feared, even courted, if the villagers wished to be sure of safety or protection.

The *koormeer* strategy, Shabaab's own name for how it planned its tactics, is in many ways the essence of a semi-territorial presence. Firstly, Shabaab expanded into a territory, often using Shabaab members of the local clan to establish safe areas under clan protection in which the organisation could consolidate its presence, most of the time in the open. In the initial stages, the Shabaab managed to avoid conflict with the only groups that could have contested their presence, namely the clan militias. Over time, the Shabaab could carefully begin to challenge the balance of power, at times providing services to the clan, at times contesting the clan militias, at times asking for financial contributions. In these ways Shabaab was able to transform into semi-territoriality, rising like a phoenix from the ashes.

Internationally speaking, the Shabaab was neglected by the wider world, which saw the Ethiopian army, correctly, as superior to the ragtag Shabaab bands in the countryside, but it failed to notice the sustainability gained by the Shabaab from taxing the locals. In fact, Shabaab's simple structures were perfectly able to survive on the income secured from local protection money or taxes collected from villages in the countryside. In these villages, Shabaab was also able to recruit locally. The money that rebuilt the Shabaab was thus not funds from the Gulf states or other far-away sources. The *koormeer* strategy progressed slowly. Shabaab had to face rivals in the countryside, often clan-based militias loyal to the Islamic courts. However, this was generally unproblematic at the start, as the Sharia court militias and the Shabaab remained part of the Sharia court alliance together.

As time went on, the relationship between the other members of the court alliance and the Shabaab grew more strained.[26] A split emerged publicly after the remains of the Sharia courts attempted to create a wider oppositional alliance from 6 to 14 September 2007. The result was the so-called Alliance for the Re-liberation of Somalia (ARS). Shabaab's old enemy Hussein Aiden became the second-in-command, and Shabaab's old rival Yusuf 'Indah Adde', Mohamed Said, became the head of defence. Secular diaspora organisations also participated in the founding meeting of the ARS. The Shabaab seems to have been thoroughly provoked by the secular participants and the fact that secular Eritrea, which had fought against the Eritrean Islamic Jihad (see chapter 3), was the host.[27] Shabaab publicly distanced itself from the meeting, and in the autumn of 2007 started to publish propaganda on online sites that was global in content, commenting upon Iraq and Palestine, and admitting that it included foreign fighters.[28] However, the differences between the ARS were not always clear to the ordinary Somali, and perhaps even less clear to the politically active Somali diaspora, many of whom had seen the Ethiopian intervention as an invasion and violation of Somalia.[29] For outsiders, too, the nuances were less clear. Many, including the current Somali prime minister, Hassan Khaire, regarded the Shabaab as part of a nationalist insurgency, a problem that would disappear as soon as the Ethiopians withdrew from Somalia.[30] Such ideas were ill informed, and became more so when there were increasing signs of a split, as for example when Fuad Shongole publicly announced in October 2007 that the Sharia courts were now 'infidels'. Another sign was the steadfast refusal of the Shabaab to use the Somali flag in their operations, since for them it was a nationalist symbol.[31]

Outside actors strengthened their presence on the ground when a Ugandan contingent of African Union troops was deployed in Somalia during the spring of 2007. Moreover, it was understood that elements of the Sharia courts had to be involved in the new government. More moderate elements of the Sharia were included in the relatively successful Djibouti peace process, starting on 9 May 2008.[32] Ethiopia also began to lose interest in its Somali adventure, downscaling its troops and leaving the insurgents in control of several areas. The thinking of the international actors was that a peace agreement with the Sharia courts would lead to an Ethiopian withdrawal, which in turn would lead to the collapse of the supposedly 'nationalist' Shabaab. However, such a view neglected both Shabaab's ideology, which sought to create unity, and the organisation's ability to discipline its members. It also neglected the clan base of the Somali army, for a change in leadership would lead to a withdrawal of its most efficient unit, the Somali Presidential Guard, at the time staffed with Majeerteen clan members from the Puntland region of the president. Additionally, it overestimated the military power of the more moderate Sharia court elements.

Finally, an agreement was reached in Djibouti which would result in an Ethiopian withdrawal and the election of the former Sharia court leader, Sharif Sheik Ahmed, as the new president of Somalia in January 2009. What was to have been a diplomatic victory became in reality a disaster when Shabaab quickly took control of the areas vacated by the Ethiopians, when the Puntlanders and the unpaid, demoralised units of the Somali army collapsed in front of them, and the moderate Sharia court militias were often neutralised by assassinations. Shabaab once again transformed itself, this time into a territorial entity, a state-like structure, with control over central Somalia. Shabaab's golden age was about to begin.

Shabaab Goes Territorial

While many international observers had expected just the opposite, the Shabaab spread rapidly in 2009. In Mogadishu, several districts fell to the Shabaab, as resistance more or less collapsed without any heavy fighting. A Yemeni commander, Khalid Rajah, even established a trench system in the border areas with the African Union and government forces.[33] The old capital of the Western-backed Transitional Federal Government, Baidoa, was 'captured' on 26 January, in the sense of Shabaab intervening against looting government troops rather than winning the city in battle.[34]

The rapid expansion into territorial control had a heavy price attached to it. Recruits flocked to the Shabaab because of its successes, and those with minimal ideological convictions, including clan fighters, would later attempt to hijack Shabaab and have it pursue a clan agenda at a more local level. Sometimes clan considerations, like Robow's protection of his fellow clansman, the warlord Hapsade, created conflict inside the Shabaab. Indeed, the organisation had to decide how to deal with clan structures, which remained important elements in governance in Somalia, though they also created cleavages. As a result, Shabaab had to enter into the business of clan mediation. The Shabaab also had to face up to the limits of its capacities. When the African Union Mission in Somalia (AMISOM) managed to stall Shabaab's attacks in Mogadishu, the front lines hardened into something resembling the Western Front in France during the First World War. This in turn meant that Shabaab had to face rivals that it could not vanquish.

In this sense, the Shabaab became more of a traditional state with borders, albeit not internationally recognised ones. Shabaab also took steps to organise a bureaucracy in the areas where it established a more permanent presence. The militia commander reigned supreme at local level. His knowledge of Sharia could often be limited and his verdicts ad hoc, but his responsibilities extended only to minor offences. However, above this level, district courts were organised as well as regional courts, though they were far from perfect. Shabaab in fact lacked the manpower to run the courts properly, and at times had to include individuals without Sharia knowledge or religious leaders of different persuasions from the Shabaab itself. At times even, these structures were not manned, yet they were still much more efficient overall than the previous justice structures run by their rivals. Shabaab also organised regional administrations, the Wilayada, or Islamic governate, with a governor (*wali*), an office of social affairs, an office of finance, an office of the judge and an office of the police (the Hisbah army). In some cases these structures were staffed with technocrats rather than global jihadists, who focused on managing the day-to-day administration rather than on global jihad. In other cases careerists, profiteers and idealists not concerned with global jihad joined this system.

The Shabaab governance structures were far from perfect, but they were more efficient than the alternatives (clan governance, warlords and the Transitional Federal Government), and the Shabaab courts were preferred to the alternatives under government control. By now, the Somali government controlled only part of Mogadishu, while Shabaab controlled a territory the size of Denmark. Shabaab carried out governance, and engaged in road building, in a way that pre-dated the Islamic State in Syria. The Shabaab was also in the business of providing justice through its court system, albeit of the harsh Sharia kind.

Yet governance also brought problems for the organisation. The wider Somali population could now more easily identify and understand Shabaab's unique ideology, as well as see the atrocities that followed from the Shabaab's implementation of Sharia. Shabaab's abuses included the destructions of Sufi shrines, the torture of human rights activists, the systematic execution of political opponents, and the banning of football.[35]

Shabaab also had to deal with the increasing power of the AMISOM forces, which were slowly building up in Mogadishu. The enemies the Shabaab had faced in the regions – non-paid Somali soldiers often more interested in looting – were of an entirely different kind from the Ugandan and Burundian forces that made up the core of AMISOM during these years. In fact, the Ugandan and Burundian forces were superior in equipment, in size and in training to the Shabaab. The AMISOM also enjoyed armoured support, as well as limited air support, and the assistance of private contractors, besides the remains of a small, unpaid, inefficient Somali army.

The AMISOM forces were a thorn in the side of the Shabaab in the few blocks they controlled in Mogadishu, and so the Shabaab attempted to move in on them and finish them off in 2010. During the so-called Ramadan offensive in 2010, which was supposed to defeat the AMISOM soldiers, Shabaab's troops were impressive. The Shabaab fielded perhaps as many as 8,000 men. However, they were attacking an enemy that was better trained and numerically superior. During the Ramadan offensive, Shabaab was defeated in the largest battlefield loss the organisation ever experienced. The losses created some disagreements within Shabaab. However, the AMISOM did not follow up Shabaab's losses and Shabaab kept its territories during 2010.

The AMISOM did, however, recognise the weakness of Shabaab, and attempted to encircle one of the major sources of Shabaab's income in Mogadishu, the Bakaara market. Slowly but steadily AMISOM rendered Shabaab's hold on the market more tenuous, almost surrounding it and ending its usefulness for taxation. In the end, territoriality in Mogadishu became too costly for Shabaab, and it gave up its hold there on 8 August 2011.

On 16 October 2011, Kenya intervened militarily in Somalia. It had over several years developed a network of local allies, which nevertheless had failed to stall Shabaab. The Kenyan decision to intervene seems to have been relatively sudden, prompted by kidnappings in the border areas. The decision-making process did not involve Uhuru Kenyatta's full cabinet, but only a few ministers.[36] The Kenyan intervention had at least two notable effects. Firstly, it turned Shabaab's focus towards Kenya. Kenya had supplied Shabaab with foreign fighters before 2011, and Shabaab had published Swahili publications on the internet as early as 2009, but now Shabaab's Swahili propaganda increased in volume. Shabaab launched attacks inside Kenya, and Shabaab leaders of Kenyan origin grew in importance within the organisation.

The radical networks in Kenya were older than the Shabaab, as were the networks in Tanzania (see chapter 8), but media exposure now brought to the fore Kenyan Shabaab leaders like Ahmad Imam Ali. Ali was an activist who first gained notice when he led protests against the leaders of one of Nairobi's oldest mosques, Masjid Pumwani Riyadha, in 2007, accusing them of corruption; later he was to take charge of the mosque.[37] It was Imam Ali who was employed by Shabaab to declare war against Kenya on 9 January 2012.[38] On 10 February 2012, Imam Ali also announced that the jihadist Muslim Youth Centre (MYC) in Nairobi had joined 'al-Qaeda East Africa' (AQEA), in a message posted on MYC's English-language blog.

The initial Kenyan intervention was slow. The Kenyans did not advance fast or far inside Somalia, but stayed in the border areas. The Kenyan intervention forces were small: around two battalions, according to the International Crisis Group.[39] Given the limited size of the Kenyan forces and the onset of the rainy season, Shabaab remained in control of the border regions for the next few months. Shabaab also struck back and attacked several targets inside Kenya's borders, including naval patrols and convoys.[40] Despite this, the Kenyan intervention presented Shabaab with a serious threat, as it had to shift its forces southwards. Furthermore, the Kenyans attempted to bring their oldest ally in Africa, Ethiopia, to intervene again, and there were random Ethiopian raids against the Shabaab. On 31 December 2011, the Ethiopian army together with local allies captured the strategic town of Beledweyne from Shabaab. A gradual expansion of the Ethiopian engagement meant that Shabaab now faced an alliance of African countries with formidable firepower and superiority in equipment and numbers. These negative developments created some anxiety in the Shabaab organisation. Management of the controlled areas became more risk-averse and the centralised taxation system seems to have broken down in 2010.[41] The defeats also strained the relationship between the Shabaab's own leaders – the withdrawals were criticised by some senior men such as Shongole.[42]

In response, the Shabaab attempted to transform its organisation. According to the International Crisis Group, officials gathered in a meeting in Barawa from 5 to 7 July and devised an administrative reform plan. Five administrative and military zones were restructured, and three regions were combined into one zone, while a rapid deployment command, the Gurmadka Degdega, was created, commanded by Omar 'Qadib' from the Isse/Dir clan.[43] Shabaab also formally joined al-Qaeda in February 2012.[44] Yet the leadership's refusal to call a general *Shura* (council) to discuss their defeats, especially the 2010 defeat in Mogadishu, led to tensions within the organisation. As Shabaab lost territories, these troubles escalated. The Shabaab lost its most economically valuable city of Kismayo (because of the port income) on 29 September 2012. The loss of excise from exports from Kismayo was not critical, and was to a certain extent offset by Shabaab's tolls on roads leading into Kismayo: it thus continued in effect to tax the port.[45] Yet the problems created pressures on the organisation. Ahmed Godane tried to call a meeting in Sakow, middle Juba, to address members of the opposition that was forming against him.[46] Several notable commanders, including Mukhtar Robow, Hassan Dahir Aweys and Omar Hamami, had grown increasingly dissatisfied with Godane. According to a later defector, Hamami, the deputy *Shura* leader at the time, was one of his fiercest critics.[47] Hamami focused his criticism against Godane on issues of military strategy, the marginalisation of foreign fighters in the organisation, the implementation of Sharia, and Shabaab's general mistreatment of other Muslims.[48] Others, like Robow, protested about the lack of inclusiveness in the organisation. However, Godane moved highly efficiently on the diverse opposition he faced and managed to decapitate it on 20 June 2013. There were some defections, including that of Hassan Dahir Aweys and, later, Mukhtar Robow, but, all in all, the organisation remained united.

Territorial losses and the transformation of the organisation from a territorial to a semi-territorial presence contributed to internal tensions in the Shabaab. Discussions of military strategy, often about tactics and the choice between holding on to and giving up territories, took their toll. The pressure on the Shabaab continued. During 2014, Operation Eagle and Operation Indian Ocean were unleashed against the organisation. On 1 September, Shabaab's leader Ahmed Godane was killed in a drone strike conducted by the United States. The potential for a destructive leadership contest arose, but this did not happen in the end. There was rivalry for leadership between Ahmad Umar 'Abu Ubaidah' (Ahmed Diriye) and Mahad 'Karate'. Karate felt that Diriye had little tactical experience, and that he came from a weak clan.[49] Karate in the end gave in under the weight of a testament from Godane, who designated Diriye as leader. Besides Godane, some Shabaab sub-commanders were assassinated by the United States, such as Aden Garar, who was killed in a drone strike on 13 March 2015.[50]

The defeats suffered by the Shabaab continued. In October 2014, the last large coastal city held by the Shabaab, Barawa, fell. Inland,

Shabaab lost its hold on some cities too. On 19 July 2015, contingents of AMISOM, including Ethiopian, Kenyan and Somalian troops, began another offensive (Operation Juba Corridor) against Shabaab, this time in Bardhere and Dinsoor. However, the Shabaab withdrew without a fight, and the two cities were left as islands in a countryside that was not controlled by any of the allies, as none of them bothered to garrison the smaller rural villages. Shabaab thus had great freedom of movement in the Somali countryside. At the same time, Shabaab was left in control of some cities in lower Juba. More importantly, there was little AMISOM control in the countryside.

During 2015, Shabaab renewed its more conventional hostilities, launching attacks against convoys and isolated company-sized AMISOM units, using far stronger forces than it had deployed since 2011. On 11 June 2015, more than a hundred Shabaab fighters ambushed an Ethiopian National Defence Force convoy escorting civilian contractors to deliver supplies for AMISOM from Mogadishu to Baidoa. There were also heavy attacks against military units. On 26 June 2015, following an initial breach of the perimeter by suicide bombers, more than a hundred Shabaab fighters overran an AMISOM base in Leego, resulting in the deaths of more than fifty Burundian soldiers. The death toll is in itself misleading as the Shabaab victory involved the rout of a full company-sized unit of the Burundian army, the largest defeat of Burundian forces in Somalia ever. The pattern was repeated in September in the battle for Janale. This time the Ugandan army was the target. The Shabaab plan was quite sophisticated, involving the disabling of a bridge before the assault in order to cut off an avenue of retreat.

By 2016, the advances of the Somali army and the AMISOM forces stopped. The few remaining cities controlled by the Shabaab remained in its hands. More importantly, the Shabaab's presence in the countryside, outside the cities, was left uncontested, apart from the odd AMISOM campaign. AMISOM started to bunker up in their bases. The Shabaab's transformation away from territoriality to semi-territoriality was in one sense completed. Its large training bases, its permanent radio stations and other more complex governance structures were now a thing of the past. Yet Shabaab was far from vanquished; it was merely transformed. This transformation had been slow and was not fully completed, as territoriality was maintained in middle Juba. In Mogadishu and the other larger cities, Shabaab operated as a clandestine network. Yet it was in the countryside supposedly conquered by AMISOM and their Somali allies where the Shabaab drew its strength, launching heavy attacks in areas where it was supposed to have been driven out.

Shabaab Resurrected: Back to Semi-territoriality

The military losses of the Shabaab from 2012 to 2016, including the loss of control of all the larger cities in south-central Somalia, did not lead to its destruction. This was confirmed by its terror activities in Mogadishu, where they were able to implement large-scale terror attacks, like the one on the Jazeera Hotel on 26 July 2015, employing a bomb of roughly 400kg of TNT or 2,000kg of homemade explosives, the largest explosive power it had employed anywhere since 2011.[51] The attack highlighted the priorities of the Shabaab, for the hotels of Mogadishu became a preferred target. In 2015, they struck at the Makka al-Mukarama Hotel (27 March 2015), Central Hotel (20 February 2015) and SYL Hotel (22 January 2015). These were combined with the detonation of car bombs, after which Shabaab commandos, often dressed in Somali military uniforms, entered the hotels and attacked guests. In these episodes there were often allegations that insiders both at the site and in the Somali security forces helped to facilitate the attackers. For the average citizen in Mogadishu, however, life had actually improved, and the attacks, being made against high-profile individuals, had implications for only a relatively small number of Mogadishu's inhabitants. Shabaab targeted hotels frequented by the government, and warned Mogadishu's citizens not to enter them.[52]

While not reaching the headlines, the impact of the Shabaab's activities in the countryside, the supposedly liberated areas, was felt more by the ordinary locals. In some villages, such as Walag on 31 May 2015, villagers were killed allegedly in punishment for transporting goods for AMISOM. On the roads, there were frequent attacks on AMISOM forces. An attack on a food aid convoy in Luuq Jeelow on 7 January 2015 is one example of how Shabaab could block the transportation of goods in the countryside. At times, Shabaab could even enforce blockades of AMISOM-held villages. For villages in areas where Shabaab had relative operational freedom, even though AMISOM was conventionally superior in numbers, villagers had to accommodate Shabaab in order to stay alive. On occasion villagers were forced to give away all their teenagers to Shabaab as recruits.[53] Several villages were also vacated by the AMISOM or government forces and subsequently reoccupied by the Shabaab, which showed the locals in the area how little protection AMISOM could really provide. At the same time, Shabaab increased its attacks against larger units of AMISOM and the Somali national forces, and routed several company-sized units. In El Adde in the Gedo region on 15 January 2016, it attacked and overran a Kenyan military company at an AMISOM forward base near the border with Kenya. This in turn led to an increasing tendency for AMISOM forces to concentrate themselves in larger and heavily fortified bases. Their withdrawal from or limited patrolling of the countryside once again enabled Shabaab to reassert control in the villages and put pressure on the locals.

The Somali allies of AMISOM also faced problems, such as the notorious failure to pay soldiers of the Somali national army. Unpaid soldiers at times mutinied, and at other times withdrew from exposed positions. From September 2015 to August 2016, the UN Monitoring Group for Somalia and Eritrea counted 17 withdrawals from villages in the southern Somali countryside, of which at least two, including the highly significant withdrawal from the port city of Merka on 5 February 2016, were due to lack of payment. Some of these withdrawals were temporary, but, as in the case of Merka, they clearly highlighted the importance for the locals of staying on friendly terms with the Shabaab, as they could quickly find themselves at the Shabaab's mercy after an AMISOM or government withdrawal.[54]

The Shabaab was not without its own losses. The United States intensified its aerial attacks on the Shabaab, and on 5 March 2016 US drones successfully targeted a Shabaab training camp in Raaso, 120 kilometres north of Mogadishu. The Shabaab lost at least 150 fighters, making it the deadliest drone strike in United States history. The US drone campaign scored other victories as well, such as the killing of Amniyat (secret service) officer Sultan Mohamed Sandhere 'Ukash' on 2 December 2015. Yet it was not the United States that scored the most prominent killing after 2015, nor AMISOM or the national forces, but one of the regional states. In late May 2016, Interim Juba Administration forces managed to kill Mohamed Kuno ('Dulyadeyn' or 'Gamadhere'), one of the major leaders behind the Garissa University College attack of 2 April 2015 that killed 148 people, mostly students, in a Kenyan border town. Kuno, himself a native of Garissa, and the military commander of Shabaab in the middle and lower Juba regions, was killed in a raid near Bulagadud, lower Juba. Such killings of senior members put pressure on Shabaab, but the resulting vacant positions were soon filled by people from the middle ranks.[55]

The Shabaab did not always have its way with pressuring locals to pay taxes. Clans collectively resisted at times, and managed to avoid taxation.[56] Nevertheless, the Somali government was relatively unwilling to provide aid to their efforts, nor did AMISOM offer help on such occasions, and local resistance towards Shabaab was left to fend for itself.

In the areas of semi-territorial and territorial control, Shabaab was able to pay its recruits regularly, according to the Monitoring Commission, from US$50 for ordinary soldiers to approximately $1,000 for senior officers and certain tax collectors, with the majority of the estimated 4,000 to 7,000 operatives receiving about $100 each. The Shabaab drew upon a mobile phone-based pay system, the Hormuud Telecom's EVC Plus service, to provide payment at the end of each Islamic calendar month. Bonuses were given for participation in larger battles. Surviving participants of the El Adde campaign each received a bonus of $200–$400.[57] New recruits could also get bonuses, as could the families of suicide bombers. Given the general situation of poverty, Shabaab could actually be a stable source of income for many, especially struggling Somali youths. This was especially the case when the organisation could maintain an open and relatively frequent presence where it had semi-territorial or full territorial control.

Not all of Shabaab's recruits joined it because of these reasons. The group also used force to recruit local villagers. At times, they could try to take advantage of clan conflicts, as in lower Shabelle, where they attempted to tap into the local Biemal clan's animosity towards the Hawiye clan-dominated Somali army. Yet in this case, they failed, as AMISOM provided an alternative to the Shabaab, giving protection to the Biemal. Yet the Shabaab also provided a semblance of order in the areas where they operated checkpoints, even the ones supposedly behind AMISOM lines. A source quoted in the United Nations arms monitoring group's report described a journey made by road from Mogadishu to Jowhar, where a receipt of payment from the first Shabaab checkpoint actually enabled the traveller to travel free through the other Shabaab checkpoints.[58] Shabaab also attempted to eliminate rival checkpoints, as they did on 21 December 2016 when they closed a checkpoint outside the village of Calol Caade, near Beledweyne. In some instances, the Shabaab even created new unarmed police units (Hisbah) in areas, such as around Brawl, which were supposed to be liberated from the Shabaab.

During 2017, all the trends of 2016 continued. There were further convoy attacks, such as that on an AMISOM convoy in Ceelgawerow near Merka on 23 October, and against a convoy on 25 October near Hoogir in the Bakool region. In Bula Xaawo, Shabaab managed to stage workshops for youth for religious purposes as well as to promote voluntary recruitment, and females were even allowed to participate.

On occasion, the clan militias resisted the Shabaab, as on 11 September in Maroodile, where they successfully repulsed the group. Clan militias sometimes provided security locally and protected clan members from Shabaab. Another island within Shabaab's semi-territorial zone was the militias loyal to Mukhtar Robow, who remained in his home area of Bay–Bakool, resisting Shabaab attempts to defeat them. In the end, Robow joined the government as Shabaab's attacks intensified. This step was celebrated as a victory by the new president of Somalia, Mohamed Abdullahi Mohamed 'Farmajo', who took power on 8 February 2017 with his new prime minister, Hassan Khaire. The two came to power on a wave of popular support. Later in the same year, a centralisation drive and lack of dialogue with the clans made them increasingly unpopular. Yet, both Farmajo and his predecessor seemed, at the time of writing, to have avoided what would have led to a major victory for the Shabaab, namely outright war between the regional states and Mogadishu.

The Shabaab continued to tax the locals in the areas in which it had a semi-territorial presence. The Shabaab also benefited from fees paid into their courts. When selling or buying farms or land, Somalis often went to a Shabaab-controlled court, even if the land was in an area under the control of the Somali state or of the regional states. This also happened with land conflicts. Moreover, the Somali state's court decisions were not properly implemented by the Somali police.[59] The juridical decisions of the Shabaab courts were seen as based on Sharia and implemented by force, whereas the Somali government's courts had a reputation for being bribable. Yet the outcomes of the courts and their rulings varied, and Shabaab did sometimes discriminate against minority clans, for example in Bay–Bakool. At times, Shabaab's superiority in law enforcement was just an image, though in many cases it was in fact better than that of the government.

Shabaab also continued to control administrative units, although these were run more cheaply and in a more rudimentary way than during their period of territoriality. Hudeeyfa Abdirahman from the Marehan clan administered lower Shabelle, while Mohamed Abu Abdalla of the Hawadle clan nominally led the administration of lower and middle Juba where Shabaab more or less held permanent control. Sheik Guled Abu Nabhan from the Galjecel clan was put in charge of Hiiraan, while Abdulkadir Hagi from the Habargidir/Saad became the leader of South Mudug. The Shabaab veteran Hassan Yaqub maintained his position in Galguduud, while perhaps the most pragmatic Shabaab leader, Kabakutukade, led middle Shabelle.[60] In Benadir, Sheik Abdifatah from the Haber Gedir clan of Hawiye held power, while Sheik Abdullahi Moallim of the Gedoow clan was the *wali* of Bay and Bakool. These administrations still engaged in clan reconciliation and conflict meditation, and could at times show surprising degrees of pragmatism. A majority of these administrative units were in theory situated in government-controlled areas, yet they maintained the ability to extract taxes from the local population.

The Shabaab was, at the time of writing, a relatively stable organisation. It had suffered defeats since its golden age of full territorial control, but its transformation into semi-territoriality had gone surprisingly smoothly. The organisation had not broken up and it did not lack the funds necessary for its operations. This successful transformation was probably enhanced by the fact that Shabaab had existed in a semi-territorial mode before; in fact it had invented a word, *koormeer*, to describe this type of existence. The example of the

Allied Democratic Forces shows that such a presence can be stable and can sustain a jihadist organisation for years. Yet, there were hopeful signs for the Shabaab as well, namely AMISOM's withdrawal, although this has, at the time of writing, been postponed several times.[61] There are already signs that AMISOM is growing more passive, similar to Ethiopian forces before their 2009 withdrawal, yet the lessons are clear: withdrawal can lead to the territorial expansion of the jihadist group. The Somali allies of AMISOM are stronger today than in 2009, yet the precedent of the transformation into territoriality in 2009 remains alive in the memory of the Shabaab leaders. Shabaab may still transform yet another time.

10

THE ISLAMIC STATE IN SOMALIA
ON THE PERIPHERY

The Islamic State in Somalia is a small, recent organisation, ironically having a semi-territorial existence on the periphery of the area of influence of Harakat al-Shabaab. Its main area of operation is in the Golis mountain range, where the presence of the government, the autonomous Puntland State under President Farole, and the Shabaab is weak, and where it can take advantage of clan allegiances in order to survive. Such an existence is in many ways necessary for survival, as it increasingly became defeated by the Shabaab in the latter's core areas. Yet, it is also active as an illegal network further south, albeit carrying out few attacks.

While the local aspect is crucial in order to understand how the entity has survived, by tapping into local clan conflicts and political rivalries, the history of the Islamic State in Somalia is also one of global impulses, of the global influence of the Islamic State and of jihadist networks in the United Kingdom. It is also tied up with the history of the Shabaab in the north and its cleavages. The Shabaab's presence was originally formed around a local clan, the Warsangeli, and its rise was fuelled by the clan's resistance to the Puntland state's attempts to gain access for international oil companies in the territories inhabited by the clan. The clan itself had for years been rather independent from both Puntland (founded in 1998) and neighbouring Somaliland, maintaining peace with both sides. Yet Puntland's role in facilitating the search for oil in Warsangeli areas created conflict, and local groups reacted angrily at what they saw as attempts by the Puntland elites to steal their resources.[1]

Resistance flared up. One of the early groups to fight Puntland was Ahmed Jeni Tag's Defenders of Sanaag Resources (DSR), a loose outfit, secular in nature, whose original resistance had little to do with the Shabaab or al-Qaeda. However, Tag was not the only guerrilla leader drawing on the animosity against Puntland. The smuggler Mohamed Said Atom, who also held a degree in East African studies, and was probably a former member of al-Ittihad al-Islamiya, began to set up militias in the area, perhaps even before the oil exploration, but would later ride on the anti-Puntland resentment.[2] At the start, Atom based his recruitment on the Warsangeli clan, but over time strengthened his connections to Shabaab, and added an Islamist ideology to his group, allegedly naming his militia Eastern Sanaag Mujahidicen in 2008–9. According to rumours, Atom also hosted visitors from the Shabaab in his camps in this period.[3] Yet, in this early phase, the situation was complex, and Atom advanced strictly Warsangeli demands in his negotiations with the government, including the release of imprisoned clan members.[4] In the period 2009–10, when Shabaab enjoyed its golden age in the south of Somalia, Atom's militias enjoyed a similar 'golden age' in the Sanaag province, and became known by the name of the area in which they mainly operated, the Galgala mountains. However, the Warsangeli were to grow closer to Puntland again. Puntland had incorporated Warsangeli leaders in their administration, including Abdullah Jama 'Ikaljiir', who gained the powerful position of minister of the interior of Puntland.[5] The general resistance towards Puntland weakened, leaving only a hard core of fighters. Atom was one of these, as was Yasin Osman Said Kilwe from the Dubays sub-clan of the Warsangeli.[6] The fighting intensified during the summer of 2010. The group gave mixed signals about their ideological leanings: as late as December 2011, they denied any Shabaab links, but nevertheless flew black flags in their camp, and made statements about implementing Sharia as a goal. However, in 2012, when the sub-group around Atom and Kilwe declared their allegiance to the Shabaab, this became quite controversial among the Warsangeli fighters in opposition to Puntland, and some even attacked the small group because of the declaration.[7]

The Puntland offensives of 2010 had forced the Galgala group, now known as Shabaab, into new clan areas: those of the Dashishle (Yalxo, Karin and Laag), and, more important for the future Islamic State, the areas of the Ali Suleban (Dahar).[8] Operations in the latter area were made easier by a new arrival, Sheikh Abdulqadir Mumin, hailing from the Ali Suleban clan of the Majeerteen. Mumin had returned from Britain in 2010, and had developed a reputation as an ideologist, a sought-after quality in the still somewhat ideologically confused northern branch of the Shabaab.

Yet Mumin also brought with him ideological traits alien to the Shabaab. His background was in the Somali diaspora. He had first lived in Sweden before moving to the United Kingdom where eventually he was granted British citizenship. He then lived in London and Leicester, developing notoriety as a firebrand preacher at extremist mosques and in videos posted online.[9] He was a visiting preacher in a mosque in London that was frequented both by Mohammed Emwazi, 'Jihadi John', who later became famous as an executioner in videos from the Islamic State in Syria/Iraq, and by Michael Adebolajo, one of the two men jailed for the meat-cleaver murder of British Army soldier Lee Rigby at Woolwich Arsenal in 2013.[10] Mumin had even participated in a press conference of the group now known as Cageprisoners Ltd, a controversial British human rights NGO, chaired by Guantánamo Bay prisoner Moazzam Begg, set up to protect the rights of detainees in the war on terror.[11]

When arriving in Puntland, Mumin was made a religious leader of the small Shabaab group.[12] Mumin was of a different calibre from the more pragmatic Atom. Indeed, Atom defected from the Shabaab on 7 June 2014, after having been removed from the leadership as early as February 2012 by the more ideologically inclined Yasin Kilwe, and fled to the south.[13] Yasin Kilwe did not last long, stepping down in 2014, after possibly delegating operational leadership to Bashir Shire Maxamed of the Dashishle clan in 2013.[14] At this stage, Shabaab consisted of a relatively small group of 400 to 500 fighters and was under considerable pressure.

An important development occurred in 2015 in the eastern part of the Golis mountains. At that time, Abdisamad Galan, a former schoolteacher from the Ali Suleban clan of the Majeerteen, was serving as governor of Puntland's Bari region. In May 2015, Galan was sacked by Puntland's President Abdiweli Mohamed Ali and replaced by Yusuf Mohamed Dhedo. The replacement initially led to violent protests, and the Puntland security forces attempted to raid Galan's house in Bosaso. According to Galan, 200 to 300 soldiers opened fire on his home. He fled, and raised an insurgency. On 21 June, a 175-strong militia, mainly hailing from the Ali Suleban, briefly entered the town of Armo, 80 kilometres south of Bosaso, before withdrawing. A battle followed, and the insurgency continued.

Galan drew heavily upon his own clan. Many members of the Ali Suleban had regarded their clan as underrepresented in Puntland politics and its civil service and in the security forces in their home areas. Indeed, Puntland had always been weak in these areas, which contained many smuggling and piracy networks. Galan hailed from the city of Qandala, the base of one of the last major pirate leaders in Somalia, Isse Yuluhow. Qandala has long-standing smuggling ties with the Yemeni port of al-Mukalla. It is also shielded by mountainous terrain to the west that makes it virtually inaccessible to the Puntland authorities, except by sea. This meant that any uprising in this inaccessible area, drawing on Ali Suleban members, would be hard to defeat. The insurgents might also ally themselves with smuggling and pirate networks interested in keeping the Puntland authorities away. For Yasin Kilwe and Bashir Shire Maxamed, this situation was of little value, for they lacked the clan background to tap into it. However, for Abdulqadir Mumin, hailing as he did from the Ali Suleban, these developments would provide major opportunities.

The Islamic State of Somalia Emerges

The pressures faced by Shabaab and the animosity towards the Puntland State were important elements in the formation of the Islamic State in Somalia. But one should not forget that Abdulqadir Mumin was an ideologist who had been very active while in the diaspora. Mumin must also have been influenced by the passivity of the al-Qaeda network and the explosive rise of the Islamic State of Iraq and Syria (ISIS), which moved into Syria against the will of the central al-Qaeda leadership. ISIS launched an offensive against

Mosul and Tikrit in Iraq in June 2014. On 29 June, ISIS leader Abu Bakr al-Baghdadi announced the formation of a caliphate stretching from Aleppo in Syria to Diyala in Iraq, cut all ties with al-Qaeda, and renamed the group the Islamic State, claiming to be a caliphate of all Muslims, from whom it demanded loyalty. The victories of the Islamic State were many, and its references to the end-time prophecies of the Quran made it attractive for foreign fighters, who joined the organisation in large numbers. There was a synergy created by the battlefield victories of the Islamic State: other organisations joined it during 2015, including the Islamic State of Sahara and Boko Haram.[15] The Islamic State also launched a number of terror attacks, including the Charlie Hebdo episode in Paris in February 2015, which gained the organisation much attention.

The Islamic State actively attempted to persuade Shabaab's members to end their allegiance to al-Qaeda. The new Islamic State affiliates in Syria, Yemen, Sinai and Iraq, as well as Boko Haram, sent videos asking the Shabaab to align with the Islamic State. A Kenyan sheikh who in the past had supported the cause of Shabaab, Hussein Hassan, also encouraged the Shabaab to turn its allegiance to the Islamic State.[16] Moreover, the Islamic State used Somali foreign fighters in the Levant to appeal to Somalis inside the Shabaab, and actually ended the recruitment of Somalis in the West to the Shabaab. These now went to Syria and the Islamic State instead.[17]

On 22 October 2015, Mumin declared allegiance to Islamic State, perhaps influenced by the developments just described. He may have been aware of sympathies among several Shabaab sub-commanders further south for the Islamic State. However, while there were some sympathisers in central Somalia, they had a hard time facing Shabaab's secret police, Amniyat. In fact, according to the United Nations Department of Safety and Security, there had been crackdown on Islamic State supporters by the Shabaab before Mumin made his declaration, with the arrest and execution of pro-Islamic State members, including five foreign fighters who had declared support for the organisation. Ironically, it was in the area fully controlled by the Shabaab, middle Juba, that these arrests took place, and where Shabaab took effective steps to stop the Islamic State over time. A senior Amniyat member was also arrested.

The Islamic State sympathisers in middle Juba managed to defend themselves on several occasions. Around Buale, there was a small battle when Shabaab attacked a group of pro-Islamic State fighters, but the latter were defeated on 11 November. Several Islamic State sympathisers tried to escape, including Shabaab's divisional commander for Buale, but their flight ended badly when their vehicle broke down. The troubles in the vinicity of Buale nevertheless continued, and on 16 November an IS supporter was killed about nine kilometres north-west of the town. Shabaab's Amniyat units conducted a sweep in the area, and made at least six arrests. In Lowdhar, three pro-IS members were killed while one managed to escape on 22 November. In the end Bashir Bu'ul (aka Maalim Yassin), the local Shabaab commander, declared that operations against the Islamic State west of Buale had been completed. Yet the clashes continued in other places in middle Juba. On 12 December, factions supporting Islamic State and al-Qaeda clashed in Rahole village, 64 kilometres south-west of Dinsoor. Shabaab also attempted more peaceful approaches to handling Islamic State sympathisers: there was, for instance, a failed mediation meeting in Booshaar on 16 December. However, in general Shabaab had arrested or killed most open Islamic State sympathisers in middle Juba by January 2016. The Shabaab had also curtailed its rivals in its areas of permanent territorial control.[18] Outside these areas, there were also clashes, as for example in Galguduud, where there were confrontations with the moderate paramilitary group al-Sunnah wal-Jama'ah and Islamic State sympathisers in Guriel, and Shabaab made arrests as well in Gedo.

As with al-Mourabitoun in Mali, the Shabaab was on the whole more vulnerable to defections to the Islamic State on its peripheries, where IS sympathisers could hide from the weaker Shabaab units in the area or sometimes run away. Admittedly, the Islamic State established a small clandestine network in Mogadishu, which managed to launch an attack with light weapons on Somali forces based in the Sinkadir district on 5 May 2016. It also made a bomb attack targeting an African Union Mission in Somalia (AMISOM) convoy in the Tridish area of Mogadishu in late April 2016. Christopher Anzalone reports that in the period from April 2016 to February 2017, fifteen attacks took place in the Banaadir region, including Mogadishu, more than in any other region of Somalia including Puntland, though in Puntland the conflict was more an outright war and less a series of terror attacks on behalf of the Islamic State.[19] The Islamic State's activities in Mogadishu were on a much smaller scale than the Shabaab attacks, involving hit-and-run attacks on AMISOM, Somali police, army bases and checkpoints, the throwing of grenades, the planting of improvised explosive devices (IEDs), the carrying out of ambushes and targeted assassinations – all the activities characteristic of a small network-based group with limited resources.[20]

Outside Mogadishu and Puntland, the Islamic State implemented a very limited number of attacks, and none in Shabaab's core areas in lower and middle Juba, and none in Gedo and Galmudug. A short while later in April 2016, however, a second, relatively strong Islamic State-affiliated group, Jahba East Africa, was to establish itself in the forests along the coast in the border areas between Kenya and Somalia. This group boasted a presence 'on the border of Somalia' and 'deep from within Tanzania'.[21] Indeed, the group was active in the media, using foreign fighters like the German Martin Andreas Mueller in their videos, until he died.[22] Jahba East Africa operated on the fringes of the Shabaab's territory in the Lamu forests of Kenya, and suffered heavy losses, among them Mueller. Even before defecting, the group had been remote from Shabaab's central command and command lines, and Shabaab's ability to control it was limited.

Jahba included both Kenyans and Tanzanians, but had few members, and faced a large Kenyan military offensive. The number of their attacks after 2016 was limited. It was the Islamic State group in the north under Mumin that would prove stronger, using clan connections and the rough terain to avoid its enemies in the Shabaab. Admittedly, it was to be a close run for the Islamic State, even in Puntland. In November Mumin and his small band of followers battled the Shabaab in the Golis mountains, barely surviving several of the clashes and in the end fleeing to the Iskushuban district in the Bari region, the homeland of Mumin's Ali Suleban clan. Yet the escape was far from successful, and Shabaab soldiers followed Mumin's group into Bari, coming to blows with it in several battles from 24 to 26 December 2015. Rumours even circulated that Mumin had been shot. He was in fact not killed, and operated as a propaganda platform for the Islamic State to Shabaab members, condemning the Shabaab killings of their own Islamic State members who had declared allegiance to the IS and calling on Shabaab fighters to disobey orders from their commanders as a result.[23] Further south, Islamic State loyalists also stressed combat ethics in their public pronouncements and claimed that Shabaab had unnecessarily targeted civilian Muslims: 'Many are easy to convince. Their [IS] doomsday narratives are very attractive, the end of times. However, at the same time Daesh only target non-Muslim, they don't target Muslims. Daesh avoids collateral damage.'[24]

Tactically, Mumin's networks and clan background gave him several advantages. According to the International Monitoring Group on Somalia, he received material support from the pirate networks of Isse Mohamoud Yusuf 'Yullux'. He also created a base camp named in honour of Abu Nu'man al-Yintari, a fighter in southern Somalia reportedly assassinated by Shabaab after he pledged allegiance to the Islamic State. Mumin did not field a substantial army but was able to survive in the face of Shabaab's own forces in the north-east, partly because of clan support. The new group established a more solid command structure, with Mahad Moalim of the Ali Suleban clan serving as the deputy commander.[25] It also managed to enlist Abdihakim Dhuqub (Ali Suleban or Ismail Ali), a veteran al-Ittihad al-Islamiya member and Mumin's cousin. In addition, the group succeeded in gaining recognition from the central Islamic State organisation, although not as a formal *wilayat*.

For the Shabaab this was an open challenge, and according to the International Monitoring Group's interviews with participants, the Shabaab attempted to send some 350 to 400 fighters, in the so-called Khalid ibn al-Walid brigade, in March 2016 to defeat Mumin. However, they were deployed far south in the Harardhere province because of fear of the international naval presence. The Puntland forces struck back in Operation Thunder. According to public statements from Puntland, 208 fighters were killed, mostly during the fighting near the town of Garacad, the rest fleeing south.

An Attempt to Gain Territorial Control? The Attack on Qandala

The Islamic State held several advantages in the north. It operated in an area with deep clan-based animosities against the central government in the Puntland region, and could draw upon the grievances of the Ali Suleban clan, some of whom, like the former governor Abdisamad Galan, were already fighting Puntland. Additionally, the Islamic State's new unit in northern Somalia acquired another advantage when, in the southern parts of Puntland, fighting broke out with the Galmudug regional state, fuelled by an old conflict. The centre of this conflict was the divided city of Galkayo, an economic hub.[26] Puntland had to prioritise this conflict, in terms of providing both soldiers and funds to purchase ammunition.

Parts of Bari are remote from the main garrisons of the Darawisha, the Puntland paramilitary force, with the city of Qandala being fourteen hours on a rough road from Bosaso. The city had never been fully under Puntland control. In fact, it was dominated by pirates from 2008 to 2013, with a strong presence of syndicates smuggling humans and arms. On the eve of the attack by the Islamic State, it had ten lightly armed police officers.[27]

On 26 October, a group of fighters from the Islamic State, estimated to have been around eighty, entered the city, walking openly about and unopposed, partly because Puntland had no military presence there.[28] The groups that could have stopped the Islamic State fighters – the cartels smuggling arms and people and the former pirates – ignored the small group, who hoisted the black flag over an old colonial building and gave a speech. However, the central Islamic State did not ignore the event, with the Amaq and al-Furat news sites publishing videos of the happenings the same day.[29]

The events were an embarrassment for Puntland, which hesitated to attack the Islamic State forces. The Ali Suleban had created several checkpoints along the road, and moves against these could have upset the negotiations already under way. Secondly, the Puntland authorities did not really know where the loyalty of the smugglers and pirates lay, especially the group of Isse Yuhulow, which had considerable firepower in the area. There were indications that the latter had provided support to the Islamic State in the past. There were also rumours of ammunition shortages among the Darwish units in the north. Lastly, it was necessary to keep watch on the Shabaab forces that were still in Galgala.

The fighting within Galkayo did, however, subside. There was a ceasefire, though it was often broken. On 8 November, heavy clashes between the parties ensued. The Puntland and the Galmudug presidents managed to calm things down. Several meetings took place, one of the largest occurring on 12 November, which included the United Nations special representative to Somalia and the Somali prime minister. Two committees were set up and an agreement was reached to schedule a further meeting on 20 November. The committees handled a flare-up of the fighting on 16 November quite efficiently, and by 18 November a demilitarised zone was created in Galkayo. Although sporadic gunfire occurred after this, the leaders of the parties managed to reduce tensions and established stronger mechanisms of communication. The negotiations with Galan also created a form of peace, and the Puntland authority approached the Ali Suleban elders. Yet preparations for a counter-attack took a long time. By late November, an offensive against Qandala was mounted with units of the Puntland Darawisha, together with the Puntland Maritime Police Force (PMPF), a relatively well-equipped coast guard force funded by the United Arab Emirates, and Ali Suleban clan militias. In the end, the major pirate leader, Isse Yusuf, also joined the Puntland forces. As in the golden age of piracy in the Caribbean, pirates were used as privateers in war, this time onshore.[30]

Slowly, this counter-attacking force approached Qandala. On 4 December, the Islamic State and the Darawisha clashed while the latter was engaged in de-mining south of Qandala. Although the PMPF had established itself at Afbashaashin, 35 kilometres south-west of Qandala, it was the Darawisha that were to see the brunt of the fighting. In the following days, the Darawisha advanced, while the Islamic State laid out mines to defend its areas. On 7 December, the Darawisha recaptured Qandala and, according to the Puntland authorities, killed 33 Islamic State fighters and wounded 35.[31]

Although the authorities may have overstated the numbers, the battle amounted in fact to a substantial loss for the Islamic State, combined with the losses it had suffered in the days before. The remaining forces fled into the mountains, later consolidating in the Ladid range. The group was relatively silent until 27 January when it ambushed a civilian truck close to Karimo, taking Darawish soldiers in the vehicle as prisoners. Three of them who had participated in the Qandala offensive were later beheaded. However, on 4 February, the Islamic State blocked the supply of water to the village of Toox to put pressure on the villagers to support them, but the Darawisha hit back. Sporadic convoy attacks continued, often using IEDs before a conventional attack, and the Islamic State entered villages relatively freely, as in Dahsaan and Jaceyl, forcing villagers to provide them with food. There was also an attack against a local representative of a large telecommunications company. After the attack on Qandala, the Islamic State gave up the attempt to hold territory and slowly transformed back into semi-territoriality. The number of attacks against Puntland forces was small, much smaller than those of the remaining Shabaab in the north-east, who were highly active throughout 2017 (though they also suffered losses).

The Islamic State in Somalia, like the Islamic State in Greater Sahara, had carved out an existence on the periphery both of rival factions loyal to al-Qaeda and of their more secular enemies. The two actively used local grievances and clan or tribal protection in order to survive. For its part, the Islamic State in Somalia did attempt to hold territory, a single city, but in the end failed, incurring in the process relatively big losses for such a small group. At the time of writing, it is suffering another loss, as the prestige of the mother organisation in Iraq–Syria has been dented by its territorial losses and the resulting loss of status. However, as the other organisations in this book show, it is possible to survive in a state of semi-territoriality for decades. Because the Islamic State in Somalia is so small, it is dependent on individuals like Mumin; and assassination attempts – like the United States attacks against the group in November 2017 – may have serious consequences for its survival. Yet the dwindling central Islamic State rewarded the group with the fully fledged status of *wilayat* in December 2017.

11

CONCLUSIONS

There are several notable insights that a comparative study of African jihadist groups unlocks. Some of them have already been revealed in chapter 2. The mechanisms for obtaining income, gaining recruits, creating cohesion and discipline will vary according to the group's territorial presence, and any policies dealing with these organisations should take this into account. The clandestine network phase is the great filter of jihadist organisations: some do not make it beyond this stage, some are defeated or seriously curtailed when operating as a clandestine network, and they end at this point. To proceed to the stage of territoriality or semi-territoriality, the jihadists' opponents need to be weak or weakened. At times, the organisation, having suffered defeats in its clandestine form, moves into a periphery, an area with fewer state institutions that may have existed for some time. Shabaab, for instance, took advantage of the anarchy in the countryside and the lack of presence of the Somali government. In some cases, organisations like Boko Haram, Ansar Dine and Shabaab managed to defeat their enemies or, in the case of Somalia, saw their withdrawal before they achieved territorial control. However, in Africa territorial control by a jihadist organisation has always resulted in foreign intervention, as the regional powers and sometimes the international actors simply do not tolerate such control. There are good reasons for this lack of tolerance, as shown by the example of various Malian jihadists and by the Shabaab, for territorial control is used to attack outsiders, and it can also help to establish new groups or reinvigorate old ones outside the area of control.

It is important to realise that jihadist groups transform over time, and it is therefore erroneous to look for the static essence of a group, an 'eternal' and unchanging Shabaab or Boko Haram. What this means is that any comparative framework needs to be based on organisational history and dynamics rather than a simple fixed typology. As this book shows, most of the organisations have, during some parts of their history, passed through similar stages, and occupied similar kinds of territorial presence. Adding to the complexity is the layer of international networks creating a diffusion of ideas and people, though this is less common than believed. Money, the influence of local conflicts over mundane matters such as cattle and resources, and old rivalries are also significant.

The most important insight of this book is perhaps the concept of semi-territoriality. Repeatedly, it has been alleged that the largest jihadist organisations in Africa have been defeated in campaigns, and vanquished. Yet they have survived. The failure to understand this phenomenon is perhaps due to an interest on the part of many observers and commentators in the spectacular, the 'funds sent from al-Qaeda' or the major terrorist attacks. However, it is not these events or financial channels that feed the jihadists. It is rather the plight of the countryside, where military doctrine focused on 'bunkering' and self-protection, a lack of will and lack of resources all ensure that there is little protection for locals, not only against bandits, but also against the jihadists. The jihadists can pressure the locals and tax them, and in turn the locals see the need to integrate with the jihadists and build a friendly relationship with them to survive. Little progress has been made on these issues: the countryside in Africa, and its local farmers and herders, are neglected, and the safety of these groups often tends to be ignored. In some cases pure geography, in combination with the limited resources of the state, hampers government efforts. However, without the provision of safety to local farmers and herders, there will be no end to the wars in the countries studied here.

The jihadists have other advantages: they often use the existence of a corrupt state in their propaganda, presenting themselves as an alternative, focusing on law and order. Yet, in the day-to-day exercise of justice, the image is somewhat (though not always) more complicated. Organisations like Boko Haram in general neglect justice provision, although rhetoric about advancing justice was important at the start, and emerged as a cause for the break-up of the organisation. Shabaab, for its part, had great difficulty in creating a court system and in preventing discrimination. The harsh punishments based on Sharia also became more notorious as territorial control grew, creating more sceptical and ambivalent feelings towards the jihadists.

The issue of 'jihad and justice' has been essential for the Islamic State's attempts at a breakthrough in Africa. This was highly important in the anti-Shabaab and al-Qaeda rhetoric launched in Somalia by some of the Islamic State's sympathisers in the south. It was also at the heart of Barnawi's attacks on Shekau during their ongoing conflict within Boko Haram. While the idea of collateral damage at times meant little for the Islamic State in the Levant, it did have meaning for important affiliates in sub-Saharan Africa.

This book dispels another myth: that of a localised al-Qaeda versus a globalised Islamic State. Both the Islamic State in the Greater Sahara and the Islamic State in Somalia are just as embedded in a local tribal/clan reality as are al-Qaeda's affiliates in their areas, if not more so; and both factions of Boko Haram maintain a local focus. Al-Qaeda's affiliates in Africa are not more 'tribalised' than the Islamic State's: they are very similar in this matter.

Such observations do suggest that this pattern can be repeated outside Africa: that the Islamic State will follow the path of al-Qaeda, with a weakened centre, perhaps operating in a semi-territorial configuration, and as increasingly locally focused affiliates, influenced by ethnic, tribal and clan dynamics as well as local conflicts. It could be argued that the Islamic State's affiliates in sub-Saharan Africa provide a special case, but it should be remembered that several of the other Islamic State affiliates in Libya, Afghanistan and Sinai are exposed to relatively similar mechanisms. The jihadists in general are also masters of taking advantage of local grievances, reinterpreting them in the light of the global jihad.

Clans and ethnic groups can act as a resource for the jihadists. A common pattern found in this book is that all the jihadists studied here gained a form of semi-territorial or territorial control, using their members who belonged to local tribes or clans to establish an initial foothold. The organisations often gained tribal or clan protection when they were weak, as was the case in Mali, Cameroon, Niger, Congo, Somalia and even Kenya. As the strength of the organisation in question grows, the tribal or clan authorities can be challenged or harnessed in an instrumental way. These initial steps into new territories are often misunderstood, with the result that the first jihadist activities are often interpreted as ethnically or tribally defined. Yet the reality is more complex, in many areas consisting of a prolonged interaction in which the tribes or clans attempt to take advantage of the radicals, while the radicals attempt to control the tribes or clans. Sometimes jihadists and tribes end up as allies against other groups. The result of this process is often hard to predict. What is certain is that tribal/clan identities are not as strong rivals to the jihadists as state structures. Jihadists can gain the upper hand in such struggles, while spaces without a state presence are far from 'ungoverned': they provide some advantages to a jihadist organisation, compared to the situation experienced by a clandestine network that is opposed by a relatively efficient state. The advantage with the latter scenario is of course the closer presence of potential targets for international terrorism.

There has been an ongoing debate between 'localists', on the one hand, who draw upon local dynamics to explain the jihadist organisations, often consisting of scholars from area studies and African studies, and 'globalists', on the other, who focus on the global links, often consisting of experts from terrorism and security studies. There have been too many simplifications in this debate. It is clear by now, thanks to documents retrieved in Afghanistan, and to defections and diaries, that there exists a comprehensive network that has stretched to most of the countries of the region. However, it is also clear that many of the dynamics explaining the activity of the organisations are local. The local elements, including personal rivalries, are highly important, and it is local sources of revenue that keep the organisations alive. None of the organisations studied in this book are 'puppets' of mother organisations such as al-Qaeda and the Islamic State: they have their own agenda, and it is unlikely that they will, for example, target the West outside of Africa. That does not mean they are without agency in the wider world, for they contribute to general discussions between the Islamic State and al-Qaeda, and to the rivalry between the two, and, in the case of the Harakat al-Shabaab, at times encourage attacks in the West through their media. A discussion of the global networks should not be neglected. They can tell us about the possibility of new jihadist groups emerging. Global links help to form strategy and tactics, and to create the potential for ideological cracks that can either lead to fragmentation or be used by aspiring leaders to build a base for their own powers.

The largest ideological crack was perhaps the emergence of the Islamic State. Yet the problems created by this emergence also illustrate the strengths of many of the organisations studied here. In the case of Jama'at Nusrat ul-Islam wal-Muslimin' and the Harakat al-Shabaab, their offshoots loyal to the Islamic State only managed to survive on the peripheries of the areas where the original organisations kept semi-territorial or territorial control. Indeed, sub-Saharan Africa was not a success for the Islamic State, with only Boko Haram among the region's larger organisations inclining in its direction, though it also fragmented in the process.

While global networks remain important, local activities and local income-generating mechanisms are much more important in understanding these organisations. The secret to the survival of the African jihadists is not mundane, global or even spectacular; it is the suffering and plight of the African herders and small farmers under the control of these groups. Their voices are often not heard, and as long as this remains so, the jihadist organisations studied in this book, some with roots already extending decades back, can continue to exist in the coming decades, while ongoing government military offensives transform them rather than truly defeating them.

NOTES

1. INTRODUCTION

1. Stig Jarle Hansen, *Al-Shabaab in Somalia: The History of an African Islamist Group 2005–2012*, London: Hurst, 2013.

2. Alex Crawford, 'Somali president says terrorists are defeated', Sky News, 2 May 2014, http://news.sky.com/story/somali-president-says-terrorists-are-defeated-10447016 (accessed 1 November 2016); David Alexander, 'U.S. confirms death of al Shabaab leader Godane in Somalia strike', Reuters, 5 September 2014, http://www.reuters.com/article/us-somalia-usa-islamist-idUSKBN0H01OO20140905 (accessed 1 November 2016); Andrew V. Pestano, 'Nigerian army says Boko Haram defeated; group's disputed leader vows to fight on', UP, 19 August 2016, http://www.upi.com/Top_News/World-News/2016/08/09/Nigerian-army-says-Boko-Haram-defeated-groups-disputed-leader-vows-to-fight-on/2041470753181/ (accessed 1 November 2016); Ryan Cummings, 'Opinion: Boko Haram and the defeat that never was', CNN, 1 January 2016, http://www.cnn.com/2016/01/01/opinions/nigeria-boko-haram-fight/ (accessed 1 November 2016).

3. John Cassidy, 'The facts about terrorism', *The New Yorker*, 24 February 2014, http://www.newyorker.com/news/john-cassidy/the-facts-about-terrorism (accessed 25 October 2016).

4. Mark Sedgwick, 'Jihadism, narrow and wide: The dangers of loose use of an important term', *Perspectives on Terrorism*, 9 (2), 2015.

5. Adekano Adesoji, 'The Boko Haram uprising and Islamic revivalism in Nigeria', *Africa Spectrum*, 45 (2), 2010, pp. 95–108.

6.   Hansen, *Al-Shabaab in Somalia*; Norman Cigar and Stephanie E. Kramer, *Al-Qaida after Ten Years of War: A Global Perspective of Successes, Failures, and Prospects*, Washington: Marine Corps, 2012; Andrew McGregor, 'Ugandan rebel movement reemerges along oil-bearing Ugandan/Congolese border', *Terrorism Monitor*, 11 (15), 2013, http://www.refworld.org/docid/5204f9e64.html (accessed 15 August 2013).

7.   Valentina Soria, 'Global jihad sustained through Africa', *UK Terrorism Analysis*, no. 2, April 2012.

8.   Mazrui quoted in Stig Jarle Hansen, Atle Mesøy and Tuncay Karadas, *The Borders of Islam*, London: Hurst, 2009, p. 111.

9.   Ahmad Salkida Maiduguri, 'The story of Nigeria's first suicide bomber', *Blueprint Magazine*, 26 June 2011, http://saharareporters.com/newspage/story-nigerias-first-suicide-bomber-blueprint-magazine; Hansen, *Al-Shabaab in Somalia*; Soria, 'Global jihad sustained through Africa'.

10. Hansen, *Al-Shabaab in Somalia*.

11. For an alarmist approach, see Douglas Farah and Richard Shultz, 'Al Qaeda's growing sanctuary', *Washington Post*, 14 July 2004, p. 19. For a more instrumentalist approach from this period, see International Crisis Group, 'Somalia: Countering terrorism in a failed state', Africa Report, no. 45, 23 May 2002.

12. In this sense it follows Jean-Luc Marret's idea of 'glocal'. See Jean-Luc Marret, 'Al-Qaeda in Islamic Maghreb: A "glocal" organization', *Studies in Conflict and Terrorism*, 31 (6), 2008.

13. Jim Berger, 'War on error', *Foreign Policy*, 2 February 2014.

14. Eyder Peralta, 'Sunni extremist group ISIS declares new Islamic Caliphate', NPR, 29 June 2014, http://www.npr.org/blogs/thetwo-way/2014/06/29/326703823/al-qaida-splinter-group-isis-declares-new-islamic-caliphate (accessed 9 July 2014).

15. Boaz Ganor, *The Counter-Terrorism Puzzle: A Guide for Decision Makers*, New Brunswick, NJ: Transaction Publishers, 2005; Boaz Ganor, 'Defining terrorism: Is one man's terrorist another man's freedom fighter?', *Police Practice and Research: An International Journal*, 3 (4), 2002.

16. Mark Sedgwick, 'Jihadism, narrow and wide: The dangers of loose use of an important term', Perspectives on Terrorism, 9 (2), 2015.

17. The definition is based on the *Oxford Living English Dictionary*: 'An organized group of people with a particular purpose, such as a business or government department', https://en.oxforddictionaries.com/definition/organization (accessed 10 November 2016).

18. See for example Jacob Zenn, 'Leadership analysis of Boko Haram and Ansaru in Nigeria', *CTC Sentinel*, 7 (2), 2014; Hansen, *Al-Shabaab in Somalia*; Virginia Comolli, *Boko Haram: Nigeria's Islamist Insurgency*,

London: Hurst, 2016; Kristof Titeca and Koen Vlassenroot, 'Rebels without borders in the Rwenzori borderland? A biography of the Allied Democratic Forces', *Journal of Eastern African Studies*, 6 (1), 2012; Aisha Ahmad, 'The security bazaar: Business interests and Islamist power in civil war Somalia', *International Security*, 39 (3), 2016; Mike Smith, *Boko Haram: Inside Nigeria's Unholy War*, London: I.B. Tauris, 2016; Laurent de Castelli, 'From sanctuary to Islamic State', *RUSI Journal*, 159 (3), 2014; Djallil Lounnas, 'Confronting al-Qa'ida in the Islamic Maghrib in the Sahel: Algeria and the Malian crisis', *Journal of North African Studies*, 19 (5), 2014; Nicholas Primo, 'No music in Timbuktu: A brief analysis of the conflict in Mali and Al Qaeda's rebirth', *Pepperdine Policy Review*, 6, 2013; Hussein Solomon, 'Mali: West Africa's Afghanistan', *RUSI Journal*, 158 (1), 2013.

19. Gregory Alonso Pirio, *The African Jihad*, Trenton, NJ: Red Sea Press, 2007.

20. Hussein Solomon, *Terrorism and Counter-terrorism in Africa: Fighting Insurgency from al-Shabaab, Ansar Dine and Boko Haram*, London: Palgrave Macmillan, 2015.

21. See Caitriona Dowd and Clionadh Raleigh, 'The myth of global Islamic terrorism and local conflict in Mali and the Sahel', *African Affairs*, 112 (448), 2013; Caitriona Dowd, 'Grievances, governance and Islamist violence in sub-Saharan Africa', *Journal of Modern African Studies*, 53 (4), 2015.

22. José Manuel Pureza, Mark Duffield, Robert Matthews, Susan Woodward and David Sogge, 'Peacebuilding and failed states, some theoretical notes', *Oficina do CES*, 250, 2007.

23. Ken Menkhaus, 'Terrorist activities in ungoverned spaces: Evidence and observations from the Horn of Africa', paper prepared for the Southern Africa and International Terrorism Workshop, 25–27 January 2007, South Africa.

24. Dowd and Raleigh, 'The myth of global Islamic terrorism', p. 506.

25. Clint Watts, Jacob Shapiro and Vahid Brown, 'Al-Qaida's (mis)adventures in the Horn of Africa', CTC Harmony Project, Special report, 2007.

26. Rebecca Evans, 'Find the white widow: Fingerprints confirm terror suspect is British mother, say Kenyan detectives', *Daily Mail*, 6 March 2012, http://www.dailymail.co.uk/news/article-2110694/Find-white-widow-Fingerprints-confirm-terror-suspect-IS-British-mother-say-Kenyan-detectives.html#ixzz34APZTxMr (accessed 10 June 2014).

27. In the latter case, a state can of course support a violent jihadist organisation clandestinely, as Eritrea did in Shabaab's early phases. See Hansen, *Al-Shabaab in Somalia*.

28. For other examples of this, see Ahmad, 'The security bazaar'; Stig Jarle Hansen, 'Civil war economies, the hunt for profit and the incentives for peace', AE Working Paper 1, 2006, University of Bath and University of Mogadishu.

29. Angel Rabasa, Steven Boraz, Peter Chalk, Kim Cragin, Theodore W. Karasik, Jennifer D.P. Moroney, Kevin A. O'Brien and John E. Peters, 'Ungoverned territories: A unique front in the war on terrorism', RAND Brief, 2007.

30. William Reno, *Warlord Politics and African States*, Boulder, CO: Lynne Rienner Publishers, 1999.

31. Paul Collier and Anke Hoeffler, 'Greed and grievance in civil war', *Oxford Economic Papers*, 56 (4), 2004; Paul Collier and Anke Hoeffler, 'On the incidence of civil war in Africa', *Journal of Conflict Resolution*, 46 (1), 2002.

32. See for example Collier and Hoeffler, 'Greed and grievance in civil war'.

33. See for example Neil Cooper, 'State collapse as business: The role of conflict trade and the emerging control agenda', *Development and Change*, 33 (5), 2002, pp. 935–955; Mats Berdal, 'How "new" are "new wars"? Global economic change and the study of civil wars', *Global Governance*, 9 (4), 2003, pp. 477–502; Mats Berdal, 'Beyond greed and grievance – and not too soon…', *Review of International Studies*, Autumn 2004.

34. See for example Roland Bensted, 'A critique of Paul Collier's "greed and grievance" thesis of civil war', *African Security*, 20 (3), 2011.

35. Andrew Lebovich, 'AQIM's Mokhtar Belmokhtar speaks out', *Al Wasat*, 21 November 2011; Raby Ould Idoumou, 'AQIM under siege', *Magharebia*, 13 January 2012.

36. Ibid.

37. For writers suggesting a weak or non-existing link, see Thomas Hegghammer, *Jihad in Saudi Arabia: Violence and Pan-Islamism since 1979*, Cambridge: Cambridge University Press, 2010; Alan B. Krueger, *What Makes a Terrorist? Economics and the Roots of Terrorism*, Princeton: Princeton University Press, 2007; Marc Sageman, *Understanding Terror Networks*, Philadelphia: University of Pennsylvania Press, 2004; James A. Piazza, 'Poverty, minority economic discrimination and domestic terrorism', *Journal of Peace Research*, 48 (3), 2011, pp. 339–353. See Atle Mesøy, 'Poverty and radicalisation into violent extremism: A causal link?', NOREF paper, January 2012, for a useful critique of these papers.

38. Alan B. Krueger, and Jitka Maleckova, 'Education, poverty, political violence and terrorism: Is there a causal connection?', NBER Working Paper 9074, 2002. For a more popularised version of the argument, see Alan B. Krueger, 'To avoid terrorism, end poverty and ignorance.

Right? Guess again!', *New York Times*, 13 December 2001, or Alan B. Krueger and Jitka Maleckova, 'The economics and the education of suicide bombers: Does poverty cause terrorism?', *New Republic*, 24 June 2002.

39.　Brynjar Lia and Katja Skjølberg, 'Causes of terrorism: An expanded and updated review of the literature', FFI Report 04307, 2005.

40.　Hansen, *Al-Shabaab in Somalia*; Steven Candia, 'ADF recruiting in Kampala, says defector', *New Vision*, 11 April 2013; M. Lowen, 'Kenyan al-Shabaab terror recruits in it for the money', BBC, 29 January 2014.

41.　Luis de la Calle and Ignacio Sánchez-Cuenca, 'Rebels without a territory: An analysis of nonterritorial conflicts in the world, 1970–1997', *Journal of Conflict Resolution*, 56 (4), 2012, pp. 580–603.

2.　DEVELOPING A TYPOLOGY OF TERRITORIAL PRESENCE

1.　For a description of the al-Qaeda network in Western Europe, see National Commission on Terrorist Attacks upon the United States, *The 9/11 Commission Report: Final Report of the National Commission on Terrorist Attacks upon the United States*, Washington DC: National Commission on Terrorist Attacks upon the United States, 2004; Petter Nesser, 'Joining jihadi terrorist cells in Europe: Exploring motivational aspects of recruitment and radicalization', in Magnus Ranstorp (ed.), *Understanding Violent Radicalization: Terrorist and Jihadist Movements in Europe*, New York: Routledge, 2010.

2.　William Reno, 'Insurgency movements in Africa', in Paul B. Rich and Isabelle Duyvesteyn (eds.), *The Routledge Handbook of Insurgency and Counterinsurgency*, London: Routledge, 2012, p. 160.

3.　Lovise Aalen, *The Politics of Ethnicity in Ethiopia: Actors, Power and Mobilization under Ethnic Federalism*, Leiden: Brill, 2011.

4.　See Ibrahim Ward, *The Price of Fear: Al-Qaeda and the Truth behind the Financial War on Terror*, New York: I.B. Tauris, 2007 for more information on the financial controls and the channels used by al-Qaeda pre-9/11.

5.　For an overview of Western Islamist terror networks, see Petter Nesser, 'Jihad in Europe: Patterns in terrorist cell formation and behavior, 1995–2010', PhD thesis, University of Oslo, 2011.

6.　Jeanne Giraldo and Harold Trinkunas, *Terrorist Financing and State Responses: A Comparative Perspective*, Stanford, CA: Stanford University Press, 2007, p. 16.

7.　Aaron Zelinsky and Martin Shubik, 'Research note: Terrorist groups as business firms: A new typological framework', *Terrorism and Political Violence*, 21 (2), 2009, pp. 327–336.

8.   Audrey Kurth Cronin, *How Terrorism Ends: Understanding the Decline and Demise of Terrorist Campaigns*, Princeton: Princeton University Press, 2010.

9.   Petter Nesser, 'How did Europe's global jihadis obtain training for their militant causes?', *Terrorism and Political Violence*, 20 (2), 2008.

10. Ibid.

11. Mia Bloom, 'Constructing expertise: Terrorist recruitment and "talent spotting" in the PIRA, al-Qaeda, and ISIS', *Studies in Conflict and Terrorism*, 20, September 2016 (online version).

12. Cronin, *How Terrorism Ends*; Leonard Weinberg and Arie Perliger, 'How terrorist groups end', *CTC Sentinel*, 3 (2), 2010, pp. 16–18; Jenna Jordan, 'When heads roll: Assessing the effectiveness of leadership decapitation', *Security Studies*, 18 (4), 2009, pp. 719–755; Seth G. Jones and Martin C. Libiki, 'How terrorist groups end', Los Angeles: RAND Report, 2008; Rogelio Alonso, 'Why do terrorists stop? Analyzing why ETA members abandon or continue with terrorism', *Studies in Conflict and Terrorism*, 34 (9), 2011, pp. 696–716; Mary Beth Altier, C.N. Thoroughgood and John Horgan, 'Turning away from terrorism: Lessons from psychology, sociology and criminology', *Journal of Peace Research*, 51 (5), 2014, pp. 647–661; Omar Ashour, 'Post-jihadism: Libya and the global transformations of armed Islamic movements', *Terrorism and Political Violence*, 23 (3), 2011, pp. 377–397; Kate Barelle, 'Pro-integration: Disengagement from and life after extremism', *Behavioral Sciences of Terrorism and Political Aggression*, 7 (2), 2015, pp. 129–142.

13. Giraldo and Trinkunas, *Terrorist Financing and State Responses*.

14. Ward, *The Price of Fear*.

15. See ibid.; Weinberg and Perliger, 'How terrorist groups end'; Jordan, 'When heads roll'; Jones and Libiki, 'How terrorist groups end'; Alonso, 'Why do terrorists stop?'; Altier, Thoroughgood and Horgan, 'Turning away from terrorism'; Ashour, 'Post-jihadism'; Barelle, ' Pro-integration'.

16. Caitriona Dowd and Clionadh Raleigh, 'The myth of global Islamic terrorism and local conflict in Mali and the Sahel', *African Affairs*, 112 (448), 2013, p. 506.

17. See chapter 6 in this book.

18. See Kavita Khory, 'Pakistan: Have the chickens come home to roost?', in Stig J. Hansen, Atle Mesøy and Tuncay Kardas, *The Borders of Islam: Exploring Huntington's Faultlines, from Al-Andalus to the Virtual Ummah*, London: Hurst, 2009.

19. J.T. Caruso, Testimony of J.T. Caruso, Acting Assistant Director, Counter-Terrorism Division, FBI, before the Subcommittee on International Operations and Terrorism, Committee on Foreign Relations, United States Senate, 18 December 2001.

20. Jonathan Schanzer, *Al Qaeda's Armies: Middle Eastern Affiliated Groups*, Washington: Washington Institute for Near East Policy, 2005. Washington, Pakistan and Saudi Arabia accepted Taliban as the government of Afghanistan from 1997, though no other countries did. On the periphery of this category lie examples such as Shabaab's existence under the Sharia courts movement in Mogadishu in 2005–6, and President Saleh's and Zia-ul-Haq's acceptance of radical jihadist-inspired groups as political allies in Yemen and Pakistan respectively.

21. Alex de Waal, 'Mission without end? Peacekeeping in the African political marketplace', *International Affairs*, 85 (1), 2009.

22. Morten Bøås and Kevin C. Dunn, *African Guerrillas: Raging against the Machine*, Boulder, CO: Lynne Rienner, 2007.

23. Steven Metz, 'Rethinking insurgency', in Rich and Duyvesteyn (eds.), *The Routledge Handbook of Insurgency and Counterinsurgency*, Abingdon and New York: Routledge, 2014.

24. Ibid. It is notable that Western countries and their special forces have used the same technique of employing non-state armed groups as tools in conflict zones. Geraint Hughes, 'Intelligence-gathering, special operations and air-strikes in modern counterinsurgency', in Rich and Duyvesteyn (eds.), *The Routledge Handbook of Insurgency and Counterinsurgency*, Abingdon and New York: Routledge, 2014.

25. Al-Qaeda had great differences with Turabism when it came to gender issues, with the general Takfirism of Wahhabism, and with the Taliban on global scope and the distant enemy. Max Taylor and Mohamed E. Elbushra, 'Research note: Hassan al-Turabi, Osama bin Laden, and al-Qaeda in Sudan', *Terrorism and Political Violence*, 18 (3), 2006, pp. 449–464; Josh Schott, 'The differences between the Taliban and al-Qaeda', *e-IR*, 2012, http://www.e-ir.info/2012/11/17/the-differences-between-the-taliban-and-al-qaeda/ (accessed 20 September 2016).

26. Interview with Sharif Hassan Sheikh Aden, 27 July 2018.

27. 'US General says Boko Haram still holds territory in Nigeria', *Sahara Reporters*, 11 March 2016, http://saharareporters.com/2016/03/11/us-general-says-boko-haram-still-holds-territory-nigeria (accessed 15 November 2016).

28. Interview by email with Somali elder, 24 November 2016.

29. See William Reno, *Corruption and State Politics in Sierra Leone*, New York: Cambridge University Press, 1995; William Reno, *Warlord Politics and African States*, Boulder, CO: Lynne Rienner, 1998.

30. Jeffrey Herbst, *States and Power in Africa: Comparative Lessons in Authority and Control*, Princeton, NJ: Princeton University Press, 2000, p. 5. An alternative strategy to attempt to control these areas is to delegate

responsibilities to private groups through funds and patronage, not dissimilar to the strategy employed by Ethiopia and the United States against the early Shabaab, pitting warlords against them.

31. Stephen Biddle, Jeffrey A. Friedman and Jacob N. Shapiro, 'Testing the surge', *International Security*, 37 (1), 2012, pp. 22–24.

32. Ibid.

33. Ibid.

34. Paul Simpson, A *Brief Guide to Stephen King*, New York: Little, Brown, 2014, p. 100.

35. Biddle, Friedman and Shapiro, 'Testing the surge', pp. 20–21.

36. For examples from Somalia, see 'Al-Shabaab and forced marriage', Landinfo, response note, 6 July 2012, http://www.landinfo.no/asset/2156 (accessed 10 September 2016).

37. For a stronger elaboration of this effect, see Macartan Humphreys and Jeremy M. Weinstein, 'Who fights? The determinants of participation in civil war', *American Journal of Political Science*, 52 (2), 2008, pp. 449–450.

38. See Stig Jarle Hansen, 'Civil war economies, the hunt for profit and the incentives for peace', 'Enemies or Allies' project, Working Paper 1, 2006, University of Bath and University of Mogadishu.

39. Interview with anonymous *amenokal*, 19 March 2018, Bamako.

40. See Alice Hills, 'Insurgency, counter-insurgency and policing', in Rich and Duyvesteyn, *The Routledge Handbook of Insurgency and Counterinsurgency*, London: Routledge, 2012, pp. 98–100.

41. Ibid., p. 98.

42. David Kilcullen, *Out of the Mountains: The Coming Age of the Urban Guerrilla*, London: Hurst, 2013, pp. 117–168.

43. Interview with an entrepreneur from Kidal, November–December 2017, conducted by anonymous researcher of the JWE project.

44. Nelson Kasfir, 'Rebel governance, constructing a field of inquiry: Definitions, scope, patterns, order, causes', in Aronja, Kasfir and Mampilly (eds.), *Rebel Governance in Civil War*, London: Cambridge University Press, 2017.

45. Stathis N. Kalyvas, 'The ontology of "political violence": Action and identity in civil wars', *Perspectives on Politics*, 1 (3), 2003.

46. Hansen, 'Civil war economies, the hunt for profit and the incentives for peace'.

47. Morten S. Hopperstad, Øyvind Gustavsen and Amund Bakke Foss, 'Dette er den enøyde terrorlederen', *VG*, 16 June 2015.

48. As will be shown later, it has been estimated that AQIM generated as much as 70 million dollars in ransom payments alone between 2006

and 2011. William Thornberry and Jaclyn Levy, 'Al-Qaeda in the Islamic Maghreb', AQAM Future Projects Case Studies Series, 4, 2011.

49. Shabaab is said to have generated some 25 million dollars from the charcoal industry in Somalia before their loss of Kismayo town in 2012, and still generates the same amount through taxing in the area. The organisation also derives a substantial income from checkpoints; see Monitoring Group on Somalia and Eritrea, 'Report of the Monitoring Group on Somalia and Eritrea pursuant to Security Council Resolution 2060 (2012): Somalia', S/2013/413, 2013, p. 38.

50. Stig Jarle Hansen, 'Somalia', *Africa Yearbook*, vol. 11, 2016, pp. 342–350.

51. There have been cases where an insurgency movement has built such structures after conquering and holding territories. See for example Zachariah C. Mampilly, *Rebel Rulers: Insurgent Governance and Civilian Life during War*, Chapel Hill, NC: Cornell University Press, 2015.

52. Brynjar Lia, 'Understanding jihadi proto-states', *Perspectives on Terrorism*, 9 (4), 2015; William McCants, *The ISIS Apocalypse: The History, Strategy, and Doomsday Vision of the Islamic State*, New York: St Martin's Press, 2016; Michael Weiss and Hassan Hassan, *ISIS: Inside the Army of Terror*, New York: Regan Arts, 2015; Jessica Stern and Jim Berger, *ISIS: The State of Terror*, New York: HarperCollins, 2016.

53. Mampilly, *Rebel Rulers*, p. 39.

54. Jim Berger, 'War on error', *Foreign Policy*, 2 February 2014.

55. Robert W. McColl, 'The insurgent state: Territorial bases of revolution', *Annals of the Association of American Geographers*, 59 (4), 1969, p. 614.

56. In the European context, see Petter Nesser, *Islamist Terrorism in Europe: A History*, London: Hurst, 2014. Thomas Hegghammer indicates that one out of nine foreign fighters are involved in terror plots. Thomas Hegghammer, 'The rise of Muslim foreign fighters: Islam and the globalization of jihad', *International Security*, 35 (3), 2010. The article does not consider the differences between organisations and is simply too old to be able to estimate the impact of the Islamic State foreign fighters. Nesser also argues that former foreign fighters play crucial parts in most European terror plots. Ideological influence, and the role the foreign fighters play in the creation of new violent jihadist organisations, and indeed their role in Africa, are under-researched.

57. Ibid.

58. Ibid.

59. See for example Paul Collier and Anke Hoeffler, 'Greed and grievance in civil war', *Oxford Economic Papers*, 56 (4), 2004, pp. 563–595.

60. For African insurgencies the degree of delegation of responsibility might vary; see Patrick Johnston, 'The geography of insurgent organization

and its consequences for civil wars: Evidence from Liberia and Sierra Leone', *Security Studies*, 17 (1), 2008.

61. Kalyvas, 'The ontology of "political violence"', pp. 475–494; Stathis Kalyvas, *The Logic of Violence in Civil War*, Cambridge: Cambridge University Press, 2006; Stathis Kalyvas and Laia Balcells, 'International system and technologies of rebellion: How the end of the Cold War shaped internal conflict', *American Political Science Review*, 104 (3), 2010, pp. 415–429; Stathis Kalyvas and Matthew Adam Kocher, 'How "free" is free riding in civil wars? Violence, insurgency, and the collective action problem', *World Politics*, 59 (2), 2007; Theodore McLauchlin, 'Desertion, terrain, and control of the home front in civil wars', *Journal of Conflict Resolution*, 58 (8), 2014.

62. Kalyvas, *The Logic of Violence in Civil War*.

63. Mancur Olson, 'Dictatorship, democracy, and development', *American Political Science Review*, 87 (3), 1993.

64. Kalyvas, *The Logic of Violence in Civil War*.

65. Olivier Roy, 'Introduction', in Virginie Collombier and Olivier Roy, *Tribes and Global Jihadism*, London: Hurst, 2018, p. 5.

66. Mohamed Husein Gaas, 'Primordialist vs. instrumentalist in Somali society: Is an alternative perspective needed?' and 'Modalities of governance and contradictions in Somalia', 2018 articles based on PhD thesis, NMBU.

67. Ibid.

68. Ibid.

69. Gabriel Koehler-Derrick, 'A false foundation? AQAP, tribes and ungoverned spaces in Yemen', Harmony Paper, CTC, West Point, 2011.

70. Roy, 'Introduction' in Collombier and Roy, *Tribes and Global Jihadism*, p. 3.

71. Claude Mbowou, 'Between the Kanuri and others', in Collombier and Roy (eds.), *Tribes and Global Jihadism*, London: Hurst, 2018, pp. 131–152.

72. Hosham Dawod, 'Iraqi tribes in the land of jihad', in Collombier and Roy (eds.), *Tribes and Global Jihadism*, London: Hurst, 2018, pp. 15–32.

73. Stephanie Pezard and Michael Shurkin, *Toward a Secure and Stable Mali: Approaches to Engaging Local Actors*, Los Angeles: RAND Corporation, 2014.

74. C.J.M. Drake, 'The role of ideology in terrorists' target selection', *Terrorism and Political Violence*, 10 (2), 1998, pp. 53–85; Ignacio Sánchez-Cuenca and Luis de la Calle, 'Domestic terrorism: The hidden side of political violence', *Annual Review of Political Science*, 12 (1), 2009, pp.

31–49; Mark Juergensmeyer, *Terror in the Mind of God: The Global Rise of Religious Violence*, Berkeley, CA: University of California Press, 2003.

75. Ideology is here defined as 'a more or less systematic set of ideas that includes the identification of a referent group (a class, ethnic, or other social group), an enunciation of the grievances or challenges that the group confronts, the identification of objectives on behalf of that group (political change – or defense against its threat), and (perhaps vaguely defined) program of action'. Francisco Gutiérrez Sanín and Elisabeth Jean Wood, 'Ideology in civil war: Instrumental adoption and beyond', *Journal of Peace Research*, 51 (2), 2014.

76. Scott Appleby, *The Ambivalence of the Sacred: Religion, Violence, and Reconciliation* (Carnegie Commission on Preventing Deadly Conflict), Lanham, MD: Rowman and Littlefield, 2002, pp. 1–19.

77. For an attempt to explore and define these terms, see Ahmad Moussalli, 'Wahhabism, Salafism and Islamism: Who is the enemy?', A Conflicts Forum Monograph, Beirut, 2009, http://conflictsforum.org/briefings/Wahhabism-Salafism-and-Islamism.pdf (accessed 15 March 2014). See also Thomas Hegghammer's critique of some of these terms. Thomas Hegghammer, 'Jihadi Salafis or revolutionaries: On religion and politics in the study of Islamist militancy', in R. Meijer (ed.), *Global Salafism: Islam's New Religious Movement*, London: Hurst, 2009, pp. 244–266.

78. Ideology here is defined as 'the basic beliefs or guiding principles of a person or group', http://www.merriam-webster.com/thesaurus/ideology (accessed 10 July 2014).

79. Mansoor Moaddel, *Class, Politics, and Ideology in the Iranian Revolution*, New York: Columbia University Press, 1993.

80. See for example Beatriz Mesa García, 'The Tuareg rebellion and al-Qaeda's role', IEES Opinion Paper, 37/12, 2012.

81. Hansen, Mesøy and Karadas, *The Borders of Islam*.

82. Sanín and Wood, 'Ideology in civil war', p. 213.

83. Ahmed Godane, Speech, 2014, http://caasimada.com/godane-oo-ka-hadlay-dagaalka-ku-soo-furmay-al-shabaab-baaq-uu-shacabka-u-diray/ (accessed 12 March 2016). Ethnic chauvinism is not alien to globalist ideologies, as demonstrated by China and the Soviet Union after the death of Stalin, which supposedly shared a universalist ideology, but still remained rivals and even had armed conflicts with each other.

84. Jacob Zenn, 'Leadership analysis of Boko Haram and Ansaru in Nigeria', *CTC Sentinel*, 7 (2), 2014. According to Abu Qaqa, alleged spokesperson of Boko Haram, there was great animosity between members from the Hausa, Fulani and Kanuri ethnic groups in the organisation, in the end leading to the domination of the Kanuri inside Boko Haram.

85. Shaukat Ali, *Administrative Ethics in a Muslim State*, Lahore: Publishers United, 1975; Mohammad al-Burray, *Management and Administration in Islam*, Riyadh: Al Dhahran, 1990.

86. Abu Bakr al-Naji, *The Management of Savagery: The Most Critical Stage through Which the Umma Will Pass*, translated by William McCants, 2006, http://azelin.files.wordpress.com/2010/08/abu-bakr-naji-the-management-of-savagery-the-most-critical-stage-through-which-the-umma-will-pass.pdf (accessed 10 April 2014).

87. Abu Ubayd al-Qurashi quoted in Michael Ryan, *Decoding al-Qaeda's Strategy: The Deep Battle against America*, New York: Columbia University Press, 2013, p. 92.

88. Robin Simcox, 'Ansar al-Sharia and governance in southern Yemen', *Current Trends in Islamist Ideology*, 14, 2013; Kamal Matinuddin, *The Taliban Phenomenon: Afghanistan 1994–1997*, Oxford: Oxford University Press, 1999, pp. 25–26; Pamela Constable, 'Taliban-style justice stirs growing anger', *Washington Post*, 10 May 2009.

89. As for example employed by the Taliban before the takeover of the Swat Valley.

90. Abdullah Azzam, *Join the Caravan*, 1987, https://archive.org/details/JoinTheCaravan (accessed 14 April 2014), p. 20.

91. Abdullah Azzam, *In Defense of the Muslim Lands*, 1979, http://www.religioscope.com/info/doc/jihad/azzam_defence_6_chap4.htm (accessed on 22 April 2014).

92. Reinhard Schulze, *Islamischer Internationalismus im 20. Jahrhundert: Untersuchungen zur Geschichte der islamischen Weltliga*, Leiden: E.J. Brill, 1990.

93. Ibid. See also the writings of Azzam for a more offensive version of loyalty to the *ummah*, through offensive jihad, to attack infidels outside the original *ummah*. Azzam, *Join the Caravan*; see also Shaykh Yusuf al-Uyari, 'The ruling on jihad and its divisions', *Series of Researches and Studies in Shari'ah*, no. 2, n.d.

94. Hegghammer, 'Jihadi Salafis or revolutionaries', p. 248.

95. Moussalli, 'Wahhabism, Salafism and Islamism'. Wahhab drew upon Ibn Taymiyyah's fatwa against the Muslim Mongols (or Tartars) in the war with the Mamluks.

96. See for example Abd al-Aziz ibn Baz, *The Necessity of Acting according to the Sunnah of the Messenger (Peace Be upon Him) and Deeming Those Who Deny It as Disbelievers*, Saudi Ministry of Information, n.d. (copy obtained by the author at the Jamia mosque in Nairobi).

97. Said Qutb, *Milestones*, Indianapolis: American Trust Publications, 1993, p. 11. Many Muslim brother scholars will strongly contest this view,

claiming that Qutb declared actions, not persons, as *takfir*; according to this interpretation, only Muslims who fail to acknowledge Allah as the only god are deemed non-Muslims by Qutb. Interview with Abdulqadir Sharif, Istanbul, 8 June 2014.

98. See Stig Jarle Hansen, *Al-Shabaab in Somalia: The History of a Militant Islamist Group 2005–2012*, London: Hurst, 2013.

99. Abubakar Shekau, Video on the abduction of the Nigerian girls, http://www.bellanaija.com/2014/05/05/end-western-education-boko-haram-leader-shekau-releases-video-watch/ (accessed 9 July 2014).

100. Marc Sageman, *Leaderless Jihad*, Philadelphia: University of Pennsylvania Press, 2007.

101. Jean-Pierre Filiu, 'Al-Qaeda in the Islamic Maghreb: Algerian challenge or global threat?', Carnegie Paper, 2009, p. 104; Hansen, *Al-Shabaab in Somalia*.

3. PROLOGUE: AL-QAEDA IN SUDAN

1. Al-Qaeda used the words 'Asian Corps' and 'African Corps' to designate two elements in the organisation; see al-Qaeda, *The Five Letters to the African Corps*, CTC Harmony Project, 2002, https://www.ctc.usma.edu/posts/letters-on-al-qaidas-operations-in-africa-original-language-2 (accessed 11 January 2018).

2. Peter Bergen and Paul Cruickshank, 'Revisiting the early al-Qaeda: An updated account of its formative years', *Studies in Conflict and Terrorism*, 35 (1), 2012; Lawrence Wright, *The Looming Tower: Al-Qaeda and the Road to 9/11*, New York: Knopf Doubleday Publishing Group, 2006; Steven Coll, *Ghost Wars: The Secret History of the CIA, Afghanistan and Bin Laden*, London: Penguin Books, 2005; Jason Burke, *Al-Qaeda: The True Story of Radical Islam*, London: I.B. Tauris, 2004; Peter L. Bergen, *The Osama bin Laden I Know*, New York: Free Press, 2006; Roland Jacquard, *In the Name of Osama bin Laden: Global Terrorism and the Bin Laden Brotherhood*, Durham, N.C.: Duke University Press, 2002; Richard Miniter, *Losing Bin Laden: How Bill Clinton's Failures Unleashed Global Terror*, Washington DC: Regnery Publishing, 2004.

3. For examples, see Michael Scheuer, *Through Our Enemies' Eyes*, Washington: Potomac Books, 2002; Rohan Gunaratna, *Inside al-Qaeda: Global Network of Terror*, New York: Columbia University Press, 2002; Ann M. Lesch, 'Osama bin Laden's "business" in Sudan', *Current History*, May 2002; Yossef Bodansky, *Bin Laden: The Man Who Declared War on America*, Roseville, CA: Prima Publishing, 2001.

4.   See Bergen, *The Osama bin Laden I Know*; Amare Tekle, 'International relations in the Horn of Africa (1991–96)', *Review of African Political Economy*, 23 (70), 1996; Shaul Shay, *The Red Sea Terror Triangle: Sudan, Somalia, Yemen, and Islamic Terror*, New Brunswick: Transaction Publishers, 2007. The documents retrieved from al-Qaeda in Pakistan and Afghanistan show a different picture, see al-Qaeda, *The Five Letters to the African Corps*.

5.   Human Rights Watch argues convincingly that the use of militias started out during Numeri's regime, as an alternative to conscription in order to fight the war in the south. See Human Rights Watch, 'Denying the honor of living: Sudan, a human rights disaster', Africa Watch Report, 65, March 1990. Other publications include Human Rights Watch, 'Sudan: In the name of God, behind the red line: Political repression in northern Sudan', London: Human Rights Watch, 1996; Jemera Rone, 'Famine in Sudan, 1998: The human rights causes', London: Human Rights Watch, 1999.

6.   Bergen, *The Osama bin Laden I Know*, p. 27.

7.   Ibid., p. 122.

8.   Ibid.

9.   There is some confusion about the funding of al-Qaeda. Some, like Jason Burke, argue that it came into existence in 1996, but primary sources seem strongly to support the above story. See Bergen and Cruickshank, 'Revisiting the early al-Qaeda', pp. 1-36, who also see the formation as the result of an increased self-confidence on behalf of Bin Laden after the battle of Lion's Den, Jaji, in 1987. Burke, *Al-Qaeda*; Bergen, *The Osama bin Laden I Know*.

10.   Wright, *The Looming Tower*, p. 134.

11.   Bergen, *The Osama bin Laden I Know*, p. 87.

12.   Wright, *The Looming Tower*.

13.   Bergen, *The Osama bin Laden I Know*, p. 116.

14.   Wright, *The Looming Tower*, pp. 144–165.

15.   Wright, *The Looming Tower*, p. 187; the invitation is mentioned in a quote from Jamal Ismail in Bergen, *The Osama bin Laden I Know*, p. 122, as well, but this was contested by Wisam al-Turabi, the wife of Hassan Turabi, in the same book. Osama bin Laden himself denied that he had formally been invited by the Sudanese, in an interview with Robert Fisk in 1993. Robert Fisk, 'Anti-Soviet warrior puts his army on the road to peace', *The Independent*, 6 December 1993, http://www.independent.co.uk/news/world/anti-soviet-warrior-puts-his-army-on-the-road-to-peace-the-saudi-businessman-who-recruited-mujahedin-1465715.html (accessed 17 December 2017). He also denied that he was invited, in

an interview with the newspaper editor Abd al-Bari Atwan; see Thomas Hegghammer, 'Dokumentasjon om al-Qaida: Intervjuer, kommunikéer og andre primærkilder, 1990–2002', FFI/RAPPORT-2002/01393, 2002. According to Osama bin Laden himself, he first visited Sudan in 1983 to look into business opportunities; see 'Usama bin Laden denies "terrorism" link', *Al-Quds al-Arabi*, 9 March 1994.

16. Quoted in Bergen, *The Osama bin Laden I Know*, p. 121; the last quote is from Burke, *Al-Qaeda*.

17. Quoted in Bergen, *The Osama bin Laden I Know*, p. 121.

18. See Lawrence Joffe, Hassan al-Turabi obituary, *Guardian*, 11 March 2016. The extent of Turabi's influence could be seen in the line-up for Bashir's first government. These appointments took place while Turabi was in prison, albeit under very lenient conditions. J. Millard Burr and Robert O. Collin, *Revolutionary Sudan*, Leiden: Brill, 2004, p. 11.

19. See Stig Jarle Hansen and Atle Mesøy, 'The Muslim Brotherhood in the wider Horn of Africa', NIBR Report, 2009, p. 12; Stig Jarle Hansen and Mohamed Husein Gaas, 'The Muslim Brotherhood in the Arab Winter', Discussion Paper, Belfer Center for Science and International Affairs, Kennedy School, Harvard, 2017.

20. See Wright, *The Looming Tower*, pp. 196, 214. If one believes Fayizah Sa'd's interview with Bin Laden, the Iranians promised to fund the maintenance of former Afghanistan veterans, but failed to do so, leading to an opening for Bin Laden and strained relations between Turabi and Iran. See Fayizah Sa'd, 'Usama bin Laden reportedly interviewed in London', *Rose al-Yusuf*, 17 June 1996; Al Jazeera, 'Al-Jazirah program on Bin Laden', Doha, Qatar, Al-Jazirah Space Channel Television in Arabic 18.05 GMT, 10 June 1999, transcribed in Foreign Broadcast Information Service, 'Compilation of Usama bin Laden statements 1994 – January 2004', FBIS Report, January 2004.

21. Burr and Collin, *Revolutionary Sudan*, p. 15. The Islamic African Relief Agency (IARA) had, for example, been established in 1980 to assist Muslim Ethiopian and Eritrean refugees in the Sudan, but served as a humanitarian cover for Sudan intelligence agents. The organisation was later, according to Burr, incorporated into the Islamic Relief Agency (ISRA), which also was active in Pakistan. See Millard Burr and Collin, *Revolutionary Sudan*, pp. 17, 53.

22. Wright, *The Looming Tower*, p. 223; Al Jazeera, 'Al-Jazirah program on Bin Laden'.

23. Peter L. Bergen, *Holy War Inc*, New York: Touchstone, 2002, p. 83.

24. Hegghammer, 'Dokumentasjon om al-Qaida', p. 18.

25. Burke, *Al-Qaeda*.

26. Interview with Hamid Turki and Sheikh Khalil Ameer Amir Mohammed Aamr, Khartoum, 24 July 2009.

27. Stig Jarle Hansen, 'Eritrean terrorism special assessment', Special report for MARISK, Maritime Security System for Risk Intelligence, Denmark, 2010.

28. Interview with Hamid Turki and Sheikh Khalil Ameer Amir Mohammed Aamr, Khartoum, 24 July 2009.

29. See Idris Abbakr Ibrahim, 'The Islamic movement in Eritrea and its political role: The case of the Eritrean Islamic Party for Justice and Development', PhD thesis, University of Malaya, Kuala Lumpur, Malaysia, 2016; Dan Connell, 'From resistance to governance: Eritrea's trouble with transition', *Review of African Political Economy*, 38 (129), 2011, p. 426; Gregory A. Pirio, *The African Jihad: Bin Laden's Quest for the Horn of Africa*, Asmara: Red Sea Press, 2007, pp. 105–119.

30. A letter to Osama bin Laden from Mohamed Othman from Eritrea, dated 1989, was found in the Sarajevo office of Benevolence International Foundation in 2002, and is presented in Bergen, *The Osama bin Laden I Know*, p. 85.

31. The sources are listed in Pirio, *The African Jihad*, p. 112.

32. According to Idris, Saudi Arabian Sheikh Abd al-Aziz ibn Baz attempted to mediate between the factions, but failed. Ibrahim, 'The Islamic movement in Eritrea'.

33. The militant wing turned into Harakat al-Islam, then changed its name to the Eritrean Islamic Reform Movement (Islah) in 2003, with a political wing called the Eritrean People's Congress. The Wefaq Party joined it in 2006. The civilian wing joined the Eritrean Democratic Alliance in 1998, and in 2004 it turned into Harakat al-Khalas al-Islami (the Eritrean Islamic Party for Justice and Development; see their webpage http://www.al-khalas.org/). The organisations, together with ELF and others, joined the Ethiopian-sponsored Eritrean Solidarity Front (ESA), which ironically was sponsored by Ethiopia. Al-Khalas and the Eritrean People's Congress also joined the Eritrean Democratic Alliance (EDA), also sponsored by Ethiopia, the ally of the United States in the war on terror, which was seen as a means to reduce Eritrean influence in Somalia (by damaging Eritrea), and thus also in theory to weaken Shabaab and al-Qaeda. See also Jonathan Miran, 'A historical overview of Islam in Eritrea', *Die Welt des Islams*, 45 (2), 2005; Connell, 'From resistance to governance'.

34. Tekle, 'International relations in the Horn of Africa', p. 505. See also al-Qaeda, 'Various admin documents and questions and translations', Harmony Project, Document AFGP-2002-801138.

35. Tekle, 'International relations in the Horn of Africa', p. 506.

36. Human Rights Watch, 'Sudan, global trade, local impact', Human Rights Watch Report, 9 (4), 1998.

37. United States District Court, Southern District of New York, 'U.S.A. v. Usama bin Laden, et al.', S (7) 98 Cr. 1023 (SDNY), trial transcript, 22 February 2001, pp. 1280–1282, Jamal al-Fadl's testimony. The second name mentioned attending the transfer meeting from Eritrean Islamic Jihad was Mohamed al-Kheir. The meeting took place in Khartoum. Fadl refers to the EIJ as 'a part of the al-Qaeda group', possibly referring to the fact that the EIJ was on the advisory committee of al-Qaeda. The EIJ never swore allegiance to Bin Laden or al-Qaeda.

38. Gunaratna, *Inside al-Qaeda*.

39. Stig Jarle Hansen, 'The changing face of the Muslim Brotherhood in Somalia', Unpublished manuscript, 2013.

40. Ibid.

41. International Crisis Group, 'Somalia's Islamists', Crisis Group Africa Report, no.100, 12 December 2005, p. 4.

42. Hansen and Mesøy, 'The Muslim Brotherhood in the wider Horn of Africa', p. 33.

43. Abdurahman Abdullahi, *The Islamic Movement in Somalia: A Case Study of Islah Movement, 1950–2000*, London: Adonis and Abbey, 2015, p. 227.

44. International Crisis Group, 'Somalia's Islamists', p. 5.

45. Ibid. These events are also well described in al-Qaeda's own documents. See al-Qaeda, 'Letters on al-Qaeda operations in Africa, first letter to Osama bin Laden', CTC Harmony Project, https://www.ctc.usma.edu/posts/letters-on-al-qaidas-operations-in-africa-original-language-2 (accessed 11 January 2018); al-Qaeda, 'Five letters to the African Corps'.

46. International Crisis Group, 'Somalia's Islamists', p. 5.

47. Al-Qaeda, 'Letters on al-Qaeda operations in Africa, first letter to Osama bin Laden'.

48. Stig Jarle Hansen, 'Faction fluctuation: The shifting allegiances within Hizbul Islam', *Jane's Intelligence Review*, 6 November 2010.

49. International Crisis Group, 'Somalia's Islamists', p. 5.

50. Ibid.

51. Ibid., p. 6.

52. Omar Taj al-Dein bin Abdullah 'Abu Belal', 'Abu Belal's report on jihad in Somalia', Harmony Project, 2002, https://www.ctc.usma.edu/posts/abu-belals-report-on-jihad-in-somalia-original-language-2 (accessed 18 January 2018).

53. Ibid.

54. Al-Qaeda, 'Letters on al-Qaeda operations in Africa, first letter to Osama bin Laden'.
55. Ken Menkhaus, 'Somalia: State collapse and the threat of terrorism', IISS Adelphi Paper, 364, 2004.
56. Saif al-Islam, 'The Ogadeni file, Operation Holding MSK', Harmony Project, Document AFGP-2002-600104, https://www.ctc.usma.edu/posts/the-ogaden-file-operation-holding-al-msk-original-language-2 (accessed 18 January 2018).
57. Ibid.
58. Ibid.
59. Salih Abdal al-Wahid, 'Report from Salih Abd-al-Wahid to Sheikh Abu-Hafs', dated 1 December 1993, in *Situation Report from al-Qaeda*, Harmony Project, https://www.ctc.usma.edu/posts/situation-report-from-somalia-original-language-2 (accessed 18 January 2018).
60. Abu al-Noor, Abu al-Haitham, Abu al-Fateh, Abu Emad al-Yamani (first aid), Abu Hamma al-Saeedy.
61. They also were in contact with Sheikh Ali Warsame.
62. Abu Haf, 'Abu Haf's report on operations in Somalia', 2002, Harmony Project, Document AFGP-2002-800597, https://www.ctc.usma.edu/posts/abu-hafs-report-on-operations-in-somalia-original-language-2 (accessed 18 January 2018).
63. Saif al-Adl, 'A short report on the trip from Nairobi', Harmony Project, Document AFGP-2002-600113, https://www.ctc.usma.edu/posts/a-short-report-on-the-trip-from-nairobi-original-language-2.
64. International Crisis Group, 'Somalia's Islamists', p. 5.
65. The exception was Islah, the Somali Muslim Brotherhood, which in general managed to maintain unity during the 1990s. From 2006 onwards this organisation encountered problems, but not to the extent of the others.
66. Human Rights Watch, 'Sudan, global trade, local impact'.
67. Ibid.
68. Many of these activists were members of the Tabliqi sect in Uganda, which had received support from Turabi since 1986. See Anneli Botha, *Terrorism in Kenya and Uganda: Radicalization from a Political Socialization Perspective*, London: Lexington Books, 2017, p. 1.
69. See Burr and Collin, *Revolutionary Sudan*.
70. Jonathan Schanzer, *Al-Qaeda's Armies*, New York: Specialist Press International, 2004, p. 99.
71. The Gia leadership under Zitouni later struck against al-Qaeda's influence, and former participants from al-Qaeda camps in Sudan or Afghanistan were systematically killed. See Maha Abedin, 'From

mujahid to activist: An interview with a Libyan veteran of the Afghan jihad', Jamestown Foundation, *Spotlight on Terror*, 3 (2), 2005.

72. Burke, *Al-Qaeda*, p. 206.

73. Molly Fletcher, 'Egyptian Islamic Jihad', Council of Foreign Relations Report, 30 May 2008, https://www.cfr.org/backgrounder/egyptian-islamic-jihad (accessed 20 August 2015).

74. 'U.S.A. v. Usama bin Laden, et al.', S (7) 98 Cr. 1023 (SDNY), pp. 1280–1282; Sa'd, 'Usama bin Laden reportedly interviewed in London'; Al Jazeera, 'Al-Jazirah program on Bin Laden'.

75. *Al-Quds al-Arabi* reports 1993 for both attacks in their interview (transcribed by FIBS). Peter Bergen, interestingly, quoting from the same interview, maintains that the first attack was in February 1994, and the last a few weeks later. J.M. Berger examines a story from one of the attackers who says that the attack was staged; Jim Berger, 'The alleged 1994 assassination attempt on Osama bin Laden: Declassified State Department cable adds color to little known Sudan incident', *Intelwire*, 12 August 2007, http://news.intelwire.com/2007/08/alleged-1994-assassination-attempt-on.html. In his 2006 book, *The Osama bin Laden I Know*, p. 135, he maintains that the attack was late in 1994.

76. 'U.S.A. v. Usama bin Laden, et al.', S (7) 98 Cr. 1023 (SDNY), pp. 1280–1282.

77. Bruce Reidel, *The Search for al-Qaeda, Its Leadership, Ideology and Future*, Washington DC: Brookings Institution Press, 2008, p. 56.

4. JAMA'AT NUSRAT UL-ISLAM WAL-MUSLIMIN': GREY BORDERS IN THE DESERT

1. For AQIM's own story of this cooperation, see AQIM, *The Dialogue of Shaykh 'Abd al 'Azīz Ḥabīb with Zakariā' Būghrārah: 'The Full Story of the Islamic Emirate of Azawad', Part 2*, Ifrīqīyyah Media, 2014.

2. Gilles Kepel, *Jihad: The Trail of Political Islam*, London: I.B. Tauris, 2006, p. 161. Boyali was a veteran of the Algerian war of independence, and was at the start alienated by the struggle between the so-called 'externals', the political leadership abroad, and the internals, the core of the guerrilla fighters. The former gained power on independence, and he was even more annoyed by the coup against Ben Bella in 1965. According to Robert Fisk, the front hardened after the police attempted to arrest Boyali. See Robert Fisk, *The Great War for Civilization: The Conquest of the Middle East*, New York: Vintage Books, 2005.

3. Martin Stone, *The Agony of Algeria*, New York: Columbia University Press, 1997, p. 181.

4. See Fisk, *The Great War for Civilization*.

5. Richard J. Chasdi, *Tapestry of Terror: A Portrait of Middle East Terrorism, 1994–1999*, New York: Lexington Books, 2003, p. 72.

6. Kepel, *Jihad*, p. 257. After Meliani, the leaders were Benameur Benaissa 'the executioner', then the Afghanistan veteran Murad Sid Ahmed, who took over from August 1993 till his death in February 1994, followed by Cherif Gousmi, who died in September 1994. See Yahia Zoubir, 'Islamists and insurgency in post-independent Algeria', in Barry Rubin (ed.), *Conflict and Insurgency in the Contemporary Middle East*, New York: Routledge, 2009; and Yahia H. Zoubir, 'The Algerian political crisis: Origins and prospects for the future of democracy', *Journal of North African Studies*, 3 (1), 1998, pp. 74–100.

7. Stone, *The Agony of Algeria*, p. 185; see also Luis Martinez, *The Algerian Civil War, 1990–1998*, London: Hurst, 2000 for more on early GIA history.

8. Jason Burke, *Al-Qaeda: The True Story of Radical Islam*, London: I.B. Tauris, 2004, p. 206.

9. There are some disagreements over this story, for example over al-Misrati's connections with al-Qaeda; some point to him as a member of the Libyan Islamic Fighting Group. However, his ties to al-Qaeda were solid and strong. See Camille Tawil, *Brothers in Arms: The Story of al-Qa'ida and the Arab Jihadists*, London: Saqi, 2011.

10. Zoubir, 'Islamists and insurgency in post-independent Algeria', p. 244.

11. Evan F. Kohlmann, 'Two decades of jihad in Algeria: The GIA, the GSPC, and al-Qaida', NEFA Foundation, May 2007.

12. Stephen Harmon, 'From GSPC to AQIM: The evolution of an Algerian Islamist terrorist group into an al-Qa'ida affiliate', *Concerned African Scholars Bulletin*, no. 85, 2010, p. 14.

13. Ibid.

14. 'GSPC rival leader Hattab reclaims title', *Terrorism Focus*, 2 (21), 2005. Later Hattab was criticised by AQIM for negotiating with the government.

15. William Thornberry and Jaclyn Levy, 'Al-Qaeda in the Islamic Maghreb', AQAM Future Projects Case Studies Series, 4, 2011.

16. Salima Mellah and Jean-Baptiste Rivoire, 'El Para, the Maghreb's Bin Laden', *Le Monde Diplomatique*, 4 February 2005.

17. Craig Whitlock, 'Missteps by U.S. in Africa revealed', *Pittsburgh Post-Gazette*, 21 May 2012. For a fascinating account of his Afghanistan experiences, see Alex Thurston, 'Mokhtar Belmokhtar's Afghanistan reminiscences', Sahel blog, 7 February 2017, https://sahelblog.

wordpress.com/2017/02/07/mokhtar-belmokhtars-afghanistan-reminiscences/ (accessed 9 August 2017).

18.   Whitlock, 'Missteps by U.S. in Africa revealed'.

19.   He was actually endorsed by al-Qaeda before AQIM, joined the Afghan jihad in 1991, and trained in al-Qaeda camps in Khowst and Jalalabad. Lianne K. Boudali, 'The GSPC: Newest franchise in al-Qa'ida's global jihad', North Africa Project, CTC, April 2007, p. 5; Andrew Wojtanik, 'Mokhtar Belmokhtar: One-eyed firebrand of North Africa and the Sahel', Jihadi Bios Project, Combating Terrorist Centre, West Point, 2015, https://www.ctc.usma.edu/v2/wp-content/uploads/2015/03/CTC_Mokhtar-Belmokhtar-Jihadi-Bio-February2015-2.pdf (accessed 7 July 2017). The history of the estrangement can also in many ways be read in the so-called Timbuktu papers, a cache of AQIM correspondence found by AP journalists in Timbuktu in 2014. See 'Al-Qaeda papers', AP, https://www.longwarjournal.org/images/al-qaida-papers-how-to-run-a-state.pdf (accessed 27 January 2018).

20.   See Andrew Lebovich, 'AQIM's Mokhtar Belmokhtar speaks out', *Al Wasat*, 21 November 2011, https://thewasat.wordpress.com/2011/11/21/aqims-mokhtar-belmokhtar-speaks-out/ (accessed 7 July 2017).

21.   Mathieu Guidère, 'The Timbuktu letters: New insights about AQIM', *Res Militaris*, 4 (1), Winter/Spring 2014, p. 4.

22.   On 11 September 2006, Ayman al-Zawahiri announced the GSPC merger with al-Qaeda. GSPC refused to participate in national reconciliation in Algeria, and also declared that it would attack Western targets, as well as targets related to these countries inside Algeria. Droukdel then formally pledged allegiance to Bin Laden. In January 2007 the GSPC adopted its new name, al-Qaeda in the Islamic Maghreb (AQIM) It is rather unclear what the name change meant, and in hindsight it seems to have involved little change in targeting and modus operandi, save for AQIM's introduction of suicide bombing, not known before in Algeria. Anneli Botha, 'Terrorism in the Maghreb: The transformation of domestic terrorism', Institute for Security Studies Monograph, 144, June 2008. There was also an increase in the activity level of the organisation after the merger. Yet AQIM refrained from attacking outside the region, and AQIM's contacts with al-Qaeda go further back than the merger. See also Harmon, 'From GSPC to AQIM', p. 16.

23.   Jean-Pierre Filiu, 'Could al-Qaeda turn African in the Sahel?', Carnegie Middle East Program, no. 112, 2010, p. 6.

24. Peter Pham, 'Foreign influences and shifting horizons: Al-Qaeda in the Islamic Maghreb', *Orbis*, 2011, p. 244; Harmon, 'From GSPC to AQIM', p. 17.

25. Peter Pham, 'The dangerous "pragmatism" of al-Qaeda in the Islamic Maghreb', *Journal of the Middle East and Africa*, 2 (15), 2011, pp. 29, 20.

26. US Embassy in Bamako, 'Cable: Tuareg and GOM officials provide details on GSPC attack and accords', 31 October 2006, 08.20 (Tuesday), WikiLeaks.

27. US Embassy in Bamako, 'Mali's unsettled north: Restive Tuaregs, restive president', 28 November 2006, 17.05 (Tuesday), WikiLeaks.

28. AQIM killed four French tourists near Aleg, Mauritania, in December 2007, and took responsibility for a drive-by shooting in front of the Israeli embassy in Nouakchott, Mauritania, in February 2008. In the summer of 2009, AQIM attacked the French embassy with a suicide bomber and assassinated a US citizen in the country. See Filiu, 'Could al-Qaeda turn African in the Sahel?', p. 6.

29. Like the Arab militia established to fight Tuareg rebel leader Ibrahim Bahanga. This was indeed an older Malian tradition. The Songhai Ganda Koy and the Ganda Iso militias had served a similar role in the 1990s, and the former continued to have a role in 2012. Stephanie Pezard and Michael Shurkin, *Toward a Secure and Stable Mali: Approaches to Engaging Local Actors*, Los Angeles: RAND Corporation, 2014, p. 4; see also Grégory Chauzal and Thibault van Damme, 'The roots of Mali's conflict', CRU Report, March 2015, https://www.clingendael.org/sites/default/files/pdfs/The_roots_of_Malis_conflict.pdf (accessed 26 January 2017).

30. Filiu, 'Could al-Qaeda turn African in the Sahel?, p. 6.

31. The latter was indicated by DEA agents infiltrating smugglers, quoted in Pham from Daniel Volman and Yahia Zoubir, 'US trans-Saharan security policy under Obama', Unpublished manuscript, 2010, p. 24.

32. Guidère, 'The Timbuktu letters'.

33. Peter Pham refers to Omar le Sahraoui, a former Polisario veteran, as well as Mohamed Salem Mohamed Ali Ould Rguibi, Mohamed Salem Hamoud and Nafii Ould Mohamed M'Barek as having participated in the 2009 kidnapping of three Spanish aid workers in the north-east of Mauritania. Omar le Sahraoui confessed to having been paid by Belmokhtar to lead the operation. Pham, 'The dangerous "pragmatism" of al-Qaeda in the Islamic Maghreb', p. 22.

34. Filiu, 'Could al-Qaeda turn African in the Sahel?, p. 8.

35. US Embassy in Bamako, 'Cable: Problem child: Algeria's growing impatience with Mali', 12 May 2009, 15.06 (Tuesday), WikiLeaks.

36. Alex Thurston, 'AQIM updates, August 6', Sahel blog, 6 August 2012, https://sahelblog.wordpress.com/2011/08/06/aqim-updates-august-6/ (accessed 22 July 2017). The Malian side had great problems in participating in the offensive.

37. Jessica M. Huckabey, 'Al-Qaeda in Mali: The defection connections', *Orbis*, 57 (3), 2013, p. 469.

38. Andrew McGregor, 'Where trafficking and terrorism intersect: A profile of Mauritanian militant Hamada Ould Kheirou', Aberfoyle International Security blog, 31 March 2014, http://www.aberfoylesecurity.com/?p=823 (accessed 13 August 2014). This writer does not agree with McGregor that MUJAO was a plot to recruit southern jihadists to AQIM; rather it was the product of a real fissure within AQIM (not within al-Qaeda, to which MUJAO stayed loyal). MUJAO's cooperation with Belmokhtar, who had a tense relationship with AQIM's leadership, cannot be taken as a sign of loyalty to AQIM's central leadership. MUJAO may have kept some channels to the central relationship, though.

39. The name MUJWA, based on the English name, is often used. See Alain Antil, 'Le Mujao, dernier venu des mouvements islamistes armés du nord Mali', Ultima Ratio blog, 2 May 2010, http://ultimaratio-blog.org/archives/4532 (accessed 12 July 2017).

40. It is interesting that the group pointed back to the older Islamists in West Africa, Usman Dan Fodio, Umar Tall and Cheikou Amadou, in the way they spoke. There were many theories about the defection of MUJAO from AQIM: some saw it as a splinter group, some as a clandestine part of AQIM meant to confuse its enemies, or a result of Algerian manipulation. See Huckabey, 'Al-Qaeda in Mali'. Others claimed that it emerged due to a quarrel over ransom money.

41. Andrew Lebovich, 'Of mergers, MUJWA, and Mokhtar Belmokhtar', *Al Wasat*, 23 August 2013. Many believed at the time that this was an offshoot from AQIM to recruit from other ethnic groups in West Africa, as well as staging attacks in other parts of West Africa. This writer finds this doubtful, and would rather emphasise MUJAO as a sign of conflict within AQIM, later also manifesting itself in Belmokhtar's resistance towards the central leadership.

42. Ag Ghali was in many ways a point of contact between many militant groups, as well as with the Malian government. See Oliver J. Walter and Dimitris Christopoulos, 'Islamic terrorism and the Malian rebellion', *Terrorism and Political Violence*, 27 (3), 2015, pp. 497–519.

43. Baz Lecocq and George Klute, 'Tuareg separatism in Mali', *International Journal*, 68 (3), 2013; Andrew Alesbury, 'A society in motion: The

Tuareg from the pre-colonial era to today', *Nomadic Peoples*, 17 (1), 2013. Significantly, the Ifoghas did not resist the French.

44. The exception was the support the rebels received from the Gaddafi regime in Libya. See Macartan Humphreys and Habaye Ag Mohamed, 'Senegal and Mali', Paper presented at the World Bank/Center for United Nations Studies Conference, Yale University, 12–15 April 2002, p. 20, http://www.columbia.edu/~mh2245/papers1/sen_mali.pdf.

45. He was a sub-commander of the Mouvement Populaire de Libération de l'Azawad (MPLA) in 1988. In 1991 the organisation lost 'Libération' and turned into Mouvement Populaire de l'Azawad (MPA). The group fragmented and had an Arab offshoot, Front Islamique et Arabe de l'Azawad (FIAA). MPA was again to fragment tribally when other parts of Kel Adagh (dominated by recruits from Imghad or Tilaqqiwin tribes) split from the Ifoghas and founded Armée Révolutionaire pour la Libération de l'Azawad (ARLA). Baz Lecocq, *Disputed Desert Decolonisation, Competing Nationalisms and Tuareg Rebellions in Northern Mali*, Leiden: Brill, 2010, p. 263.

46. US Embassy in Bamako, 'Cable: Tribal fault lines within the Tuareg of northern Mali', 6 March 2008, 14.21 (Thursday), WikiLeaks.

47. Lecocq, *Disputed Desert Decolonisation, Competing Nationalisms and Tuareg Rebellions in Northern Mali*, p. 243; Peter Beaumont, 'The man who could determine whether the West is drawn into Mali's war', *The Guardian*, 27 October 2012, https://www.theguardian.com/world/2012/oct/27/mali-one-man-determine-war (accessed 18 June 2017).

48. Lecocq, *Disputed Desert Decolonization, Competing Nationalisms and Tuareg Rebellions in Northern Mali*, p. 243.

49. Ibid.

50. Ag Ghali refers to the period till 2009 as 'the stage of getting to know the mujahideen'. See Alex Thurston, 'Mali: Iyad Ag Ghali's loose relationship with Salafism', Sahel blog, 5 April 2017, https://sahelblog.wordpress.com/2017/04/05/mali-iyad-ag-ghalis-loose-relationship-with-salafism/ (accessed 18 June 2017).

51. Lecocq and Klute, 'Tuareg separatism in Mali'.

52. US Embassy in Bamako, 'Cable: Tribal fault lines within the Tuareg of northern Mali', 6 March 2008.

53. The organisation was also known as Alliance Nationale des Touareg du Mali (ANTM) and Mali-Niger Tuareg Alliance (MNTA).

54. Much of the MNLA's platform derived from the MNA, created in November 2010.

55. Lawrence E. Cline, 'Nomads, Islamists, and soldiers: The struggles for northern Mali', *Studies in Conflict and Terrorism*, 36 (8), 2013, p. 622.

56. The Ifoghas line has been prominent in Tuareg politics. Often their *amenokal* functioned as a Tuareg *amenokal*. Kidal Ifoghas were at the centre of the first Tuareg rebellion, the second Tuareg rebellion, and the 2006 attacks in Ménaka and Kidal.

57. William Lloyd George, 'The man who brought the black flag to Timbuktu', *Foreign Policy*, 22 October 2012.

58. The news website Tawassoul.net reported the existence of the organisation.

59. Iyad Ag Ghali, 'Ansar Dine ne connaît que le Mali et la Charia', *Jeune Afrique*, 8 April 2012.

60. See Huckabey, 'Al-Qaeda in Mali', p. 470. At times individuals switched between the organisations. Ansar Dine's Omar Ould Hamaha openly affiliated with MUJAO in mid-2012, becoming its spokesperson, and at that time even aided Ansar Dine's attempt to gain local recruits. Some AQIM leaders may have pretended to be part of Ansar Dine because of Alghabass Ag Intallah, the son of the Ifoghas *amenokal*, who turned from MNLA to Ansar Dine, but ended up forming the Islamic Movement of Azawad (MIA in French) in January 2013. He was intolerant of AQIM in the cities that his forces controlled.

61. Ansar Dine, 'Iyad Ag Ghaly, le leader d'Ansar Dine, se met en scène', 15 March 2012, http://www.jeuneafrique.com/176967/politique/vid-o-mali-iyad-ag-ghaly-le-leader-d-ansar-dine-se-met-en-sc-ne/ (accessed 22 June 2017).

62. As in the case of one of the first AQIM units mobilised for Ansar Dine, led by an Ifogha named Abdelkrim al-Targui. See International Crisis Group, 'Mali: Avoiding escalation', Africa Report, no. 189, 18 July 2012, p. 16.

63. International Crisis Group, 'Mali', p. 14.

64. Ibid., p. 15.

65. Jean-Bertrand Pinatel, 'The crisis in Mali, the diplomatic maneuvers', Geopolitics, Geo Strategy Analyses and Debates, http://www.geopolitique-geostrategie.com/the-crisis-in-mali-the-diplomatic-maneuver (accessed 9 August 2017); 'Al-Qaeda papers', AP, n.d., https://www.longwarjournal.org/images/al-qaida-papers-how-to-run-a-state.pdf (accessed 27 January 2018).

66. 'Dialogues with the youth of Ansar Al-Din Movement in Timbuktu', *Al-Akhbar News Agency*, 3 May 2012, p. 1; Military commander of Ansar al-Din, 'Our war is not for independence, it is for Islam', Kavkaz Center, 10 April 2012, http://kavkazcenter.com/eng/content/2012/04/10/16087.shtml (accessed 20 October 2014).

67. 'Sahara Media interview with Sanda bin Bouamama al-Timbukti, a commander in Ansar al-Din movement', Sahara Media, 12 April 2012;

'Interview with Iyad Ag Ghaly, amir of Jamaat Ansar al-Din', *Sahara Media*, 12 November 2012.

68. International Crisis Group, 'Mali', p. 16.

69. Ibid. However, some, like the traditional chief (*amenokal*) of the Kel Adagh (higher up in the tribal hierarchy above the *amenokal* of the Ifoghas, Intallah Ag Attaher), remained loyal to MNLA. His older brother Mohamed, being the first-born, and the more 'serious' of the two, still had a strong claim at this point in time.

70. 'Update 1: Mali Tuareg leaders call off Islamist pact', *Reuters*, 1 June 2012, http://www.reuters.com/article/mali-rebels-idUSL5E8H1CXZ20120601 (accessed 9 June 2017); see also 'Press release: Ansar al-Dine and MNLA agreement', MNLA, 2012.

71. 'Update 1: Mali Tuareg leaders call off Islamist pact', *Reuters*, 1 June 2012.

72. Ahmed Ould al-Nada, 'Interview with Sanda Ould Bouamama, media official of Ansar al-Din', *Al-Akhbar News Agency*, 16 April 2012.

73. Anne Look, 'Mali rebel groups merge, plan to create Islamic State', *VOA Africa*, 27 May 2012, voattps://blogs.voanews.com/breaking-news/2012/05/27/mali-rebel-groups-merge-plan-to-create-islamic-state/ (accessed 8 August 2017).

74. Alex Thurston, 'Mali: Clashes between the MNLA and Ansar Dine', Sahel blog, 8 June 2012, https://sahelblog.wordpress.com/2012/06/08/mali-clashes-between-the-mnla-and-ansar-dine/ (accessed 8 August 2017).

75. Peggy Bruguière, 'Backed by popular support, Mali's Islamists drive Tuareg from Gao', France24, 29 June 2012, http://observers.france24.com/en/20120629-mali-backed-popular-support-islamists-drive-tuareg-separatists-north-city-gao (accessed 8 August 2017).

76. Thurston, 'Political shifts in northern Mali'.

77. 'Mali Islamists claim Menaka victory against rebels', BBC News Africa, 2012, http://www.bbc.com/news/world-africa-20404519 (accessed 8 August 2017).

78. Interview with anonymous *amenokal*, 19 March 2018, Bamako.

79. 'Mali Islamists claim Menaka victory against rebels'.

80. Ibid.

81. Ibid. This might have been bragging from AQIM's side. Adam Sandor (in email with the writer) indicates that Ag Intallah prevented AQIM from entering Kidal at the time. The writer is not able to fully establish if the AQIM claims are true, but they nevertheless show an interesting rhetoric focusing on justice provision.

82. Ibid.

83. Othman Ag Othman, 'Implementation of the Sharia in Azawad', Sahara Media, 25 June 2012, https://www.youtube.com/watch?v=oAq3GT_3Htk (accessed 28 August 2017).

84. Othman Ag Othman, 'Interview with the Sheikh Mohammed al-Hussein, judge of Timbuktu city', Sahara Media, 15 July 2012.

85. Interview with local civil servant in Kidal, November–December 2017, conducted by anonymous researcher for the JWE project.

86. May Ying Welsh, 'Making sense of Mali's armed groups', *Al Jazeera*, 17 January 2013, http://www.aljazeera.com/indepth/features/2013/01/20131139522812326.html (accessed 28 August 2017); Derek Henry Flood, 'Between Islamization and secession: The contest for northern Mali', *CTC Sentinel*, 5 (7), 2013.

87. Ibid.

88. Bill Roggio, 'West African jihadists flock to northern Mali', Threat Matrix, 28 September 2012, http://www.longwarjournal.org/archives/2012/09/west_african_jihadists_flock_t.php (accessed 8 August 2017); Bill Roggio, 'Foreign jihadists continue to pour into Mali', *Threat Matrix*, 27 October 2012, http://www.longwarjournal.org/archives/2012/10/foreign_jihadists_continue_to.php (accessed 8 August 2017).

89. International Crisis Group, 'Mali: Reform or relapse', Crisis Group Africa Report, no. 210, 2014.

90. International Crisis Group, 'Central Mali: An uprising in the making?', Crisis Group Africa Report, no. 238, 2016, p. 7.

91. Ibid., p. 10.

92. United Nations Security Council Resolution 2085 (2012), 20 December 2012, https://www.un.org/ga/search/view_doc.asp?symbol=S/RES/2085%20%282012%29 (accessed 17 July 2017). The resolution actually sanctioned an African force.

93. Sergei Boeke and Bart Schuurman, 'Operation Serval: A strategic analysis of the French intervention in Mali 2013–2014', *Journal of Strategic Studies*, 28 (6), 2015, p. 812.

94. Ibid.

95. Olivier Tramond and Philippe Seigneur, 'Operation Serval: Another Beau Geste of France in sub-Saharan Africa?', *Military Review*, November–December 2014, p. 80.

96. Ibid.

97. Ibid.

98. Ibid., p. 81.

99. Boeke and Schuurman, 'Operation Serval', p. 815.

100. Ibid.

101. Ibid.
102. Tramond and Seigneur, 'Operation Serval', p. 82.
103. Ibid.
104. Boeke and Schuurman, 'Operation Serval', p. 816.
105. In March, the contingent, which had been deployed on 17 January, consisted of 6,000 men, with Chad fielding 2,000 troops, Nigeria 1,000, Togo 700, Niger 700 and Senegal 500, apart from several smaller contingents, followed by 140 men from Togo though these seem to have been deployed mainly as a rearguard. Marek Brylonek, 'Security crisis in the Sahel region', *Scientific Quarterly*, 3 (92), 2013, p. 56. The planning for the West African force had started as early as June 2012, based on forces from the ECOWAS: it was to be named the ECOWAS Mission in the Republic of Mali, and to consist of 5,000 troops. Lack of funding created problems, and the deployment dragged on. By the end of 2012 the force was renamed the African-Led International Support Mission in Mali (AFISMA). For smaller contributions to the early MINUSMA, see Claire Mills. 'In brief: International military forces in Mali', House of Commons Brief, SN06615, 2013.
106. Brylonek, 'Security crisis in the Sahel region', p. 60.
107. International Crisis Group, 'Central Mali', p. 9.
108. Simon Allison, 'Think again: Did France's intervention work in Mali?', *ISS Daily*, 1 July 2014.
109. Boeke and Schuurman, 'Operation Serval', p. 802.
110. Brylonek, 'Security crisis in the Sahel region', p. 56.
111. International Crisis Group, 'Central Mali', p. 14. According to the International Crisis Group, the MNLA based itself more on Idnan and Chamanamas militants, while the HCUA tended to represent the Ifoghas of Kidal.
112. AQIM, 'A disciplinary letter from al-Qaida's HR Department', AQIM, 3 October 2012.
113. Belmokhtar argued that Sharia implementation in northern Mali had been essential, and actually asked for help from Mauritanian imams to come to the aid of 'Azawad', secular MNLA's secular name for their independent Tuareg-dominated entity.
114. See https://www.memri.org/jttm/amid-reports-having-left-aqim-mokhtar-belmokhtar-announces-new-group-threatens-against-military; and Daveed Gartenstein-Ross, 'Is Algeria's kidnapper a "common criminal"? Look again', *Globe and Mail*, 22 January 2013, https://www.theglobeandmail.com/opinion/is-algerias-kidnapper-a-common-criminal-look-again/article7618417/.

115. See https://thewasat.wordpress.com/2013/01/23/primer-on-jihadi-players-in-algeria-mali/; for the original video see https://www.youtube.com/watch?v=xdnsZHDjwqc. Thanks to Ann Stenersen and Henrik Graterud for helping me get access to the video.

116. Ibid.

117. Andrew Lebovich, 'The local face of jihadism in northern Mali', *CTC Sentinel*, 6 (6), 2013. Hamaha also stated that Belmokhtar had left AQIM; see Baba Ahmed, 'Leader of al-Qaeda unit in Mali quits AQIM', *Daily Star*, 3 December 2013.

118. 'Belmokhtar's militants "merge" with Mali's MUJAO', BBC News Africa, 22 August, http://www.bbc.com/news/world-us-canada-23796920 (accessed 8 August 2017). The new name, al-Mourabitoun, was a reference to the Almoravids, a medieval dynasty that had ruled large parts of the Sahel and reinvigorated the Muslims in Spain in their battles with the Christians. The dynasty had figured quite prominently in previous AQIM propaganda. See Lianne Kennedy Boudali, 'Leveraging history in AQIM communications', *CTC Sentinel*, 2 (4), 2009.

119. Aziz Mohamed, 'Les services de sécurité algériens ont réussi à identifier les preneurs d'otages algériens et français au Sahel', *El Watan*, 5 July 2013, http://maliactu.net/sahel-aqmi-a-cree-un-groupe-special-pour-les-otages/ (accessed 8 August 2017).

120. Leela Jacinto, 'Al-Qaeda leader Abou Zeid "killed in Mali"', France24, 5 March 2013, http://www.france24.com/en/20130323-france-confirms-death-top-al-qaeda-leader-abou-zeid-mali (accessed 8 August 2017).

121. The statements about Belmokhtar leaving AQIM came from the somewhat unstable Omar Ould Hamaha, who frequently changed organisational affiliation, and from local rumours, not from Belmokhtar himself, although he never publicly refuted Hamaha's statements. Belmokhtar, on the other hand, dedicated terror attacks to AQIM leaders who had been killed, including his rival Abu Zeid.

122. AQIM, 'A disciplinary letter from al-Qaida's HR Department'.

123. Laura Grossman, 'Ansar Dine leader resurfaces, urges expulsion of France from Mali', FDD's Long War Journal, 12 August 2013, http://www.longwarjournal.org/archives/2014/08/iyad_ag_ghaly_re-eme.php (accessed 8 August 2017).

124. Bill Roggio and Caleb Weiss, 'French troops kill MUJAO founder during raid in Mali', FDD's Long War Journal, December 2014, http://www.longwarjournal.org/archives/2014/12/us_wanted_malian_jih.php (accessed 8 August 2017).

125. International Crisis Group, 'Mali: Reform or relapse', p. 9.

126. Roggio and Weiss, 'French troops kill MUJAO founder during raid in Mali'.

127. AQIM,

قيادي بإمارة الصحراء "القاعدة" في مهرجان خطابي بأزواد

MIQA, https://www.youtube.com/watch?v=varUnZIk0Vg&feature=youtube (accessed 8 August 2017); see also Rida Lyammouri, 'AQIM making noise again in Timbuktu region, northern Mali', The Maghreb and Sahel, Sand, Tea, and Guns blog, 3 December 2015, https://maghrebandsahel.wordpress.com/2016/06/01/mali-aqim-and-security-related-incidents-in-may-2016/ (accessed 8 August 2017).

128. Interview with the mayor of Timbuktu, July–September 2017, conducted by local anonymous researchers, for the JWE project.

129. Interview with traditional leader, Timbuktu, July–September 2017, conducted by local anonymous researchers, for the JWE project.

130. Interview with traditional leader, Timbuktu, July–September 2017, conducted by local anonymous researchers, for the JWE project.

131. Interview with entrepreneur A, Kidal, November–December 2017, conducted by local anonymous researchers for the JWE project.

132. Ibid.

133. Interview with entrepreneur B, Kidal, November–December 2017, conducted by local anonymous researchers for the JWE project.

134. International Crisis Group, 'Mali: Reform or relapse', p. 10.

135. International Crisis Group, 'Mali: Last chance in Algiers', Crisis Group Africa Briefing, no. 104, 18 November 2014, p. 12.

136. Jacques Follorou, 'Jihadists return to northern Mali a year after French intervention', The Guardian, 11 March 2014, https://www.theguardian.com/world/2014/mar/11/mali-jihadists-return-after-france-mission; (accessed 8 August 2017); Serge Daniel, 'Jihadists announce blood-soaked return to northern Mali', AFP, 9 October 2014, https://www.yahoo.com/news/jihadists-announce-blood-soaked-return-northern-mali-044311121.html (accessed 8 August 2017).

137. International Crisis Group, 'Central Mali: An uprising in the making?', p. 10.

138. Andrew McGregor, 'The Fulani crisis: Communal violence and radicalization in the Sahel', CTC Sentinel, 10 (2), 2017. It seems likely that McGregor probably overestimated the problems between Koufa and Ansar Dine in this article, as Koufa led his organisation into union with Ansar Dine just months after McGregor's article.

139. Katibat Macina, 'First video of Katibat Macina, message from Jamaat Ansar Dine', Katibat Macina, 18 May 2016, http://jihadology.net/2016/05/18/new-video-message-from-jamaat-

an%E1%B9%A3ar-al-din-first-video-of-katibat-macina/ (accessed 8 August 2017).

140. As in the 28 June 2015 Fakola attack, where Malian sources implicated the Macina Liberation Front, while Ansar Dine took public responsibility. See Alex Thurston, 'Partial list of recent jihadist attacks in southern and central Mali', Sahel blog, 30 June 2015, https://sahelblog.wordpress. com/2015/06/30/partial-list-of-recent-jihadist-attacks-in-southern-and-central-mali/ (accessed 23 August 2017).

141. International Crisis Group, 'Central Mali: An uprising in the making?', p. 14.

142. Jacob Zenn, 'The Sahel's militant "melting pot": Hamadou Kouffa's Macina Liberation Front (FLM)', *Terrorism Monitor*, 13 (22), 2015. Zenn also has a useful overview of the attacks in central Mali.

143. Tor A. Benjaminsen and Boubacar Ba, 'Why do pastoralists in Mali join jihadist groups? A political ecological explanation', *Journal of Peasant Studies*, 2018, doi: 10.1080/03066150.2018.1474457, p. 13.

144. Ibid., p. 10.

145. Rukmini Callimachi and Nabih Bulos, 'Mali hotel attackers are tied to an Algerian Qaeda leader', *International New York Times*, 21 November 2015; 'The Radisson Blue siege', *The Economist*, 28 November 2015. See also Mourabitoun's statement on the attack, 'Claiming Bamako, Mali hotel attack', 21 November 2015. Thanks to Christopher Anzalone for helping me get access to this statement.

146. See, for example, Ansar Dine, 'Ambushing Mali army south of the river', 30 September 2016. Thanks to Christopher Anzalone for helping me get access to this statement. See also Caleb Weiss, 'Al-Qaeda group strikes in northern Mali', FDD's Long War Journal, 26 December 2015.

147. Interview with businessman A from the transport sector in Timbuktu, July–September 2017, conducted by local anonymous researchers, for the JWE project.

148. Interview with businessman B from the transport sector in Timbuktu, July–September 2017, conducted by local anonymous researchers, for the JWE project.

149. Interview with businessman C from the transport sector in Timbuktu, July–September 2017, conducted by local anonymous researchers, for the JWE project.

150. Héni Nsaibia, 'Jihadist groups in the Sahel region formalize merger', The Jihadica blog, 27 March 2017, http://jihadology.net/2017/03/27/guest-post-jihadist-groups-in-the-sahel-region-formalize-merger/ (accessed 25 January 2017).

151. Rida Lyammouri, 'AQIM never really abandoned Timbuktu, Mali', The Maghreb and Sahel, Sand, Tea, and Guns blog, 6 February 2016, https://maghrebandsahel.wordpress.com/2016/02/06/aqim-never-really-abandoned-timbuktu-mali/ (accessed 4 October 2018). The CMA consists of three parts: the High Council for the Unity of Azawad (HCUA), the Arab Movement of Azawad (French acronym, MAA), and the National Movement for the Liberation of Azawad (French acronym, MNLA). Basically it consists of the more secular rebels from 2012.

5. THE ISLAMIC STATE IN THE GREATER SAHARA: ON THE PERIPHERY OF THE PERIPHERY

1.   'Qui est Walid Abou Adnan Sahraoui, le porte-parole du MUJAO?', *La Tribune du Sahara*, 26 March 2013.

2.   Ibid. He was allegedly the grandchild of the famous Western Saharan activist Hatri Ould Said Ould Yumani.

3.   Other Sahrawites were to feature in MUJAO later, like Abdelhakim Sahraoui and Aboul Qaaqaa Sahraoui.

4.   Andrew McGregor, 'Where trafficking and terrorism intersect: A profile of Mauritanian militant Hamada Ould Kheirou', Aberfoyle International Security blog, 31 March 2014, http://www.aberfoylesecurity.com/?p=823 (accessed 13 August 2014). Kheirou had been arrested by Mauritanian authorities in 2005, but escaped prison in 2006, and probably fled to Senegal, later joining Belmokhtar in Mali.

5.   There were many theories about the defection of MUJAO from AQIM. Some saw it as a splinter group, some as a clandestine part of AQIM made to confuse its enemies, or a result of Algerian manipulation. See Jessica M. Huckabey, 'Al-Qaeda in Mali: The defection connections', *Orbis*, 57 (3), 2013. Others claimed that it emerged due to a quarrel over ransom money.

6.   Adib Bencherif, 'From resilience to fragmentation: Al-Qaeda in the Islamic Maghreb and jihadist group modularity', *Terrorism and Political Violence*, 29 (6), 2017, p. 9. For other explanations, see Wolfram Lacher, 'Organized crime and conflict in the Sahel-Sahara region', Carnegie Endowment, blog, 13 September 2012, http://carnegieendowment.org/2012/09/13/organized-crime-and-conflict-in-sahel-sahara-region-pub-49360 (accessed 10 September 2017); Abu al-Ma'ali, 'Al-Qaeda and its allies in the Sahel and Sahara', Al Jazeera Centre for Studies Report, 1 May 2012.

7.   Islamic State in the Sahara, الأزوادية النصرة الإسلامية دولة, 5 July 2014 (thanks to Adam Egal for translations). Abu al-Walid al-Sahrawi,

'Statement from the military commander of Jama'at al-Tawhid wa al-Jihad in West Africa, Abu al-Walid al-Sahrawi', MUJAO, 27 July 2013; 'Interview with commander Ahmed Ould Aamir aka Ahmed al-Talmasi Amir of the Osama bin Laden brigade and member of Majlis Shura of Jama'at al-Tawhid wa al-Jihad in West Africa', Al-Akhbar News Agency.

8. The name itself might have been a compromise, with its Moroccan connotations, as the al-Murabitoun dynasty in Western Sahara (Almoravid) originated in Morocco. But the name also refers to Belmokhtar's old group, which was called by the nickname al-Mulathimun ('the masked ones'). See Bill Roggio, 'Al-Qaeda group led by Belmokhtar, MUJAO unite to form al-Murabitoon', *Threat Matrix*, 22 August 2013, http://www.longwarjournal.org/archives/2013/08/al_qaeda_groups_lead_by_belmok.php (accessed 10 September 2017).

9. The original leader of the organisation was Abu Bakr al-Masri. After he was killed in April 2014, the new leader became Ahmed Ould Amer (Ahmed al-Tilemsi).

10. Rida Lyammouri, 'Key events that led to tensions between Mokhtar Belmokhtar and Adnan Abu Walid al-Sahrawi before splitting', The Maghreb and Sahel, Sand, Tea, and Guns blog, 7 December 2015, https://maghrebandsahel.wordpress.com/2015/12/ (accessed 1 September 2017).

11. Ibid.

12. Tore Refslund Hamming, 'The al-Qaeda–Islamic State rivalry: Competition yes, but no competitive escalation', *Terrorism and Political Violence*, 1, 2017.

13. Ibid.

14. 'Bay'a to Abu Bakr al-Baghdadi', جماعة المرابطون تؤكد بيعتها لخليفة المسلمين", Murabitoun (Sahrawi faction), 19 May 2015. From Christopher Anzalone's archive.

15. Ibid.

16. Connor Gaffey, 'ISIS expands into the Sahel, Africa's migration hub', *Newsweek*, 24 November 2016.

17. 'Le Jihadiste algérien Mokhtar Belmokhtar devient chef d'al-Qaïda en Afrique de l'Ouest', *PressAfrik*, 15 September 2015, http://www.pressafrik.com/Le-jihadiste-algerien-Mokhtar-Belmokhtar-devient-chef-d-al-Qaida-en-Afrique-de-l-Ouest_a139316.html (accessed 15 September 2017).

18. Al-Qaeda in the Islamic Maghreb, 'New statement from al-Qā'idah in the Islamic Maghrib: "Important: Denying the death of the Amīr of Greater Sahara"', Al-Andalus Media Foundation, 4 April 2013, http://jihadology.net/?s=islamic+state+in+the+greater+sahara (accessed

15 September 2017); 'Mali – Urgent: L'émir d'al-Mourabitoune gravement blessé dans des affrontements', Maliactu.net, 17 June 2015, http://maliactu.net/mali-urgent-lemir-dal-mourabitoune-gravement-blesse-dans-des-affrontements/ (accessed 15 September 2017). The latter article contains a confirmation by tribal leaders.

19. 'Ménaka: L'Etat islamique à la manœuvre', *Malijet*, 20 July 2017.

20. Ibid.

21. Thomas Joscelyn and Caleb Weiss, 'Report: Head of the Islamic State's Sahara branch threatens Morocco', *Threat Matrix*, 6 May 2016, http://www.longwarjournal.org/archives/2016/05/report-head-of-the-islamic-states-sahara-branch-threatens-morocco.php (accessed 15 September 2017).

22. Madjid Zerrouky, 'Un groupe lié à l'Etat islamique revendique une première attaque dans le Sahel', *Le Monde Afrique*, 5 September 2016, http://www.lemonde.fr/afrique/article/2016/09/05/un-groupe-lie-a-l-etat-islamique-revendique-une-premiere-attaque-dans-le-sahel_4992882_3212.html#ByKSg7dvsYUXuCf2.99 (accessed 15 September 2017).

23. Carole Kouassi, 'Niger: l'EI revendique l'assaut contre la prison de Koutoukalé', Africanews, 19 October 2016, http://fr.africanews.com/2016/10/19/niger-l-ei-revendique-l-assaut-contre-la-prison-de-koutoukale/ (accessed 15 September 2017).

24. 'Burkina Faso: Ansaroul Islam pledging allegiance to the Islamic State? Maybe or maybe not', Menastream, 16 April 2017, http://menastream.com/burkina-faso-ansaroul-islam-pledging-allegiance-to-the-islamic-state-maybe-or-maybe-not/ (accessed 1 September 2017); I. Khalou, 'Mali: Amadou Kouffa et l'Etat islamique: Creuse un trou pour ton ennemi, mais pas trop profond, on ne sait jamais', Maliactu.net, 6 January 2017, http://maliactu.net/mali-amadou-kouffa-et-letat-islamique-creuse-un-trou-pour-ton-ennemi-mais-pas-trop-profond-on-ne-sait-jamais/.

25. 'Burkina Faso: Ansaroul Islam pledging allegiance to the Islamic State? Maybe or maybe not'; Khalou, 'Mali: Amadou Kouffa et l'Etat islamique'.

26. Khalou, 'Mali: Amadou Kouffa et l'Etat islamique'.

6. BOKO HARAM/THE ISLAMIC STATE IN WEST AFRICA: FROM TERRITORIALITY TO FRAGMENTATION?

1. Institute for Economics and Peace, *Global Terrorism Index*, Institute for Economics and Peace, Oxford, 2014, p. 53.

2. Stig Jarle Hansen, *Al-Shabaab in Somalia*, London: Hurst, 2013, p. 89; Jacob Zenn, 'Boko Haram's international connections', *CTC Monitor*, January 2013; Ryan Cummings, 'A jihadi takeover bid in Nigeria? The evolving relationship between Boko Haram and al-Qa'ida', *CTC Sentinel*, 10 (11), 2017. Newly declassified documents taken from Osama bin Laden's compound in Abbottabad in 2011 provide evidence for the AQIM–Boko Haram link.

3. Abdulbasit Kassim and Michael Nwankpa, *The Boko Haram Reader: From Nigerian Preachers to the Islamic State*, London: Hurst, 2018 is the best collection of original sources of Boko Haram texts.

4. A comparison between Boko Haram's declaration of a caliphate with Shabaab's video on the death of Ahmed Abdi Godane is enlightening; Boko Haram Media Section, 'Boko Haram declares a new caliphate in northeastern Nigeria', Boko Haram, 2014, https://www.youtube.com/watch?v=Rl4IgD--nKg (accessed 20 January 2015); Shabaab Media Section, 'Dilkii Axmed Godane iyo Alshabaab oo Xaqijisay kuna dhawaaqday Amiir Cusub', Harakat al-Shabaab, 2014, https://www.youtube.com/watch?v=tn34K2wdbeQ (accessed 20 January 2015): The comparison does not hold true for the whole of Boko Haram's existence. Mohammed Yusuf's publications were theologically advanced, and Boko Haram's publications grew more sophisticated over 2014.

5. Actually, the different views can even be found in the same edited volumes. For the first view, see Osumah Oarhe, 'Responses of the Nigerian defense and intelligence establishments to the challenge of Boko Haram', in Ioannis Mantzikos (ed.), *Boko Haram: Anatomy of a Crisis*, Bristol: e-International Relations, 2013; for the second view, see Freedom Onuoha, 'Understanding Boko Haram's attacks on telecommunication infrastructure', in Mantzikos, *Boko Haram*, or Isioma Madike, 'Boko Haram: Rise of a deadly sect', *National Mirror*, 19 June 2011, http://www.nationalmirroronline.net/sunday-mirror/big_read/14548.html (accessed 5 November 2012). For the last view, see Jideofor Adibe, 'What do we really know about Boko Haram?', in Mantzikos, *Boko Haram*.

6. International Crisis Group, 'Curbing violence in Nigeria (II): The Boko Haram insurgency', Crisis Group Africa Report, no. 216, 3 April 2014, pp. 7–12.

7. Adetoro Rasheed Adenrele, 'Boko Haram insurgency in Nigeria as a symptom of poverty and political alienation', *Journal of Humanities and Social Science*, 3 (5), 2012, p. 22.

8. Ibid., p. 23; Hannah Hoechner, 'Traditional Quranic students (almajirai) in Nigeria: Fair game for unfair accusations?', in Marc-Antoine Pérouse

de Montclos (ed.), *Boko Haram: Islamism, Politics, Security and the State in Nigeria*, West African Politics and Society Series, 2, 2014.

9. Adenrele, 'Boko Haram insurgency in Nigeria as a symptom of poverty and political alienation', p. 22; see also Alex Thurston, *Boko Haram: The History of an African Jihadist Movement*, Princeton: Princeton University Press, 2018, p. 29, probably the most comprehensive book on the organisation.

10. Sani Tukur, 'Ex-Gov Sheriff, accused of sponsoring Boko Haram, ready to face justice', *Premium Times*, 3 September 2014, http://www.premiumtimesng.com/news/headlines/167706-ex-gov-sheriff-accused-of-sponsoring-boko-haram-ready-to-face-justice.html#sthash.xJ4QodiG.dpbs (accessed 26 November 2014).

11. Ibid.

12. Gilles Kepel, *The War for Muslim Minds: Islam and the West*, Cambridge, MA: Belknap Press, 2004; Olivier Roy, *Den globaliserede Islam*, Copenhagen: Vandkunsten, 2004; Quintan Wiktorowicz, 'Introduction: Islamic activism and social movement theory', in Q. Wiktorowicz (ed.), *A Social Movement Theory Approach*, Bloomington, IN: Indiana University Press, 2004.

13. Onuoha, 'Understanding Boko Haram's attacks on telecommunication infrastructure'.

14. Ibid.

15. Ibid.

16. Marc-Antoine Pérouse de Montclos, 'Boko Haram and politics: From insurgency to terrorism', in De Montclos, *Boko Haram*.

17. The sub-group rejoined Boko Haram in 2005. Interview with Farid Esack, Pretoria, 19 January 2015.

18. Thurston, *Boko Haram*, pp. 13–18. Thurston also has an excellent section on the etymology of these terms.

19. Interview with N1, Maiduguri, 5 October 2018.

20. Interview with female student from Bama, Maiduguri, 4 October 2018.

21. Interview with member of the Shabaab, Maiduguri, 5 October 2018; interview with sheikh and friend of Ali Husseini, Maiduguri, 6 October, 2018; interview with sheikh of a neighbouring mosque, 7 October 2018.

22. Ibid., p. 23.

23. Thurston refers to a first wave of Salafisation in the 1970s, the wave described in the text in this book being the second wave; see ibid., p. 61.

24. According to Human Rights Watch, the Nigerian police believed that Mohammed Yusuf was the spiritual leader of the 'Taliban' groups, but he contested it. He was also on hajj in Saudi Arabia for parts of 2003 and

2004, when many of the attacks in question took place. Human Rights Watch, 'Spiraling violence: Boko Haram attacks and security force abuses in Nigeria', Human Rights Watch Report, October 2012, p. 31, http://www.hrw.org/sites/default/files/reports/nigeria1012webwcover_0.pdf (accessed 1 January 2015).

25. Thurston, *Boko Haram*, p. 84.

26. Ibid., pp. 95, 161, 118. On page 118 Thurston refers to original documents, making the claims of Ali's role in the leadership of the group more credible. However, the claim that Ali received support from al-Qaeda is unsubstantiated by primary sources.

27. According to one eyewitness, Husseini claimed that Yusuf was the leader of the group when confronted by him, but it should be remembered that Yusuf remained the formal leader of the Shabaab and that Husseini's claim could have been an attempt to underline that the Kanamma group remained part of the Shabaab: the Kanamma group had previously attempted to remove Yusuf as leader of the Shabaab, and Yusuf expressed criticism of the group at several meetings.

28. Ahmed Murtada, 'The Boko Haraam group in Nigeria: Its beginnings, principles and actions', *Al Qirat*, 12, 2012. Mohammed Ali could have been the first leader or a co-leader with Mohammed Yusuf. Mohammed Ali was in the end killed in unclear circumstances in the guesthouse of a local Salafist sheikh.

29. Interview with member of the Shabaab, Maiduguri, 5 October 2018; interview with sheikh and friend of Ali Husseini, Maiduguri, 6 October, 2018; interview with sheikh of a neighbouring mosque, 7 October 2018.

30. Ibid.

31. Kassim and Nwankpa, *The Boko Haram Reader*, p. 14.

32. For example, Yusuf's debate with Isa Ali Ibrahim Pantami; see ibid., pp. 29–50.

33. US Embassy in Abuja, 'Extremist attacks continue into the night', Cable 09ABUJA1379, WikiLeaks, 2009, https://search.wikileaks.org/plusd/cables/09ABUJA1379_a.html (accessed 25 January 2017).

34. Interview with former Yusufia, 1, Maiduguri, 5 October 2018.

35. Human Rights Watch, 'Spiraling violence', p. 25.

36. Interview with member of the Shabaab, Maiduguri, 5 October 2018.

37. See Osama bin Laden, 'Declaration of war against the Americans occupying the land of the two Holy Places', 1996, http://www.pbs.org/newshour/updates/military/july-dec96/fatwa_1996.html (accessed 16 March 2013); Osama bin Laden, 'Jihad against the Jews and Crusaders', World Islamic Front Statement, 1998, http://www.

fas.org/irp/world/para/docs/980223-fatwa.htm (accessed 16 March 2013), for examples of how Taymiyyah was used by al-Qaeda. For the problems with al-Qaeda's use of Taymiyyah, see Camille Mulcaire, 'Assessing al-Qaeda from the teachings of Ibn Taymiyya', *e-IR*, 2013, http://www.e-ir.info/2013/10/15/assessing-al-qaeda-from-the-teachings-of-ibn-taymiyya/ (accessed 23 November 2014).

38. Interview with sheikh, Maiduguri, 7 October 2017.

39. Ibid.

40. Interview with businessman from the Mafoni area and Shekau's neighbour, Maiduguri, 4 October 2018.

41. Interview with woman from Bama, 4 October 2018.

42. De Montclos, 'Boko Haram and politics'; Thurston, *Boko Haram*, p. 12; Johannes Harnischfeger, 'Boko Haram and its critics: Observation from the Yobe state', in De Montclos, *Boko Haram*.

43. Kassim and Nwankpa, *The Boko Haram Reader*, p. 28. Sheriff later claimed that the appointment was due to Foi's governance experience.

44. Interview with Maiduguri NGO worker, 6 January 2017, by email.

45. International Crisis Group, 'Curbing violence in Nigeria (II)', p. 11. In 2007 Ali Modu Sheriff, Governor of Borno from 2003 to 2011, appointed Buji Foi, an influential Boko Haram member, as Commissioner of Islamic Affairs. See Integrated Regional Information Networks (IRIN), 'What will follow Boko Haram?', 24 November 2011, http://www.refworld.org/docid/4ed388292.html (accessed 2 September 2014).

46. Interview with former Boko Haram member (2009–11), Maiduguri, 7 October 2018.

47. Interview with person attending the Markas mosque, 6 October 2018.

48. Kassim and Nwankpa, *The Boko Haram Reader*.

49. George Goreman, 'Nigerian Taliban leader killed in custody', FDD's Long War Journal, 31 July 2009, http://www.longwarjournal.org/archives/2009/07/nigerian_taliban_lea.php.

50. Isa Umar Gusau, 'Boko Haram: How it all began', *Sunday Trust*, 2 August 2009, http://sundaytrust.com.ng/index.php/the-arts/35-people-in-the-news/people-in-the-news/5869-boko-haram-how-it-all-began (accessed 1 November 2014).

51. This points to the showdown between the government and Boko Haram, when the police attempted to arrest Boko Haram members in Bauchi in early June, as the major escalation trigger, not the Biu-Maiduguri incident. See Murray Last, 'The pattern of dissent: Boko Haram in Nigeria 2009', *Annual Review of Islam in Africa*, 2009, p. 10.

52. Gusau, 'Boko Haram: How it all began'.

53. Abdulkareem Mohammed and Mohammed Haruna, *The Paradox of Boko Haram*, Lagos: Moving Image, 2010.

54. Gusau, 'Boko Haram: How it all began'.

55. US Embassy in Abuja, 'Nigerian Islamist extremists launch attacks in 4 towns', Cable 09ABUJA1377, WikiLeaks, 2009, https://search.wikileaks.org/plusd/cables/09ABUJA1377_a.html.

56. 'Boko Haram vows to continue attack', RFI, 30 July 2009, http://www1.rfi.fr/actuen/articles/115/article_4552.asp,

57. Timothy Ola, 'Boko Haram: How 3 pastors were beheaded, eyewitness', *Daily Sun*, 6 August 2009. Archived from the original on 12 August 2009: 'The result of the 26–30 July events was that 3,500 people were internally displaced, more than 1,264 children orphaned, and over 392 women widowed. In addition, 28 police officers and five prison warders, as well as an undisclosed number of soldiers, had been killed. Properties destroyed include 48 buildings, three primary schools, more than 12 churches and a magistrate's court.'

58. US Embassy in Abuja, 'Muslim and Christian leaders criticize Boko Haram and GON, cites poverty as a key issue', Cable 09ABUJA1422, WikiLeaks, 2009, https://search.wikileaks.org/plusd/cables/09ABUJA1422_a.html.

59. Human Rights Watch, 'Spiraling Violence', p. 31.

60. See David Smith, 'Nigerian "Taliban" offensive leaves 150 dead', *The Guardian*, 27 July 2009. See also the last recorded interview with Yusuf (in custody): 'Boko Haram leader Mohammed Yusuf interrogation before his execution by Nigerian security agents', https://www.youtube.com/watch?v=ePpUvfTXY7w (accessed 25 January 2018).

61. Jacob Zenn, 'Leadership analysis of Boko Haram and Ansaru in Nigeria', *CTC Sentinel*, 24 February 2014. The flight of Boko Haram activists was corroborated by Stig Jarle Hansen, *Al-Shabaab in Somalia*; see also Thurston, *Boko Haram*, p. 163.

62. Jacob Zenn, 'A brief look at Ansaru's Khalid al-Barnawi: AQIM's bridge into northern Nigeria', *Militant Leadership Monitor*, 4 (3), 2013.

63. Interview with woman from Bama, Maiduguri, 4 October 2018.

64. Not all leaders fled outside Nigeria. Aminu Tashen-Ilimi, allegedly given 40 million naira to buy arms from the Niger Delta, either fled from the organisation or stayed in Kaduna as head of a clandestine cell. For indications of the internal conflicts, see Sharon Bean, 'The founding of Boko Haram and its spread to 32 Nigerian states', *Terrorism Monitor*, 24 March 2010; 'Boko Haram's divided house', *The Nigerian Voice*, 24 July 2011.

65. Ely Karmon, 'Boko Haram's international reach', *Perspectives on Terrorism*, 8 (1), 2014.

66. Michael Baca, 'Nigeria: The Borno and Kanuri roots of Boko Haram', African Arguments, 3 January 2015, http://www.ocnus.net/artman2/publish/Africa_8/Nigeria---the-Borno-and-Kanuri-Roots-of-Boko-Haram.shtml (accessed 21 January 2015). It should be noted that Nigerian intelligence could be over-reporting ethnic factors in Boko Haram in order to fragment it (thanks to Professor Hamid Bobboyi for making this point to me).

67. Quoted from Karmon, 'Boko Haram's international reach', p. 6.

68. Interview with woman from Bama, Maiduguri, 4 October 2018.

69. Freedom Onuoha, 'The 9/7 Boko Haram attack on Bauchi prison: A case of intelligence failure', *Peace and Conflict Monitor*, 2 November 2010.

70. 'Islamist leader Shekau "hiding in the desert"', AFP, 16 June 2010, http://www.iol.co.za/news/africa/islamist-leader-shekau-hiding-in-the-desert-1.490069#.VL-o1E0cSYY (accessed 21 January 2015). The video was distributed, like many other videos of Shekau that emerged in the period, through mobile telephones in the region.

71. Kassim and Nwankpa, *The Boko Haram Reader*, p. 297.

72. Thurston, *Boko Haram*, p. 16. Prior to 2009, three of Mohammed Ali's followers had lived and trained with AQIM's Sahara unit, and there is hard evidence for contact from 2009 and onwards; see Thurston's footnotes.

73. Ibid., pp. 175–176.

74. Onuoha, 'The 9/7 Boko Haram attack on Bauchi prison'.

75. Alex Thurston, 'Nigeria: Boko Haram assassinations', Sahel blog, 13 October 2010, https://sahelblog.wordpress.com/2010/10/13/nigeria-boko-haram-assassinations/ (accessed 22 January 2015).

76. Ibid.

77. Alex Thurston, 'Quick items: Boko Haram and al-Shabaab', Sahel blog, 6 December 2010, https://sahelblog.wordpress.com/2010/10/22/quick-items-boko-haram-and-al-shabab/ (accessed 22 January 2015).

78. Interview with businessman from the Mafoni area, Maiduguri, 4 October 2018.

79. International Crisis Group, 'Curbing violence in Nigeria'.

80. Alex Thurston, 'Boko Haram battles police in Maiduguri', Sahel blog, 6 December 2010, https://sahelblog.wordpress.com/2010/12/06/boko-haram-battles-police-in-maiduguri/ (accessed 22 January 2015).

81. Stig Jarle Hansen, 'African jihadis: Media strategies', Report for the Canadian Defense Academy, 2014.

82. Zenn, 'Leadership analysis of Boko Haram and Ansaru in Nigeria'; Hansen, *Al-Shabaab*.

83. Zenn, 'Leadership analysis of Boko Haram and Ansaru in Nigeria'. An article on the split was published in the glossy *Al Risalah* magazine; see Abu Usamatul Ansary, 'A message from Nigeria', *Al Risalah*, 4, 2017, https://azelin.files.wordpress.com/2017/01/al-risacc84lah-magazine-4.pdf (accessed 5 February 2018).

84. Ibid.

85. Adam Nossiter, 'In Nigeria, a deadly group's rage has local roots', *New York Times*, 25 February 2012.

86. Hansen, 'African jihadis: Media strategies'.

87. Human Rights Watch, 'Spiraling violence', p. 31.

88. John Campbell, 'To battle Nigeria's Boko Haram, put down your guns', *Foreign Policy*, September 2011.

89. Minika Mark, 'Boko Haram ready for peace talks with Nigeria, says alleged sect member', *The Guardian*, 1 November 2012.

90. Ibid. See also Kassim and Nwankpa, *The Boko Haram Reader*, p. 345.

91. Daniel E. Agbiboa, 'Peace at daggers drawn? Boko Haram and the state of emergency in Nigeria', *Studies in Conflict and Terrorism*, 37 (1), 2014, p. 46.

92. Ibid., p. 47.

93. Ibid., p. 41.

94. Thurston, *Boko Haram*, p. 213.

95. Agbiboa, 'Peace at daggers drawn?', p. 48.

96. Jim Sanders, 'The military balance in northeast Nigeria', *Africa in Transition*, 16 September 2014, http://blogs.cfr.org/campbell/2014/09/16/the-military-balance-in-northeast-nigeria/ (accessed 30 April 2015).

97. Interview with secretary of the vigilantes, Maiduguri, 7 October 2018; interview with businessman from the Mafoni area, Maiduguri, 4 October 2018.

98. Human Rights Watch, 'Nigeria: Massive destruction, deaths from military raid', Human Rights Watch news release, 1 May 2013, http://www.hrw.org/news/2013/05/01/nigeria-massive-destruction-deaths-military-raid (accessed 30 April 2015).

99. Virginia Comolli, *Boko Haram: Nigeria's Islamist Insurgency*, London: Hurst, 2016.

100. Ola' Audu, 'Boko Haram: Shekau claims responsibility for attack on Giwa barracks, threatens to attack universities, civilian-JTF', *Premium Times*, 24 March 2014, http://www.premiumtimesng.com/news/157374-boko-haram-shekau-claims-responsibility-attack-giwa-barracks-threatens-attack-universities-civilian-jtf.html (accessed 9 April 2017).

101. Human Rights Watch, '"Those terrible weeks in their camp": Boko Haram violence against women and girls in northeast Nigeria', Human Rights Watch Report, 3 October 2014.

102. International Crisis Group, 'Curbing violence in Nigeria (II)', p. 17.

103. TRAC, 'Boko Haram: Coffers and coffins; a Pandora's box – the vast financing options for Boko Haram', May 2014, http://www.trackingterrorism.org/article/boko-haram-coffers-and-coffins-pandoras-box-vast-financing-options-boko-haram; 'Nigeria: Boko Haram "taking over" northern Borno state', *Daily Trust*, 20 April 2013, http://allafrica.com/stories/201304200127.html.

104. Ibid.

105. For an overview of the losses of leaders, see International Crisis Group, 'Curbing violence in Nigeria (II)', p. 22. The group still maintains that Boko Haram is fragmented today, but this writer maintains that organised military efforts, the very efficient military campaigns conducted by Boko Haram in Borno from 2013 onwards, and increasing centralisation of media efforts, all indicate a trend towards centralisation. Independent cells probably exist outside Borno and the north-east, but their activities are so limited that they are of less importance.

106. Stig Jarle Hansen, 'A trend analysis of Boko Haram over the last year, as well as the Nigerian army and its performance', Risk Intelligence Brief, 2015.

107. 'Boko Haram declares "Islamic state" in northern Nigeria', BBC News, 25 August 2014, http://english.alarabiya.net/en/perspective/alarabiya-studies/2014/09/03/ (accessed 9 April 2017).

108. Human Rights Watch, '"Those terrible weeks in their camp"', p. 3.

109. Interview with an NGO worker in Lake Chad area, Maiduguri, 5 October 2018.

110. Interview with secretary of the vigilantes, Maiduguri, 7 October 2018.

111. Simon Allison, 'In Nigeria, Boko Haram follows in the footsteps of Iraq's Islamic State', *Daily Maverick*, 14 August 2014.

112. Hansen, 'A trend analysis of Boko Haram over the last year'.

113. Jama'at Ahl al-Sunna li-l-Da'wah wal-Jihad, 'Applications of the rulings of Islam in the Islamic State of East Africa', 2015, https://www.youtube.com/watch?v=dZI2KlHvg9A (accessed 9 January 2017).

114. Abubakar Shekau, 'A message to the Ummah', Jama'at Ahl al-Sunna li-l-Da'wah wal-Jihad, 2014, https://www.youtube.com/watch?v=Vm2LdvevMBU (accessed 9 January 2017).

115. Interview with former Boko Haram fighter (2015–17), 6 October 2018, Maiduguri.

116. For traces of Boko Haram's activities in Chad, see Abdel Aziz, 'Beheading in Chad', in Kassim and Nwankpa, *The Boko Haram Reader*, pp. 429–434.

117. 'Nigeria's Boko Haram: Baga destruction "shown in images"', BBC, 15 January 2015, http://www.bbc.com/news/world-africa-30826582 (accessed 9 December 2017).

118. Abu Musab al-Barnawi, 'About the events in the city of Baga', al-Urwah-al-Wuthqa Foundation, 27 January 2015, http://jihadology. net/2015/01/27/al-urwah-al-wuthqa-foundation-presents-a-new-video-message-from-from-boko-%e1%b8%a5arams-jamaat-ahl-al-sunnah-li-dawah-wa-l-jihad-interview-with-the-official-spokesma/ (accessed 9 December 2017).

119. Kassim and Nwankpa, *The Boko Haram Reader*.

120. Claude Mbowou, 'Between the "Kanuri" and others', in Virginie Collombier and Olivier Roy (eds.), *Tribes and Global Jihadism*, London: Hurst, 2018, pp. 131–152; Thurston, *Boko Haram*, pp. 245–248.

121. See, for example, Laura Grossman, 'Analysis: Boko Haram loses ground, but remains in the fight', FDD's Long War Journal, 23 March 2015, http://www.longwarjournal.org/archives/2015/03/boko-haram-loses-ground-but-remains-in-the-fight.php (accessed 30 April 2015).

122. Abubakar Shekau, 'Jama'at _Ahl_al-Sunnah_li-l-Da'wah_wal-Jihad_ Pledges_Allegiance_to_Caliph_of_the_Muslims_Abu-Bakr_al-Baghdadi', @urwa_wuthqa (Twitter), 7 March 2015.

123. Richard Barrett, 'The Islamic State', The Soufan Group Report, 2014, http://www.google.no/url?sa=t&rct=j&q=&esrc=s&source=web& cd=1&ved=0CB0QFjAA&url=http%3A%2F%2Fsoufangroup. com%2Fwp-content%2Fuploads%2F2014%2F10%2FTSG-The-Islamic-State-Nov14.pdf&ei=9Vs-VZ_8FciuswG35oGYAw&usg=AF QjCNFMbXX-OrKwKdmBQEWSdrDTbtoggQ&bvm=bv.91665533 ,d.bGg (accessed 30 April 2015).

124. Sarah al-Mukhtar, 'How Boko Haram courted and joined the Islamic State', *New York Times*, 10 June 2015.

125. See, for example, 'Is Islamic State shaping Boko Haram media?', BBC, 7 April 2015, http://www.bbc.com/news/world-africa-31522469 (accessed 28 April 2015).

126. Jacob Zenn, 'Wilayat West Africa reboots for the caliphate', *CTC Sentinel*, 8 (8), 2015; Cummings, 'A jihadi takeover bid in Nigeria?'

127. See, for example, Michael Weiss and Hassan Hassan, *ISIS: Inside the Army of Terror*, New York: Regan Arts, 2015.

128. Abu Musab al-Barnawi, 'We will get out of our misery harder and stronger, God willing', *al-Naba*, 41, 2016.

129. Abubakar Shekau, 'Message to the world', 3 August 2016, http://jihadology.net/2016/08/03/new-audio-message-from-abu-bakr-al-shekau-message-to-the-world/ (accessed 9 December 2017).

130. 'New Boko Haram leader, al-Barnawi, accuses Abubakar Shekau of killing fellow Muslims, living in luxury', *Sahara Reporters*, 5 August 2016, http://saharareporters.com/2016/08/05/new-boko-haram-leader-al-barnawi-accuses-abubakar-shekau-killing-fellow-muslims-living/ (accessed 9 December 2017).

131. Interview with former Boko Haram fighter (2015–17), 6 October 2018, Maiduguri.

132. 'Boko Haram: Shekau loses ground to al-Barnawi in battle of supremacy', 360 News, 14 December 2017, https://www.360nobs.com/2017/12/boko-haram-shekau-loses-grounds-al-barnawi-battle-supremacy/ (accessed 10 January 2018).

133. Interview with former Boko Haram fighter (2015–17), 6 October 2018, Maiduguri.

134. 'Terrorists raid Borno village for food, medical supplies', Pulse News Agency, 6 March 2017, http://www.pulse.ng/news/local/boko-haram-terrorists-raid-borno-village-for-food-medical-supplies-id6430975.html (accessed 10 January 2018).

7. THE ALLIED DEMOCRATIC FORCES: OPPORTUNISTS IN DISGUISE?

1.   See, for example, Lindsay Scorgie-Porter, 'Economic survival and borderland rebellion: The case of the Allied Democratic Forces on the Uganda-Congo border', *Journal of the Middle East and Africa*, 6 (2), 2015, pp. 191–213.

2.   Kristof Titeca and Koen Vlassenroot, 'Rebels without borders in the Rwenzori borderland? A biography of the Allied Democratic Forces', *Journal of Eastern African Studies*, 6 (1), 2012; Gérard Prunier, 'Rebel movements and proxy warfare in Uganda, Sudan and the Congo (1986–99)', *African Affairs*, 103 (412), 2004; Scorgie-Porter, 'Economic survival and borderland rebellion'; Andrew McGregor, 'Oil and jihad in Central Africa: The rise and fall of Uganda's ADF', *Terrorism Monitor*, 5 (24), 2007.

3.   On 30 June 1962, Isaya Mukirania, father of the current king (after a Rwenzori kingdom was established in 2008), and Peter Mupalya and Yeremia Kawamala, both Bamba representatives in the Toro kingdom, walked out of the Orukurato (Toro Kingdom parliament) allegedly over issues of lack of equality, starting the process that led to the rebellion.

See Felix Basiime, Thembo Kahungu Misairi and Geoffrey Mutegeki Araali, 'The Bakonjo–Bamba clashes: Looking beyond the fights', *Daily Monitor*, 14 July 2012.

4. Prunier, 'Rebel movements and proxy warfare', p. 368.
5. Ibid.
6. Ibid.
7. Ibid.
8. Ibid., p. 374.
9. Kirsten Alnaes, 'Rebel ravages in Bundibugyo', in Bruce Kapferer and Bjørn Enge Bertelsen (eds.), *Crisis of the State: War and Social Upheaval*, London: Berghahn Books, 2009, p. 104.
10. Ibid.
11. International Crisis Group, 'Eastern Congo: The ADF–NALU's lost rebellion', Africa Briefing, no. 93, 2012, p. 4.
12. Mike Ssegawa, 'The aftermath of the attack on Uganda Muslim Supreme Council', *Daily Monitor*, 3 August 2015.
13. Ibid.
14. It should be noted that the Nakasero mosque had a tradition of violent clashes after it became estranged from Jamil Mukulu and his group, usually over internal leadership positions.
15. The sect left Nakasero and set up base in Makindye, Madirisa; later they shifted their headquarters to Sheikh Kimera's plot in Mengo near Lubiri. According to Mike Ssegawa, Sheikh Muzafalu Mulinde was elected as head, Sheikh Mukulu became the chief judge, Sheikh Ismail Buikwe became the leader of Dawa, and Sheikh Sharif Mukyotala became treasurer.
16. Els De Temmerman, 'ADF rebellion: Guerilla to urban terrorism', *New Vision*, 21 May 2007.
17. Ibid.
18. Titeca and Vlassenroot, 'Rebels without borders in the Rwenzori borderland?', pp. 154–176.
19. After Kabila launched his war, Hosea was cut off in Goma. Hosea was then replaced by Mzee Fenahasi Kisokeranio, from NALU. John Thawite, 'Uganda: 'Benz spills ADF secrets', *All Africa*, 31 December 2000, https://allafrica.com/stories/200101020459.html (accessed 10 October 2018).
20. Interview with MP from Beni, Goma, 10 July 2018.
21. Interview with *mwami* (traditional king), Goma, 7 July 2018.
22. Perhaps the most famous were the attacks on the Kasese district in Uganda, when the cities of Mpondwe and Bwera were captured and held for some days. Gérard Prunier, 'The geopolitical situation in the

Great Lakes Area in light of the Kivu crisis', Writenett, 1 February 1997, http://www.refworld.org/docid/3ae6a6be0.html (accessed 18 December 2015); International Crisis Group, 'North Kivu: Into the quagmire? An overview of the current crisis in North Kivu', ICG Kivu Report, no. 1, 1998.

23. Ibid.
24. Scorgie-Porter, 'Economic survival and borderland rebellion', p. 211.
25. Ibid.
26. 'Uganda: IRIN Special Report on the ADF rebellion', IRIN News, 1999.
27. See Bright Malere, 'ADF rebels: My abduction, camp life and escape', New Vision, 4 September 2013.
28. Howard Adelman and Govind C. Rao (eds.), War and Peace in Zaire-Congo: Analyzing and Evaluating Intervention, 1996–1997, Trenton, NJ: Africa World Press, 2003.
29. International Crisis Group, 'How Kabila lost his way', ICG Congo Report, no. 3, 21 May 1999, p. 10.
30. Ali B. Ali-Dinar, 'IRIN Special Report on the ADF rebellion', IRIN News, 8 December 1999, http://www.africa.upenn.edu/Hornet/irin-120899c.html (accessed 10 February 2018). According to the former ADF chief of staff, Commander Benz, Abdallah Yusuf Kabanda was ADF's leader, Jamil Mukulu and Hosea were second-in-command, the latter being later replaced by Fenahasi Kisokeranio. Other commanders included Henry Matovu, Benz himself and the legendary Kasangaki Kiwewa Swaib Kigozi, aka 'Commander Tiger'. Immigration and Refugee Board of Canada, 'The Allied Democratic Front (ADF) in Uganda including leaders, goals, objectives, and whether or not members and supporters are harassed by the government (1995–2002)', UGA38401.E, 2003. Another notable commander was Henry Matovu Birungi, aka Commander Cobra. Another line-up is listed by Hans Romkema: Abdallah Yusuf Kabanda is here given as a military commander under Mukulu. He was said to have a deputy chief, Dr Kyeyune. Isiko Barahu was listed as chief of military general headquarters, together with Mohammed Kayiira as chief of administration and director of military intelligence, Mohammed Batambuze as army commander, Commander Tiger as overall field commander, Hassan Musa as chief of military operations and logistics, and Mohammed Isabirye. See Hans Romkema, 'Opportunities and constraints for the disarmament and repatriation of foreign armed groups in the Democratic Republic of Congo', Report commissioned by the Secretariat of the MDRP, 2007.

31. Ibid., pp. 70–79.
32. Ibid.
33. Ibid.
34. Ibid.
35. Scorgie-Porter, 'Economic survival and borderland rebellion', p. 200.
36. McGregor, 'Oil and jihad in Central Africa', p. 3.
37. Scorgie-Porter, 'Economic survival and borderland rebellion'.
38. Ibid., p. 198.
39. Ibid.
40. African Rights, *Avoiding an Impasse: Understanding Conflicts in Western Uganda*, Kampala: African Rights, 2001; Lucy Hovil and Eric Werker, 'Portrait of a failed rebellion: An account of rational, sub-optimal violence in western Uganda', *Rationality and Society*, 17 (5), 2005; see also Titeca and Vlassenroot, 'Rebels without borders in the Rwenzori borderland?', p. 159 for civilian losses in its early phase.
41. Ibid., p. 163.
42. Ibid., p. 200. According to Lindsay Scorgie-Porter, 'Community leaders in Eringeti reported that the ADF taxed chainsaws U.S.$200 per year and issued fines of U.S.$500 to those accessing such areas without "permission".'
43. International Crisis Group, 'Eastern Congo: The ADF–NALU's lost rebellion', p. 6.
44. Interview with MP from Beni, Goma, 10 July 2018.
45. Ibid.
46. Ibid.
47. Taken from the appendix of the Group of Experts on the Democratic Republic of the Congo, 'Final report of the Group of Experts on the Democratic Republic of the Congo', Security Council Report S/2012/348, Annex 6, 2012.
48. McGregor, 'Oil and jihad in Central Africa'.
49. The people who paid the bail were Mustapha Kamau and Jacob Musyoka, the latter a friend of Sylvester Opiyo. Musyoka disappeared, together with Opiyo, in Molo in May 2012, and this contributed to the anger that manifested itself in Mombasa after the Muslim cleric Aboud Rogo died in August in a drive-by shooting, basically because many believed the two had been killed by the Kenyan government. However, the sister of Opiyo claims to have been in contact with him after his disappearance and said that he fled to Somalia. See Group of Experts on the Democratic Republic of the Congo, 'Final report of the Group of Experts on the Democratic Republic of the Congo', Security Council Report S/2012/843, 2012, p. 30, for details of the bail itself.

50. Group of Experts on the Democratic Republic of the Congo, 'Final report of the Group of Experts on the Democratic Republic of the Congo', Security Council Report S/2015/19, 2015.

51. Ibid.

52. Ibid., p. 156.

53. Ibid.

54. Ibid.

55. Group of Experts on the Democratic Republic of the Congo, 'Final report of the Group of Experts on the Democratic Republic of the Congo', Security Council Report S/2016/466, 2016, p. 166. The man in question was Colonel Richard Bisamaza, who defected from the Congolese army in 2013. He denied the allegations himself.

56. Ibid. The militia in question was André Mbonguma Kitobi's.

57. Risdel Kasasira, 'Who is ADF's Jamil Mukulu?', *The Monitor*, 7 August 2015.

58. Group of Experts on the Democratic Republic of the Congo, 'Midterm report of the Group of Experts on the Democratic Republic of the Congo', Security Council Report S/2016/1102, 2016, p. 90.

59. Group of Experts on the Democratic Republic of the Congo, 'Midterm report of the Group of Experts on the Democratic Republic of the Congo', Security Council Report S/2017/672/Rev.

60. Interview with Nande journalist, Goma, 6 June 2018.

61. Interview with Ugandan security service official, Kampala, 12 June 2018.

8. AL-HIJRA/AL-MUHAJIROUN, AND THEIR UNCLEAR FRINGES

1. In Kenya there are exceptions, as in the north-east (along the Somali border), where state institutions and law enforcement agencies are weaker, as well as in the north, such as Turkana. In the north-east, the Harakat al-Shabaab have operated relatively openly; see chapter 9.

2. The Mpeketoni attack was used to attack the opposition in Kenya. See David M. Anderson and Jacob McKnight, 'Kenya at war: Al-Shabaab and its enemies in Eastern Africa', *African Affairs*, 114 (454), 2015.

3. Søren Gilsaa, 'Salafism(s) in Tanzania: Theological roots and political subtext of the Ansar al-Sunna', *Islamic Africa*, 6, 2015, pp. 30–49; Anneli Botha, 'Radicalization in Kenya, recruitment to al-Shabaab and the Mombasa Republican Council', ISS Paper, no. 265, 2015.

4. See Barbara Brents and Deo S. Mishgeni, 'Terrorism in context: Race, religion, party, and violent conflict in Zanzibar', *The American Sociologist*, Summer 2004.

5. Abu Hassan An-Nairobi, 'Madonda Yasiopona', *Gaidi Mtaani*, 2, 2012.

6. Marie-Aude Fouéré, *Remembering Julius Nyerere in Tanzania: History, Memory, Legacy*, Dar es Salaam: Mkukina Nyota Publishers, 2015, p. 175.

7. Stig Jarle Hansen, 'Uamsho, Shabaab and the threat of terrorism in Tanzania', *Strategic Insights*, 59, 2015, p. 16.

8. BBC, 'Zanzibar clashes over missing cleric Sheik Farid Hadi', BBC, 18 October 2012, http://www.bbc.com/news/world-africa-19997774 (accessed 29 October 2015).

9. Joop Koopman, 'Is Tanzania radical Islam's next target?', *Huffington Post*, 4 June 2014, http://www.huffingtonpost.com/joop-koopman/is-tanzania-radical-islam_b_4725828.html (accessed 29 October 2015).

10. Andre LeSage, 'The rising terrorist threat in Tanzania: Domestic Islamist militancy and regional threats', *Strategic Forum*, September 2014.

11. Ioannis Gatsiounis, 'After al-Shabaab', *Current Trends in Islamic Ideology*, 14, 2013, p. 82.

12. Arye Oded, *Islam and Politics in Kenya*. Boulder, CO: Lynne Rienner Publishers, 2000.

13. See Great Britain, 'Kenya Protectorate Order in Council, 1920', S.R.O. 1920, no. 2343, S.R.O. & S.I. Rev. VIII, 1920.

14. Richard Stren, 'Factional politics and central control in Mombasa, 1960–1969', *Canadian Journal of African Studies*, 4 (1), 1970, p. 38.

15. Stig Jarle Hansen, Stian Lid and Clifford Collin Omondi Okwany, 'Countering violent extremism in Somalia and Kenya: Actors and approaches', NIBR Report, 2016, p. 10.

16. Parselelo Kantai, 'Kenya's Mombasa Republican Council: The coast calls for freedom', Africa Report, 17 May 2012, https://web.archive.org/web/20120702202413/http://www.theafricareport.com/index.php/20120517501811752/east-horn-africa/kenya-s-mombasa-republican-council%E2%80%A9-the-coast-calls-for-freedom-501811752.html (accessed 18 December 2017).

17. James Macharia, 'Insight: Separatist storm brewing on Kenya's coast', Reuters World News, 23 July 2012, https://uk.reuters.com/article/uk-kenya-coast-mrc/insight-separatist-storm-brewing-on-kenyas-coast-idUKBRE86M0H820120723, (accessed 18 December 2017).

18. Botha, 'Radicalization in Kenya, recruitment to al-Shabaab and the Mombasa Republican Council', p. 3; Kamau Muthoni and Patrick Beja, 'Mombasa Republican Council (MRC) now demands dialogue with state after major victory in court', *The Standard*, 26 July 2016, https://www.standardmedia.co.ke/article/2000209821/mombasa-republican-council-mrc-now-demands-dialogue-with-state-after-major-victory-in-court (accessed 18 December 2017).

19. For example, see Abu Hassan An-Nairobi, 'Madonda Yasiopona'.
20. David Ochami, 'How fiery cleric Rogo developed, propagated extremism', *The Standard*, 1 September 2012, https://www.standardmedia.co.ke/?articleID=2000065268&story_title=How-fiery-cleric-Rogo-developed,-propagated-extremism- (accessed 18 December 2017).
21. Arye Oded, 'Islamic extremism in Kenya: The rise and fall of Sheikh Khalid Balala', *Journal of Religion in Africa*, 26 (4), 1996.
22. Arye Oded, 'Islamic extremism in Kenya', RIMA Occasional Papers, 1 (14), 2013.
23. Patric Beja, 'I was declared stateless while in Germany', *The Standard*, 7 June 2015, https://www.standardmedia.co.ke/article/2000168245/i-was-declared-stateless-while-in-germany (accessed 19 December 2017). Balala, who was allowed to return to Kenya after five years, maintains that the party was not Islamist, but focused on protecting the rights of Kenya's Muslim population. It is notable that elements of the party also joined the oppositional Ford Kenya.
24. Oded, 'Islamic extremism in Kenya, the case of Sheik Khalid Balala', p. 412.
25. Matthew Rosenberg, 'Al-Qaeda skimming charity money', AP, 7 June 2004, https://www.cbsnews.com/news/al-qaeda-skimming-charity-money/ (accessed 18 December 2017). Rogo was accused of being involved in the 2002 al-Qaeda Paradise Hotel attack, but was acquitted by the Kenyan courts. See 'Mombasa bombing trial collapses', BBC, 9 June 2005, http://news.bbc.co.uk/2/hi/africa/4075988.stm (accessed 19 December 2017).
26. The mosque was founded by the family of former Mombasa mayor Ali Taib, but the Taib family quitted the running of the mosque around the period Rogo became part of it. Ishaq Jumbe, 'History of the controversial Musa mosque', *The Standard Digital*, 3 February 2014, https://www.standardmedia.co.ke/article/2000103809/history-of-the-controversial-musa-mosque (accessed 27 December 2017).
27. Ibid. See also Citizen TV, 'The troubled Masjid Musa', Citizen TV, 10 February 2014, https://www.youtube.com/watch?v=ZMHBnMaWR24 (accessed 27 December 2017).
28. See, for example, Phil Hatcher Moore's interviews with Masjid Musa frequenters: Phil Hatcher Moore, 'Islamism on the Kenyan coast', Philmoore info blog, 7 October 2013, http://philmoore.info/blog/2013/10/islamism-on-the-kenyan-coast (accessed 27 December 2017); Cyrus Ombati, 'Police name Kenyan suspects luring youth to join al-Shabaab', *The Standard Digital*, 18 August 2015, https://www.

standardmedia.co.ke/article/2000173237/police-name-kenyan-suspects-luring-youth-to-join-al-shabaab (accessed 27 December 2017).

29. Rob Jillo, 'Two Kenyans charged with terrorism', Capital FM, 22 December 2010, https://www.capitalfm.co.ke/news/2010/12/two-kenyans-charged-with-terrorism/ (accessed 27 December 2017).

30. Nyambega Gisesa, 'Ten things you didn't know about Sheikh Abubakar Shariff alias Makaburi', The Standard Digital, 2 April 2014, https://www.standardmedia.co.ke/article/2000108421/ten-things-you-didn-t-know-about-sheikh-abubakar-shariff-alias-makaburi (accessed 18 December 2017).

31. It contributed to Rogo's radicalisation, according to Hassan Omer Hassan, former deputy head of the government-funded Kenya National Commission on Human Rights. Tom Odula, 'Shooting of cleric who bombed Israeli hotel highlights growing Islamism in Mombasa', Times of Israel, 6 September 2012, https://www.timesofisrael.com/mombasa-cleric-who-tried-to-bomb-israeli-hotel-killed-in-drive-by-shooting/ (accessed 27 December 2017). This contradicts the sources describing his friendship with Fazul in Siyu before 2002.

32. Monitoring Group on Somalia and Eritrea, 'Report of the Monitoring Group on Somalia and Eritrea submitted in accordance with Resolution 1916 (2010)', S/2011/433, 18 July 2011.

33. Ibid., p. 142. This point is often missed; there was a stream of foreign fighters going to Somalia before the Kenyan intervention in Somalia in 2011.

34. Group interview with three anonymous sheikhs formerly involved in the Pumwani mosque, 7 January 2016.

35. Interview with Ole Hassan Nadu, 3 January 2016.

36. Monitoring Group on Somalia and Eritrea, 'Report of the Monitoring Group on Somalia and Eritrea submitted in accordance with Resolution 1916 (2010)', p. 140.

37. The Monitoring Group enclosed a copy of the founding charter of the MYC; see ibid., pp. 149–156.

38. Kenya Muslim Youth Alliance, 'We don't trust anyone, strengthening relationship is the key to reducing violent extremism in Kenya', Special Report, 2016, p. 19, http://www.international-alert.org/sites/default/files/Kenya_ViolentExtremism_EN_2016.pdf (accessed 28 December 2017).

39. Monitoring Group on Somalia and Eritrea, 'Report of the Monitoring Group on Somalia and Eritrea submitted in accordance with Resolution 1916 (2010)', pp. 159–167.

40. Ibid., p. 145.

41. Ibid., p. 140.

42. Interview with Clifford Collins, community worker in Majengo at the time, 21 December 2017. Collins claims that Opiyo was the leader of the MYC while other sources claim that Opiyo led the resource centre of the organisation. See Anneli Botha, *Terrorism in Kenya and Uganda: Radicalization from a Political Socialization Perspective*, London: Lexington Books, 2017, p. 12.

43. See, for example, Imam Ali, 'And whoever does so among you – then it is those who are the wrongdoers', Kataib Media, 29 July 2017, http:// jihadology.net/category/individuals/ideologues/a%E1%B8%A5mad-iman-ali/ (accessed 27 December 2017); Imam Ali, 'Interview on the general elections in Kenya, Part 1', Kataib Media, 26 July 2017, http://jihadology.net/2017/07/26/new-video-message-from-%e1%b8%a5arakat-al-shabab-al-mujahidins-a%e1%b8%a5mad-iman-ali-interview-on-the-general-elections-in-kenya-part-1/ (accessed 27 December 2017).

44. Whitney Eulich, 'Mombasa riots stretch into second day as extremist group tries to rally Muslims', *Christian Science Monitor*, 28 August 2012, https://www.csmonitor.com/World/Security-Watch/terrorism-security/2012/0828/Mombasa-riots-stretch-into-second-day-as-extremist-group-tries-to-rally-Muslims (accessed 27 December 2017). Several other sheikhs were killed and went missing. Muhammad Kassim was, for example, declared missing in April 2012. In April 2014 Sheikh Abubakar Shariff 'Makaburi' was killed.

45. Human Rights Watch, 'Deaths and disappearances: Abuses in counterterrorism operations in Nairobi and in northeastern Kenya', Human Rights Watch Report, 7 (20), 2016, https://www.hrw. org/report/2016/07/20/deaths-and-disappearances/abuses-counterterrorism-operations-nairobi-and (accessed 27 December 2017).

46. Jonathan Horowitz, 'Trouble looms as Kenya struggles to combat terrorism', *World Post*, 2014, https://www.huffingtonpost.com/jonathan-horowitz/kenya-terrorism_b_5028058.html (accessed 27 December 2017).

47. KTN, 'Masjid Musa parliamentary statement, 18th February 2014', KTN, 18 February 2014, https://www.youtube.com/watch?v=0rEL89OIqn4 (accessed 27 December 2017).

48. See, for example, Harakat al-Shabaab, 'New statement from Ḥarakat al-Shabāb al-Mujāhidīn: "Shaykh Aboud Rogo's death: A catalyst for change"', Kataib Media, 27 August 2012, http://jihadology. net/2012/08/27/new-statement-from-%e1%b8%a5arakat-al-

shabab-al-mujahidin-shaykh-aboud-rogos-death-a-catalyst-for-change/ (accessed 27 December 2017); 'Biography of the martyred figures in East Africa #3: Shaykh 'Abūud Rūghū', 2013, http://jihadology.net/2013/03/26/new-release-biography-of-the-flags-of-the-martyrs-in-east-africa-3-shaykh-abuud-rughu/ (accessed 27 December 2017).

49. The names of the two mosques were changed. See Philip Mwakio, 'Teenager picked to act as new Masjid Musa imam', *The Standard Digital*, 24 January 2015, https://www.standardmedia.co.ke/article/2000148985/teenager-picked-to-act-as-new-masjid-musa-imam (accessed 27 December 2017).

50. Martin Wachira, 'Why Joho was almost beaten by angry youth, barred from mosque', *The Pulse*, 18 May 2017, http://www.pulselive.co.ke/news/electionske-why-joho-was-almost-beaten-by-angry-youth-barred-from-mosque-id6696212.html (accessed 27 December 2017).

51. Wachira Mwangi, 'Mosque reopens for prayers as caretaker calls for sobriety', *Daily Nation*, 6 December 2014, http://www.nation.co.ke/news/Mosque-reopens-for-prayers-as-caretaker-calls-for-sobriety/1056-2547472-ch9tbsz/index.html (accessed 27 December 2017).

52. Monitoring Group on Somalia and Eritrea, 'Report of the Monitoring Group on Somalia and Eritrea submitted in accordance with Resolution 1916 (2010)', p. 140.

53. Fredrick Nzes, 'Al-Hijra: Al-Shabab's affiliate in Kenya', *CTC Sentinel*, 7 (5), 2014, p. 24.

54. For example, Muslim Youth Centre, 'New statement from the Muslim Youth Center: "On Abū Manṣūr al-Amrīkī"', MYC, 14 September 2013, http://jihadology.net/category/the-muslim-youth-center/ (accessed 27 December 2017). There are many other examples available on this link.

55. Nick Owens, 'Fugitive Samantha Lewthwaite – the "white widow" of 7/7 – writes chilling online blog', *The Mirror*, 1 July 2102, http://www.mirror.co.uk/news/uk-news/fugitive-samantha-lewthwaite---the-white-946967 (accessed 27 December 2017).

56. IGAD Security Sector Program (ISSP) and Sahan Foundation, 'Al-Shabaab as a transnational security threat', IGAD Special Report, 2016, p. 23.

57. Reuters, 'Nairobi explosions: At least 12 killed, more than 70 wounded in attacks on bus, market', Reuters/AFP/ABC, 16 May 2014, http://www.abc.net.au/news/2014-05-16/deadly-twin-bomb-blasts-rock-nairobi/5459300 (accessed 27 December 2017).

58. IGAD Security Sector Program (ISSP) and Sahan Foundation, 'Al-Shabaab as a transnational security threat', p. 23 and relevant footnotes as well.

59. Botha, 'Radicalization in Kenya, recruitment to al-Shabaab and the Mombasa Republican Council'.

60. John Mwangi, 'The process and trends of youth radicalization in Kenya's Mombasa and Nairobi counties', Paper presented at the 3rd MISR Graduate Students' Conference, 28–29 July 2017.

61. Ngala Chome, 'Lessons from Kenya's coast and why extremism is a global burden', *The Standard Digital*, 26 February 2017, https://www.standardmedia.co.ke/article/2001230736/lessons-from-kenya-s-coast-and-why-extremism-is-a-global-burden (accessed 27 December 2017).

62. Kenyan schools teach English as a main language, and Swahili as a secondary language. In Tanzania, the latter is the primary language.

63. For an example, see Mujahiroun, 'Statement on the Tanzanian spy', Mujahiroun Tanga, 3 April 2016, https://somalianews.files.wordpress.com/2016/04/ampressrelease3.pdf (accessed 27 December 2017).

64. Calvins Onsarigo, 'Terror suspect Ali Hamis Mzomo shot dead in Likoni', *The Star*, 8 December 2017, https://www.the-star.co.ke/news/2017/12/08/terror-suspect-ali-hamis-mzomo-shot-dead-in-likoni_c1681959 (accessed 27 December 2017).

65. Zhou Xin, 'Kenya foils terror attack in coast region, recover weapons', Xinhua, 20 December 2017, http://news.xinhuanet.com/english/2017-12/20/c_136840917.htm (accessed 27 December 2017); Dominic Wabala, 'Al-Shabaab returnee's horrid tales of sex slavery', *The Standard Digital*, 10 December 2017, https://www.standardmedia.co.ke/article/2001262655/al-shabaab-returnee-s-horrid-tales-of-sex-slavery (accessed 27 December 2017).

66. Hansen, 'Uamsho, Shabaab and the threat of terrorism in Zanzibar'.

67. Thomas Ndaluka and Frans Wijsen, *Religion and State in Tanzania Revisited: Reflections from 50 Years of Independence*, Münster: Lit Verlag, 2014, p. 69.

68. Al-Muhajiroun, 'Protecting our sheiks', al-Muhajiroun, 2015, http://jihadology.net/2015/03/03/new-article-from-al-muhajirun-in-east-africa-a-message-to-tanzania-protecting-our-clerics/ (accessed 29 October 2015).

69. Felicitas Becker, 'Rural Islamism during the war on terror: A Tanzanian case study', *African Affairs*, 105 (421), 2006; Simon Turner, 'These young men show no respect for local customs: Globalization, youth and Islamic revival in Zanzibar', DIIS Working Paper, 4, 2008, p. 17.

70. There has been debate over the role of Saudi scholarships. Some writers like Søren Gilsaa, Centre of African Studies, University of Copenhagen, argue that the Saudi influence was part of a longer tradition of influence from abroad, starting in the nineteenth century, and became a reformist strain in Tanzania, which was consolidated in the 1970s. Søren Gilsaa, 'Islamic reform and politics in Tanzania: Situating the Ansar al-Sunna in Tanzania's historical politics of Islam', Paper presented at the 3rd European Conference on African Studies in Leipzig, 2009. He does, however, fail to adequately explain why these currents were consolidated in the 1970s and why almost all the leaders of AMYC had a background in Saudi institutions.

71. Gilsaa, 'Salafism(s) in Tanzania', pp. 38–39.

72. Ibid., pp. 47, 57; Gerard C. van de Bruinhorst, *Raise Your Voices and Kill Your Animals*, Amsterdam: Amsterdam University Press, 2007, p. 96.

73. Ibid.; Gilsaa, 'Salafism(s) in Tanzania', p. 48.

74. Ibid.

75. Ibid., p. 48; Monitoring Group on Somalia and Eritrea, 'Report of the Monitoring Group on Somalia and Eritrea pursuant to Security Council Resolution, 2002 (2011)', 2012, p. 94.

76. The Monitoring Group lists the following individuals: Omar Suleiman, Nur Abubakar Maulana 'Abu Maulana', Kassim Mafuta, Juma Hekka, Khamis Abubakar Khamis and Ali Said.

77. David Smith and Abdalle Ahmed, 'Al-Shabaab leader "responsible for Garissa attack" is Kenyan', *The Guardian*, 3 April 2015.

78. Stig Jarle Hansen, *Al-Shabaab in Somalia*, London: Hurst, 2013.

79. Abdulhakim Omar and Fuad Barahiyan, the brother of Sheikh Salim. See Monitoring Group on Somalia and Eritrea, 'Report of the Monitoring Group on Somalia and Eritrea pursuant to Security Council Resolution, 2002 (2011)', 2012, p. 95.

80. Ibid.

81. Ibid., p. 94

82. *The Citizen*, 'Muslim cleric tells converts to bury their Christian parents as if they were dead dogs', *The Citizen*, 7 January 2013.

83. See https://www.facebook.com/Ansaar-Muslim-Youth-Centre-611677848964221/ (accessed 29 October 2015).

84. Van de Bruinhorst, *Raise Your Voices and Kill Your Animals*, p. 96; see also Salim Abdulrahim Barahiyan, 'Makosa ya Msingi yaliyomo ndani ya Katiba ya Jamhuri ya Muungano wa Tanzania kwa mtazamo wa Kiislamu by Sheikh Salim Barahiyan, by Ahmed Ahlusuna TV Mwanza TZ', Ansar Muslim Youth Centre, 2011, https://www.youtube.com/watch?v=tuevjePBMl0 (accessed 29 October 2015).

85. Deodatus Balile, 'Tanzania dismantles al-Shabaab child indoctrination camp in Tanga region', *All Africa*, 15 November 2013.

86. Valentine Marc Nkwame, 'Muslim Council suspends Sheikh Ally Kisiwa', *Arusha Times*, 2 July 2004.

87. Cynthia Mwilolezi, 'Arusha bombing incidents suspects finally in court', *The Guardian*, 2014, http://www.ippmedia.com/frontend/?l=70602; *Pesa Times*, 'Police arrest more suspects behind Arusha bomb blasts', *Pesa Times*, 1 August 2014, http://pesatimes.co.tz/news/governance/police-arrest-more-suspects-behind-arusha-bomb-blasts/Tanzania/.

88. Al-Mujahiroun, 'The tormentors', *Shaheed Biography*, 2015, http://jihadology.net/2015/02/20/new-issue-of-the-magazine-amka-magazine-1/.

89. Frank Aman, 'TPDF officer killed, 2 others and 3 cops injured in shoot-outs with "terrorists"', *Guardian on Sunday*, 15 February 2015.

90. *The Citizen*, 'Police must deal with terror threats soberly', *The Citizen*, 22 April 2015.

91. 'Waiganaji wa kiislam Tanzania', 2015, https://www.youtube.com/watch?v=m6J3D4Dedq8 (accessed 2 November 2015).

92. See Felix Njini, 'Tanzanian police arrest nine al-Shabaab suspects at local mosque', *Bloomberg News*, 15 April 2015, http://www.bloomberg.com/news/articles/2015-04-15/tanzanian-police-arrest-nine-al-shabaab-suspects-at-local-mosque (accessed 2 November 2015); Elisa Lopez Lucia, 'Islamist radicalisation and terrorism in Tanzania', Helpdesk Report, 18 May 2015.

93. See *Pesa Times*, '17 lost children found in Moshi', *Pesa Times*, 9 March 2015, http://pesatimes.co.tz/news/crime-and-court/17-lost-children-found-in-moshi/tanzania (accessed 2 November 2015).

94. Nyasha K. Mutizwa, 'Trial of nearly 200 jihadists in Mozambique', Africanews, 10 May 2018, http://www.africanews.com/2018/10/05/trial-of-nearly-200-jihadists-in-mozambique/ (accessed 10 October 2018).

9. THE HARAKAT AL-SHABAAB: FROM TERRITORIALITY TO SEMI-TERRITORIALITY

1. Stig Jarle Hansen, *Al-Shabaab in Somalia*, London: Hurst, 2013, p. 21. Sahal was later celebrated on the Shabaab-affiliated Kataib webpage, now closed down.

2. Interview, Mogadishu, 5 April 2017.

3. Hansen, *Al-Shabaab in Somalia*, p. 24.

4. Ibid., pp. 21, 25.

5. Stig Jarle Hansen, 'Somalia, al-Shabaab and the accidental jihadist', in Morten Bøås and Kevin C. Dunn (eds.), *Africa's Insurgents: Navigating the Evolving Landscape*, Boulder, CO: Lynne Rienner, 2017, p. 188.

6. Stig Jarle Hansen, 'Civil war economies, the hunt for profit and the incentives for peace', Enemies or Allies Working Paper, 1, 2006.

7. Stig Jarle Hansen, 'Somalia: Grievance, religion, clan, and profit', in Stig Jarle Hansen, Atle Mesøy and Tuncay Kardas, *The Borders of Islam*, London: Hurst, 2009.

8. Scott Thomas, 'Building communities of character: Foreign aid policy and faith-based organizations', *SAIS Review of International Affairs*, 24 (2), 2004, pp. 133–148.

9. Hansen, *Al-Shabaab in Somalia*, p. 33.

10. Hansen, 'Civil war economies, the hunt for profit and the incentives for peace'.

11. Hansen, *Al-Shabaab in Somalia*, p. 34.

12. Ibid., p. 35.

13. Abu Mansoor al-Amerki [Omar Hamami], *The Story of an American Jihadi, Part I*, Mogadishu: Hamami, 2012, p. 58.

14. Hansen, *Al-Shabaab in Somalia*, p. 35. The new organisation remained under the umbrella of the Sharia courts, and included non-Mogadishu components such as the Raskamboni Brigade, led by Hassan al-Turki and Ahmed Madobe (who left after the end of the ICU), as well as representatives of more fundamentalist Islamic courts.

15. Ibid., p. 36.

16. Ibid.

17. Ibid.

18. Hansen, 'Somalia, al-Shabaab and the accidental jihadist', p. 190.

19. Stig Jarle Hansen, 'Sharia courts holds sway in Mogadishu', *Foreign Report*, 10, 2006.

20. Hansen, *Al-Shabaab in Somalia*, p. 51.

21. Human Rights Watch, 'Somalia: War crimes in Mogadishu: UN should address civilian protection', Human Rights Watch, 13 August 2007, https://www.hrw.org/news/2007/08/13/somalia-war-crimes-mogadishu (accessed 27 November 2017).

22. Al-Amerki [Omar Hamami], *The Story of an American Jihadi, Part I*.

23. Ibid.

24. Hansen, *Al-Shabaab in Somalia*, p. 54.

25. Hansen, 'Somalia, al-Shabaab and the accidental jihadist', p. 190.

26. Hansen, *Al-Shabaab in Somalia*, p. 56.

27. Ibid., p. 57.

28. Ibid.

29. Personal communication, Mohamed Elmi, 1 February 2007, Mogadishu.

30. Conversations with the writer, 11 February 2007.

31. Hansen, *Al-Shabaab in Somalia*, p. 63.

32. Apuuli Phillip Kasaija, 'The UN-led Djibouti peace process for Somalia 2008–2009: Results and problems', *Journal of Contemporary African Studies*, 28 (10), 2010.

33. Hansen, *Al-Shabaab in Somalia*, p. 76.

34. Ibid., p. 77.

35. See Human Rights Watch, 'Harsh war, harsh peace: Abuses by al-Shabaab, the Transitional Federal Government, and AMISOM in Somalia', Human Rights Watch Report, 19 April 2010.

36. International Crisis Group, 'The Kenyan intervention in Somalia', Africa Report, no. 184, 2012.

37. 'A portrait of a jihadist, born and bred in Mogadishu', *Daily Nation*, 30 January 2012, http://www.nation.co.ke/lifestyle/dn2/What--happened--to-this-man-/957860-1315980-3x7nxez/index.html (accessed 28 November 2017).

38. 'Al-Shabaab propaganda video declares jihad against Kenya', *Daily Nation*, 9 January 2012, http://www.nation.co.ke/News/Al+Shabaab+propaganda+video+declares+Jihad+against+Kenya+/-/1056/1302644/-/jip6qkz/-/index.html (accessed 29 November 2017).

39. Hansen, *Al-Shabaab in Somalia*, p. 5.

40. Katherine Zimmerman, 'Timeline: Operation Linda Nchi', Critical Threats, 24 October 2011, https://www.criticalthreats.org/analysis/timeline-operation-linda-nchi#MonthOne (accessed 29 November 2017).

41. Ashley Jackson and Abdi Aynte, 'Talking to the other side: Humanitarian negotiations with al-Shabaab in Somalia', Humanitarian Policy Group Working Paper, Overseas Development Institute, 18 December 2013, p. 18.

42. Seth G. Jones, Andrew M. Liepman and Nathan Chandler, 'Counterterrorism and counterinsurgency in Somalia: Assessing the campaign against the Shabaab', RAND Research Report, RR-1539-OSD, 2016, p. 21.

43. International Crisis Group, 'Somalia: Al-Shabaab – It will be a long war', Crisis Group Africa Briefing, no. 99, 26 June 2014, p. 10.

44. Harakat al-Shabaab, 'Glad tidings: Announcement of Harakat al-Shabaab al-Mujahidin officially joining al-Qaidah', Global Islamic Media Front, 9 February 2012.

45. Stig Jarle Hansen, 'An in-depth look at al-Shabaab's internal divisions', *CTC Sentinel*, 7 (2), 2014.

46. Interview with Zachariah, 15 January 2016, Mogadishu.

47. Ibid.

48. Hansen, 'An in-depth look at al-Shabaab's internal divisions'.

49. Interview with anonymous person, Mogadishu, 13 February 2016; Monitoring Group on Somalia and Eritrea, 'Report of the Monitoring Group on Somalia and Eritrea pursuant to Security Council Resolution 2182 (2014): Somalia', Report S/2015/801, 2015, pp. 26–27.

50. Ibid.

51. Monitoring Group on Somalia and Eritrea, 'Report of the Monitoring Group on Somalia and Eritrea pursuant to Security Council Resolution 2182 (2014): Somalia', p. 322.

52. This is a United Nations estimate, and relatively unreliable. See United Nations DESA / Population Division, 'The 2017 revision of world population prospects', United Nations interactive page, https://esa. un.org/unpd/wpp/ (accessed 1 December 2017). There are higher estimates as well: 'The evolving urban form', *Demographia World Urban Areas*, 13th annual edition, April 2017 (accessed 1 December 2017); Landinfo, 'Somalia: Violence, fatalities, perpetrators and victims in Mogadishu', Query response, 27 February 2017, https://landinfo.no/ id/114.0 (accessed 5 December 2017).

53. Monitoring Group on Somalia and Eritrea, 'Report of the Monitoring Group on Somalia and Eritrea pursuant to Security Council Resolution 2182 (2014): Somalia', p. 246.

54. Ibid., pp. 82–84.

55. Alan Yuhas, 'Two major al-Shabaab leaders killed in US airstrike and raid by Somali forces', *The Guardian*, 1 June 2016, https://www.theguardian. com/world/2016/jun/01/al-shabaab-leaders-killed-airstrike-raid-somalia-abdullahi-haji-daud-mohamed-dulyadin (accessed 1 December 2017).

56. 'Minister: 22 killed as residents, al-Shabaab clash over Zakah', *Shabelle News*, 22 February 2016, http://allafrica.com/stories/201602230290. html (accessed 1 December 2017); 'Locals clash with al-Shabaab over alms collection, 4 people killed', *Goobjoog News*, 11 May 2016, http:// goobjoog.com/english/locals-clash-al-shabaab-alms-collection-10-people-killed/ (accessed 1 December 2017).

57. Monitoring Group on Somalia and Eritrea, 'Report of the Monitoring Group on Somalia and Eritrea pursuant to Security Council Resolution 2182 (2014): Somalia', pp. 82–84.

58. Ibid.

59. Interview with Professor Yahya Ibrahim, by email, 8 September 2017. This was also the information found by the Norwegian Landinfo in 2017. Conversation with Landinfo officials after their fact-finding mission to Mogadishu.

60. Formally, Kabakutukade holds power, but he is often alleged to be dominated by Abu Daud, a returning member of the diaspora.

61. Paul Williams, 'Somalia's African Union mission has a new exit strategy. But can troops actually leave?', *Washington Post*, 30 November 2017, https://www.washingtonpost.com/news/monkey-cage/wp/2017/11/30/somalias-african-union-mission-has-a-new-exit-strategy-but-can-troops-actually-exit/?utm_term=.4fe90563766b (accessed 5 December 2017).

10. THE ISLAMIC STATE IN SOMALIA: ON THE PERIPHERY

1.   Monitoring Group on Somalia, 'Report of the Monitoring Group on Somalia submitted in accordance with Resolution 1811 (2008)', Report S/2008/769, 2008, p. 33.

2.   A local interviewed in an article by Reuters claimed that Atom started to recruit in 2005. See Abdi Sheik, 'Islamist rebels vow jihad on Somalia's Puntland', Reuters, 28 July 2010, https://www.reuters.com/article/ozatp-somalia-conflict-puntland-20100728-idAFJOE66R0F220100728 (accessed 7 December 2017). For an article claiming Atom as a champion of local (Warsangeli) rights, see Mohamud Haji Ahmed, 'Galgala: Farole's Waterloo', *Hiiran News*, 28 August 2010, https://www.hiiraan.com/op4/2010/aug/15736/galgala_farole_s_waterloo.aspx (accessed 6 December 2017).

3.   Monitoring Group on Somalia, 'Report of the Monitoring Group on Somalia submitted in accordance with Resolution 1811 (2008)', p. 45.

4.   Ibid.

5.   Stig Jarle Hansen, *Al-Shabaab in Somalia*, London: Hurst, 2013, p. 123.

6.   Bill Roggio, 'Somali Islamist group formally declares allegiance to Shabaab, al-Qaeda', FDD's Long War Journal, 25 February 2012, https://www.longwarjournal.org/archives/2012/02/somali_islamist_grou.php (accessed 6 December 2017).

7.   Hansen, *Al-Shabaab in Somalia*, p. 125.

8.   Monitoring Group on Somalia and Eritrea, 'Somalia: Report of the Monitoring Group on Somalia and Eritrea submitted in accordance with Resolution 2002 (2011)', Report S/2012/544, 2012, p. 172.

9.   'Who is this Islamic State's Abdulqadir Mumin in Somalia?', AFP, 2 September 2016, http://www.theeastafrican.co.ke/news/Who-is-

this-Islamic-State-Abdulqadir-Mumin-in-Somalia/2558-3366896-u8y2ah/index.html (accessed 6 December 2017).

10. Colin Freeman, 'British extremist preacher linked to Lee Rigby killer emerges as head of Islamic State in Somalia', *The Telegraph*, 5 April 2016, http://www.telegraph.co.uk/news/2016/04/29/british-extremist-preacher-linked-to-lee-rigby-killer-emerges-as/ (accessed 6 December 2017).

11. Andrew Gilligan, 'Cage: The extremists peddling lies to British Muslims to turn them into supporters of terror', *The Telegraph*, 28 February 2015, http://www.telegraph.co.uk/news/uknews/terrorism-in-the-uk/11442602/Cage-the-extremists-peddling-lies-to-British-Muslims-to-turn-them-into-supporters-of-terror.html (accessed 6 December 2017).

12. 'Shabaab appoints new leaders for Puntland', *Somalia Report*, 20 July 2012, http://piracyreport.com/index.php/post/3534/Shabaab_Appoints_New_Leaders_for_Puntland (accessed 6 December 2017).

13. 'Why al-Shabaab ally "Atom" surrendered to the Somali government', Somalia Newsroom, 9 June 2014, https://somalianewsroom.com/2014/06/09/why-al-shabaab-ally-atom-surrendered-to-the-somali-government/ (accessed 6 December 2017).

14. Monitoring Group on Somalia and Eritrea, 'Report of the Monitoring Group on Somalia and Eritrea pursuant to Security Council Resolution 2060 (2012): Somalia', Report S/2013/440, 2013, p. 69.

15. Robyn Kriel and Lillian Leposo, 'In video, Somali ISIS members court al-Shabaab', CNN Online, 22 May 2015, http://edition.cnn.com/2015/05/22/world/somalia-isis-al-shabaab-video/ (accessed 6 December 2017).

16. Alexander Meleagrou-Hitchens, 'Al-Shabab fighters in Somalia', *Foreign Affairs*, 8 October 2015.

17. Kriel and Leposo, 'In video, Somali ISIS members court al-Shabaab'.

18. 'Suspected leader of pro-IS al-Shabab faction reported killed', VOA, 22 November 2015, https://www.voanews.com/a/somalia-suspected-leader-of-pro-islamic-state-al-shabab-faction-reported-killed/3069114.html (accessed 6 December 2017).

19. Christopher Anzalone, 'JTIC brief: The expansion of the Islamic State in East Africa', *Jane's Terrorism and Insurgency Monitor*, 27 March 2017.

20. Ibid.

21. Ibid.

22. Caleb Weiss, 'Shabaab defectors claim German jihadist is dead', *Threat Matrix*, 2 July 2016, https://www.longwarjournal.org/archives/2016/07/shabaab-defectors-claim-german-jihadist-is-dead.

php (accessed 6 December 2017); see also 'From the heart of jihad', Jabha East Africa, 29 Ramadan 1437/2016, file:///C:/Users/stigha/Downloads/jabha-east-africa-22from-the-heart-of-jihacc84d22.pdf; http://jihadology.net/category/jahba-east-africa/ (accessed 6 December 2017).

23. See Islamic State in Somalia, 'New video message from Jund al-Khilāfah in Somalia: The Commander Shaykh Abū Nu'man Military Training Camp', Furat Media, 16 April 2016; http://jihadology.net/2016/04/15/new-video-message-from-jund-al-khilafah-in-somalia-the-commander-shaykh-abu-numan-military-training-camp/ifriqiyyah/ (accessed 6 December 2017); Islamic State in Somalia, 'Eid on the frontiers (Thughur) of Somalia', Furat Media, 16 September 2016. Thanks to Christopher Anzalone for providing the videos.

24. Interview with anonymous community leader from Garissa, 5 January 2016.

25. Having defected from al-Shabaab as late as December 2015, Moalim had previously been assigned as the deputy head of finance for al-Shabaab north-east (ASNE) in the Golis mountains.

26. Farsamada, 'Renewed Fighting between Galmudug and Puntland erupts in Galkayo', Radio Dalsan, 6 November 2016, https://www.radiodalsan.com/2016/11/06/renewed-fighting-between-galmudug-and-puntland-erupts-in-galkayo/ (accessed 7 December 2017).

27. Interview with anonymous Bari police commander, 27 December 2017.

28. 'Puntland pro-Isil group occupies Qandala town, Bari', Vates Corp Special Report, 4 November 2016, https://vatescorp.com/index.php/blog/item/27-special-report-20161104-puntland-pro-isil-group-occupies-qandala-town-bari-region (accessed 7 December 2017).

29. Caleb Weiss, 'Islamic State fighters withdraw from captured Somali port town', *Threat Matrix*, 28 October 2016, https://www.longwarjournal.org/archives/2016/10/islamic-state-fighters-withdraw-from-captured-somali-port-town.php (accessed 7 December 2017).

30. Interview with anonymous Bari police commander, 27 December 2017.

31. UN Department of Safety and Security, Somalia, 'Situation Report, 7 December 2016', DSS Daily Situation Report, 2016.

BIBLIOGRAPHY

Aalen, Lovise, *The Politics of Ethnicity in Ethiopia: Actors, Power and Mobilization under Ethnic Federalism*, Leiden: Brill, 2011.

Abdullahi, Abdurahman, *The Islamic Movement in Somalia: A Case Study of Islah Movement, 1950–2000*, London: Adonis and Abbey, 2015.

Abedin, Maha, 'From mujahid to activist: An interview with a Libyan veteran of the Afghan jihad', Jamestown Foundation, *Spotlight on Terror*, 3 (2), 2005.

Adelman, Howard and Govind C. Rao (eds.), *War and Peace in Zaire-Congo: Analyzing and Evaluating Intervention, 1996–1997*, Trenton, NJ: Africa World Press, 2003.

Adenrele, Adetoro Rasheed, 'Boko Haram insurgency in Nigeria as a symptom of poverty and political alienation', *Journal of Humanities and Social Science*, 3 (5), 2012.

Adesoji, Adekano, 'The Boko Haram uprising and Islamic revivalism in Nigeria', *Africa Spectrum*, 45 (2), 2010.

Adibe, Jideofor, 'What do we really know about Boko Haram?', in Ioannis Mantzikos (ed.), *Boko Haram: Anatomy of a Crisis*, Bristol: e-International Relations, 2013.

Adl, Saif al-, 'A short report on the trip from Nairobi', Harmony Project, Document AFGP-2002-600113, https://www.ctc.usma.edu/posts/a-short-report-on-the-trip-from-nairobi-original-language-2.

AFP, 'Islamist leader Shekau "hiding in the desert"', AFP, 16 June 2010, http://www.iol.co.za/news/africa/islamist-leader-shekau-hiding-in-the-desert-1.490069#.VL-o1E0cSYY (accessed 21 January 2015).

AFP, 'Who is this Islamic State's Abdulqadir Mumin in Somalia?', AFP, 2 September 2016, http://www.theeastafrican.co.ke/news/Who-is-this-Islamic-State-Abdulqadir-Mumin-in-Somalia/2558-3366896-u8y2ah/index.html (accessed 6 December 2017).

African Rights, *Avoiding an Impasse: Understanding Conflicts in Western Uganda*, Kampala: African Rights, 2001.

Ag Ghali, Iyad, 'Ansar Dine ne connaît que le Mali et la Charia', *Jeune Afrique*, 8 April 2012.

Ag Othman, Othman, 'Implementation of the Sharia in Azawad', Sahara Media, 25 June 2012, https://www.youtube.com/watch?v=oAq3GT_3Htk (accessed 28 August 2017).

Ag Othman, Othman, 'Interview with the Sheikh Mohammed al-Hussein, judge of Timbuktu city', Sahara Media, 15 July 2012.

Agbiboa, Daniel, E., 'Peace at daggers drawn? Boko Haram and the state of emergency in Nigeria', *Studies in Conflict and Terrorism*, 37 (1), 2014.

Ahmad, Aisha, 'The security bazaar: Business interests and Islamist power in civil war Somalia', *International Security*, 39 (3), 2016.

Ahmed, Baba, 'Leader of al-Qaeda unit in Mali quits AQIM', *Daily Star*, 3 December 2013.

Ahmed, Mohamud Haji, 'Galgala: Farole's Waterloo', *Hiiran News*, 28 August 2010, https://www.hiiraan.com/op4/2010/aug/15736/galgala_farole_s_waterloo.aspx (accessed 6 December 2017).

Al Jazeera, 'Al-Jazirah program on Bin Laden', Doha, Qatar, Al-Jazirah Space Channel Television in Arabic 18.05 GMT, 10 June 1999, transcribed in Foreign Broadcast Information Service, 'Compilation of Usama bin Laden statements 1994 – January 2004', FBIS Report, January 2004.

Al-Akhbar News Agency, 'Dialogues with the youth of Ansar al-Din Movement in Timbuktu', Al-Akhbar News Agency, 3 May 2012.

Alesbury, Andrew, 'A society in motion: The Tuareg from the pre-colonial era to today', *Nomadic Peoples*, 17 (1), 2013.

Alexander, David, 'U.S. confirms death of al Shabaab leader Godane in Somalia strike', Reuters, 5 September 2014, http://www.reuters.com/article/us-somalia-usa-islamist-idUSKBN0H01OO20140905 (accessed 1 November 2016).

Ali, Imam, 'And whoever does so among you – then it is those who are the wrongdoers', Kataib Media, 29 July 2017, http://jihadology.net/category/individuals/ideologues/a%E1%B8%A5mad-iman-ali/ (accessed 27 December 2017)

Ali, Imam, 'Interview on the general elections in Kenya, Part 1', Kataib Media, 26 July 2017, http://jihadology.net/2017/07/26/new-video-message-from-%e1%b8%a5arakat-al-shabab-al-mujahidins-a%e1%b8%a5mad-iman-ali-interview-on-the-general-elections-in-kenya-part-1/ (accessed 27 December 2017).

Ali, Shaukat, *Administrative Ethics in a Muslim State*, Lahore: Publishers United, 1975.

Ali-Dinar, Ali B., 'IRIN Special Report on the ADF rebellion', IRIN News, 8 December 1999, http://www.africa.upenn.edu/Hornet/irin-120899c. html (accessed 10 February 2018).

Allison, Simon, 'In Nigeria, Boko Haram follows in the footsteps of Iraq's Islamic State', *Daily Maverick*, 14 August 2014.

Allison, Simon, 'Think again: Did France's intervention work in Mali?', *ISS Daily*, 1 July 2014.

Al-Muhajiroun, 'Protecting our sheiks', al-Muhajiroun, 2015, http:// jihadology.net/2015/03/03/new-article-from-al-muhajirun-in-east-africa-a-message-to-tanzania-protecting-our-clerics/ (accessed 29 October 2015).

Al-Mujahiroun, 'The tormentors', *Shaheed Biography*, 2015, http:// jihadology.net/2015/02/20/new-issue-of-the-magazine-amka-magazine-1/.

Alnaes, Kirsten, 'Rebel ravages in Bundibugyo', in Bruce Kapferer and Bjørn Enge Bertelsen (eds.), *Crisis of the State:War and Social Upheaval*, London: Berghahn Books, 2009.

Alonso, Rogelio, 'Why do terrorists stop? Analyzing why ETA members abandon or continue with terrorism', *Studies in Conflict and Terrorism*, 34 (9), 2011.

Al-Qaeda, 'Letters on al-Qaeda operations in Africa, first letter to Osama bin Laden', CTC Harmony Project, https://www.ctc.usma.edu/posts/ letters-on-al-qaidas-operations-in-africa-original-language-2 (accessed 11 January 2018).

Al-Qaeda, *The Five Letters to the African Corps*, CTC Harmony Project, 2002, https://www.ctc.usma.edu/posts/letters-on-al-qaidas-operations-in-africa-original-language-2 (accessed 11 January 2018).

Al-Qaeda in the Islamic Maghreb, 'New statement from al-Qā'idah in the Islamic Maghrib: "Important: Denying the death of the Amīr of Greater Sahara"', Al-Andalus Media Foundation, 4 April 2013, http://jihadology. net/?s=islamic+state+in+the+greater+sahara (accessed 15 September 2017).

Al-Quds al-Arabi, 'Usama bin Laden denies "terrorism" link', *Al-Quds al-Arabi*, 9 March 1994.

Altier, Mary Beth, C.N. Thoroughgood and John Horgan, 'Turning away from terrorism: Lessons from psychology, sociology and criminology', *Journal of Peace Research*, 51 (5), 2014.

Aman, Frank, 'TPDF officer killed, 2 others and 3 cops injured in shoot-outs with "terrorists"', *Guardian on Sunday*, 15 February 2015.

Amerki, Abu Mansoor al- [Omar Hamami], *The Story of an American Jihadi, Part I*, Mogadishu: Hamami, 2012.

Anderson, David M. and Jacob McKnight, 'Kenya at war: Al-Shabaab and its enemies in Eastern Africa', *African Affairs*, 114 (454), 2015.

Ansar Dine, 'Iyad Ag Ghaly, le leader d'Ansar Dine, se met en scène', 15 March 2012, http://www.jeuneafrique.com/176967/politique/vid-o-mali-iyad-ag-ghaly-le-leader-d-ansar-dine-se-met-en-sc-ne/ (accessed 22 June 2017).

Ansary, Abu Usamatul, 'A message from Nigeria', *Al Risalah*, 4, 2017, https://azelin.files.wordpress.com/2017/01/al-risacc84lah-magazine-4.pdf (accessed 5 February 2018).

Antil, Alain, 'Le Mujao, dernier venu des mouvements islamistes armés du Nord Mali', Ultima Ratio blog, 2 May 2010, http://ultimaratio-blog.org/archives/4532 (accessed 12 July 2017).

Anzalone, Christopher, 'JTIC brief: The expansion of the Islamic State in East Africa', *Jane's Terrorism and Insurgency Monitor*, 27 March 2017.

AP, 'Al-Qaeda papers', AP, https://www.longwarjournal.org/images/al-qaida-papers-how-to-run-a-state.pdf (accessed 27 January 2018).

Appleby, Scott, *The Ambivalence of the Sacred: Religion, Violence, and Reconciliation (Carnegie Commission on Preventing Deadly Conflict)*, Lanham, MD: Rowman and Littlefield, 2002.

AQIM, 'A disciplinary letter from al-Qaida's HR Department', AQIM, 3 October 2012.

AQIM, *The Dialogue of Shaykh 'Abd al 'Azīz Ḥabīb with Zakarīā' Būghrārah: 'The Full Story of the Islamic Emirate of Azawad'*, Part 2, Ifrīqīyyah Media, 2014.

Ashour, Omar, 'Post-jihadism: Libya and the global transformations of armed Islamic movements', *Terrorism and Political Violence*, 23 (3), 2011.

Audu, Ola', 'Boko Haram: Shekau claims responsibility for attack on Giwa barracks, threatens to attack universities, civilian-JTF', *Premium Times*, 24 March 2014, http://www.premiumtimesng.com/news/157374-boko-haram-shekau-claims-responsibility-attack-giwa-barracks-threatens-attack-universities-civilian-jtf.html (accessed 9 April 2017).

Aziz, Abdel, 'Beheading in Chad', in Abdulbasit Kassim and Michael Nwankpa, *The Boko Haram Reader: From Nigerian Preachers to the Islamic State*, London: Hurst, 2018.

Azzam, Abdullah, *In Defense of the Muslim Lands*, 1979, http://www.religioscope.com/info/doc/jihad/azzam_defence_6_chap4.htm (accessed on 22 April 2014).

Azzam, Abdullah, *Join the Caravan*, 1987, https://archive.org/details/JoinTheCaravan (accessed 14 April 2014).

Baca, Michael, 'Nigeria: The Borno and Kanuri roots of Boko Haram', African Arguments, 3 January 2015, http://www.ocnus.net/artman2/publish/Africa_8/Nigeria---the-Borno-and-Kanuri-Roots-of-Boko-Haram.shtml (accessed 21 January 2015).

Balile, Deodatus, 'Tanzania dismantles al-Shabaab child indoctrination camp in Tanga region', All Africa, 15 November 2013.

Barelle, Kate, 'Pro-integration: Disengagement from and life after extremism', Behavioral Sciences of Terrorism and Political Aggression, 7 (2), 2015.

Barnawi, Abu Musab al-, 'About the events in the city of Baga', al-Urwah-al-Wuthqa Foundation, 27 January 2015, http://jihadology.net/2015/01/27/al-urwah-al-wuthqa-foundation-presents-a-new-video-message-from-from-boko-%e1%b8%a5arams-jamaat-ahl-al-sunnah-li-dawah-wa-l-jihad-interview-with-the-official-spokesma/ (accessed 9 December 2017).

Barnawi, Abu Musab al-, 'We will get out of our misery harder and stronger, God willing', al-Naba, 41, 2016.

Barrett, Richard, 'The Islamic State', The Soufan Group Report, 2014, http://www.google.no/url?sa=t&rct=j&q=&esrc=s&source=web&cd=1&ved=0CB0QFjAA&url=http%3A%2F%2Fsoufangroup.com%2Fwp-content%2Fuploads%2F2014%2F10%2FTSG-The-Islamic-State-Nov14.pdf&ei=9Vs-VZ_8FciuswG35oGYAw&usg=AFQjCNFMbXX-OrKwKdmBQEWSdrDTbtoggQ&bvm=bv.91665533,d.bGg (accessed 30 April 2015).

Basiime, Felix, Thembo Kahungu Misairi and Geoffrey Mutegeki Araali, 'The Bakonjo, Bamba clashes: Looking beyond the fights', Daily Monitor, 14 July 2012.

BBC News Africa, 'Belmokhtar's militants "merge" with Mali's MUJAO', BBC News Africa, 22 August, http://www.bbc.com/news/world-us-canada-23796920 (accessed 8 August 2017).

BBC News, 'Boko Haram declares "Islamic state" in northern Nigeria', BBC News, 25 August 2014, http://english.alarabiya.net/en/perspective/alarabiya-studies/2014/09/03/ (accessed 9 April 2017).

BBC, 'Is Islamic State shaping Boko Haram media?', BBC, 7 April 2015, http://www.bbc.com/news/world-africa-31522469 (accessed 28 April 2015).

BBC News Africa, 'Mali Islamists claim Menaka victory against rebels', BBC News Africa, 2012, http://www.bbc.com/news/world-africa-20404519 (accessed 8 August 2017).

BBC, 'Mombasa bombing trial collapses', BBC, 9 June 2005, http://news.bbc.co.uk/2/hi/africa/4075988.stm (accessed 19 December 2017).

BBC, 'Nigeria's Boko Haram: Baga destruction "shown in images"', BBC, 15 January 2015, http://www.bbc.com/news/world-africa-30826582 (accessed 9 December 2017).

BBC, 'Zanzibar clashes over missing cleric Sheik Farid Hadi', BBC, 18 October 2012, http://www.bbc.com/news/world-africa-19997774 (accessed 29 October 2015).

Bean, Sharon, 'The founding of Boko Haram and its spread to 32 Nigerian states', *Terrorism Monitor*, 24 March 2010.

Beaumont, Peter, 'The man who could determine whether the West is drawn into Mali's war', *The Guardian*, 27 October 2012, https://www.theguardian.com/world/2012/oct/27/mali-one-man-determine-war (accessed 18 June 2017).

Becker, Felicitas, 'Rural Islamism during the war on terror: A Tanzanian case study', *African Affairs*, 105 (421), 2006.

Beja, Patric, 'I was declared stateless while in Germany', *The Standard*, 7 June 2015, https://www.standardmedia.co.ke/article/2000168245/i-was-declared-stateless-while-in-germany (accessed 19 December 2017).

'Belal, Abu', Omar Taj al-Dein bin Abdullah, 'Abu Belal's report on jihad in Somalia', Harmony Project, 2002, https://www.ctc.usma.edu/posts/abu-belals-report-on-jihad-in-somalia-original-language-2 (accessed 18 January 2018).

Bencherif, Adib, 'From resilience to fragmentation: Al-Qaeda in the Islamic Maghreb and jihadist group modularity', *Terrorism and Political Violence*, 29 (6), 2017.

Benjaminsen, Tor A. and Boubacar Ba, 'Why do pastoralists in Mali join jihadist groups? A political ecological explanation', *Journal of Peasant Studies*, 2018, doi: 10.1080/03066150.2018.1474457.

Bensted, Roland, 'A critique of Paul Collier's "greed and grievance" thesis of civil war', *African Security*, 20 (3), 2011.

Berdal, Mats, 'Beyond greed and grievance – and not too soon …', *Review of International Studies*, Autumn 2004.

Berdal, Mats, 'How "new" are "new wars"? Global economic change and the study of civil wars', *Global Governance*, 9 (4), 2003.

Bergen, Peter L., *Holy War Inc*, New York: Touchstone, 2002.

Bergen, Peter L., *The Osama bin Laden I Know*, New York: Free Press, 2006.

Bergen, Peter and Paul Cruickshank, 'Revisiting the early al-Qaeda: An updated account of its formative years', *Studies in Conflict and Terrorism*, 35 (1), 2012.

Berger, Jim, 'The alleged 1994 assassination attempt on Osama bin Laden: Declassified State Department cable adds color to little known Sudan incident', *Intelwire*, 12 August 2007, http://news.intelwire.com/2007/08/alleged-1994-assassination-attempt-on.html.

Berger, Jim, 'War on error', *Foreign Policy*, 2 February 2014.

Biddle, Stephen, Jeffrey A. Friedman and Jacob N. Shapiro, 'Testing the surge', *International Security*, 37 (1), 2012.

Bloom, Mia, 'Constructing expertise: Terrorist recruitment and "talent spotting" in the PIRA, al-Qaeda, and ISIS', *Studies in Conflict and Terrorism*, 20, September 2016 (online version).

Bøås, Morten and Kevin C. Dunn, *African Guerrillas: Raging against the Machine*, Boulder, CO: Lynne Rienner, 2007.

Bodansky, Yussef, *Bin Laden, the Man Who Declared War on America*, Roseville, CA: Prima Publishing, 2001.

Boeke, Sergei and Bart Schuurman, 'Operation Serval: A strategic analysis of the French intervention in Mali 2013–2014', *Journal of Strategic Studies*, 28 (6), 2015.

Boko Haram Media Section, 'Boko Haram declares a new caliphate in northeastern Nigeria', Boko Haram, 2014, https://www.youtube.com/watch?v=Rl4IgD--nKg (accessed 20 January 2015).

Botha, Anneli, 'Radicalization in Kenya, recruitment to al-Shabaab and the Mombasa Republican Council', ISS Paper, no. 265, 2015.

Botha, Anneli, 'Terrorism in the Maghreb: The transformation of domestic terrorism', Institute for Security Studies Monograph, 144, June 2008.

Botha, Anneli, *Terrorism in Kenya and Uganda: Radicalization from a Political Socialization Perspective*, London: Lexington Books, 2017.

Boudali, Lianne Kennedy, 'Leveraging history in AQIM communications', *CTC Sentinel*, 2 (4), 2009.

Boudali, Lianne K., 'The GSPC: Newest franchise in al-Qa'ida's global jihad', North Africa Project, CTC, April 2007.

Brents, Barbara and Deo S. Mishgeni, 'Terrorism in context: Race, religion, party, and violent conflict in Zanzibar', *The American Sociologist*, Summer 2004.

Bruguière, Peggy, 'Backed by popular support, Mali's Islamists drive Tuareg from Gao', France24, 29 June 2012, http://observers.france24.com/en/20120629-mali-backed-popular-support-islamists-drive-tuareg-separatists-north-city-gao (accessed 8 August 2017).

Brylonek, Marek, 'Security crisis in the Sahel region', *Scientific Quarterly*, 3 (92), 2013.

Burke, Jason, *Al-Qaeda: The True Story of Radical Islam*, London: I.B. Tauris, 2004.

Burr, J. Millard and Robert O. Collin, *Revolutionary Sudan*, Leiden: Brill, 2004.

Burray, Mohammad al-, *Management and Administration in Islam*, Riyadh: Al Dhahran, 1990.

Calle, Luis de la and Ignacio Sánchez-Cuenca, 'Rebels without a territory: An analysis of nonterritorial conflicts in the world, 1970–1997', *Journal of Conflict Resolution*, 56 (4), 2012.

Callimachi, Rukmini and Nabih Bulos, 'Mali hotel attackers are tied to an Algerian Qaeda leader', *International New York Times*, 21 November 2015.

Campbell, John, 'To battle Nigeria's Boko Haram, put down your guns', *Foreign Policy*, September 2011.

Candia, Steven, 'ADF recruiting in Kampala, says defector', *New Vision*, 11 April 2013.

Cassidy, John, 'The facts about terrorism', *The New Yorker*, 24 February 2014, http://www.newyorker.com/news/john-cassidy/the-facts-about-terrorism (accessed 25 October 2016).

Castelli, Laurent de, 'From sanctuary to Islamic State', *RUSI Journal*, 159 (3), 2014.

Chasdi, Richard J., *Tapestry of Terror: A Portrait of Middle East Terrorism, 1994–1999*, New York: Lexington Books, 2003.

Chauzal, Grégory and Thibault van Damme, 'The roots of Mali's conflict', CRU Report, March 2015, https://www.clingendael.org/sites/default/files/pdfs/The_roots_of_Malis_conflict.pdf (accessed 26 January 2017).

Chome, Ngala, 'Lessons from Kenya's coast and why extremism is a global burden', *The Standard Digital*, 26 February 2017, https://www.standardmedia.co.ke/article/2001230736/lessons-from-kenya-s-coast-and-why-extremism-is-a-global-burden (accessed 27 December 2017).

Cigar, Norman and Stephanie E. Kramer, *Al-Qaida after Ten Years of War: A Global Perspective of Successes, Failures, and Prospects*, Washington: Marine Corps, 2012.

Citizen TV, 'The troubled Masjid Musa', Citizen TV, 10 February 2014, https://www.youtube.com/watch?v=ZMHBnMaWR24 (accessed 27 December 2017).

Citizen, The, 'Muslim cleric tells converts to bury their Christian parents as if they were dead dogs', *The Citizen*, 7 January 2013.

Citizen, The, 'Police must deal with terror threats soberly', *The Citizen*, 22 April 2015.

Cline, Lawrence E., 'Nomads, Islamists, and soldiers: The struggles for northern Mali', *Studies in Conflict and Terrorism*, 36 (8), 2013.

Coll, Steven, *Ghost Wars: The Secret History of the CIA, Afghanistan and Bin Laden*, London: Penguin Books, 2005.

Collier, Paul and Anke Hoeffler, 'Greed and grievance in civil war', *Oxford Economic Papers*, 56 (4), 2004.

Collier, Paul and Anke Hoeffler, 'On the incidence of civil war in Africa', *Journal of Conflict Resolution*, 46 (1), 2002.

Comolli, Virginia, *Boko Haram: Nigeria's Islamist Insurgency*, London: Hurst, 2016.

Connell, Dan, 'From resistance to governance: Eritrea's trouble with transition', *Review of African Political Economy*, 38 (129), 2011.

Constable, Pamela, 'Taliban-style justice stirs growing anger', *Washington Post*, 10 May 2009.

Cooper, Neil, 'State collapse as business: The role of conflict trade and the emerging control agenda', *Development and Change*, 33 (5), 2002.

Crawford, Alex, 'Somali president says terrorists are defeated', Sky News, 2 May 2014, http://news.sky.com/story/somali-president-says-terrorists-are-defeated-10447016 (accessed 1 November 2016).

Cummings, Ryan, 'A jihadi takeover bid in Nigeria? The evolving relationship between Boko Haram and al-Qa'ida', *CTC Sentinel*, 10 (11), 2017.

Cummings, Ryan, 'Opinion: Boko Haram and the defeat that never was', CNN, 1 January 2016, http://www.cnn.com/2016/01/01/opinions/nigeria-boko-haram-fight/ (accessed 1 November 2016).

Daily Nation, 'A portrait of a jihadist, born and bred in Mogadishu', *Daily Nation*, 30 January 2012, http://www.nation.co.ke/lifestyle/dn2/What--happened--to-this-man-/957860-1315980-3x7nxez/index.html (accessed 28 November 2017).

Daily Nation, 'Al-Shabaab propaganda video declares jihad against Kenya', *Daily Nation*, 9 January 2012, http://www.nation.co.ke/News/Al+Shabaab+propaganda+video+declares+Jihad+against+Kenya+/-/1056/1302644/-/jip6qkz/-/index.html (accessed 29 November 2017).

Daily Trust, 'Nigeria: Boko Haram "taking over" northern Borno state', *Daily Trust*, 20 April 2013, http://allafrica.com/stories/201304200127.html.

Daniel, Serge, 'Jihadists announce blood-soaked return to northern Mali', AFP, 9 October 2014, https://www.yahoo.com/news/jihadists-announce-blood-soaked-return-northern-mali-044311121.html (accessed 8 August 2017).

Dawod, Hosham, 'Iraqi tribes in the land of jihad', in Virginie Collombier and Olivier Roy (eds.), *Tribes and Global Jihadism*, London: Hurst, 2018.

De Temmerman, Els, 'ADF rebellion: Guerilla to urban terrorism', *New Vision*, 21 May 2007.

De Waal, Alex, 'Mission without end? Peacekeeping in the African political marketplace', *International Affairs*, 85 (1), 2009.

Dowd, Caitriona, 'Grievances, governance and Islamist violence in sub-Saharan Africa', *Journal of Modern African Studies*, 53 (4), 2015.

Dowd, Caitriona and Clionadh Raleigh, 'The myth of global Islamic terrorism and local conflict in Mali and the Sahel', *African Affairs*, 112 (448), 2013.

Drake, C.J.M., 'The role of ideology in terrorists' target selection', *Terrorism and Political Violence*, 10 (2), 1998.

Economist, The, 'The Radisson Blue siege', *The Economist*, 28 November 2015.

Eulich, Whitney, 'Mombasa riots stretch into second day as extremist group tries to rally Muslims', *Christian Science Monitor*, 28 August 2012, https://www.csmonitor.com/World/Security-Watch/terrorism-security/2012/0828/Mombasa-riots-stretch-into-second-day-as-extremist-group-tries-to-rally-Muslims (accessed 27 December 2017).

Evans, Rebecca, 'Find the white widow: Fingerprints confirm terror suspect is British mother, say Kenyan detectives', *Daily Mail*, 6 March 2012, http://www.dailymail.co.uk/news/article-2110694/Find-white-widow-Fingerprints-confirm-terror-suspect-IS-British-mother-say-Kenyan-detectives.html#ixzz34APZTxMr (accessed 10 June 2014).

Farah, Douglas and Richard Shultz, 'Al Qaeda's growing sanctuary', *Washington Post*, 14 July 2004.

Farsamada, 'Renewed Fighting between Galmudug and Puntland erupts in Galkayo', Radio Dalsan, 6 November 2016, https://www.radiodalsan.com/2016/11/06/renewed-fighting-between-galmudug-and-puntland-erupts-in-galkayo/ (accessed 7 December 2017).

Filiu, Jean-Pierre, 'Al-Qaeda in the Islamic Maghreb: Algerian challenge or global threat?', Carnegie Paper, 2009.

Filiu, Jean-Pierre, 'Could al-Qaeda turn African in the Sahel?', Carnegie Middle East Program, no. 112, 2010.

Fisk, Robert, 'Anti-Soviet warrior puts his army on the road to peace', *The Independent*, 6 December 1993, http://www.independent.co.uk/news/world/anti-soviet-warrior-puts-his-army-on-the-road-to-peace-the-saudi-businessman-who-recruited-mujahedin-1465715.html (accessed 17 December 2017).

Fisk, Robert, *The Great War for Civilization: The Conquest of the Middle East*, New York: Vintage Books, 2005.

Fletcher, Molly, 'Egyptian Islamic Jihad', Council of Foreign Relations Report, 30 May 2008, https://www.cfr.org/backgrounder/egyptian-islamic-jihad (accessed 20 August 2015).

Flood, Derek Henry, 'Between Islamization and secession: The contest for northern Mali', *CTC Sentinel*, 5 (7), 2013.

Follorou, Jacques, 'Jihadists return to northern Mali a year after French intervention', *The Guardian*, 11 March 2014, https://www.theguardian.com/world/2014/mar/11/mali-jihadists-return-after-france-mission; (accessed 8 August 2017).

Fouéré, Marie-Aude, *Remembering Julius Nyerere in Tanzania: History, Memory, Legacy*, Dar es Salaam: Mkukina Nyota Publishers, 2015.

Freeman, Colin, 'British extremist preacher linked to Lee Rigby killer emerges as head of Islamic State in Somalia', *The Telegraph*, 5 April 2016, http://www.telegraph.co.uk/news/2016/04/29/british-extremist-preacher-linked-to-lee-rigby-killer-emerges-as/ (accessed 6 December 2017).

Gaas, Mohamed Husein, 'Primordialist vs. instrumentalist in Somali society: Is an alternative perspective needed?' and 'Modalities of governance and contradictions in Somalia', 2018 essay based on PhD thesis, NMBU.

Gaffey, Connor, 'ISIS expands into the Sahel, Africa's migration hub', *Newsweek*, 24 November 2016.

Ganor, Boaz, 'Defining terrorism: Is one man's terrorist another man's freedom fighter?', *Police Practice and Research: An International Journal*, 3 (4), 2002.

Ganor, Boaz, *The Counter-Terrorism Puzzle: A Guide for Decision Makers*, New Brunswick, NJ: Transaction Publishers, 2005.

Gartenstein-Ross, Daveed, 'Is Algeria's kidnapper a "common criminal"? Look again', *Globe and Mail*, 22 January 2013, https://www.theglobeandmail.com/opinion/is-algerias-kidnapper-a-common-criminal-look-again/article7618417/.

Gatsiounis, Ioannis, 'After al-Shabaab', *Current Trends in Islamic Ideology*, 14, 2013.

Gilligan, Andrew, 'Cage: The extremists peddling lies to British Muslims to turn them into supporters of terror', *The Telegraph*, 28 February 2015, http://www.telegraph.co.uk/news/uknews/terrorism-in-the-uk/11442602/Cage-the-extremists-peddling-lies-to-British-Muslims-to-turn-them-into-supporters-of-terror.html (accessed 6 December 2017).

Gilsaa, Søren, 'Islamic reform and politics in Tanzania: Situating the Ansar al-Sunna in Tanzania's historical politics of Islam', Paper presented at the 3rd European Conference on African Studies in Leipzig, 2009.

Gilsaa, Søren, 'Salafism(s) in Tanzania: Theological roots and political subtext of the Ansar al-Sunna', *Islamic Africa*, 6, 2015.

Giraldo, Jeanne and Harold Trinkunas, *Terrorist Financing and State Responses: A Comparative Perspective*, Stanford, CA: Stanford University Press, 2007.

Gisesa, Nyambega, 'Ten things you didn't know about Sheikh Abubakar Shariff alias Makaburi', *The Standard Digital*, 2 April 2014, https://www.standardmedia.co.ke/article/2000108421/ten-things-you-didn-t-know-about-sheikh-abubakar-shariff-alias-makaburi (accessed 18 December 2017).

Goobjoog News, 'Locals clash with al-Shabaab over alms collection, 4 people killed', *Goobjoog News*, 11 May 2016, http://goobjoog.com/english/

locals-clash-al-shabaab-alms-collection-10-people-killed/ (accessed 1 December 2017).

Goreman, George, 'Nigerian Taliban leader killed in custody', FDD's Long War Journal, 31 July 2009, http://www.longwarjournal.org/archives/2009/07/nigerian_taliban_lea.php.

Grossman, Laura, 'Analysis: Boko Haram loses ground, but remains in the fight', FDD's Long War Journal, 23 March 2015, http://www.longwarjournal.org/archives/2015/03/boko-haram-loses-ground-but-remains-in-the-fight.php (accessed 30 April 2015).

Grossman, Laura, 'Ansar Dine leader resurfaces, urges expulsion of France from Mali', FDD's Long War Journal, 12 August 2013, http://www.longwarjournal.org/archives/2014/08/iyad_ag_ghaly_re-eme.php (accessed 8 August 2017).

Group of Experts on the Democratic Republic of the Congo, 'Final report of the Group of Experts on the Democratic Republic of the Congo', Security Council Report S/2012/348, 2012.

Group of Experts on the Democratic Republic of the Congo, 'Final report of the Group of Experts on the Democratic Republic of the Congo', Security Council Report S/2012/843, 2012.

Group of Experts on the Democratic Republic of the Congo, 'Final report of the Group of Experts on the Democratic Republic of the Congo', Security Council Report S/2015/19, 2015.

Group of Experts on the Democratic Republic of the Congo, 'Final report of the Group of Experts on the Democratic Republic of the Congo', Security Council Report S/2016/466, 2016.

Group of Experts on the Democratic Republic of the Congo, 'Midterm report of the Group of Experts on the Democratic Republic of the Congo', Security Council Report S/2016/1102, 2016.

Group of Experts on the Democratic Republic of the Congo, 'Midterm report of the Group of Experts on the Democratic Republic of the Congo', Security Council Report S/2017/672/Rev.

Guidère, Mathieu, 'The Timbuktu letters: New insights about AQIM', Res Militaris, 4 (1), Winter/Spring 2014.

Gunaratna, Rohan, Inside al-Qaeda: Global Network of Terror, New York: Columbia University Press, 2002.

Gusau, Isa Umar, 'Boko Haram: How it all began', Sunday Trust, 2 August 2009, http://sundaytrust.com.ng/index.php/the-arts/35-people-in-the-news/people-in-the-news/5869-boko-haram-how-it-all-began (accessed 1 November 2014).

Gutiérrez Sanín, Francisco and Elisabeth Jean Wood, 'Ideology in civil war: Instrumental adoption and beyond', Journal of Peace Research, 51 (2), 2014.

Haf, Abu, 'Abu Haf's report on operations in Somalia', 2002, Harmony Project, Document AFGP-2002-800597, https://www.ctc.usma.edu/posts/abu-hafs-report-on-operations-in-somalia-original-language-2 (accessed 18 January 2018).

Hamming, Tore Refslund, 'The al-Qaeda–Islamic State rivalry: Competition yes, but no competitive escalation', *Terrorism and PoliticalViolence*, 1, 2017.

Hansen, Stig Jarle, 'A trend analysis of Boko Haram over the last year, as well as the Nigerian army and its performance', Risk Intelligence Brief, 2015.

Hansen, Stig Jarle, 'African jihadis: Media strategies', Report for the Canadian Defense Academy, 2014.

Hansen, Stig Jarle, *Al-Shabaab in Somalia:The History of a Militant Islamist Group 2005–2012*, London: Hurst, 2013.

Hansen, Stig Jarle, 'An in-depth look at al-Shabaab's internal divisions', *CTC Sentinel*, 7 (2), 2014.

Hansen, Stig Jarle, 'Civil war economies, the hunt for profit and the incentives for peace', 'Enemies or Allies' project, Working Paper 1, University of Bath and University of Mogadishu, 2006.

Hansen, Stig Jarle, 'Eritrean terrorism special assessment', Special report for MARISK, Maritime Security System for Risk Intelligence, Denmark, 2010.

Hansen, Stig Jarle, 'Faction fluctuation:The shifting allegiances within Hizbul Islam', *Jane's Intelligence Review*, 6 November 2010.

Hansen, Stig Jarle, 'Sharia courts holds sway in Mogadishu', *Foreign Report*, 10, 2006.

Hansen, Stig Jarle, 'Somalia, al-Shabaab and the accidental jihadist', in Morten Bøås and Kevin C. Dunn (eds.), *Africa's Insurgents: Navigating the Evolving Landscape*, Boulder, CO: Lynne Rienner, 2017.

Hansen, Stig Jarle, 'Somalia: Grievance, religion, clan, and profit', in Stig Jarle Hansen, Atle Mesøy andTuncay Kardas, *The Borders of Islam*, London: Hurst, 2009.

Hansen, Stig Jarle, 'Somalia', *AfricaYearbook*, vol. 11, 2016.

Hansen, Stig Jarle, 'The changing face of the Muslim Brotherhood in Somalia', Unpublished manuscript, 2013.

Hansen, Stig Jarle, 'Uamsho, Shabaab and the threat of terrorism inTanzania', *Strategic Insights*, 59, 2015.

Hansen, Stig Jarle, 'War economies, the hunt for profit and the incentives for peace', Enemies or AlliesWorking Paper, 1, 2006.

Hansen, Stig Jarle and Atle Mesøy, 'The Muslim Brotherhood in the wider Horn of Africa', NIBR Report, 2009.

Hansen, Stig Jarle and Mohamed Husein Gaas, 'The Muslim Brotherhood in the Arab Winter', Discussion Paper, Belfer Center for Science and International Affairs, Kennedy School, Harvard, 2017.

Hansen, Stig Jarle, Atle Mesøy and Tuncay Karadas, *The Borders of Islam*, London: Hurst, 2009.

Hansen, Stig Jarle, Stian Lid and Clifford Collin Omondi Okwany, 'Countering violent extremism in Somalia and Kenya: Actors and approaches', NIBR Report, 2016.

Harakat al-Shabaab, 'New statement from Ḥarakat al-Shabāb al-Mujāhidīn: "Shaykh Aboud Rogo's death: A catalyst for change"', Kataib Media, 27 August 2012, http://jihadology.net/2012/08/27/new-statement-from-%e1%b8%a5arakat-al-shabab-al-mujahidin-shaykh-aboud-rogos-death-a-catalyst-for-change/ (accessed 27 December 2017).

Harmon, Stephen, 'From GSPC to AQIM: The evolution of an Algerian Islamist terrorist group into an al-Qa'ida affiliate', *Concerned African Scholars Bulletin*, no. 85, 2010.

Harnischfeger, Johannes, 'Boko Haram and its critics: Observation from the Yobe state', in Marc-Antoine Pérouse de Montclos (ed.), *Boko Haram: Islamism, Politics, Security and the State in Nigeria*, West African Politics and Society Series, 2, 2014.

Hegghammer, Thomas, 'Dokumentasjon om al-Qaida: Intervjuer, kommunikéer og andre primærkilder, 1990–2002', FFI/RAPPORT-2002/01393, 2002.

Hegghammer, Thomas, *Jihad in Saudi Arabia: Violence and Pan-Islamism since 1979*, Cambridge: Cambridge University Press, 2010.

Hegghammer, Thomas, 'Jihadi Salafis or revolutionaries: On religion and politics in the study of Islamist militancy', in R. Meijer (ed.), *Global Salafism: Islam's New Religious Movement*, London: Hurst, 2009.

Hegghammer, Thomas, 'The rise of Muslim foreign fighters: Islam and the globalization of jihad', *International Security*, 35 (3), 2010.

Herbst, Jeffrey, *States and Power in Africa: Comparative Lessons in Authority and Control*, Princeton, NJ: Princeton University Press, 2000.

Hills, Alice, 'Insurgency, counter-insurgency and policing', in Rich and Duyvesteyn (eds.), *The Routledge Handbook of Insurgency and Counterinsurgency*, London: Routledge, 2012.

Hoechner, Hannah, 'Traditional Quranic students (almajirai) in Nigeria: Fair game for unfair accusations?', in Marc-Antoine Pérouse de Montclos (ed.), *Boko Haram: Islamism, Politics, Security and the State in Nigeria*, West African Politics and Society Series, 2, 2014.

Hopperstad, Morten S., Øyvind Gustavsen and Amund Bakke Foss, 'Dette er den enøyde terrorlederen', *VG*, 16 June 2015.

Horowitz, Jonathan, Trouble looms as Kenya struggles to combat terrorism', *World Post*, 2014, https://www.huffingtonpost.com/jonathan-horowitz/kenya-terrorism_b_5028058.html (accessed 27 December 2017).

Hovil, Lucy and Eric Werker, 'Portrait of a failed rebellion: An account of rational, sub-optimal violence in western Uganda', *Rationality and Society*, 17 (5), 2005.

Huckabey, Jessica M., 'Al-Qaeda in Mali: The defection connections', *Orbis*, 57 (3), 2013.

Hughes, Geraint, 'Intelligence-gathering, special operations and air-strikes in modern counterinsurgency', in Rich and Duyvesteyn (eds.), *The Routledge Handbook of Insurgency and Counterinsurgency*, Routledge: New York, 2014.

Human Rights Watch, 'Deaths and disappearances: Abuses in counterterrorism operations in Nairobi and in northeastern Kenya', Human Rights Watch Report, 7 (20), 2016, https://www.hrw.org/report/2016/07/20/deaths-and-disappearances/abuses-counterterrorism-operations-nairobi-and (accessed 27 December 2017).

Human Rights Watch, 'Denying the honor of living: Sudan, a human rights disaster', Africa Watch Report, 65, March 1990.

Human Rights Watch, 'Harsh war, harsh peace: Abuses by al-Shabaab, the Transitional Federal Government, and AMISOM in Somalia', Human Rights Watch Report, 19 April 2010.

Human Rights Watch, 'Nigeria: Massive destruction, deaths from military raid', Human Rights Watch news release, 1 May 2013, http://www.hrw.org/news/2013/05/01/nigeria-massive-destruction-deaths-military-raid (accessed 30 April 2015).

Human Rights Watch, 'Somalia: War crimes in Mogadishu: UN should address civilian protection', Human Rights Watch, 13 August 2007, https://www.hrw.org/news/2007/08/13/somalia-war-crimes-mogadishu (accessed 27 November 2017).

Human Rights Watch, 'Spiraling violence: Boko Haram attacks and security force abuses in Nigeria', Human Rights Watch Report, October 2012, http://www.hrw.org/sites/default/files/reports/nigeria1012webwcover_0.pdf (accessed 1 January 2015).

Human Rights Watch, 'Sudan, global trade, local impact', Human Rights Watch Report, 9 (4), 1998.

Human Rights Watch, 'Sudan: In the name of God, behind the red line: Political repression in northern Sudan', London: Human Rights Watch, 1996.

Human Rights Watch, '"Those terrible weeks in their camp": Boko Haram violence against women and girls in northeast Nigeria', Human Rights Watch Report, 3 October 2014.

Humphreys, Macartan and Habaye Ag Mohamed, 'Senegal and Mali', Paper presented at the World Bank/Center for United Nations Studies Conference, Yale University, 12–15 April 2002, http://www.columbia.edu/~mh2245/papers1/sen_mali.pdf.

Humphreys, Macartan and Jeremy M. Weinstein, 'Who fights? The determinants of participation in civil war', *American Journal of Political Science*, 52 (2), 2008.

Ibn Baz, Abd al-Aziz, *The Necessity of Acting according to the Sunnah of the Messenger (Peace Be upon Him) and Deeming Those Who Deny It as Disbelievers*, Saudi Ministry of Information, n.d.

Ibrahim, Idris Abbakr, 'The Islamic movement in Eritrea and its political role: The case of the Eritrean Islamic Party for Justice and Development', PhD thesis, University of Malaya, Kuala Lumpur, Malaysia, 2016.

Idoumou, Raby Ould, 'AQIM under siege', *Magharebia*, 13 January 2012.

IGAD Security Sector Program (ISSP) and Sahan Foundation, 'Al-Shabaab as a transnational security threat', IGAD Special Report, 2016.

Immigration and Refugee Board of Canada, 'The Allied Democratic Front (ADF) in Uganda including leaders, goals, objectives, and whether or not members and supporters are harassed by the government (1995–2002)', UGA38401.E, 2003.

Institute for Economics and Peace, *Global Terrorism Index*, Institute for Economics and Peace, Oxford, 2014.

Integrated Regional Information Networks (IRIN), 'What will follow Boko Haram?', 24 November 2011, http://www.refworld.org/docid/4ed388292.html.

International Crisis Group, 'Central Mali: An uprising in the making?', Crisis Group Africa Report, no. 238, 2016.

International Crisis Group, 'Curbing violence in Nigeria (II): The Boko Haram insurgency', Crisis Group Africa Report, no. 216, 3 April 2014.

International Crisis Group, 'Eastern Congo: The ADF–NALU's lost rebellion', Africa Briefing, no. 93, 2012.

International Crisis Group, 'How Kabila lost his way', ICG Congo Report, no. 3, 21 May 1999.

International Crisis Group, 'Mali: Avoiding escalation', *Africa Report*, no. 189, 18 July 2012.

International Crisis Group, 'Mali: Last chance in Algiers', Crisis Group Africa Briefing, no. 104, 18 November 2014.

International Crisis Group, 'Mali: Reform or relapse', Crisis Group Africa Report, no. 210, 2014.

International Crisis Group, 'North Kivu: Into the quagmire? An overview of the current crisis in North Kivu', ICG Kivu Report, no. 1, 1998.

International Crisis Group, 'Somalia: Al-Shabaab – It will be a long war', Crisis Group Africa Briefing, no. 99, 26 June 2014.

International Crisis Group, 'Somalia: Countering terrorism in a failed state', *Africa Report*, no. 45, 23 May 2002.

International Crisis Group, 'Somalia's Islamists', Crisis Group Africa Report, no.100, 12 December 2005.

International Crisis Group, 'The Kenyan intervention in Somalia', Africa Report, no. 184, 2012.

IRIN News, 'Uganda: IRIN Special Report on the ADF rebellion', IRIN News, 1999.

Islam, Saif al-, 'The Ogadeni file, Operation Holding MSK', Harmony Project, Document AFGP-2002-600104, https://www.ctc.usma.edu/posts/the-ogaden-file-operation-holding-al-msk-original-language-2 (accessed 18 January 2018).

Islamic State in Somalia, 'Eid on the frontiers (Thughur) of Somalia', Furat Media, 16 September 2016.

Islamic State in Somalia, 'New video message from Jund al-Khilāfah in Somalia: The Commander Shaykh Abū Nu'man Military Training Camp', Furat Media, 16 April 2016.

Jacinto, Leela, 'Al-Qaeda leader Abou Zeid "killed in Mali"', France24, 5 March 2013, http://www.france24.com/en/20130323-france-confirms-death-top-al-qaeda-leader-abou-zeid-mali (accessed 8 August 2017).

Jackson, Ashley and Abdi Aynte, 'Talking to the other side: Humanitarian negotiations with al-Shabaab in Somalia', Humanitarian Policy Group Working Paper, Overseas Development Institute, 18 December 2013.

Jacquard, Roland, *In the Name of Osama bin Laden: Global Terrorism and the Bin Laden Brotherhood*, London: Duke University Press, 2002.

Jillo, Rob, 'Two Kenyans charged with terrorism', Capital FM, 22 December 2010, https://www.capitalfm.co.ke/news/2010/12/two-kenyans-charged-with-terrorism/ (accessed 27 December 2017).

Joffe, Lawrence, Hassan al-Turabi obituary, *The Guardian*, 11 March 2016.

Johnston, Patrick, 'The geography of insurgent organization and its consequences for civil wars: Evidence from Liberia and Sierra Leone', *Security Studies*, 17 (1), 2008.

Jones, Seth G. and Martin C. Libiki, 'How terrorist groups end', RAND Report, Los Angeles, 2008.

Jones, Seth G., Andrew M. Liepman and Nathan Chandler, 'Counterterrorism and counterinsurgency in Somalia: Assessing the campaign against the Shabaab', RAND Research Report, RR-1539-OSD, 2016.

Jordan, Jenna, 'When heads roll: Assessing the effectiveness of leadership decapitation', *Security Studies*, 18 (4), 2009.

Joscelyn, Thomas and Caleb Weiss, 'Report: Head of the Islamic State's Sahara branch threatens Morocco', *Threat Matrix*, 6 May 2016, http://www.longwarjournal.org/archives/2016/05/report-head-of-the-islamic-states-sahara-branch-threatens-morocco.php (accessed 15 September 2017).

Juergensmeyer, Mark, *Terror in the Mind of God: The Global Rise of Religious Violence*, Berkeley, CA: University of California Press, 2003.

Jumbe, Ishaq, 'History of the controversial Musa mosque', *The Standard Digital*, 3 February 2014, https://www.standardmedia.co.ke/article/2000103809/history-of-the-controversial-musa-mosque (accessed 27 December 2017).

Kalyvas, Stathis N., *The Logic of Violence in Civil War*, Cambridge: Cambridge University Press, 2006.

Kalyvas, Stathis N., 'The ontology of "political violence": Action and identity in civil wars', *Perspectives on Politics*, 1 (3), 2003.

Kalyvas, Stathis N. and Laia Balcells, 'International system and technologies of rebellion: How the end of the Cold War shaped internal conflict', *American Political Science Review*, 104 (3), 2010.

Kalyvas, Stathis N. and Matthew Adam Kocher, 'How "free" is free riding in civil wars? Violence, insurgency, and the collective action problem', *World Politics*, 59 (2), 2007.

Kantai, Parselelo, 'Kenya's Mombasa Republican Council: The coast calls for freedom', Africa Report, 17 May 2012, https://web.archive.org/web/20120702202413/http://www.theafricareport.com/index.php/20120517501811752/east-horn-africa/kenya-s-mombasa-republican-council%E2%80%A9-the-coast-calls-for-freedom-501811752.html (accessed 18 December 2017).

Karmon, Ely, 'Boko Haram's international reach', *Perspectives on Terrorism*, 8 (1), 2014.

Kasaija, Apuuli Phillip, 'The UN-led Djibouti peace process for Somalia 2008–2009: Results and problems', *Journal of Contemporary African Studies*, 28 (10), 2010.

Kasasira, Risdel, 'Who is ADF's Jamil Mukulu?', *The Monitor*, 7 August 2015.

Kasfir, Nelson, 'Rebel governance, constructing a field of inquiry: Definitions, scope, patterns, order, causes', in Aronja, Kasfir and Mampilly (eds.), *Rebel Governance in Civil War*, London: Cambridge University Press, 2017.

Kassim, Abdulbasit and Michael Nwankpa, *The Boko Haram Reader: From Nigerian Preachers to the Islamic State*, London: Hurst, 2018.

Katibat Macina, 'First video of Katibat Macina, message from Jamaat Ansar Dine', Katibat Macina, 18 May 2016, http://jihadology.net/2016/05/18/new-video-message-from-jamaat-an%E1%B9%A3ar-al-din-first-video-of-katibat-macina/ (accessed 8 August 2017).

Kenya Muslim Youth Alliance, 'We don't trust anyone, strengthening relationship is the key to reducing violent extremism in Kenya', Special

Report, 2016, http://www.international-alert.org/sites/default/files/Kenya_ViolentExtremism_EN_2016.pdf (accessed 28 December 2017).

Kepel, Gilles, *Jihad: The Trail of Political Islam*, London: I.B. Tauris, 2006.

Kepel, Gilles, *The War for Muslim Minds: Islam and the West*, Cambridge, MA: Belknap Press, 2004.

Khalou, I., 'Mali: Amadou Kouffa et l'Etat islamique: Creuse un trou pour ton ennemi, mais pas trop profond, on ne sait jamais', Maliactu. net, 6 January 2017, http://maliactu.net/mali-amadou-kouffa-et-letat-islamique-creuse-un-trou-pour-ton-ennemi-mais-pas-trop-profond-on-ne-sait-jamais/.

Khory, Kavita, 'Pakistan: Have the chickens come home to roost?', in Stig J. Hansen, Atle Mesøy and Tuncay Kardas, *The Borders of Islam*, London: Hurst, 2009.

Kilcullen, David, *Out of the Mountains: The Coming Age of the Urban Guerrilla*, London: Hurst, 2013.

Koehler-Derrick, Gabriel, 'A false foundation? AQAP, tribes and ungoverned spaces in Yemen', Harmony Paper, CTC, West Point, 2011.

Kohlmann, Evan F., 'Two decades of jihad in Algeria: The GIA, the GSPC, and al-Qaida', NEFA Foundation, May 2007.

Koopman, Joop, 'Is Tanzania radical Islam's next target?', *Huffington Post*, 4 June 2014, http://www.huffingtonpost.com/joop-koopman/is-tanzania-radical-islam_b_4725828.html (accessed 29 October 2015).

Kouassi, Carole, 'Niger: l'EI revendique l'assaut contre la prison de Koutoukalé', Africanews, 19 October 2016, http://fr.africanews.com/2016/10/19/niger-l-ei-revendique-l-assaut-contre-la-prison-de-koutoukale/ (accessed 15 September 2017).

Kriel, Robyn and Lillian Leposo, 'In video, Somali ISIS members court al-Shabaab', CNN Online, 22 May 2015, http://edition.cnn.com/2015/05/22/world/somalia-isis-al-shabaab-video/ (accessed 6 December 2017).

Krueger, Alan B., 'To avoid terrorism, end poverty and ignorance. Right? Guess again!', *New York Times*, 13 December 2001.

Krueger, Alan B., *What Makes a Terrorist? Economics and the Roots of Terrorism*, Princeton: Princeton University Press, 2007.

Krueger, Alan B. and Jitka Maleckova, 'Education, poverty, political violence and terrorism: Is there a causal connection?', NBER Working Paper 9074, 2002.

Krueger, Alan B. and Jitka Maleckova, 'The economics and the education of suicide bombers: Does poverty cause terrorism?', *New Republic*, 24 June 2002.

KTN, 'Masjid Musa parliamentary statement, 18th February 2014', KTN, 18 February 2014, https://www.youtube.com/watch?v=0rEL89OIqn4 (accessed 27 December 2017).

Kurth, Audrey, *How Terrorism Ends: Understanding the Decline and Demise of Terrorist Campaigns*, Princeton: Princeton University Press, 2010.

Lacher, Wolfram, 'Organized crime and conflict in the Sahel-Sahara region', Carnegie Endowment, blog, 13 September 2012, http://carnegieendowment.org/2012/09/13/organized-crime-and-conflict-in-sahel-sahara-region-pub-49360 (accessed 10 September 2017).

Landinfo, 'Al-Shabaab and forced marriage', Landinfo, response note, 6 July 2012, http://www.landinfo.no/asset/2156 (accessed 10 September 2016).

Landinfo, 'Somalia: Violence, fatalities, perpetrators and victims in Mogadishu', Query response, 27 February 2017, https://landinfo.no/id/114.0 (accessed 5 December 2017).

Last, Murray, 'The pattern of dissent: Boko Haram in Nigeria 2009', *Annual Review of Islam in Africa*, 2009.

Lebovich, Andrew, 'AQIM's Mokhtar Belmokhtar speaks out', *Al Wasat*, 21 November 2011, https://thewasat.wordpress.com/2011/11/21/aqims-mokhtar-belmokhtar-speaks-out/ (accessed 7 July 2017).

Lebovich, Andrew, 'Of mergers, MUJWA, and Mokhtar Belmokhtar', *Al Wasat*, 23 August 2013.

Lebovich, Andrew, 'The local face of jihadism in northern Mali', *CTC Sentinel*, 6 (6), 2013.

Lecocq, Baz, *Disputed Desert Decolonisation, Competing Nationalisms and Tuareg Rebellions in Northern Mali*, Leiden: Brill, 2010.

Lecocq, Baz and George Klute, 'Tuareg separatism in Mali', *International Journal*, 68 (3), 2013.

LeSage, Andre, 'The rising terrorist threat in Tanzania: Domestic Islamist militancy and regional threats', *Strategic Forum*, September 2014.

Lesch, Ann M., 'Osama bin Laden's "business" in Sudan', *Current History*, May 2002.

Lia, Brynjar, 'Understanding jihadi proto-states', *Perspectives on Terrorism*, 9 (4), 2015.

Lia, Brynjar and Katja Skjølberg, 'Causes of terrorism: An expanded and updated review of the literature', FFI Report 04307, 2005.

Lloyd George, William, 'The man who brought the black flag to Timbuktu', *Foreign Policy*, 22 October 2012.

Look, Anne, 'Mali rebel groups merge, plan to create Islamic State', *VOA Africa*, 27 May 2012, voattps://blogs.voanews.com/breaking-news/2012/05/27/mali-rebel-groups-merge-plan-to-create-islamic-state/ (accessed 8 August 2017).

Lounnas, Djallil, 'Confronting al-Qa'ida in the Islamic Maghrib in the Sahel: Algeria and the Malian crisis', *Journal of North African Studies*, 19 (5), 2014.

Lowen, M., 'Kenyan al-Shabaab terror recruits in it for the money', BBC, 29 January 2014.

Lucia, Elisa Lopez, 'Islamist radicalisation and terrorism in Tanzania', Helpdesk Report, 18 May 2015.

Lyammouri, Rida, 'AQIM making noise again in Timbuktu region, northern Mali', The Maghreb and Sahel, Sand, Tea, and Guns blog, 3 December 2015, https://maghrebandsahel.wordpress.com/2016/06/01/mali-aqim-and-security-related-incidents-in-may-2016/ (accessed 8 August 2017).

Lyammouri, Rida, 'AQIM never really abandoned Timbuktu, Mali', The Maghreb and Sahel, Sand, Tea, and Guns blog, 6 February 2016, https://maghrebandsahel.wordpress.com/2016/02/06/aqim-never-really-abandoned-timbuktu-mali/ (accessed 4 October 2018).

Lyammouri, Rida, 'Key events that led to tensions between Mokhtar Belmokhtar and Adnan Abu Walid al-Sahrawi before splitting', The Maghreb and Sahel, Sand, Tea, and Guns blog, 7 December 2015, https://maghrebandsahel.wordpress.com/2015/12/ (accessed 1 September 2017).

Ma'ali, Abu al-, 'Al-Qaeda and its allies in the Sahel and Sahara', Al Jazeera Centre for Studies Report, 1 May 2012.

Macharia, James, 'Insight: Separatist storm brewing on Kenya's coast', Reuters World News, 23 July 2012, https://uk.reuters.com/article/uk-kenya-coast-mrc/insight-separatist-storm-brewing-on-kenyas-coast-idUKBRE86M0H820120723 (accessed 18 December 2017).

Madike, Isioma, 'Boko Haram: Rise of a deadly sect', *National Mirror*, 19 June 2011, http://www.nationalmirroronline.net/sunday-mirror/big_read/14548.html (accessed 5 November 2012).

Maiduguri, Ahmad Salkida, 'The story of Nigeria's first suicide bomber', *Blueprint Magazine*, 26 June 2011, http://saharareporters.com/news-page/story-nigerias-first-suicide-bomber-blueprint-magazine. The Story Of Nigeria's First Suicide Bomber-BluePrint Magazine The Story Of Nigeria's First Suicide Bomber-BluePrint Magazine

Malere, Bright, 'ADF rebels: My abduction, camp life and escape', *New Vision*, 4 September 2013.

Malijet, 'Ménaka: L'Etat islamique à la manœuvre', *Malijet*, 20 July 2017.

Mampilly, Zachariah C., *Rebel Rulers: Insurgent Governance and Civilian Life during War*, Chapel Hill, NC: Cornell University Press, 2015.

Mark, Monica, 'Boko Haram ready for peace talks with Nigeria, says alleged sect member', *The Guardian*, 1 November 2012.

Marret, Jean-Luc, 'Al-Qaeda in Islamic Maghreb: A "glocal" organization', *Studies in Conflict and Terrorism*, 31 (6), 2008.

Martinez, Luis, *The Algerian Civil War, 1990–1998*, London: Hurst, 2000.

Matinuddin, Kamal, *The Taliban Phenomenon: Afghanistan 1994–1997*, Oxford: Oxford University Press, 1999.

Mbowou, Claude, 'Between the "Kanuri" and others', in Virginie Collombier and Olivier Roy (eds.), *Tribes and Global Jihadism*, London: Hurst, 2018.

McCants, William, *The ISIS Apocalypse: The History, Strategy, and Doomsday Vision of the Islamic State*, New York: St Martin's Press, 2016.

McColl, Robert W., 'The insurgent state: Territorial bases of revolution', *Annals of the Association of American Geographers*, 59 (4), 1969.

McGregor, Andrew, 'Oil and jihad in Central Africa: The rise and fall of Uganda's ADF', *Terrorism Monitor*, 5 (24), 2007.

McGregor, Andrew, 'The Fulani crisis: Communal violence and radicalization in the Sahel', *CTC Sentinel*, 10 (2), 2017.

McGregor, Andrew, 'Ugandan rebel movement reemerges along oil-bearing Ugandan/Congolese border', *Terrorism Monitor*, 11 (15), 2013, http://www.refworld.org/docid/5204f9e64.html (accessed 15 August 2013).

McGregor, Andrew, 'Where trafficking and terrorism intersect: A profile of Mauritanian militant Hamada Ould Kheirou', Aberfoyle International Security blog, 31 March 2014, http://www.aberfoylesecurity.com/?p=823 (accessed 13 August 2014).

McLauchlin, Theodore, 'Desertion, terrain, and control of the home front in civil wars', *Journal of Conflict Resolution*, 58 (8), 2014.

Meleagrou-Hitchens, Alexander, 'Al-Shabab fighters in Somalia', *Foreign Affairs*, 8 October 2015.

Mellah, Salima and Jean-Baptiste Rivoire, 'El Para, the Maghreb's Bin Laden', *Le Monde Diplomatique*, 4 February 2005.

Menastream, 'Burkina Faso: Ansaroul Islam pledging allegiance to the Islamic State? Maybe or maybe not', Menastream, 16 April 2017, http://menastream.com/burkina-faso-ansaroul-islam-pledging-allegiance-to-the-islamic-state-maybe-or-maybe-not/ (accessed 1 September 2017).

Menkhaus, Ken, 'Somalia: State collapse and the threat of terrorism', IISS Adelphi Paper, 364, 2004.

Menkhaus, Ken, 'Terrorist activities in ungoverned spaces: Evidence and observations from the Horn of Africa', Paper prepared for the Southern Africa and International Terrorism Workshop, 25–27 January 2007, South Africa.

Mesa García, Beatriz, 'The Tuareg rebellion and al-Qaeda's role', IEES Opinion Paper, 37/12, 2012.

Mesøy, Atle, 'Poverty and radicalisation into violent extremism: A causal link?', NOREF paper, January 2012.

Metz, Steven, 'Rethinking insurgency', in Rich and Duvesteyn (eds.), *The Routledge Handbook of Insurgency and Counterinsurgency*, London: Routledge, 2014.

Mills, Claire, 'In brief: International military forces in Mali', House of Commons Brief, SN06615, 2013.

Miniter, Richard, *Losing Bin Laden: How Bill Clinton's Failures Unleashed Global Terror*, Washington DC: Regnery Publishing, 2004.

Miran, Jonathan, 'A historical overview of Islam in Eritrea', *Die Welt des Islams*, 45 (2), 2005.

Moaddel, Mansoor, *Class, Politics, and Ideology in the Iranian Revolution*, New York: Columbia University Press, 1993.

Mohamed, Aziz, 'Les services de sécurité algériens ont réussi à identifier les preneurs d'otages algériens et français au Sahel', *El Watan*, 5 July 2013, http://maliactu.net/sahel-aqmi-a-cree-un-groupe-special-pour-les-otages/ (accessed 8 August 2017).

Mohammed, Abdulkareem and Mohammed Haruna, *The Paradox of Boko Haram*, Lagos: Moving Image, 2010.

Monitoring Group on Somalia, 'Report of the Monitoring Group on Somalia submitted in accordance with Resolution 1811 (2008)', Report S/2008/769, 2008.

Monitoring Group on Somalia and Eritrea, 'Report of the Monitoring Group on Somalia and Eritrea submitted in accordance with Resolution 1916 (2010)', S/2011/433, 18 July 2011.

Monitoring Group on Somalia and Eritrea, 'Report of the Monitoring Group on Somalia and Eritrea pursuant to Security Council Resolution, 2002 (2011)', 2012.

Monitoring Group on Somalia and Eritrea, 'Somalia: Report of the Monitoring Group on Somalia and Eritrea submitted in accordance with Resolution 2002 (2011)', Report S/2012/544, 2012.

Monitoring Group on Somalia and Eritrea, 'Report of the Monitoring Group on Somalia and Eritrea pursuant to Security Council Resolution 2060 (2012): Somalia', Report S/2013/440, 2013.

Monitoring Group on Somalia and Eritrea, Report of the Monitoring Group on Somalia and Eritrea pursuant to Security Council Resolution 2060 (2012): Somalia, S/2013/413, 2013.

Monitoring Group on Somalia and Eritrea, 'Report of the Monitoring Group on Somalia and Eritrea pursuant to Security Council Resolution 2182 (2014): Somalia', Report S/2015/801, 2015.

Moore, Phil Hatcher, 'Islamism on the Kenyan coast', Philmoore info blog, 7 October 2013, http://philmoore.info/blog/2013/10/islamism-on-the-kenyan-coast (accessed 27 December 2017)

Moussalli, Ahmad, 'Wahhabism, Salafism and Islamism: Who is the enemy?', A Conflicts Forum Monograph, Beirut, 2009, http://conflictsforum. org/briefings/Wahhabism-Salafism-and-Islamism.pdf (accessed 15 March 2014).

Mujahiroun, 'Statement on the Tanzanian spy', Mujahiroun Tanga, 3 April 2016, https://somalianews.files.wordpress.com/2016/04/ ampressrelease3.pdf (accessed 27 December 2017).

Mukthar, Sarah al-, 'How Boko Haram courted and joined the Islamic State', New York Times, 10 June 2015.

Mulcaire, Camille, 'Assessing al-Qaeda from the teachings of Ibn Taymiyya', e-IR, 2013, http://www.e-ir.info/2013/10/15/assessing-al-qaeda-from-the-teachings-of-ibn-taymiyya/ (accessed 23 November 2014).

Murtada, Ahmed, 'The Boko Haraam group in Nigeria: Its beginnings, principles and actions', Al Qirat, 12, 2012.

Muslim Youth Centre, 'New statement from the Muslim Youth Center: "On Abū Manṣūr al-Amrīkī"', MYC, 14 September 2013, http://jihadology. net/category/the-muslim-youth-center/ (accessed 27 December 2017).

Muthoni, Kamau and Patrick Beja, 'Mombasa Republican Council (MRC) now demands dialogue with state after major victory in court', The Standard, 26 July 2016, https://www.standardmedia.co.ke/article/2000209821/ mombasa-republican-council-mrc-now-demands-dialogue-with-state-after-major-victory-in-court (accessed 18 December 2017).

Mutizwa, Nyasha K., 'Trial of nearly 200 jihadists in Mozambique', Africanews, 10 May 2018, http://www.africanews.com/2018/10/05/ trial-of-nearly-200-jihadists-in-mozambique/ (accessed 10 October 2018).

Mwakio, Philip, 'Teenager picked to act as new Masjid Musa imam', The Standard Digital, 24 January 2015, https://www.standardmedia.co.ke/ article/2000148985/teenager-picked-to-act-as-new-masjid-musa-imam (accessed 27 December 2017).

Mwangi, John, 'The process and trends of youth radicalization in Kenya's Mombasa and Nairobi counties', Paper presented at the 3rd MISR Graduate Students' Conference, 28–29 July 2017.

Mwangi, Wachira, 'Mosque reopens for prayers as caretaker calls for sobriety', Daily Nation, 6 December 2014, http://www.nation.co.ke/news/ Mosque-reopens-for-prayers-as-caretaker-calls-for-sobriety/1056-2547472-ch9tbsz/index.html (accessed 27 December 2017).

Mwilolezi, Cynthia, 'Arusha bombing incidents suspects finally in court', The Guardian, 2014, http://www.ippmedia.com/frontend/?l=70602.

Nada, Ahmed Ould al-, 'Interview with Sanda Ould Bouamama, media official of Ansar al-Din', Al-Akhbar News Agency, 16 April 2012.

Nairobi, Abu Hassan an-, 'Madonda Yasiopona', *Gaidi Mtaani*, 2, 2012.

Naji, Abu Bakr al-, *The Management of Savagery: The Most Critical Stage through Which the Umma Will Pass*, translated by William McCants, 2006, http://azelin.files.wordpress.com/2010/08/abu-bakr-naji-the-management-of-savagery-the-most-critical-stage-through-which-the-umma-will-pass.pdf (accessed 10 April 2014).

National Commission on Terrorist Attacks upon the United States, *The 9/11 Commission Report: Final Report of the National Commission on Terrorist Attacks upon the United States*, Washington DC: National Commission on Terrorist Attacks upon the United States, 2004.

Ndaluka, Thomas and Frans Wijsen, *Religion and State in Tanzania Revisited: Reflections from 50 Years of Independence*, Münster: Lit Verlag, 2014.

Nesser, Petter, 'How did Europe's global jihadis obtain training for their militant causes?', *Terrorism and Political Violence*, 20 (2), 2008.

Nesser, Petter, *Islamist Terrorism in Europe: A History*, London: Hurst, 2014.

Nesser, Petter, 'Jihad in Europe: Patterns *in terrorist cell formation and behavior, 1995–2010*', PhD thesis, University of Oslo, 2011.

Nesser, Petter, 'Joining jihadi terrorist cells in Europe: Exploring motivational aspects of recruitment and radicalization', in Magnus Ranstorp (ed.), *Understanding Violent Radicalization: Terrorist and Jihadist Movements in Europe*, New York: Routledge, 2010.

Nigerian Voice, 'Boko Haram's divided house', *The Nigerian Voice*, 24 July 2011.

Njini, Felix, 'Tanzanian police arrest nine al-Shabaab suspects at local mosque', *Bloomberg News*, 15 April 2015, http://www.bloomberg.com/news/articles/2015-04-15/tanzanian-police-arrest-nine-al-shabaab-suspects-at-local-mosque (accessed 2 November 2015)

Nkwame, Valentine Marc, 'Muslim Council suspends Sheikh Ally Kisiwa', *Arusha Times*, 2 July 2004.

Nossiter, Adam, 'In Nigeria, a deadly group's rage has local roots', *New York Times*, 25 February 2012.

Nsaibia, Héni, 'Jihadist groups in the Sahel region formalize merger', The Jihadica blog, 27 March 2017, http://jihadology.net/2017/03/27/guest-post-jihadist-groups-in-the-sahel-region-formalize-merger/ (accessed 25 January 2017).

Nzes, Fredrick, 'Al-Hijra: Al-Shabab's affiliate in Kenya', *CTC Sentinel*, 7 (5), 2014.

Oarhe, Osumah, 'Responses of the Nigerian defense and intelligence establishments to the challenge of Boko Haram', in Ioannis Mantzikos (ed.), *Boko Haram: Anatomy of a Crisis*, Bristol: e-International Relations, 2013.

Ochami, David, 'How fiery cleric Rogo developed, propagated extremism', *The Standard*, 1 September 2012, https://www.standardmedia. co.ke/?articleID=2000065268&story_title=How-fiery-cleric-Rogo-developed,-propagated-extremism- (accessed 18 December 2017).

Oded, Arye, 'Islamic extremism in Kenya: The rise and fall of Sheikh Khalid Balala', *Journal of Religion in Africa*, 26 (4), 1996.

Oded, Arye, 'Islamic extremism in Kenya', RIMA Occasional Papers, 1 (14), 2013.

Oded, Arye, *Islam and Politics in Kenya.* Boulder, CO: Lynne Rienner Publishers, 2000.

Odula, Tom, 'Shooting of cleric who bombed Israeli hotel highlights growing Islamism in Mombasa', *Times of Israel*, 6 September 2012, https://www. timesofisrael.com/mombasa-cleric-who-tried-to-bomb-israeli-hotel-killed-in-drive-by-shooting/ (accessed 27 December 2017).

Ola, Timothy, 'Boko Haram: How 3 pastors were beheaded, eyewitness', *Daily Sun*, 6 August 2009.

Olson, Mancur, 'Dictatorship, democracy, and development', *American Political Science Review*, 87 (3), 1993.

Ombati, Cyrus, 'Police name Kenyan suspects luring youth to join al-Shabaab', *The Standard Digital*, 18 August 2015, https://www.standardmedia. co.ke/article/2000173237/police-name-kenyan-suspects-luring-youth-to-join-al-shabaab (accessed 27 December 2017).

Onsarigo, Calvins, 'Terror suspect Ali Hamis Mzomo shot dead in Likoni', *The Star*, 8 December 2017, https://www.the-star.co.ke/news/2017/12/08/terror-suspect-ali-hamis-mzomo-shot-dead-in-likoni_c1681959 (accessed 27 December 2017).

Onuoha, Freedom, 'The 9/7 Boko Haram attack on Bauchi prison: A case of intelligence failure', *Peace and Conflict Monitor*, 2 November 2010.

Onuoha, Freedom, 'Understanding Boko Haram's attacks on telecommunication infrastructure', in Ioannis Mantzikos (ed.), *Boko Haram: Anatomy of a Crisis*, Bristol: e-International Relations, 2013.

Owens, Nick, 'Fugitive Samantha Lewthwaite – the "white widow" of 7/7 – writes chilling online blog', *The Mirror*, 1 July 2102, http://www. mirror.co.uk/news/uk-news/fugitive-samantha-lewthwaite---the-white-946967 (accessed 27 December 2017).

Peralta, Eyder, 'Sunni extremist group ISIS declares new Islamic Caliphate', NPR, 29 June 2014, http://www.npr.org/blogs/thetwo-way/2014/06/29/326703823/al-qaida-splinter-group-isis-declares-new-islamic-caliphate (accessed 9 July 2014).

Pérouse de Montclos, Marc-Antoine (ed.), *Boko Haram: Islamism, Politics, Security and the State in Nigeria*, West African Politics and Society Series, 2, 2014.

Pesa Times, '17 lost children found in Moshi', *Pesa Times*, 9 March 2015, http://pesatimes.co.tz/news/crime-and-court/17-lost-children-found-in-moshi/tanzania (accessed 2 November 2015).

Pesa Times, 'Police arrest more suspects behind Arusha bomb blasts', *Pesa Times*, 1 August 2014, http://pesatimes.co.tz/news/governance/police-arrest-more-suspects-behind-arusha-bomb-blasts/Tanzania/.

Pestano, Andrew V., 'Nigerian army says Boko Haram defeated; group's disputed leader vows to fight on', UP, 19 August 2016, http://www.upi.com/Top_News/World-News/2016/08/09/Nigerian-army-says-Boko-Haram-defeated-groups-disputed-leader-vows-to-fight-on/2041470753181/ (accessed 1 November 2016).

Pezard, Stephanie and Michael Shurkin, *Toward a Secure and Stable Mali: Approaches to Engaging Local Actors*, Los Angeles: RAND Corporation, 2014.

Pham, Peter, 'Foreign influences and shifting horizons: Al-Qaeda in the Islamic Maghreb', *Orbis*, 2011.

Pham, Peter, 'The dangerous "pragmatism" of al-Qaeda in the Islamic Maghreb', *Journal of the Middle East and Africa*, 2 (15), 2011.

Piazza, James A., 'Poverty, minority economic discrimination and domestic terrorism', *Journal of Peace Research*, 48 (3), 2011.

Pinatel, Jean-Bertrand, 'The crisis in Mali, the diplomatic maneuvers', Geopolitics, Geo Strategy Analyses and Debates, http://www.geopolitique-geostrategie.com/the-crisis-in-mali-the-diplomatic-maneuver (accessed 9 August 2017).

Pirio, Gregory A., *The African Jihad: Bin Laden's Quest for the Horn of Africa*, Asmara: Red Sea Press, 2007.

PressAfrik, 'Le Jihadiste algérien Mokhtar Belmokhtar devient chef d'al-Qaïda en Afrique de l'Ouest', *PressAfrik*, 15 September 2015, http://www.pressafrik.com/Le-jihadiste-algerien-Mokhtar-Belmokhtar-devient-chef-d-al-Qaida-en-Afrique-de-l-Ouest_a139316.html (accessed 15 September 2017).

Primo, Nicholas, 'No music in Timbuktu: A brief analysis of the conflict in Mali and Al Qaeda's rebirth', *Pepperdine Policy Review*, 6, 2013.

Prunier, Gérard, 'Rebel movements and proxy warfare in Uganda, Sudan and the Congo (1986–99)', *African Affairs*, 103 (412), 2004.

Prunier, Gérard, 'The geopolitical situation in the Great Lakes Area in light of the Kivu crisis', Writenett, 1 February 1997, http://www.refworld.org/docid/3ae6a6be0.html (accessed 18 December 2015).

Pulse News Agency, 'Terrorists raid Borno village for food, medical supplies', Pulse News Agency, 6 March 2017, http://www.pulse.ng/news/local/boko-haram-terrorists-raid-borno-village-for-food-medical-supplies-id6430975.html (accessed 10 January 2018).

Pureza, José Manuel, Mark Duffield, Robert Matthews, Susan Woodward and David Sogge, 'Peacebuilding and failed states, some theoretical notes', *Oficina do CES*, 250, 2007.

Qutb, Said, *Milestones*, Indianapolis: American Trust Publications, 1993.

Rabasa, Angel, Steven Boraz, Peter Chalk, Kim Cragin, Theodore W. Karasik, Jennifer D.P. Moroney, Kevin A. O'Brien and John E. Peters, 'Ungoverned territories: A unique front in the war on terrorism', RAND Brief, 2007.

Reidel, Bruce, *The Search for al-Qaeda, Its Leadership, Ideology and Future*, Washington DC: Brookings Institution Press, 2008.

Reno, William, *Corruption and State Politics in Sierra Leone*, New York: Cambridge University Press, 1995.

Reno, William, 'Insurgency movements in Africa', in Paul B. Rich and Isabelle Duyvesteyn (eds.), *The Routledge Handbook of Insurgency and Counterinsurgency*, London: Routledge, 2012.

Reno, William, *Warlord Politics and African States*, Boulder, CO: Lynne Rienner Publishers, 1998.

Reuters, 'Nairobi explosions: At least 12 killed, more than 70 wounded in attacks on bus, market', Reuters/AFP/ABC, 16 May 2014, http://www.abc.net.au/news/2014-05-16/deadly-twin-bomb-blasts-rock-nairobi/5459300 (accessed 27 December 2017).

Reuters, 'Update 1: Mali Tuareg leaders call off Islamist pact', Reuters, 1 June 2012, http://www.reuters.com/article/mali-rebels-idUSL5E8H1CXZ20120601 (accessed 9 June 2017).

RFI, 'Boko Haram vows to continue attack', RFI, 30 July 2009, http://www1.rfi.fr/actuen/articles/115/article_4552.asp.

Roggio, Bill, 'Al-Qaeda group led by Belmokhtar, MUJAO unite to form al-Murabitoon', *Threat Matrix*, 22 August 2013, http://www.longwarjournal.org/archives/2013/08/al_qaeda_groups_lead_by_belmok.php (accessed 10 September 2017).

Roggio, Bill, 'Foreign jihadists continue to pour into Mali', *Threat Matrix*, 27 October 2012, http://www.longwarjournal.org/archives/2012/10/foreign_jihadists_continue_to.php (accessed 8 August 2017).

Roggio, Bill, 'Somali Islamist group formally declares allegiance to Shabaab, al-Qaeda', FDD's Long War Journal, 25 February 2012, https://www.longwarjournal.org/archives/2012/02/somali_islamist_grou.php (accessed 6 December 2017).

Roggio, Bill, 'West African jihadists flock to northern Mali', Threat Matrix, 28 September 2012, http://www.longwarjournal.org/archives/2012/09/west_african_jihadists_flock_t.php (accessed 8 August 2017).

Roggio, Bill and Caleb Weiss, 'French troops kill MUJAO founder during raid in Mali', FDD's Long War Journal, December 2014, http://www.

longwarjournal.org/archives/2014/12/us_wanted_malian_jih.php (accessed 8 August 2017).

Romkema, Hans, 'Opportunities and constraints for the disarmament and repatriation of foreign armed groups in the Democratic Republic of Congo', Report commissioned by the Secretariat of the MDRP, 2007.

Rone, Jemera, 'Famine in Sudan, 1998: The human rights causes', London: Human Rights Watch, 1999.

Rosenberg, Matthew, 'Al-Qaeda skimming charity money', AP, 7 June 2004, https://www.cbsnews.com/news/al-qaeda-skimming-charity-money/ (accessed 18 December 2017).

Roy, Olivier, Den globaliserede Islam, Copenhagen: Vandkunsten, 2004.

Ryan, Michael, Decoding al-Qaeda's Strategy: The Deep Battle against America, NewYork: Columbia University Press, 2013.

Sa'd, Fayizah, 'Usama bin Laden reportedly interviewed in London', Rose al-Yusuf, 17 June 1996.

Sageman, Marc, Leaderless Jihad, Philadelphia: University of Pennsylvania Press, 2007.

Sageman, Marc, Understanding Terror Networks, Philadelphia: University of Pennsylvania Press, 2004.

Sahara Media, 'Interview with Iyad Ag Ghaly, amir of Jamaat Ansar al-Din', Sahara Media, 12 November 2012.

Sahara Media, 'Sahara Media interview with Sanda bin Bouamama al-Timbukti, a commander in Ansar al-Din movement', Sahara Media, 12 April 2012.

Sahara Reporters, 'US General says Boko Haram still holds territory in Nigeria', Sahara Reporters, 11 March 2016, http://saharareporters.com/2016/03/11/us-general-says-boko-haram-still-holds-territory-nigeria (accessed 15 November 2016).

Sahrawi, Abu al-Walid al-, 'Statement from the military commander of Jamaat al-Tawhid wa al-Jihad in West Africa, Abu al-Walid al-Sahrawi', MUJAO, 27 July 2013.

Sánchez-Cuenca, Ignacio and Luis de la Calle, 'Domestic terrorism: The hidden side of political violence', Annual Review of Political Science, 12 (1), 2009.

Sanders, Jim, 'The military balance in northeast Nigeria', Africa in Transition, 16 September 2014, http://blogs.cfr.org/campbell/2014/09/16/the-military-balance-in-northeast-nigeria/ (accessed 30 April 2015).

Schanzer, Jonathan, Al Qaeda's Armies: Middle Eastern Affiliated Groups, Washington: Washington Institute for Near East Policy, 2005.

Schanzer, Jonathan, Al-Qaeda's Armies, NewYork: Specialist Press International, 2004.

Scheuer, Michael, *Through Our Enemies' Eyes*, Washington: Potomac Books, 2002.

Schott, Josh, 'The differences between Taliban and al-Qaeda', *e-IR*, 2012, http://www.e-ir.info/2012/11/17/the-differences-between-the-taliban-and-al-qaeda/ (accessed 20 September 2016).

Schulze, Reinhard, *Islamischer Internationalismus im 20. Jahrhundert: Untersuchungen zur Geschichte der islamischen Weltliga*, Leiden: Brill, 1990.

Scorgie-Porter, Lindsay, 'Economic survival and borderland rebellion: The case of the Allied Democratic Forces on the Uganda-Congo border', *Journal of the Middle East and Africa*, 6 (2), 2015.

Sedgwick, Mark, 'Jihadism, narrow and wide: The dangers of loose use of an important term', *Perspectives on Terrorism*, 9 (2), 2015.

Shabaab Media Section, 'Dilkii Axmed Godane iyo Alshabaab oo Xaqijisay kuna dhawaaqday Amiir Cusub', Harakat al-Shabaab, 2014, https://www.youtube.com/watch?v=tn34K2wdbeQ (accessed 20 January 2015).

Shabelle News, 'Minister: 22 killed as residents, al-Shabaab clash over Zakah', *Shabelle News*, 22 February 2016, http://allafrica.com/stories/201602230290.html (accessed 1 December 2017)

Shay, Shaul, *The Red Sea Terror Triangle: Sudan, Somalia, Yemen, and Islamic Terror*, New Brunswick: Transaction Publishers, 2007.

Sheik, Abdi, 'Islamist rebels vow jihad on Somalia's Puntland', Reuters, 28 July 2010, https://www.reuters.com/article/ozatp-somalia-conflict-puntland-20100728-idAFJOE66R0F220100728 (accessed 7 December 2017)

Shekau, Abubakar, 'A message to the Ummah', Jama'at Ahl al-Sunna li-l-Da'wah wal-Jihad, 2014, https://www.youtube.com/watch?v=Vm2LdvevMBU (accessed 9 January 2017).

Shekau, Abubakar, 'Message to the world', 3 August 2016, http://jihadology.net/2016/08/03/new-audio-message-from-abu-bakr-al-shekau-message-to-the-world/ (accessed 9 December 2017).

Simcox, Robin, 'Ansar al-Sharia and governance in southern Yemen', *Current Trends in Islamist Ideology*, 14, 2013.

Simpson, Paul, *A Brief Guide to Stephen King*, New York: Little, Brown, 2014.

Smith, David, 'Nigerian "Taliban" offensive leaves 150 dead', *The Guardian*, 27 July 2009.

Smith, David and Abdalle Ahmed, 'Al-Shabaab leader "responsible for Garissa attack" is Kenyan', *The Guardian*, 3 April 2015.

Smith, Mike, *Boko Haram: Inside Nigeria's Unholy War*, London: I.B. Tauris, 2016.

Solomon, Hussein, 'Mali: West Africa's Afghanistan', *RUSI Journal*, 158 (1), 2013.

Solomon, Hussein, *Terrorism and Counter-terrorism in Africa: Fighting Insurgency from al-Shabaab, Ansar Dine and Boko Haram*, London: Palgrave Macmillan, 2015.

Somalia Newsroom 'Why al-Shabaab ally "Atom" surrendered to the Somali government', Somalia Newsroom, 9 June 2014, https://somalianewsroom.com/2014/06/09/why-al-shabaab-ally-atom-surrendered-to-the-somali-government/ (accessed 6 December 2017).

Somalia Report, 'Shabaab appoints new leaders for Puntland', *Somalia Report*, 20 July 2012, http://piracyreport.com/index.php/post/3534/Shabaab_Appoints_New_Leaders_for_Puntland (accessed 6 December 2017).

Soria, Valentina, 'Global jihad sustained through Africa', *UK Terrorism Analysis*, no. 2, April 2012.

Ssegawa, Mike, 'The aftermath of the attack on Uganda Muslim Supreme Council', *Daily Monitor*, 3 August 2015.

Stern, Jessica and Jim Berger, *ISIS: The State of Terror*, New York: HarperCollins, 2016.

Stone, Martin, *The Agony of Algeria*, New York: Columbia University Press, 1997.

Stren, Richard, 'Factional politics and central control in Mombasa, 1960–1969', *Canadian Journal of African Studies*, 4 (1), 1970.

Tawil, Camille, *Brothers in Arms: The Story of al-Qa'ida and the Arab Jihadists*, London: Saqi, 2011.

Taylor, Max and Mohamed E. Elbushra, 'Research note: Hassan al-Turabi, Osama bin Laden, and al-Qaeda in Sudan', *Terrorism and Political Violence*, 18 (3), 2006.

Tekle, Amare, 'International relations in the Horn of Africa (1991–96)', *Review of African Political Economy*, 23 (70), 1996.

Terrorism Focus, 'GSPC rival leader Hattab reclaims title', *Terrorism Focus*, 2 (21), 2005.

Thawite, John, 'Uganda: 'Benz spills ADF secrets', *All Africa*, 31 December 2000, https://allafrica.com/stories/200101020459.html (accessed 10 October 2018).

Thomas, Scott, 'Building communities of character: Foreign aid policy and faith-based organizations', *SAIS Review of International Affairs*, 24 (2), 2004.

Thornberry, William and Jaclyn Levy, 'Al-Qaeda in the Islamic Maghreb', AQAM Future Projects Case Studies Series, 4, 2011.

Thurston, Alex, 'AQIM updates, August 6', Sahel blog, 6 August 2012, https://sahelblog.wordpress.com/2011/08/06/aqim-updates-august-6/ (accessed 22 July 2017).

Thurston, Alex, *Boko Haram: The History of an African Jihadist Movement*, Princeton: Princeton University Press, 2018.

Thurston, Alex, 'Boko Haram battles police in Maiduguri', Sahel blog, 6 December 2010, https://sahelblog.wordpress.com/2010/12/06/boko-haram-battles-police-in-maiduguri/ (accessed 22 January 2015).

Thurston, Alex, 'Mali: Clashes between the MNLA and Ansar Dine', Sahel blog, 8 June 2012, https://sahelblog.wordpress.com/2012/06/08/mali-clashes-between-the-mnla-and-ansar-dine / (accessed 8 August 2017).

Thurston, Alex, 'Mali: Iyad Ag Ghali's loose relationship with Salafism', Sahel blog, 5 April 2017, https://sahelblog.wordpress.com/2017/04/05/mali-iyad-ag-ghalis-loose-relationship-with-salafism/ (accessed 18 June 2017).

Thurston, Alex, 'Mokhtar Belmokhtar's Afghanistan reminiscences', Sahel blog, 7 February 2017, https://sahelblog.wordpress.com/2017/02/07/mokhtar-belmokhtars-afghanistan-reminiscences/ (accessed 9 August 2017).

Thurston, Alex, 'Nigeria: Boko Haram assassinations', Sahel blog, 13 October 2010, https://sahelblog.wordpress.com/2010/10/13/nigeria-boko-haram-assassinations/ (accessed 22 January 2015).

Thurston, Alex, 'Partial list of recent jihadist attacks in southern and central Mali', Sahel blog, 30 June 2015, https://sahelblog.wordpress.com/2015/06/30/partial-list-of-recent-jihadist-attacks-in-southern-and-central-mali/ (accessed 23 August 2017).

Thurston, Alex, 'Quick items: Boko Haram and al-Shabaab', Sahel blog, 6 December 2010, https://sahelblog.wordpress.com/2010/10/22/quick-items-boko-haram-and-al-shabab/ (accessed 22 January 2015).

Titeca, Kristof and Koen Vlassenroot, 'Rebels without borders in the Rwenzori borderland? A biography of the Allied Democratic Forces', *Journal of Eastern African Studies*, 6 (1), 2012

TRAC, 'Boko Haram: Coffers and coffins; a Pandora's box – the vast financing options for Boko Haram', May 2014, http://www.trackingterrorism.org/article/boko-haram-coffers-and-coffins-pandoras-box-vast-financing-options-boko-haram.

Tramond, Olivier and Philippe Seigneur, 'Operation Serval: Another Beau Geste of France in sub-Saharan Africa?', *Military Review*, November–December 2014.

Tribune du Sahara, La, 'Qui est Walid Abou Adnan Sahraoui, le porte-parole du MUJAO?', *La Tribune du Sahara*, 26 March 2013.

Tukur, Sani, 'Ex-Gov Sheriff, accused of sponsoring Boko Haram, ready to face justice', *Premium Times*, 3 September 2014, http://www.

premiumtimesng.com/news/headlines/167706-ex-gov-sheriff-accused-of-sponsoring-boko-haram-ready-to-face-justice.html#sthash.xJ4QodiG.dpbs (accessed 26 November 2014).

Turner, Simon, 'These young men show no respect for local customs: Globalization, youth and Islamic revival in Zanzibar', DIIS Working Paper, 4, 2008.

UN Department of Safety and Security, Somalia, 'Situation Report, 7 December 2016', DSS Daily Situation Report, 2016.

US Embassy in Abuja, 'Extremist attacks continue into the night', Cable 09ABUJA1379, WikiLeaks, 2009, https://search.wikileaks.org/plusd/cables/09ABUJA1379_a.html (accessed 25 January 2017).

US Embassy in Abuja, 'Muslim and Christian leaders criticize Boko Haram and GON, cites poverty as a key issue', Cable 09ABUJA1422, WikiLeaks, 2009, https://search.wikileaks.org/plusd/cables/09ABUJA1422_a.html.

US Embassy in Abuja, 'Nigerian Islamist extremists launch attacks in 4 towns', Cable 09ABUJA1377, WikiLeaks, 2009, https://search.wikileaks.org/plusd/cables/09ABUJA1377_a.html.

US Embassy in Bamako, 'Cable: Problem child: Algeria's growing impatience with Mali', 12 May 2009, 15.06 (Tuesday), WikiLeaks.

US Embassy in Bamako, 'Cable: Tribal fault lines within the Tuareg of northern Mali', 6 March 2008, 14.21 (Thursday), WikiLeaks.

US Embassy in Bamako, 'Cable: Tuareg and GOM officials provide details on GSPC attack and accords', 31 October 2006, 08.20 (Tuesday), WikiLeaks.

US Embassy in Bamako, 'Mali's unsettled north: Restive Tuaregs, restive president', 28 November 2006, 17.05 (Tuesday), WikiLeaks.

Uyari, Shaykh Yusuf al-, 'The ruling on jihad and its divisions', *Series of Researches and Studies in Shari'ah*, no. 2, n.d.

Van de Bruinhorst, Gerard C., *Raise Your Voices and Kill Your Animals*, Amsterdam: Amsterdam University Press, 2007.

Vates Corp, 'Puntland pro-Isil group occupies Qandala town, Bari', Vates Corp Special Report, 4 November 2016, https://vatescorp.com/index.php/blog/item/27-special-report-20161104-puntland-pro-isil-group-occupies-qandala-town-bari-region (accessed 7 December 2017).

VOA, 'Suspected leader of pro-IS al-Shabab faction reported killed', VOA, 22 November 2015, https://www.voanews.com/a/somalia-suspected-leader-of-pro-islamic-state-al-shabab-faction-reported-killed/3069114.html (accessed 6 December 2017).

Volman, Daniel and Yahia Zoubir, 'US trans-Saharan security policy under Obama', Unpublished manuscript, 2010.

Wabala, Dominic, 'Al-Shabaab returnee's horrid tales of sex slavery', *The Standard Digital*, 10 December 2017, https://www.standardmedia.

co.ke/article/2001262655/al-shabaab-returnee-s-horrid-tales-of-sex-slavery (accessed 27 December 2017).

Wachira, Martin, 'Why Joho was almost beaten by angry youth, barred from mosque', *The Pulse*, 18 May 2017, http://www.pulselive.co.ke/news/electionske-why-joho-was-almost-beaten-by-angry-youth-barred-from-mosque-id6696212.html (accessed 27 December 2017).

Wahid, Salih Abdal al-, 'Report from Salih Abd-al-Wahid to Sheikh Abu-Hafs', dated 1 December 1993, in *Situation Report from al-Qaeda*, Harmony Project, https://www.ctc.usma.edu/posts/situation-report-from-somalia-original-language-2 (accessed 18 January 2018).

Walter, Oliver J. and Dimitris Christopoulos, 'Islamic terrorism and the Malian rebellion', *Terrorism and Political Violence*, 27 (3), 2015.

Ward, Ibrahim, *The Price of Fear: Al-Qaeda and the Truth behind the Financial War on Terror*, New York: I.B. Tauris, 2007.

Watts, Clint, Jacob Shapiro and Vahid Brown, 'Al-Qaida's (mis)adventures in the Horn of Africa', CTC Harmony Project, Special report, 2007.

Weinberg, Leonard and Arie Perliger, 'How terrorist groups end', *CTC Sentinel*, 3 (2), 2010.

Weiss, Caleb, 'Al-Qaeda group strikes in northern Mali', FDD's Long War Journal, 26 December 2015.

Weiss, Caleb, 'Islamic State fighters withdraw from captured Somali port town', *Threat Matrix*, 28 October 2016, https://www.longwarjournal.org/archives/2016/10/islamic-state-fighters-withdraw-from-captured-somali-port-town.php (accessed 7 December 2017).

Weiss, Caleb, 'Shabaab defectors claim German jihadist is dead', *Threat Matrix*, 2 July 2016, https://www.longwarjournal.org/archives/2016/07/shabaab-defectors-claim-german-jihadist-is-dead.php (accessed 6 December 2017).

Weiss, Michael and Hassan Hassan, *ISIS: Inside the Army of Terror*, New York: Regan Arts, 2015.

Welsh, May Ying, 'Making sense of Mali's armed groups', *Al Jazeera*, 17 January 2013, http://www.aljazeera.com/indepth/features/2013/01/20131139522812326.html (accessed 28 August 2017).

Whitlock, Craig, 'Missteps by U.S. in Africa revealed', *Pittsburgh Post-Gazette*, 21 May 2012.

Wiktorowicz, Quintan, 'Introduction: Islamic activism and social movement theory', in Q. Wiktorowicz (ed.), *A Social Movement Theory Approach*, Bloomington, IN: Indiana University Press, 2004.

Williams, Paul, 'Somalia's African Union mission has a new exit strategy. But can troops actually leave?', *Washington Post*, 30 November 2017, https://www.washingtonpost.com/news/monkey-cage/wp/2017/11/30/

somalias-african-union-mission-has-a-new-exit-strategy-but-can-troops-actually-exit/?utm_term=.4fe90563766b (accessed 5 December 2017).

Wojtanik, Andrew, 'Mokhtar Belmokhtar: One-eyed firebrand of North Africa and the Sahel', Jihadi Bios Project, Combating Terrorist Centre, West Point, 2015, https://www.ctc.usma.edu/v2/wp-content/uploads/2015/03/CTC_Mokhtar-Belmokhtar-Jihadi-Bio-February2015-2.pdf (accessed 7 July 2017).

Wright, Lawrence, *The Looming Tower: Al-Qaeda and the Road to 9/11*, New York: Knopf Doubleday Publishing Group, 2006.

Yuhas, Alan, 'Two major al-Shabaab leaders killed in US airstrike and raid by Somali forces', *The Guardian*, 1 June 2016, https://www.theguardian.com/world/2016/jun/01/al-shabaab-leaders-killed-airstrike-raid-somalia-abdullahi-haji-daud-mohamed-dulyadin (accessed 1 December 2017).

Zelinsky, Aaron and Martin Shubik, 'Research note: Terrorist groups as business firms: A new typological framework', *Terrorism and Political Violence*, 21 (2), 2009.

Zenn, Jacob, 'A brief look at Ansaru's Khalid al-Barnawi: AQIM's bridge into northern Nigeria', *Militant Leadership Monitor*, 4 (3), 2013.

Zenn, Jacob, 'Boko Haram's international connections', *CTC Monitor*, January 2013.

Zenn, Jacob, 'Leadership analysis of Boko Haram and Ansaru in Nigeria', *CTC Sentinel*, 7 (2), 2014.

Zenn, Jacob, 'The Sahel's militant "melting pot": Hamadou Kouffa's Macina Liberation Front (FLM)', *Terrorism Monitor*, 13 (22), 2015.

Zenn, Jacob, 'Wilayat West Africa reboots for the caliphate', *CTC Sentinel*, 8 (8), 2015.

Zerrouky, Madjid, 'Un groupe lié à l'Etat islamique revendique une première attaque dans le Sahel', *Le Monde Afrique*, 5 September 2016, http://www.lemonde.fr/afrique/article/2016/09/05/un-groupe-lie-a-l-etat-islamique-revendique-une-premiere-attaque-dans-le-sahel_4992882_3212.html#ByKSg7dvsYUXuCf2.99 (accessed 15 September 2017).

Zimmerman, Katherine, 'Timeline: Operation Linda Nchi', Critical Threats, 24 October 2011, https://www.criticalthreats.org/analysis/timeline-operation-linda-nchi#MonthOne (accessed 29 November 2017).

Zoubir, Yahia, 'Islamists and insurgency in post-independent Algeria', in Barry Rubin (ed.), *Conflict and Insurgency in the Contemporary Middle East*, New York: Routledge, 2009.

Zoubir, Yahia H., 'The Algerian political crisis: Origins and prospects for the future of democracy', *Journal of North African Studies*, 3 (1), 1998.

INDEX

Tumushabe (Benz): 131
Turabi, Hassan: 63–4, 128–9; allies
of, 56–7; founder of PAIC, 54–5
Turki, Hamid: 56, 59; Harakat Ras
Kamboni (militia), 168
Tutsi (ethnic group): 134
Twitter: 153–4

Uganda: 4, 15, 50, 61, 127, 129,
131, 133–5; Bakono-Baamba
population of, 128–9; borders of,
27; Buganda, 128; Bundibugyo,
135; Bunyoro, 129; Busoga, 129;
Independence of (1962), 128;
Kabarole, 135; Kampala, 135;
Kasese, 135; Kayera Gorge, 131;
military of, 127, 129, 135, 174;
Mpondwe Attack (1996), 134;
Rwenzururu, 138; Toro, 128–9
Uganda Muslim Freedom Fighters
(UMFF): formation of, 131;
members of, 61
Ugandan Muslim Supreme Council
(USMC): 130; Tabliqi attacks
against, 130–1
Umar, Ahmad (Abu Ubaidah/
Ahmed Diriye): 177
Umaru, Sanni: 111
ummah: 31, 41, 44, 46–8, 147, 159
United Arab Emirates (UAE): 132
United Kingdom (UK): 147, 156,
185; 7/7 Attacks, 154; Leicester,
187; London, 154, 187
United Nations (UN): 111, 127,
133, 138–9, 158, 182, 194;
Department of Safety and
Security, 189; Development
Programme (UNDP), 170;
Disarmament, Repatriation,
Resettlement and Reintegration
Program (DDRRR), 138;

International Support Mission
in Mali (AFISMA), 79;
Mission for the Referendum in
Western Sahara (MINURSO),
95; Monitoring Group for
Somalia and Eritrea, 29, 180;
Multidimensional Integrated
Stabilisation Mission in
Mali (MINUSMA), 80, 96;
Organisation Stabilisation
Mission in the Democratic
Republic of the Congo
(MONUSCO), 137; Resolution
2085 (2012), 79; Resolution
2100 (2013), 80; Security
Council (UNSC), 79–80
United States of America (USA):
18, 26–7, 62–3, 130, 138,
158–9, 180–1; 9/11 Attacks,
2, 4, 9, 18–19, 22, 48, 56, 164,
182; Central Intelligence Agency
(CIA), 62; Special Forces, 97
University of Maiduguri: 101
Usman dan Fodio: founder of
Sokoto Caliphate, 3

Vlassenroot, Koen: observations of
ADF, 128

de Waal, Alex: 23
Wadi al-Aqiq: 55
al-Wahhab, Abd: founder of
Wahhabism, 47
Wahhabism: 4, 42, 44, 48, 56, 58;
neo-Wahhabism, 42, 44
Warsame, Ali: 59
Warsangeli (clan): Dubays (sub-
clan), 186; relationship with
Islamic State in Somalia, 185–6;
territory held by, 186
Waxdah: 58